CW01081448

Previous Page: Detail, College Chapel. This page: Chapel Cloister

Portrait of Garrett Óg Fitzgerald, founder of the 1518 College

WE REMEMBER MAYNOOTH
A COLLEGE ACROSS FOUR CENTURIES

Edited by

Salvador Ryan
& John-Paul Sheridan

Dublin
Messenger Publications
2020

Cover image of Saint Patrick was taken by:
Stuart McNamara, Corporate Photographers Dublin

Designed by Messenger Publications Design Department
Typeset in Plantin & Athelas
Printed by Hussar Books

Messenger Publications,
37 Leeson Place, Dublin D02 E5V0
www.messenger.ie

Pugin East Cloister

Table of Contents

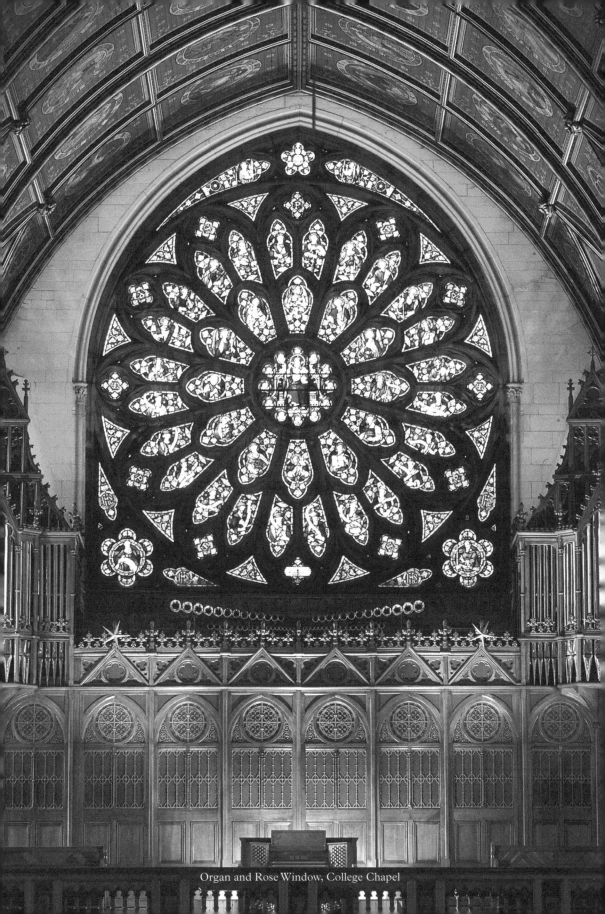

Organ and Rose Window, College Chapel

Above: Maynooth College Chapel spire from Carton House
Facing page (page 19): Detail – Lady Chapel, College Chapel

PREFACE
and
ACKNOWLEDGEMENTS

In his memoir, *I Remember Maynooth*, first published in 1937, and in a revised edition in 1945, Neil Kevin, Professor of English, made the following remarks as Maynooth College approached its 150th anniversary:

> Maynooth College begins to be old. One of the signs of age, a failing memory begins to be noticeable. Already clues are missing, and when conversation turns to reminiscence, there are doubts and gaps … what is lacking to us is not a historian, but a diarist who would have written for us between the lines of history – and not one diarist, but a sequence of them.

On the occasion of its 225th anniversary, this volume sets out to fulfil, at least in part, Neil Kevin's desire for a sequence of diarists. Certainly, some of the contributions gathered here recall historic events of the college's life, but most of the essays are written 'between the lines of history'.

This volume is a benefaction of memory. Each contribution here is a bestowal to future generations conjured from the minds and hearts of past generations. It is a paean offered for those no longer with us, whose names are evoked and honoured.

The editors wish to acknowledge the encouragement and support of the College President, Professor Michael Mullaney and the generous publication grant from the D'Alton Fund.

We offer our sincere thanks to all the contributors for their time and effort in not only revisiting memories, but also committing them to paper or screen. We acknowledge, in particular, Denis Bergin for his enthusiastic support throughout

Detail – Russell Library

this publishing project, and for allowing us to use material from his interview with Msgr Brendan Devlin and the interviews with Aidan and Noeleen Ryan.

We are most grateful to all those who have entrusted us with precious photos. To Stuart McNamara of Corporate Photographers, Dublin, for permission to use the picture of St Patrick on the cover and to Dominic McNamara for facilitating this. To Liam O'Brien for the image of St Joseph's Square on the back cover and a number of other images within this volume. To Professor Thomas O'Connor and the Clericus project for assistance with obtaining images of college class-pieces.

We thank the following for their assistance: the college authorities for the use of material from the College Archive and for the assistance of the archivist, Anna Porter; the staff at the Russell Library for sourcing and presenting material; to Peter Fallon of Gallery Press for permission to reproduce the Frank McGuinness poem in memory of Professor Barbara Hayley and to Bill Tinley for granting us permission to publish his poem in honour of Professor Peter Connolly. We have made every effort otherwise to secure rights and permissions for the material presented here and trust that appropriate image and literary credits are cited in each case.

To the staff at Messenger Publications who have been enthusiastic about this project from the very beginning and have supported our efforts to produce a volume far greater and more expansive than we initially envisaged, we owe a deep debt of gratitude; and, in particular, to Cecilia West, Paula Nolan, Kate Kiernan and Carolanne Henry for their professionalism and courtesy in seeing this volume through to press.

When we first issued our call for contributions to this volume, we aimed for a wide representation of past students and staff within these pages. We are delighted with the response of so many who have agreed to write and share their reflections on college life. Needless to say, the views, thoughts and opinions expressed in the various articles belong solely to the individual authors and not necessarily to the editors of this volume or to Maynooth College itself.

Finally, while the reminiscences contained here comprise a multiplicity of snapshots of student and staff life Maynooth College, an institution that is now 225 years old, we will have fully realised our aim only if it inspires others to more consciously record for posterity the treasure chest of stories of its past, most of which will otherwise never be written down, remaining (but finitely) within the minds of the living.

Salvador Ryan and John-Paul Sheridan
Friday, 19 June 2020

St Joseph's Square

REMEMBERING MAYNOOTH

An Exercise in Indulgence, Acknowledgement, Balance and Preservation

Denis Bergin

t is a few days before Christmas. The waking bell rings earlier than usual and by six o'clock there is a steady stream of black-clad and -hatted young men passing under the arches and moving towards the college gate, where a fleet of double-decker Dublin buses is waiting. Here and there in the darkness are also some smaller vehicles, minibuses whose drivers rose at two or three o'clock in the morning in Kerry or Mayo or Donegal, and whose mission is to bring the pride of their communities back to the bosom of their families. The buses fill with hundreds of passengers, and the Dublin-bound masses are deposited near the Castle Hotel, where they can enjoy a traditional breakfast before making their own way home, perhaps with a little shopping or cinema interlude on the way. By nightfall almost every corner of Ireland will have welcomed one of these valiant followers of a centuries-old path to priestly service.

That typical memory from the mid-1960s, the last years of an institution's singular historic mission as the National Seminary, reminds us of the power and importance of remembering the places, events and relationships from a formative period of our lives. At its simplest, such remembering indulges our sense of nostalgia. At its most powerful it provides, if we are lucky, the information on which future generations may depend for the compilation of a broader and more definitive account, whether of a community, a place or, indeed, an entire era. With that may come a guarantee against being forgotten as the social landscape changes, and a sense of contribution to the balancing of any negative perceptions that may have arisen in the writing of 'the first draft of history', the typical mission of the mass media in the twenty-first century.

Nowhere is that more evident than in the case of Maynooth College, which has one of the most complex and varied life stories of any educational institution. Memories of it, whether formal or informal, whether expressed in traditional print or in transient social media, or whether driven by nostalgia or a need to record relevant facts, can range over the whole gamut of human emotions and responses, from the shallow to the deeply spiritual, the sorrowful to the elated, and the playful to the serious.

From its very beginning 225 years ago, the Royal College of St Patrick at Maynooth has had its share of remembrancers, not all of them viewing their experience in the most favourable light. The original foundation, promoted and bankrolled by the British government to counter the influence of revolutionary Europe on the future priests educated there for Irish dioceses, had significant opposition. That opposition often expressed itself in political diatribes and in the writings of disenchanted former students, and indeed of some who had persevered but subsequently left the priesthood. One early commentator, an ordained priest who left Ireland for America but later managed a circus, studied law and married twice, was of this opinion: 'I am sorry to say, from my knowledge of Roman Catholic priests that there is not a more corrupt, licentious body of men in the world.'

By the middle of the nineteenth century, opinion had settled, and as Maynooth developed its role as a major force in the affairs of the Irish Church, only the modest variations in beliefs, plans, allegiances, attitudes and even personal habits of the professorial classes gave a sense of conflict or controversy. Some of these variations related to serious theological movements and undercurrents within the Church itself; some related to the political situation in Ireland into the twentieth century, and the issues of the land question, Home Rule, conscription and the Troubles. None was serious enough to cause a disturbance worthy of extensive chronicling at the time, though some are likely to be the focus now of research by a whole new generation of post-graduate students in the vast expanses of the academy that now occupies both sides of the Kilcock Road.

As the century ended, John Healy's straightforward centenary history dominated the field of factual accounts of Maynooth's progress, though there were also interesting and more nostalgic contributions to the *Irish Ecclesiastical Record* by the enigmatic Dean John Gunn and the more visible Dean Cornelius Mulcahy.

These modest efforts pre-date another group of more formidable publications – the reminiscences of Professor Walter McDonald, published posthumously in 1923; Professor Neil Kevin, writing in mid-professorial career and initially under a pseudonym, in 1935; and Professor Denis Meehan, appearing in print in 1949 and again in 1964, by which time he had entered a Californian monastery and could afford to be daring in chronicling the foibles of former colleagues.[1]

---

1   Walter McDonald, *Reminiscences of a Maynooth Professor* (London: Jonathan Cape, 1925); Neil Kevin, *I Remember Maynooth* (London: Longmans, Green and Co., 1938); Denis Meehan, *Window on Maynooth* (Dublin: Clonmore and Reynolds, 1949).

There were occasional nostalgic pieces by alumni in *Vexilla Regis* from 1951, when a group of laymen, who had studied at Maynooth but left '*ad vota saecularia*', got together with enthusiastic episcopal approval to promote the cause of their often forlorn ilk. A typical example of the scholarly treatises to be found in its pages is a five-page essay on college slang.

The student magazine *The Silhouette* often produced whimsical accounts of contemporary student life, written from the coalface, that can make for nostalgia-inducing reading several decades on. In a conservative age, and a strictly-controlled intellectual environment, there was never going to be anything too controversial in its pages, though it was sometimes hijacked for slightly nefarious purposes by regional schools of cynics, many of them from Northern dioceses, and particularly the notorious Derry clique. The evocation of oral exams in theology using the styles of Hemingway ('In the room it was cool' ...), Joyce and Beckett remains a personal favourite.

As another century drew to a close, serious histories of the institution prepared at the hands of college presidents began to appear – Tomás Ó Fiaich's compact Irish-language volume in 1972, Jeremiah Newman's works on the college in the Georgian (1979) and Victorian (1984) periods and Patrick Corish's bicentenary history (1995).[2]

By then the seismic changes in Maynooth's make-up, intake and status from the 1960s onwards had changed the context in which the campus was to be viewed by its former students, though the outside world took a little time to take note.

The hostels that began to sprout on the site across the Kilcock Road in the later years of that decade were relentlessly modern, creating a residential complex that could have been on any university site anywhere. One of my first significant writing assignments was to produce a special issue of the magazine *Education Environment* on the low-profile (in every sense) development in 1973, in what may have been the only extensive media coverage of the project.

Only the Divine Word Missionaries, who had commissioned the ultra-modernist, Japan-based, Czech-American architect Antonin Raymond, struck a singular note: their plan

2 Tomas Ó Fiaich, *Má Nuad* (Má Nuad: An Sagart, 1972); Jeremiah Newman, *Maynooth and Georgian Ireland* (Galway: Kenny's Bookshop & Art Gallery, 1979); Jeremiah Newman, *Maynooth and Victorian Ireland* (Galway: Kenny's Bookshop & Art Gallery, 1983); Patrick J. Corish, *Maynooth College 1795–1995* (Dublin: Gill & Macmillan, 1995).

called for 100 single rooms for students, ten priests' rooms (bedroom, study, shower), three big reception rooms, two small reception rooms, ten parlours, a language lab, a library with 25,000 volumes, six piano practice rooms, a swimming pool, a boiler house, and a chapel to seat 182 people with a sanctuary for thirty concelebrants. A smaller version, negotiated by the order's Irish collaborator, Robinson, Keefe and Devane, was eventually built.

A decade or so later, the John Paul II Library, strategically located at the borders of the old world and the new, became the first intrusion of the dynamic of change in the traditional campus configuration, although the Aula Maxima nearby maintained its doughty presence and its nostalgic potential.

Surprisingly, the current 'remembering' industry in regard to Maynooth College is a very active one, with over a dozen separate history-related publications of one type or another appearing in the past twenty years alone. Many of these are informal guides or factual presentations on aspects of the college's physical presence – architecture, artwork, ecclesiastical treasures, scientific equipment.

A new category of reference has sprung up with the arrival of autobiographies of Maynooth alumni and former professors who treat of their seminary experience, even if briefly – William Treacy, the college's oldest alumnus, a pioneer of evangelisation via modern media and still active in Seattle at 100, and Denis O'Callaghan, a former professor of moral theology who spent over thirty years in the college as student and academic, are pertinent examples.

As the various sub-divisions and individual institutions '*apud* Maynooth' – National Seminary, Pontifical University, secular university – have developed their own identities and administrations, they present a completely new aspect and focus when compared with their older versions. A scattergun approach to the location of the various faculty offices and administrative support facilities across both North and South Campuses makes it difficult to provide or sense any feeling of institutional integrity or its negative counterpart, isolation.

That, it may be said, is a good thing, allowing an enlightening mixture of student types and

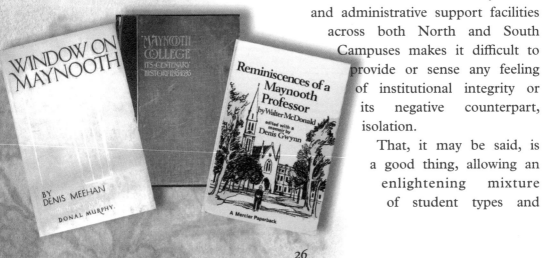

experiences in areas like the main refectory (now rechristened Pugin Hall) and drawing students at Maynooth University away from the relentless modernity of the North Campus. A walk through St Joseph's Square, or a stroll through the Junior Garden, offer a calming contrast to the more intense proceedings in the National Centre for Geocomputation or the Innovation Value Institute further north.

One of the small mysteries of the new set-up is that there is no readily accessible public space for private prayer or liturgical worship – St Mary's Oratory, though often accessible, is removed from the main arteries of student passage, and primarily serves the seminary community; and St Joseph's Oratory, which is at the intersection of the college and local community, is closed except on special occasions.

The growth of social media and the production of corporate publications for the 'new Maynooth' has turned the chronicling of student life and concerns into an instant production line, catalogued quickly by year and faculty. The documented incidents come thick and fast, but they are often transient and nondescript in both nature and medium, echoing the themes of commonplace undergraduate doings everywhere. The daring pre-vacation escapade, the quirky professorial lapse, the telling student put-down, the raucous celebration – are all fair game for the modern memory machine.

Occasionally there may appear the inspiring mentor, the uplifting experience, the critical insight, the spiritual moment, the unexpected bonding. But the pace of recording these experiences, and the transient nature of the media in which they are recorded, often militates against even the briefest of nostalgic recollection, much less mature consideration or the drawing of worthwhile conclusions.

Despite the emergence of this exciting modern vista, both physical and virtual, for student and alumni engagement at Maynooth, the fascination with the institution of the 'closed' era remains. The occasional narratives and sparse memoirs of those years would suggest that these were times and circumstances to be endured rather than to be enjoyed, where rising above a frugal and isolated existence was the continual challenge, and where only the company of fellow sufferers consoled the aspiring cleric, already heavily regimented and disciplined, usually by superiors with no talent or remit for fraternal communication.

The result is often the characterisation of a Maynooth overwhelmingly repressive in its purpose and actuality, despite the rationale for the enterprise often being seen in official circles, and even accepted by the students themselves, as of the boot camp variety (one spiritual director of the time saw seminary training as being akin to taking pieces of wood and boring out the knots in them). Despite the fact that, compared to other forms of third-level education and residential professional training at the time, the only thing that the old Maynooth seemed to lack was a student culture based on extreme socialising, extensive drinking and rampant lecture-avoiding; the limitations on personal freedom were often seen as trumping any advantages of concentration, spiritual formation and rural peace.

It was a situation brought home as recently as 2016 when an initiative to mark the fiftieth anniversary of the NUI graduation of a typical Maynooth class of the period, over 50 per cent of whom had left the seminary or the priesthood, was discussed with the *Irish Times*.

The original point of departure for the exercise was this: although Maynooth might have thought of itself, quite legitimately, as a place where future priests were educated, the reality was that up to half of its intake would not persevere in the effort. Yet these men would go out into the world with many of the same commitments and insights as their ordained confrères and represented a significant resource for the missionary role of the Church and the well-being of rural and urban communities (many alumni became principals or vice-principals of secondary or community schools).

However, by 2016 the effects of repeated allegations of 'strange goings-on' in Maynooth had begun to make themselves felt. In that environment it was difficult to steer the *Irish Times* towards a sympathetic appraisal of the situation, though the conditions that obtained fifty years previously had nothing to do with the more recent news stories.

Despite the professional attentions of the journalist involved, and the sincerity and openness of the two class members she talked to in person, the emailed opinions of others and a certain amount of sub-editorial licence made the overall result overwhelmingly negative. A photo editor requested 'anything black', to reflect the prevailing tenor of the piece.

Subsequent reactions of class members to the publication often painted a different picture. They saw their experience as pretty much in line with, if not superior to, a university education available anywhere else, with the advantage of time to focus on and assimilate the knowledge offered in a calm, undisturbed environment. Several noted the excellence of their professors and the educational process and suggested that they might even be regarded as world class.

In fact, the tradition of academic achievement in Maynooth, and the contribution of the college to national cultural and scientific advancement, has never been promoted satisfactorily. First it has to be remembered, and to be remembered, it has to be recorded. In that regard, Maynooth is at a disadvantage. Some of that is caused by the fact that Maynooth professors often passed out of the college in mid-life on appointment to parishes or as bishops, and their later mission obscured the success of the earlier. The other reason may be an almost pathological aversion to documenting individual lives, often driven by the humility of the potential subject. The result is that there is only a very small body of work that allows any assessment of the day-to-day academic and administrative workings of the college down through the years. Yet, when we look at the reputations and contributions of men like O'Brien, Ó Gramhnaigh, Ó Floinn and Ó Fiannachta in Irish; Corish, Ó Fiaich and Comerford in History; Callan, de Brún, McLaughlin, McConnell and McGreevy in Science, whether at national or international level, Maynooth can hold its own with any other Irish educational institution in the last 200 years.

In fact, one of the conundrums of Maynooth, that in many cases the strength of its scholarship in the arts and sciences outshone, at least by the standards of the secular world, its performance in the core subjects of its mission – Theology, Canon Law, Sacred Scripture – has been less vaunted. Those fields are too vast to cover here, though it has to be said that the era of the Second Vatican Council produced luminaries – Cremin, McDonagh, McNamara, Flanagan, O'Callaghan, Harrington – who had a profound effect on all shades of opinion in the Irish Church. However, in an interesting indication of appropriateness of academic background for the position of president, only a handful of appointments to that position have been made from the ranks of mainstream theologians in the more than 200 years of the college's existence (the others have been canon lawyers, Scripture scholars, classicists, sociologists and historians).

Another aspect of negativity regarding Maynooth is the association of the college with episcopal control of areas way beyond the simple matters of educational administration or theological orthodoxy. This is an accusation that is not new – it is encapsulated at its most extreme in Ian Paisley's reference fifty years ago to the political influence of 'the potbellied bishops of Maynooth'.

The fact that for most of its life as an institution Maynooth was simply a convenient official gathering place for the Irish hierarchy, with no dedicated meeting facilities or administrative support on site – except a row of rooms on Long Corridor reserved for the bishops' very occasional use, with their names inscribed on the doors – belies that assumption.

In fact, it is not generally acknowledged that the Church Corporate has a far greater presence in Maynooth today than it has ever had, with a custom-built conference facility for bishops' meetings in the Columba Centre (the former

Senior Infirmary), and more than a dozen episcopal commissions and related agencies having full-scale office set-ups throughout the South Campus.

There is also a suggestion that the Irish hierarchy has been dominated by appointments from the Maynooth professorial staff, thereby giving the college an undue influence in the control of the Irish Church. In fact, although 75 per cent of Irish bishops in the twentieth century had been educated at Maynooth, fewer than 25 per cent had been on the staff there.

There is even less awareness and acknowledgement of another overwhelming fact in regard to the college: the Irish hierarchy have given to the nation a superb secular university in which there is no hint of territorial claim on behalf of the Catholic faith or the Catholic Church in Ireland. Along the way, and particularly in the transitional decades between 1967 and 1997, when NUI Maynooth came into being as an independent entity, the college authorities made more than a dozen professorial appointments in the arts and sciences, almost all of them lay and many of them non-Catholic. In the June 1971 meeting of the hierarchy alone, five women were appointed to junior lectureships.

The ultimate result of their munificence could have been an institution hobbled by constraining regulation and intellectual straitjacketing; yet what has been produced is a bright, diverse, adventurous and totally modern academic community that not only holds its own in the marketplace of Irish and European third-level education, but has made successful efforts to blend into its activities the academic traditions of its predecessor and contemporary institutions on the site. It is, moreover, one of the most open and accessible campuses in Ireland, visited every day by dozens of local community members for recreation and inspiration.

Distracting historic perceptions of Maynooth as an engine of intellectual repression or an oppressing ecclesiastical power base aside, the issue now is whether the purpose of remembering Maynooth has gone beyond nostalgic indulgence to a point where it is essential to preserve the institutional memory of the college in the face of a declining presence and influence, both of college and Church, in modern society.

If that is achieved, a secondary but equally felicitous outcome may be that the documentation of Maynooth's history can play a role in balancing the perception of a Church damaged by revelations of abusive behaviour and failures of administration, discipline and governance. These revelations have had a damning effect on the reputation of an institution whose very purpose for so long was to create conditions where piety and knowledge could be cultivated side by side, and then imbibed and dispersed to the four corners of the world with conviction, justice and charity towards all.

It may be that public opinion and media comment will continue to pillory Maynooth for the sins of a previous generation, and that it will take some time for both college and Church to repair the damage and restore balance to their perception in the vast panorama of Irish political, social and intellectual history.

What is certain is this: any attempt to research the history of Ireland on either a macro or micro scale has to take account of the role of Maynooth in almost every aspect of Ireland's cultural and spiritual life, and, through the work of its alumni, both clerical and lay, in the well-being and development of almost every community on this island over the 225 years of the college's existence.

As one of those who remembers striding through the darkness in the early hours of a pre-Christmas morning fifty-plus years ago, I will continue to experience a wave of nostalgia as I walk across St Joseph's Square of a sunlit evening, heading towards a comfortable guest room in Long Corridor or New House, near the more spartan ones I occupied as a student in the early 1960s.

For me there is an added nostalgic factor. Less than four years after I left Maynooth, I was working on a small publishing project that involved historical research by a group of undergraduate seminarians in the college. On the day of a meeting there to progress the work, I met, in the most fateful of circumstances, the academic director of a US college-level cultural exchange group in Dublin and suggested that she accompany me to view an important centre of intellectual and spiritual influence. She agreed, and we have been husband and wife now for forty-seven years. It was not an outcome that the founding fathers of Maynooth might have intended for those who passed under the hallowed portals, but for me the impact of that relationship, both personally and in terms of my outreach to the world, has been as great as if I had pursued to the end the original purpose of my entry to the college.

MAYNOOTH
A Continuing Landscape of Learning

Geraldine Castle, Maynooth

Colm Lennon

In a watercolour of c. 1800 by an unknown artist the newly established St Patrick's College is depicted, centred on Stoyte House, and framed by the ruined FitzGerald castle on the right and the parish church of St Mary on the left. When a commonality of interests in Ireland between the royal government and the Roman Catholic bishops, supported by the Catholic gentry, led to the foundation of the college in 1795, Maynooth was chosen as its location as being within both the ecclesiastical purview of Dublin and the sphere of munificence of the family of FitzGerald, dukes of Leinster, then seated at Carton House. The figures in the picture, including the academics, are shown within a landscape shaped by Geraldine influence. Stoyte House had been the site of the FitzGeralds' council house, the castle was their principal residence in the Middle Ages and St Mary's incorporated their collegiate establishment, set up in 1518.

For a brief period in the early sixteenth century, there was at least some prospect that the castle and earlier college at Maynooth might have become a major centre of learning in Ireland, which then lacked a university. Although this vision faded rapidly after the 1530s with the decline of the FitzGeralds as premier family and the suppression of the religious houses, reflections on the topography and history of these Geraldine precincts give rise to questions as to the academic milieu that predated the politico-religious upheavals of the early modern period, and the resultant changes and continuities down to 1795.

The medieval castle of Maynooth was not only part of the defences of the English Pale but was also at the centre of the FitzGerald system of patronage of English and Gaelic secular and religious culture. Reflecting their ties to Renaissance Florence and other parts of Europe, the FitzGeralds possessed 'one of the richest earl's houses under the crown of England', containing in the 1510s valuable plate, precious jewels and furnishings, and also an important library of books and manuscripts in Latin, French, English and Irish. In the collection were the earliest printed books in Ireland, including Thomas More's *Utopia*. As well as works of theology, devotion and philosophy, there were versions of classical authors, secular literature including romances and poetry, and also the writings in English and Irish translation of Giraldus Cambrensis, the famous twelfth-century ancestor of the family. Contemporary religious controversies were represented in the form of printed refutations by Thomas More and King Henry VIII of Martin Luther's religious views. The Maynooth library reflects the noble family's openness to international scholarly trends, including the Christian humanism of Erasmus, as well as their engagement with Ireland's Gaelic and Norman heritage.

Within 100 metres of the castle keep, the Anglican church now occupies the site of the College of the Blessed Virgin Mary of 1518, where previously the castle chapel had stood. When founding their college as part of a vogue for such institutions in late medieval Europe, the FitzGerald earls intended it primarily as a chantry whose priests would intercede for the good of their souls, but there may also have been an aspiration to establish a school or academy of higher learning, as happened under the sponsorship of contemporary aristocrats elsewhere. The Geraldine college of priests and choristers at Maynooth had added significance, being located within the ambit of the vice-regal court of the Kildares. It had a larger than average complement of twelve collegiate personnel, including up to seven priests or fellows, and five clerks and choristers. Through administrative links with St Patrick's Cathedral, the Earl of Kildare and the Archbishop of Dublin disposed jointly of substantial secular and spiritual resources. Mention of 'other works of piety' in the foundation charter adumbrated perhaps a wider role for the college. A programme of building work was embarked upon by the ninth Earl of Kildare, which produced a beautifully refitted collegiate church of St Mary, as well as a place of residence for the collegiate clergy, all funded by a substantial landed endowment.

Any plans for the development of an academy at Maynooth were thwarted by the fall of the Kildare Geraldines after the insurrection of Thomas FitzGerald, briefly tenth earl, in 1534. Although the family was restored in the mid-century,

Linocut of the Geraldine Castle by Susan Durack

they were never again as influential as they had been during their period of ascendancy as chief governors. Moreover, the castle, church and other college buildings were severely damaged in the siege and capture of the Maynooth fortress in 1535, necessitating much expensive repair work. Simultaneously, the introduction of the Reformation from the 1530s undermined the *raison d'être* of collegiate chantries by rejecting the efficacy of priestly intercession for the souls in Purgatory, though in Ireland most of these institutions survived, apart from St Mary's, Maynooth. The liberal Erasmian reform movement that underpinned many educational advances was stunted by the confessional divisions that opened up in northern European countries, including Ireland, where the imposition of an Anglican state church in 1560 rendered illegal the religion of the Catholic majority.

This changing regime in church and state was crystallised in the guardianship of the Maynooth estates by Richard Boyle, Earl of Cork and leading colonist in early seventeenth-century Ireland. He arranged the marriage of his daughter to the sixteenth Earl of Kildare, and, as part of his social aspirations, undertook the restoration of Maynooth Castle and church. The castle was partly rebuilt with a new manor house and other edifices. As to the church, which had been put to profane uses, the Earl of Cork engaged in a refurbishment programme, replacing the windows, plastering and whitewashing the interior and installing comfortable pews, thus ensuring a suitable burial place for members of his own and the FitzGerald family. Thereafter the church at Maynooth functioned as a centre of Protestant worship for the parishioners of Maynooth. The suite of new and restored buildings, secular and ecclesiastical, embodied the ascendancy of new English Protestantism, as reflected in a plaque, dated 1630, over the southern gate of the castle, impaling the arms of Boyle and FitzGerald and extolling Richard as builder and restorer.

While much of the work was undone during the turbulence of the 1640s, substantial town development was overseen by the FitzGeralds, now dukes of Leinster, from their estate and house at Carton in the eighteenth century. When, with the legalising of native Catholic education, a national seminary and lay college were proposed, Maynooth was ideally placed to benefit, with its improved communications with Dublin and the west of Ireland, and the patronage of the Leinster family. Settled at the former hub of Geraldine rule, the new institution evoked their spiritual and cultural legacy. Denominationally of its age, St Patrick's was animated by the same religious zeal as characterised its collegiate predecessor at Maynooth. Its international scholarly curriculum was redolent of the rich collection in the old castle library.

ST MARY'S

The Parish Church that Looks Like Part of the College

Patrick Comerford

t Mary's, the Church of Ireland parish church in Maynooth, is incorporated into the outer wall of St Patrick's College, and while few students or graduates may have been inside the church, many still think it is part of the college buildings.

The church was originally built as a private chapel for Maynooth Castle when it was one of the principal residences of the FitzGeralds of Kildare.

At the arrival of the Anglo-Normans, the church at Laraghbryan was included in Strongbow's list of church properties belonging to the Diocese of Glendalough in 1173. Soon after, however, Laraghbryan became subservient to St Mary's, Maynooth, which was built by the FitzGerald family.

Maynooth was part of a pocket of churches and parishes in this part of north Kildare that were in the diocese of Glendalough. St Mary's became a prebendal church of St Patrick's Cathedral, Dublin, in October 1248, at the request of Maurice FitzGerald. Richard de Carren was the priest of the parish at the time. From then on, the tithes of the parish supported one of the canons of the cathedral, and this canon, the prebendary of Maynooth, was also the incumbent (parish priest or rector) of Maynooth. Medieval rectors and prebendaries included John de Sandford, later dean of St Patrick's and Archbishop of Dublin; and Alexander de Bicknor, also a future archbishop.

Gerald FitzGerald, ninth Earl of Kildare, built and endowed a college at Maynooth in 1518, rebuilt the castle chapel and attached it to his college. However, at the Reformation, what had become the 'King's College of Maynooth' was suppressed and the chapel became the Church of Ireland parish church of Maynooth.

St Mary's Church, like other churches of the day, suffered in the Reformation conflicts, and rectors were appointed and removed on a whim, depending on the religious fashions of the day. Edward Dillon, who was also dean of Kildare, was put to death as a rebel in the castle in 1535; Richard Johnson was pensioned off at the suppression of the cathedral chapter of St Patrick's in 1547, was reappointed

St Mary's Church, Maynooth

in 1555, was deprived again within six or seven weeks, and was appointed for a third time in 1572. In between, John Doyne spent less than a year at Maynooth before he was dismissed on charges of adultery.

Later, it was said, the church fell into disrepair and was used for keeping cattle. However, St Mary's was extensively renovated in the 1630s by Richard Boyle, Earl of Cork, father-in-law of George FitzGerald (1612–1660), sixteenth Earl of Kildare. At the same time, Boyle was rebuilding Maynooth Castle.

During the wars of the 1640s, both the castle and the church fell into ruin. The FitzGeralds returned to appointing parish clergy after the Caroline Restoration. Robert Price, who had survived the Cromwellian era, became the Restoration Bishop of Ferns, and his successor, Thomas Price, who was prebendary of Maynooth and Bishop of Kildare at the same time (1661–67), became Archbishop of Cashel (1667–78).

For much of the time, however, many rectors of Maynooth were absentees, pluralists, or both, and the real liturgical and pastoral work in the parish became the burden of the vicars or curates they appointed. However, the benign interest of the FitzGeralds ensured the parish did not suffer from clerical negligence, and a new schoolhouse was built beside the church in 1702.

James FitzGerald (1722–1773), first Duke of Leinster and father of Lord Robert FitzGerald, repaired St Mary's Church in 1770, shortly after he had built Leinster House in Dublin, and the church was used by the Church of Ireland parish once again. The church was restored or repaired by the FitzGerald family in 1828, again in 1859 by Augustus Frederick FitzGerald (1791–1874), third Duke of Leinster. Throughout these times, the FitzGeralds retained the right to appoint priests to the church until disestablishment.

The large east window is unusual because it is made of wood and set in stone. During the restoration in 1770, this window was taken from the church in Laraghbryan, which had fallen into ruin. Other windows came from the castle's council chamber. The back end of the church and churchyard contains the last fragments of the medieval curtain wall of the castle.

From 1821 to 1875, the fifteenth-century tower was a mausoleum for the third Duke of Leinster, who lived at Carton, his wife Lady Charlotte Augusta Stanhope (1791–1874), duchess of Leinster, and seven members of their family. Before that, the family was buried in St Brigid's Cathedral, Kildare.

One clergyman was also buried here: Canon George Dacre Blacker came to the parish in 1838 and was rector and prebendary of Maynooth from 1841 to 1871. His death coincided with disestablishment, and the pulpit is also his memorial. The positions of rector of Maynooth and prebendary of Maynooth were separated at disestablishment, and the patronage of the FitzGerald family was abolished.

A medieval font from St Coca's Church in Kilcock was moved to St Mary's in 1991. The small organ, dating from around 1820, is one of the few untouched Telford organs in Ireland. The church plate includes a large silver flagon and an alms dish given by Mary FitzGerald, Countess of Kildare, in 1744, and a chalice and paten dating from 1697. The church still exhibits prayer books from 1860 that identified the pews of the Duke of Leinster and his family.

The area on the north side of the church, behind the vestry, was a parish school from 1770 to 1859, when it was moved to the Geraldine Hall near the Royal Canal. The school closed in 1935.

The parish of Maynooth was transferred to the diocese of Meath in 1940 and joined to the Dunboyne group of parishes. The present rector, the Reverend Eugene Griffin, who was appointed in 2018, is also the treasurer's vicar or a minor canon of St Patrick's Cathedral. The present prebendary of Maynooth in St Patrick's, Canon Mark Gardner, was appointed in 2012.

PROFESSOR LOUIS DELAHOGUE'S HAPPY BIRTHDAY

16 January 1812

Donal McMahon

The early years of Maynooth College were a time of rapid, often precarious growth in a turbulent period of Irish and European history. Shortage of money, overcrowded living conditions and occasional tensions between the French professors and the Irish students made for trying times for everyone, including the 'embattled presidents'.[1] The fifth of these, however, Patrick Everard (1810–12), continued so well in Maynooth the good work he had been doing in his school in England that the dean, Andrew Hart (1811–12), could now talk about the 'present happy situation of the house, a hint of the President's wishes [being] sufficient to lead the students to do anything'.[2]

One impressive thing they did was answer very well in their Christmas exams of January 1812 (all oral in those days), so well, indeed, that their Professor of Dogmatic Theology, Louis Delahogue, was almost lost for words. He admits as much in the speech he gave to the students on 16 January in one of the lecture halls. On this occasion he spoke to them in English, a language he obviously did not master as well as the language normally used in class, Latin, or, of course, his native French – English, as Patrick Corish puts it, 'that still halted a little'.[3] However, it is precisely to the speaker's less-than-perfect command of the language that we may owe this precious piece of ephemera since, not being used to speaking in public in English, he must have felt the need to make a quick draft beforehand of the text of his speech.

> I cannot find too expressive words to testify to you my satisfaction on every respect for your numerous attendance during all the days, your constant attention, and your answer to the different questions proposed to you.[4]

1 Patrick J. Corish, *Maynooth College 1795–1995* (Dublin: Gill & Macmillan, 1995), p. 42.
2 Ibid., p. 50.
3 Ibid., p. 53.
4 Clogher Diocesan Archives, DIORC/1/2/G/69, on deposit in the Public Record Office of Northern Ireland and published by permission of the Deputy Keeper of the Records. Corish (pp. 53–54) quotes from the text as transcribed in part by John Forsythe ('Clogher Diocesan Archives', *Archivium Hibernicum*, 43 (1988),

Delahogue Manuscript

'In the manner in which those days of examination have been spent,' he went on, 'you will reap more advantage from them than from the two months perhaps of lectures in this hall.' How so? 'On account of the revision of all the matters [cf. French '*matières*', subjects] by which you know perfectly the connexion of all the questions, all the proofs and all the objections.' He can only urge them to keep this up: 'I exhort you, gentlemen, to continue.'

He now develops this theme of hard work and the fruits thereof on both a human and a religious level. To illustrate the idea of everyone working together towards the same end while, given their different abilities, competing with each other, he resorts to a military metaphor:

> I consider the three courses of divinity as three divisions of the same army which are to be in competition one with another for places of honour. You are acquainted enough with your respective talents to know what you have to hope or to fear. I will say only that it seems to me that in every division they [for 'there'?] are rivals not to be desprised [sic].[5]

Then, as now, some will do better than others and win a prize – the first prize list appeared in 1799.[6] Delahogue asks whether there are any 'motives of emulation'

3–24 (pp. 22–23)) and, describing it as a 'brouillon' (i.e. draft), summarises it in 'Les séminaires irlandais du continent, la Révolution française et les origines du collège de Maynooth' *Études irlandaises*, 23 (1998), 121–35 (p. 133)). Jottings in vacant spaces on the two manuscript pages (each used on both sides) include 'tear in pieces – torn', 'complacancy' [sic], 'timeo hominem unius libri' [I fear the man of just one book].

5   For 'desprised' see OED 'disprize' (obsolete or archaic). We may translate as 'underestimated'.
6   Corish, p. 38.

for the many students not 'proclaimed in the list of honour'. His answer, drawing on God's words to Abraham in Genesis 15:1 ('*merces tua magna nimis*' – 'your reward will be very great') and on the parable of the talents (Matthew 25:14–30), proposes a far higher kind of honours list than the military or academic:

> They [for 'there'?] are certainly, and the most able to incite them to neglect nothing to improve themselves according to their respective talents. This motive is the greatest reward possible, <u>Deus ipse merces magna nimis</u>, qui unumquemque remunaturus est habita ratione non talentorum illi a patrefamilias commissorum ad usuram sed eorum quae ipse ex pecunia ipsi ad hoc commissa lucraturus fuerit.
>
> God himself will be the very great reward, who will honour each one not on the basis of talents entrusted to him by the master of the house to be deposited for interest but on the basis of those which he will have earned himself from the money given him [by God] for that purpose.[7]

He ends by referring to his own life: 'I am satisfied. I have a reward and a very sufficient reward, because Almighty God knew my intentions and he will reward me for it.'

We have here, so far, a very nice tribute to hard-working students, one that develops finally into a kind of uplifting sermon. Then comes the announcement, as big a surprise to the class that day, no doubt, as to us readers today:

> Gentlemen, this day ~~I begin my which~~ is my Birthday permitt me ~~on that~~ to adress to you some words on that account. I begin the 73 year of my age. 30 years ago at what time I enjoyed of [cf. Fr.'*jouir de*'] every commodities of life, very sufficient income, honorable situation, and general estime of the Bishops of France, at what time if I was to look what was to be my situation at an advanced age, I foresaw what is called in Latin <u>otium cum dignitate</u> [leisure with dignity] and perhaps I had too much complacancy in that idea. All these hopes <u>in uno instanti sicut fumus evanescunt</u>.[8]

All these hopes 'in one instant disappeared like smoke'. He who had reached

---

7   Delahogue's reference to 'interest' ('usura'), a word used just once in the parable, focuses the discussion on the servant with one talent (v. 27). In applying the parable to an academic context and substituting moral effort for material gain, he encourages the student without a prize to keep trying to 'improve himself' with the gifts he has, where the option open to his scriptural equivalent had been to deposit his money ('pecunia') with the bankers for interest ('usura'). ('Servant' and 'student' are to be understood today, of course, in inclusive terms.)

8   The text given here (indicating the revisions of the first sentence only) is an exact transcription of the original. 'I begin the 73 year of my age' indicates that he is seventy-two and was therefore born in 1740. Corish (1998), however, describes him as being seventy-three ('à l'occasion de son soixante-treizième anniversaire'), which gives us 1739 as the year of his birth, the year found in all the Maynooth sources (e.g. the panel at the entrance to the cemetery), as opposed to 1740 in the French ones (e.g. the catalogue of the Bibliothèque nationale de France). Now, Delahogue declares in his will that he was born 'at Paris in January 1740' (John Forsythe, 'Clogher Diocesan Papers (2)', *Archivium Hibernicum*, 44 (1989), 5–70 (p. 62)). Therefore, when he died in May 1827, he was eighty-seven, not eighty-eight as in the Maynooth sources (Corish, p. 31, following John Healy, *Maynooth College: Its Centenary History* (Dublin, 1895), p. 195).

the highest places of honour in French life suddenly found himself, at the age of fifty-two, driven from Paris during the September massacres and forced to flee abroad. In the words of his obituarist, 'On the third [of September 1792], he quitted the scene of his well-earned reputation and former happiness, now turned into a theatre of massacre and blood.'[9] 'In the general destruction I never had any concern for my private loss,' he tells the students. (After six years in England, he found a welcome in Ireland when appointed Professor of Moral Theology in Maynooth, moving to the chair of Dogmatic Theology in 1801. He declined an invitation to return to the Sorbonne in 1816, choosing instead to spend the rest of his days in his adopted homeland. He died on 9 May 1827 aged eighty-seven and was buried in the college cemetery.) He concludes his speech by expressing his thanks to God who opened up the path that led him to Maynooth:

> But, Gentlemen, I had great many thanks to return to Almighty God who [inserted: 'in that general dest.'] has procured me such an honourable situation as that – to have been called to teach the young clergymen of Ireland. I neglected nothing to fulfill my duty for the greatest advantage of them.[10]

And, finally, he tells of a third reason for celebration: 'I have the satisfaction to have finished the fourth Tractatus, *De Trinitate et Incarnatione*.' The professor had gathered his lecture notes together to provide yet another useful textbook for future students.

The announcement of the exam results falling on the same day as his birthday led Professor Delahogue to digress for once, we may suppose, into personal reminiscence. His congratulations on their performance in the exams were, no doubt, very gratefully received by the students, but how taken aback and even moved they must have been to hear him then share with them the news of his birthday, along with the exact age, and go on to tell them about the major challenges he had faced in his life and, with God's help, had overcome!

The dean, Andrew Hart, may very well have raised his glass in the refectory that evening to congratulate his esteemed former professor on his birthday – with maybe a pleasantry about their ages being the same, only the other way

---

9   Anon., 'Death of the Rev. Dr. Delahogue', in *The Freeman's Journal*, 16 May 1827, p. 4.
10 The word 'dest.' is an abbreviation of 'destruction'. For 'has procured' (< Fr passé composé) we may read 'procured'. The inclusion of a not easily decipherable verb omitted in Forsythe (1988, p.23) and, following him, Corish (1995, p.54), adds to the ringing words Delahogue uses to summarise his work in Ireland: 'called to *teach* the young clergymen of Ireland'. (There is a nice reciprocity between the teacher who 'neglect[s] nothing' in his duty towards the students and the students who 'neglect nothing to improve themselves'.) Another memorable mention of Ireland is found in the second edition of *Tractatus De Religione* (Paris, 1815, first published Dublin, 1808): in a note to the reader (p. [i]), the publisher tells how the author '[was] forced by the change of affairs in France to leave his homeland for Ireland' ('*rerum Gallicanarum conversione coactus patria secedere in Hiberniam*').

round! – and wish him many more years of dedicated service to the college. Little did he know that, after resigning from Maynooth in July, he himself was to enjoy only a few years as parish priest of Saggart, Rathcoole and Newcastle in west Dublin. He died on 20 November 1815, aged thirty. Delahogue attended his funeral and, the following day, delivered a moving address to the students – this time, in Latin.[11] He also composed the Latin epitaph as seen today, adapted, under the life-sized effigy of Fr Andrew that surmounts his grave in the Church of the Nativity of the Blessed Virgin Mary, Saggart.[12] The writer, a parishioner of Saggart, likes to look over at the dean every now and then, and remembers the French professor too in his thoughts and prayers.[13]

11 Clogher Diocesan Archives, DIORC/1/3/4, on deposit in the Public Record Office of Northern Ireland and, by permission of the Deputy Keeper of the Records, translated and published online by Donal McMahon at https://saggartparish.blogspot.com/search?q=delahogue.

12 Donal McMahon, 'Zealous Exertions: Fr Andrew Hart and St Finian's Church', in *St Finian's Church, Newcastle Lyons, 1813–2013* (Newcastle, Dublin: St Finian's Bicentenary Book Committee, 2013), pp. 27–31.

13 He will think of him especially when he celebrates the same birthday in 2020 as Delahogue's in 1812 and looks back, as he did, on the course of his life: he too followed a path that led to an 'honourable situation' in Maynooth where, for nearly forty years, he did the best he could, in his subject, 'to teach the young clergymen of Ireland'.

MAYNOOTH MAKES PEACE
WITH THACKERAY

Engraving St Patrick's College

Donal McMahon

aynooth College has quite different memories of what two of Victorian England's most famous writers, John Henry Newman (1801–1890) and William Makepeace Thackeray (1811–1863), had to say about it. The first is remembered fondly for the high praise he gave to the College President, Charles Russell, in his *Apologia ProVita Sua* (1864), while the second's very name is (going by the records up to now) almost unmentionable, such is the enduring painful effect of what he said about the college in his *Irish Sketch Book* (1843) after a short visit to it during his tour of Ireland the previous year. In this auspicious year of its history and taking my cue from the 'Makepeace' in his name, I would like to explore here the possibility of a rapprochement between Maynooth and Thackeray.

Newman's tribute occurs at a key moment in the account he gives of his conversion: '[M]y dear friend, Dr Russell […] had, perhaps, more to do with my conversion than any one else. […] [H]e was always gentle, mild, unobtrusive, uncontroversial. He let me alone.'[1] Every word is weighed carefully by a writer, now sixty-three, looking back over decades spent perfecting the craft. Thackeray, on the other hand, around half that age at his time of writing, is scraping a living from journalism, '[his] trade [being] to write books and sell the same – a chapter

1   John Henry Newman, *Apologia Pro Vita Sua* (London: Penguin Books, 1994), pp. 178–79.

for a guinea, a line for a penny' – to provide for his Irish-born wife in an asylum in Paris and his two young children in the care of his mother, also in Paris.[2] But, of course, these extenuating circumstances cannot, of themselves, absolve him of the charge of writing in an offensive and unjust way about the college.

'Thackeray has some unkind things to say in general about Maynooth here and there in his *Irish Sketch Book*. […] Perhaps it is best to draw a veil over his remarks,' writes Denis Meehan in 1949. The language becomes less diplomatic in the final chapter ('Concerning Sources'), where the *Sketch Book* (noted incorrectly as being published in 1852) is described as containing 'a brief and blistering account of a visit to the College [which is] particularly hard to read, even dispassionately, after the lapse of a century, without forming harsh judgments about Thackeray'.[3] Jeremiah Newman delivers one such judgement in 1979: '[T]he College was visited by William Makepeace Thackeray who did a vitriolic diatribe on it.'[4] Finally, in 1995, drawing the veil fully aside, Patrick Corish takes Thackeray determinedly to task:

> Thackeray, visiting in 1842, raged about what he saw as slatternliness everywhere in Ireland, but was apoplectic about 'the supreme dirt and filth of Maynooth – that can but belong to one place, even in Ireland … Ruin so needless, filth so disgusting, such a look of lazy squalor, no Englishman who has not seen can conceive'.[5]

While the use of terms like 'raged' and 'apoplectic' to describe the style of the writing is open to debate, Corish proceeds, quite properly, to call the content into question by citing alternative documentary evidence: '[O]ther visitors, while they stress the poverty, do not support Thackeray's charge of dirt and slatternliness outstanding even by Irish standards – Johnson in 1844, for example, or Head in 1852.'[6]

The mistake in the publication date of the *Sketch Book* found in the final chapter of Meehan ('Concerning Sources') is repeated in 'Tuilleadh Léitheoireachta' at the end of Tomás Ó Fiaich's *Má Nuad* (1972), Sir F. Head being listed (correctly) as also having published in 1852.[7] Unfortunately, it also

2   Since editions of *The Irish Sketch Book* are not easily available in hard copy, I refer to the following edition: M. A. [Michael Angelo] Titmarsh, *The Irish Sketch Book* (London: Chapman and Hall, 1857, first published 1843), online (and searchable) at https://archive.org/stream/irishsketchbook100thac?ref=ol#page/n5/mode/2up. Thackeray signs the dedication to Charles Lever (p. [vii]) with his real name. The words quoted are on p. 258.
3   Denis Meehan, *Window on Maynooth* (Dublin: Clonmore and Reynolds, 1949), pp. 50, 173.
4   Jeremiah Newman, *Maynooth and Georgian Ireland* (Galway: Kenny's Bookshops, 1979), p. 252.
5   Patrick J. Corish, *Maynooth College 1795–1995* (Dublin: Gill & Macmillan, 1995), p. 106, quoting two different passages of the *Sketch Book*, pp. 309 and 357.
6   Ibid. While 'slattern' and 'slatternly' are each found once in the *Sketch Book*, 'slatternliness' is not found at all.
7   Tomás Ó Fiaich, *Má Nuad* (Má Nuad: An Sagart, 1972), lch. 104.

finds its way into the appendix ('A Note on Sources') to Corish's indispensable bicentenary history:

> Two books with sharply contrasting approaches appeared in 1852. W. M. Thackeray's *Irish Sketch Book* is sourly critical, unjustly so it is reasonable to speculate, especially if judged against his contemporary, Sir Francis Bond Head, whose life as a colonial administrator had given him a capacity for detail of an almost photographic quality. The long chapter on Maynooth (*A Fortnight in Ireland*, pp. 66–69) is indeed a good substitute for a photographic album.[8]

Now the case against Thackeray here has two flaws: an error of fact regarding the year of publication (begging the question, 'Has the writer forgotten that the book is a depiction of pre-Famine Ireland?') and a failure to consider the Maynooth chapter in Head in the context of the overall argument of that book, one that emerges slowly, cumulatively and, finally, devastatingly from the details assembled meticulously along the way:

> Are the Priesthood of Ireland the cause of the moral degradation of Ireland? I reply, 'They are!' [. . .] I calmly defy all the talents, ability, sophistry, artifice, and indignation of the Irish priesthood to repel the evidence I am about to adduce [against] a clergy who – *I will prove it* – have brought scandal on the sacred character of the Catholic Church, who have disgraced the cloth they wear etc.

And it was in Maynooth that 'the cheap wholesale manufacture' of this priesthood took place![9] A valid judgement of a book's worth is reached, then, not on the evidence of one photo-like chapter or one or two 'sourly critical' paragraphs, but on the evidence offered by the whole book, both for and against. And in the case of Thackeray, there is a good deal for.

Newman certainly thought so. Three days before receiving a copy (on 30 December 1863) of Kingsley's defamatory article in *Macmillan's Magazine* that was to be the occasion for his *Apologia*, Newman learned of Thackeray's sudden death on Christmas Eve at the age of fifty-two. He expresses his feelings in two letters written on the 27th:

> [I write] to express the piercing sorrow that I feel at Thackeray's death. You know I never saw him [but] one saw in his books the workings of his mind. [...] A new work of his had been advertised and I had looked forward with pleasure to reading it. [...] His last (fugitive)

---

8   Corish, p. 493. A different view, penned as boldly as any of Thackeray's, was expressed by the Maynooth theologian Patrick Murray (1811–1882) soon after the book's publication in November: 'Sir F. Head is a keen, shrewd observer [...] but he is evidently deficient in the thinking faculty. His book is worthless' (*Essays Chiefly Theological*, 4 vols (Dublin, 1850–53), iv (1853), 31).

9   Sir Francis B. Head, *A Fortnight in Ireland* (London: John Murray, 1852), pp. 251, 394.

William Makepeace Thackeray

pieces in the *Cornhill* have been almost sermons. [...] [From second letter] He is said to have had such drawings to Catholicity.[10] Thackeray's biographer Gordon Ray quotes Oratorian Ignatius Ryder as saying that 'Newman was fond of Thackeray, reading faithfully everything that he wrote, down to the last unfinished work'.[11] Indeed, 1848 saw the appearance of a novel by each of them, *Vanity Fair* and *Loss and Gain: The Story of a Convert*.

Thackeray, for his part, is on record as having (O his prophetic soul!) called Newman a saint. An anonymous young lady made notes of a conversation between Thackeray and his friend Charles Bray in 1855: '[Thackeray] talked of Newman. Called him a saint, in a way that was a blessing to hear, so heartily and truly did he utter it.'[12] A similar generosity of spirit can be found in the *Sketch Book* when, for example, he expresses the hope that 'no Irish reader will be offended at my speaking of this poverty, not with scorn or ill-feeling, but with hearty sympathy and good-will'.[13] And conscious, no doubt, of maybe overstepping the mark when he writes of the college in his typical free-rein style, he immediately appeals to the reader's understanding: 'I hope these words will not be taken hostilely.'[14]

The institutional memory of Maynooth shows that they were. Now, given that Maynooth holds Newman in high regard, and that Newman holds Thackeray in equally high regard, then ... but let us not resort to logic. Rather let us open the *Sketch Book* again, that vivid and (for the right reasons!) unforgettable depiction of the lives of our forebears in Ireland's pre-calamitous times, joining the author, say, at the moment when he visits the women's room in the North Dublin Union Workhouse: 'Some of the poor old creatures began to stand up as we came in – I can't say how painful such an honour seemed to me.'[15]

---

10 Charles Stephen Dessain (ed.), *The Letters and Diaries of John Henry Newman*, vol. xx (London: Nelson, 1970), pp. 566, 569.
11 Edward Short, *Newman and His Contemporaries* (London: T&T Clark, 2011), p. 245.
12 Philip Collins (ed.), *Thackeray: Interviews and Recollections*, vol. 1 (London: Macmillan, 1983), p. 139.
13 *Irish Sketch Book*, p. 91. John A. Gamble acknowledges the hearty sympathy: 'Whatever one thinks about Thackeray, and no matter how provocative he is, it is apparent that his heart was touched by the poverty of the Irish people' (*The Irish Sketch Book 1842* (Belfast: The Blackstaff Press, 1985), p. ix).
14 Ibid., p. 358. The words in question come in the final chapter describing his visit to the college in the autumn of 1842. They constitute the main part of the case against Thackeray as outlined here (see Note 5, 'Ruin so needless etc.').
15 Ibid., p. 366. Thackeray's encounter near Westport with the glass-blower, a 'poor starving lonely man' (p. 230), is another example of an unforgettable, even haunting moment.

MAYNOOTH COLLEGE AND QUEEN VICTORIA'S VISIT TO IRELAND, 1849

Terence Dooley

n 10 August 1849, during her first visit to Ireland, Queen Victoria visited Carton House in Maynooth, the Palladian mansion of Augustus Frederick FitzGerald, third Duke of Leinster. The Duke was one of Victoria's regular Irish communicants, and one for whom she had a high personal regard, recording in her diary: 'The Duke is one of the kindest and best of men.' The visit was important to him, politically and socially, for, as Thomas Nelson has pointed out, it 'was public proof that the quiet and diligent loyalty' of Leinster and his father, William, before him 'had dissipated any lingering doubts about the allegiance of the FitzGeralds in the wake of the very public rebellion of the 1st duke's son, Lord Edward, in 1798.'

Three years before the rebellion, William, second Duke of Leinster, had provided the lands for the establishment of the Royal College of St Patrick; according to Patrick Corish, he was a liberal Whig whose active good will induced the trustees to build in Maynooth instead of Dublin. In the first half century, the relationship between the FitzGeralds and the college was amiable. Augustus had followed his father's footsteps as a liberal Whig who had supported O'Connell's Catholic Emancipation movement (though not repeal), and it was no surprise, therefore, that of the 200 or so elite guests   aristocracy, gentry, Catholic and Protestant strong farmers, clergymen and professionals drawn from Maynooth and the surrounding countryside, eager to see the young Queen and to be seen – amongst them were Msgr Laurence Renehan (1798–1857), College President, and the elderly Daniel Murray (1768–1852), Archbishop of Dublin. They were all treated to a 'Magnificent Dejeuner' of sumptuous delicacies and luxuries, and entertained by military bands, Sheridan, 'the Kilcock piper', and a well-choreographed 'peasants' dance on the front lawn. Included in the thousands more who flooded into the village by train and lined the roads were around 100 seminarian students. Later that evening, Victoria recorded in her diary that the students 'did not make a very attractive impression'.

The year before the visit, there was a minor spat between Murray and Renehan over the latter's failure to turn up at the lord lieutenant's levee in Dublin Castle. Murray, who had very good relations with successive lords lieutenant, and who, according to Thomas O'Connor, had 'respect for legally established authority' (though O'Connell 'feared that he was over-trusting in his dealings with the government'), wrote in tones of subtle rebuke: 'Observations have lately reached me from different quarters expressing surprise and regret that the President of the Royal College of Maynooth was not among those who, on a recent occasion, thought it right to testify their respect for Her Majesty by appearing at the levée of her Representatives'. He was displeased by the rumour that Renehan had somewhere said if he attended the levee he would 'not be able to govern the college'. Murray complained: 'This if it had a shadow of truth in it would be a sad tale for Maynooth.' That year, Murray had reissued decrees forbidding his clergy from becoming involved in politics.

Renehan's reply was clothed in equal measures of deference and defiance: his absence at the levee, he said, was 'merely from habit and without any distinct motive'; previous presidents had not attended at Dublin Castle except on 'very extraordinary occasion'. 'But,' he continued, 'should Your Grace and the Trustees advise me to the contrary, and authorize me ... I shall feel a pride and a pleasure in following whatever course your Lordships may recommend as most becoming the President of a purely Ecclesiastical College, and most expressive of loyalty to the Queen and of respect to the Irish Viceroy.'

In the grander scheme of things, the spat was minor. Murray and Renehan had much in common: a respect for established authority, a desire to keep their priests and students out of politics, and a political shrewdness necessary to get things done.

In the summer of 1849, the episcopacy was divided on how to welcome the Queen. On 24 July, Archbishop John MacHale of Tuam wrote to Murray urging that a formal address should be presented by the bishops to Victoria in which 'the terrible suffering of her subjects, as well as of the cruel neglect with which they have been treated by her ministers' be laid bare. However, Murray drafted instead an address of warm welcome that paid 'profound homage' to Victoria. The worst social calamity to afflict Ireland was not to be made a point of contention; the address read: 'On an occasion so truly cheering as the present, we will not place before Your Majesty a detail of the many woes of our suffering poor, the thought of which we know pressed already so severely on Your Majesty's parental heart.' MacHale immediately rejected the address and fourteen of the twenty-seven bishops refused to sign it. Murray sent MacHale's criticism to the lord lieutenant, Lord Clarendon: 'Your Excellency will perceive

Carton House, 1894

by the accompanying letter what I have to endure from some of my Brethern.'

In response to the bishops' address, Victoria prayed that 'all classes of my subjects will unite with mutual charity and concord in providing the progressive and permanent prosperity of the country'. It was a standard response but within the context of the famine conditions that still prevailed it had ambivalent resonances. While the guests at Carton feasted at the 'Magnificent Dejeuner', an estimated 141 people in Maynooth were suffering from cholera and typhus and at least forty-seven of them subsequently died. On the same page of the *Leinster Express* that the bishops' address to Victoria appeared, the New East India Tea Company provided prices for a range of luxuries, including teas, coffee, claret, champagne, wines and spirits; the George Hotel at Menai Bridge in Wales invited Irish families 'desirous of combining comfort and quietness' to vacation there; while elsewhere in the paper it was reported that local markets were busy with 'fat cattle' and 'fat sheep ... all sold ... at remunerating prices to graziers'. Insensitivity to the suffering of the poor went far beyond Victoria and the British government, or the resident aristocracy and gentry.

Murray could not be accused of insensitivity to the plight of the suffering. From the outset, he had been extremely diligent in running one of the most impressive famine relief schemes that had operated at national level; thus, his failure to make the suffering of the poor a contentious issue in the bishops' address was likely motivated by his ideological belief that more could be achieved working with the British administration than against it. He clearly also had something of a soft spot for royalty. As soon as he had heard from his Dublin Castle contacts about the Queen's visit to Carton, he wrote to Renehan: 'I am far from thinking it improbable that some of the Royal party will look in on the college. Perhaps even the amiable little Queen may take it into her head to do so.' Of course, she never did, nor did she stay overnight at Carton, another local myth. However, a possible visit must have influenced Renehan to compose an 'Address from the College of Maynooth', which he signed on behalf of the 'President, Masters, Professors and Students'. Taking his cue from Murray's address, his deferential tone offered the 'most loyal, dutiful, and affectionate welcome', and paid 'homage of devoted loyalty'. The essence of the address was to express gratitude ' ... that our college is indebted for an endowment suited to the importance of ecclesiastical education, the wants of a numerous people, and the dignity of a great empire'. While Renehan's address could easily be interpreted as political sycophancy, he was, like Murray, commonsensical enough to know who helped butter the Maynooth bread. In August 1849, the building of A. W. N. Pugin's Gothic edifice was 'far advanced', at a cost in excess of the £30,000 provided under the Maynooth College Grant of 1845. The college trustees could not use this state funding in any other way, but it is likely that the construction work, which lasted almost the entire period of the famine, offered some respite to Maynooth and surrounding areas.

Unfortunately, there seems to be no evidence of the provenance of Renehan's address – Corish, Healy and Newman do not mention it in their histories, and there is no reference to it in the Renehan papers in the Maynooth College archives – or who amongst the college trustees, staff, and students supported or opposed Renehan. In that summer of 1849, staff and students of the college were divided over immediate theological questions concerning the Immaculate Conception, and historical questions over O'Connellite politics (even though the Liberator had died in 1847). In August, there was only about one fifth of the clerical population in the college because of summer vacation, so even if all those in residence signed Renehan's address it could not be taken as a true reflection of majority attitudes. But if the 'amiable little Queen' had visited the college, as Murray had hoped, how might she have been received? Patrick Corish had heard stories that during the prayer sung for the monarch after High Mass each Sunday, some students had replaced '*Domine salvam fac Reginam*' with '*Domine salvam whack Reginam*'. The anecdote certainly suggested division. However, Corish speculated that if Victoria had visited it was 'likely that courtesy would have won in the actual presence of royalty'. He was a historian who did not need banks of statistics to explain human nature.

Further Reading

R. V. Comerford, 'Grievance, scourge or shame? The complexity of attitudes to Ireland's Great Famine', in Christian Noack, Lindsay Janssen, Vincent Comerford (eds.), *Holodomor and Gorta Mór: Histories, Memories And Representations of Famine in Ukraine and Ireland* (London, 2013)

Patrick J. Corish, *Maynooth College 1795–1995* (Dublin: Gill & Macmillan, 1995).

John Healy, *Maynooth College: its Centenary History* (Dublin, 1895).

James Loughlin, *The British Monarchy and Ireland: 1800 to the Present* (Cambridge: Cambridge University Press, 2007).

Walter McDonald, *Reminiscences of a Maynooth Professor*, ed. Denis Gwynn (Cork, 1967 ed.).

David Murphy, 'Renehan, Laurence F', *Dictionary of Irish Biography* [*DIB*]. *Reign of Queen Victoria* (Cork, 2001).

Thomas Nelson, 'Lord Frederick FitzGerald (1857–1924) and local politics in county Kildare', in Patrick Cosgrove et al. (eds.), *Aspects of Irish Aristocratic Life: Essays on the FitzGeralds and Carton* (Dublin: University College Dublin Press, 2014), pp. 197–209.

Jeremiah Newman, *Maynooth and Georgian Ireland* (Galway: Kenny's Bookshop and Art Galleries, 1979)

E. R. Norman, 'The Maynooth question of 1845', *Irish Historical Studies*, 15, no. 60 (1967), pp. 407–37.

Thomas O'Connor, 'Murray, Daniel', *DIB*.

REMEMBERING NICHOLAS CALLAN
(1799–1864)

Niall McKeith

icholas Joseph Callan was born on 22 December 1799, the fifth child in a family of six or seven, at Darver, between Drogheda and Dundalk. His initial education was at an academy in Dundalk, run by a Presbyterian clergyman, William Nelson. His local parish priest, Fr Andrew Levins, took him in hand as an altar boy and Mass server, and saw him start the priesthood at Navan seminary. He entered Maynooth College in 1816 and was to remain there for almost the rest of his life.

In his third year at Maynooth, Callan studied natural and experimental philosophy under Dr Cornelius Denvir, who would later to become Bishop of Down and Connor. Denvir introduced the experimental method into his teaching and had an interest in electricity and magnetism. After ordination as priest in 1823, Callan went to Rome, where he studied at the Sapienza University, obtaining a doctorate in divinity in 1826. While in Rome, he became acquainted with the work carried out by Luigi Galvani (1737–1798) and Alessandro Volta (1745–1827), pioneers in the study of electricity. On the resignation of Dr Denvir, Callan was appointed to the chair of Natural Philosophy in Maynooth in 1826, and he remained in that post until his death in 1864.

Callan's major claim to fame is as the inventor of the induction coil. Following earlier experiments, he discovered in 1836 that when a current sent by battery through a 'primary' coil (a small number of turns of thick copper wire around

Image: Blue Plaque outside Callan Hall

a soft-iron core) was interrupted, a high voltage current was produced in an unconnected 'secondary' coil (a large number of turns of fine wire). Callan sent a replica of his coil to William Sturgeon (1783–1850) in London in 1837, and it was exhibited to members of the Electrical Society there to their great amazement.

In view of the great importance of Callan's invention of the induction coil, one might wonder why he was forgotten, and his invention attributed to a German-born Parisian instrument maker, Heinrich Ruhmkorff (1803–1877). The answer is simple. Maynooth was a theological university where science was the Cinderella of the curriculum. Callan's colleagues often told him that he was wasting his time. In such an atmosphere, Callan's pioneering work was simply forgotten after his death. Like all instrument makers, he put his name on every instrument he made. 'Ruhmkorff Coil' got into the textbooks. It was never challenged until1936, when Professor P. J. McLaughlin published his researche on Callan's publications, which proved incontrovertibly that the inventor of the induction coil was Nicholas Callan of Maynooth. The first acknowledgement of Callan as its inventor was in the 1953 edition of Gregory and Hadley's *Textbook of Physics*, revised by George Lodge, senior science master at St Columba's College, Rathfarnham. There is reference to Callan as inventor of the induction coil in the 1903 *Encyclopedia Britannica*. While working on electromagnetic engines in 1838, Callan may also have discovered the principle of the self-excited dynamo, though he did not follow up this line of research. In his words, he found that 'by moving with the hand some of the electromagnets, sparks are obtained from the wires coiled around them, even when the engine is no way connected to the voltaic battery'.

With the need to produce reliable batteries for his researches in electromagnetism, Callan carried out important work in this area, inventing the 'Maynooth' battery in 1854, and a single fluid cell in 1855. Previous batteries had used expensive platinum, or unsatisfactory carbon, for one of their plates, and zinc for the other. Callan found that he could use inexpensive cast iron instead of platinum or carbon. In the Maynooth battery, the outer casing was of suitably treated cast iron, and the zinc plate was immersed in a porous pot in the centre. This required two different fluids, on the inside and outside of the porous pot. However, Callan also found that he could make a simple and useful battery by dispensing with the porous pot and the two fluids, using a single solution instead. This was the forerunner of the lead acid battery that we know today. The outer casing of the battery was made of iron and, as his laboratory was in the damp basement of Stoyte House, the iron began to rust. He began to

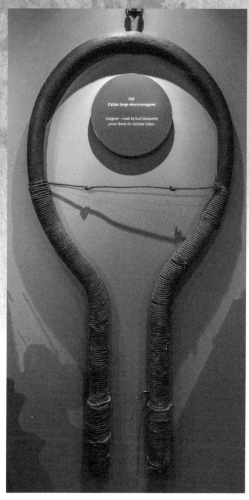

Callan's Large Electromagnet (1836),
Science Museum

see if he could devise a method of preventing the iron rusting. He invented the process of galvanisation and discovered and patented the means of protecting iron from rusting. His patent with Queen Victoria's seal is on display in the college museum.

Callan used students to measure voltage. He would make fifteen students hold hands and the two on each end would have to hold on to the output terminals of his giant coil. He determined the size of the voltage he was generating by how high the student jumped. In one of these experiments, he rendered one of the students unconscious. That student went on to be Archbishop Walsh of Dublin

Callan's Giant Induction Coil (1859–1863), Science Museum

NICOLAO CALLAN

QUI PROFESSOR PHILOSOPHIAE NATURALIS

TOTUM SE INVESTIGATIONI PHAENOMENORUM MAGNETICORUM

PER ANNOS FERE XL DICANS

HEIC ADINVENTIONES NOTABILES

PRAESERTIM SPIRAM AD VIM ELECTRICAM INDUCTAM AUGENDAM

EXCOGITAVIT

ANNO MCMLXIV AB EIUS DISCESSU CENTENARIO

Plaque commemorating the centenary of the death of Nicholas Callan, 1964

in 1916. The incident is mentioned in his biography. Callan was forbidden to use students in his experiments in future.

There is a story that Callan rode to Birr to see the giant telescope. On arrival at the castle, he was told that Lord Ross was too busy to see him and he had to return to Maynooth. Some time later Lord Ross arrived at the college gate to see Callan's large coil. The message sent down from Callan suggested that Lord Ross should return to Birr and point his telescope in the direction of Maynooth and he just might 'see' the giant coil. Another illustration of his sense of humour was to use his large electromagnet in a tug of war with six of the strongest men in the village. A metal plate, a keeper, was placed across the magnet, which was capable of lifting several tons. A rope was tied to the keeper and the men would try to pull with all their might to break the power of the magnet. When they could not, and when they huffed and puffed, Callan would switch off the current to the coil and the men would all fall to the ground to the great amusement of the general populace.

Callan apparently had little or no interest in money. Although he patented the principle of galvanisation, there is no record of his receiving any royalties from his invention.

In the chapter of McLaughlin's book on Callan as a priest he was described as one of 'these great and good men' whose 'blessed examples of ecclesiastical virtue' made a mark on the young levites. He was amiable, modest and retiring, and was noted for his 'child-like tenderness and large benevolence'. Acquaintances found him grave in manner, sometimes not 'with you', yet at the same time 'not without genuine humour'.

Recently Callan's work has been better acknowledged; firstly by the Institute of Physics, which awarded him their blue plaque for his contribution in the field of physics. The Institute of Electronic and Electrical Engineers awarded him their bronze plaque for his contribution in the field of electricity. Indeed, Callan is the first Irish person to be awarded this honour. These plaques are mounted at the entrance to the largest lecture theatre on the South Campus, Callan Hall. In the year 2000 the Irish government, as part of the millennium celebrations, issued a series of postage stamps, one of which featured Nicholas Callan and his giant induction coil.

Further Reading

P. J. McLaughlin, *Nicholas Callan, Priest-Scientist, 1799–1864* (London: Clonmore & Reynolds, 1965; republished at St Patrick's College Maynooth by Niall McKeith in 2000).

100 YEARS OF MAYNOOTH

An Account of Centenary Celebrations in June 1895

Barbara McCormack

Detail, College Chapel from
Healy's *Centenary History*

The Royal College of Maynooth was established in June 1795 by an act of the Irish Parliament 'for the better education of persons professing the popish or Roman Catholic religion'. In June 1895, the college marked its centenary with an ambitious programme of celebrations, including banquet dinners, lectures, and a fireworks display.[1] The Board of Trustees resolved to mark the centenary at their meeting in June 1894 and appointed a committee to oversee the celebrations, consisting of members of the Catholic hierarchy, college staff and two priests from each diocese. The first meeting of the Centenary Committee, chaired by Cardinal Michael Logue and attended

---

1 For a detailed account of proceedings see John Healy's *A Record of the Centenary Celebrations held in Maynooth College in June, 1895* (Dublin, 1896).

by over forty members, took place on 4 October 1894.[2] It established a number of subcommittees to manage various practical aspects of the celebrations, which would take place over three days from 25–27 June 1895. This included a banquet committee, an invitation and reception committee, a religious functions committee, and a book committee.

The college sent a formal address to Pope Leo XIII regarding the upcoming celebrations in early May 1895, and issued invitations to prelates around the world, including those in England, Scotland, the US, Australia, Italy, France, Belgium, Spain, Portugal, Germany, Austria, Hungary and Switzerland. Among the large number of responses received by the college, were congratulatory addresses from Pope Leo XIII, Cardinal Vaszary (primate of Hungary), Cardinal Gibbons (archbishop of Baltimore) Cardinal Bourret (bishop of Rodez), Archbishop Corrigan of New York, Archbishop Vignan of Lyons and Archbishop Williams of Boston. Several universities sent a formal address to mark the centenary, including the University of Salamanca in Spain, the Gregorian University of Rome, Georgetown University in the US, the Catholic Universities of Paris and Lyon, and the University of Freiburg in Switzerland. Religious bodies and institutions also sent formal addresses, including the monasteries of Monte Cassino (Italy), Maredsous (Belgium), Solesmes (France), Einsiedeln (Switzerland) and Melk (Austria).

A resolution of the trustees in October 1894 agreed to the issuing of a pastoral letter from the Catholic hierarchy outlining the current financial position of the college and encouraging the funding of free places for students as an 'excellent form of promoting religion'.[3] The only politician invited to the celebrations was Mr Justin McCarthy, chairman of the National Party.[4] McCarthy preceded John Dillon as leader of the Irish National Federation (INF), which had emerged as a national party following the Parnellite split and which enjoyed considerable support from the Catholic clergy.

The large number of attendees at the celebrations necessitated the scheduling of additional trains from Broadstone to Maynooth.[5] The celebrations began with Pontifical Vespers, officiated by the Archbishop of Dublin and presided over by Cardinals Logue and Vaughan, followed by Benediction during which the choir sang *O Sacrum Convivium*. A banquet dinner took place at half-past five, with music performed by the String Band of the Second Battalion Rifle Brigade, and at eight o'clock Dr Lennon, Professor of Natural Philosophy, delivered a lecture on 'The production and transmission of electric energy'. Guests were invited to

2   *Cork Examiner*, 6 October 1894.
3   Ibid., p. 697.
4   Ibid., p. 696.
5   *The Freeman's Journal*, 20 June 1895.

attend a concert in the Aula Maxima before retiring for the evening.

The second day of the celebrations began at ten o'clock with a solemn Mass of thanksgiving, sung by the Archbishop of Dublin, followed by Benediction and a *Te Deum*. After lunch at two o'clock an academic meeting took place in the Aula Maxima at which the Most Rev. Dr Healy, coadjutor Bishop of Clonfert and author of *Maynooth College: Its Centenary History*, delivered a lecture on the history of the college. A centenary banquet for 350 guests took place in the students' refectory at six o'clock and there was a fireworks display on the college grounds at ten o'clock. The final day of celebrations began with Pontifical High Mass at ten in the morning for benefactors of the college, sung by the Archbishop of Tuam. An academic meeting in the Aula Maxima and lunch at half past two rounded off the celebrations. The students enjoyed their own banquet at six o'clock that evening.

During the celebrations, the Very Rev. Gaffney proposed the establishment of a society for past students and friends of the college. Cardinal Logue outlined the benefits of establishing such a society, which included the interchange of views amongst priests, the generation of financial support for the college following disestablishment, and the creation of a monument to celebrate the centenary.[6] Dr Walter McDonald read a paper on the benefits of the society, which noted the need for priests to remain 'intellectually active' at a time when members of the laity were becoming increasingly educated.[7]

The centenary celebrations received positive coverage in the press, with one newspaper describing the college as 'a lasting memorial of the unconquerable devotion and piety of this Irish Nation'.[8] Another account referred to the college as 'the greatest civilising factor in Ireland from the Irish standpoint', adding that 'Maynooth has supplied patriots as well as priests to Ireland'.[9]

Hundreds of priests and other members of religious orders enjoyed the centenary celebrations; however, many of the students at Maynooth were probably preoccupied with exam preparations, the Board of Trustees having refused a request from the student body to cancel the examinations in light of the festivities.

6   *The Cork Examiner*, 28 June 1895.
7   *The Cork Examiner*, 28 June 1895.
8   *The Evening Herald*, 24 June 1895.
9   *The Irish Daily Independent*, 26 June 1895.

College Seal from Healy's *Centenary History*

A FITTING FAREWELL

Heinrich Bewerunge's Music for the Re-interment of Eugene O'Growney, 27 September 1903

Darina McCarthy

No hymn, of all those we heard again and again from the college choir, will echo through the chambers of the mind as vibrantly as will that opening peal of harmony on which was lifted up the words, 'Sicut locutus est per os sanctorum'. All over the world, men who once stood there will find stirring again in their memory the springing, staccato line of notes that went hurrying along to join the superb swell of heavenly harmony at the close of every verse. The kith and kin of the dead, who lie beneath the little headstones there, will remember it to the end, for it will have made a path through their hearts as it did through ours.[1]

eil Kevin's description refers to a setting of the canticle 'Benedictus' by Heinrich Bewerunge (1862–1923), first Professor of Gregorian chant and Organ at St Patrick's College Maynooth. The genesis of this piece of music provides an opportunity to recall two great men of Maynooth: Bewerunge and his colleague Eugene O'Growney (1863–1899). Both were prevented from fulfilling their mature potential, the former through the exigencies of the First World War and the latter through illness, and Ireland was a poorer nation for their loss.

O'Growney, with Douglas Hyde and nationalist Gaelic scholar Eoin MacNeill (1867–1945), was a founder member of the Gaelic League, and he was appointed Professor of Celtic Literature and Language at Maynooth in 1891. His appointment and Bewerunge's within three years of each other in two newly revitalised departments created a natural link between music and Irish.

1 Neil Kevin, *I Remember Maynooth* (London: Longmans, Green & Co., 1938), p.162.

Rev. Prof. Heinrich Bewerunge

They were demonstrative of the college's efforts to advance and improve its programme of studies. These young professors, less than a year apart in age, were symbolic of a concord between Gaelic identity and Catholic identity, creating a bridge between the traditional Catholic hierarchy and the secular movements of cultural nationalism.

Bewerunge's attraction to Ireland's national music was evident from his time as editor of the church music journal *Lyra Ecclesiastica*, where he included a number of articles on Irish music. Later, he undertook pioneering work in ethnomusicology through his advocacy of melodic preservation and his unique analysis of Irish airs. He led media discussions concerning the difficulty in notating traditional Irish melodies using the staff system, and the distinctions in folk song performance between native Irish peasantry and stage performers.

In the secular sphere, he taught organ, chant studies, theory and harmony privately as well as at the Leinster School of Music. His early musicological achievements included the publication of Ireland's first music periodical, the *Irish Musical Monthly*. He assisted in the establishment of an Irish branch of the International Musical Society; he was a member of the Incorporated Society of Musicians, the Dublin Orchestral Society, the Dublin Musical Society, the Gaelic League, the Irish Folk Song Society and the Feis Ceoil Association, serving his turn on committees for many of these organisations. His activities placed him within a social and cultural milieu that represented an advancing Ireland, associating with figures such as conductor and composer Michele Esposito (1855–1929), musician and historian W. H. Grattan Flood (1857–1928), dramatist and patron of the arts Edward Martyn (1859–1923), and Douglas Hyde (1860–1949), Gaelic League founder and first president of Ireland.

Bewerunge's international profile increased during the early twentieth century as he presented at conferences abroad and published in European and American journals. Following his appointment at University College Dublin in 1914, he was poised to become the single most influential figure in Irish music education, holding professorships in the National Seminary and the National University. However, the upward trajectory of his career was abruptly terminated by the outbreak of the First World War: he was visiting his family in Germany at the time and was unable to return. He was finally permitted to return to Ireland in 1920, but his deteriorating health prevented him from resuming his scholarly activities and he died in 1923.

Like Bewerunge, O'Growney's work-rate was significant within Maynooth and beyond. To facilitate his student lectures, he compiled an Irish grammar, two Irish reading primers, and part of a composition manual. He was also required by the Maynooth trustees to deliver six public lectures annually on Irish literature and archaeology. Shortly before his appointment at Maynooth, he was appointed editor of *Irisleabhar na Gaedhilge*, the organ of the Gaelic Union. Additionally, the Archbishop of Dublin, William Walsh, encouraged O'Growney to publish a language learning series in the *Weekly Freeman* and *Irisleabhar na Gaedhilge*; these were later compiled in book form as *Simple Lessons in Irish* and became a fundamental tool for Irish beginners. Their aim was to teach pronunciation through phonetics, and were aimed primarily at students who undertook the study of Irish without the assistance of a teacher. They were described by Michael O'Hickey, O'Growney's successor at Maynooth, as

Bewerunge's *Benedictus*

'probably the greatest individual service ever rendered to the Irish language movement'.[2]

O'Growney suffered from tuberculosis and his health began to fail in 1894. He took leave of absence from Maynooth and moved to the drier, warmer climate of California. En route, he completed the second volume of *Simple Lessons*, and wrote the third volume while in America. His health did not improve; he resigned from his Maynooth post in 1896 and died in 1899 at the age of thirty-six. A campaign to repatriate his body sparked a wave of nationalistic sentiment on both sides of the Atlantic, and the Californian branch of the Gaelic League raised sufficient funds to arrange his return to Ireland. His final journey brought

2   Michael P. O'Hickey, 'Father O'Growney', in *Irish Ecclesiastical Record*, November 1899, p. 438.

him from Los Angeles to Maynooth four years after his death; his remains were venerated through public processions and requiem Masses in Los Angeles, San Francisco, Chicago, New York, Cork, Dublin and Maynooth. The solemnities encompassing his return to Ireland were a nexus for political, socio-economic and religious constituents of the Gaelic revival, uniting radical and moderate elements in a brief communion to honour the priest whose Irish language primers made him a household name.

The last portion of O'Growney's pilgrimage was from Dublin to Maynooth, his alma mater, on Sunday, 27 September 1903. Special trains brought approximately 500 members of the Gaelic League and thousands of other mourners, who were met at the railway station by St Patrick's College staff and students. The procession to the college was led by the Maynooth contingent, numbering about 600. The hearse was next, followed by branches of the Gaelic League, leading members of the revivalist movement, and great crowds who were kept in check by hurlers with their camáns. As the cavalcade moved up Leinster Street, turned left and up towards the college gates, the choir sang a *Miserere*, a setting of Psalm 50 composed by Bewerunge for the occasion. Even-numbered verses were chanted, and odd-numbered verses were harmonised in sixteenth-century fauxbourdon style. The psalm's twenty verses brought the hearse to the college gates, and the procession moved in silence to the square, where the students arranged themselves behind a black-draped pulpit. The choir then sang the *Benedictus* canticle, a setting also composed by Bewerunge for the occasion and which Neil Kevin described so vividly. Like the *Miserere*, the *Benedictus* was in fauxbourdon style with alternating chanted and harmonised verses. As the coffin was placed on a bier and the rest of the mourners filed in, the students sang 'Marbhna Eoghan Uí Ghramhnaigh', a caoineadh in Irish composed by a Maynooth student and set to an old Irish air with Bewerunge's assistance. After the funeral oration, delivered in Irish, the body was brought into the College Chapel, and O'Growney was finally back with his own community. Vespers were chanted and the choir sang Bewerunge's *Magnificat*, the third piece he composed for these unique, emotionally charged ceremonials.

Final liturgies were celebrated the following morning in the chapel, which was draped with black to mark the solemnity of the occasion. Four bishops and about 200 priests from around Ireland were in attendance, as well as Maynooth's staff and students. Bewerunge presided over the choir; his usual *schola* of approximately fourteen men was augmented by another nine former choir members. Lauds from the Office for the Dead was sung (including Bewerunge's *Miserere* and *Benedictus*), followed by solemn requiem Mass. O'Growney's body was then brought in procession around the grounds of the college, the casket and bier drawn by black-plumed horses, preceded by priests bearing lighted tapers, and followed by a long line of students in soutanes and surplices. As O'Growney was laid to rest in the church tower, Douglas Hyde and other dignitaries bade their final farewell by kissing the casket.

Throughout the twelve decades since its first performance, and for all its repetition at many funerals and liturgies, Bewerunge's requiem *Benedictus* has lost none of its affective power. It has indeed made a path through our hearts and become part of the fabric of Maynooth's traditions.

Afterword

The New York Gaelic League raised funds to erect a monument over O'Growney's grave, and on the day of the final requiem Mass, Michael O'Hickey proposed the idea that such a monument should take the form of a simple early Irish chapel. Douglas Hyde and Edward Martyn chose a design submitted by the architect William A. Scott, and this memorial was erected adjacent to the Maynooth graveyard. W. A. Scott is the present writer's great-great-uncle.

In 1963, ceremonies were held at Maynooth to celebrate the centenary of O'Growney's birth. RTÉ archives have forty seconds of film footage from this occasion, showing a long line of seminarians processing from the chapel towards the graveyard, and Sinéad de Valera, wife of President Éamon de Valera, laying a wreath at the O'Growney monument. The footage can be viewed at: *www.rte.ie/archives/2018/0813/984788-father-eugene-ogrowney*

O'Growney's repatriation ceremonies were extensively covered in the newspapers. More substantial sources for further information on the life and death of O'Growney include:

Timothy G. McMahon, *Grand Opportunity: The Gaelic Revival and Irish Society 1893–1910* (New York: Syracuse University Press, 2008).

Agnes O'Farrelly, *Leabhar an Athar Eoghan* (Dublin: M.H. Gill & Son, 1904).

Michael P. O'Hickey, 'Father O'Growney', in *Irish Ecclesiastical Record*, November 1899, pp. 426–443.

SEANMÓIRÍ MUIGHE NUADHAD I–III
(1906–08)

Ciarán Mac Murchaidh

A small but highly important project begun in Maynooth around the latter end of 1904 or early 1905, which came to fruition in the period 1906–08, must represent one of the earliest manifestations of the practice of 'crowd-sourcing' in the world of Irish-language studies. The project in question, *Seanmóirí Muighe Nuadhad* (The Maynooth Sermons), was initiated by a group of clerical students involved in the college's Irish-language society, Cuallacht Choilm Cille. Their plan was to publish a selection of sermons in the Irish language on a diverse range of themes from the Murphy and Renehan manuscript collections held in the college library. The resulting initiative led to the publication of three volumes: volume 1, published in 1906 by Browne & Nolan (of Nassau Street, Dublin), and volumes 2 and 3, published in 1907 and 1908 by M. H. Gill (of O'Connell Street, Dublin). There were fourteen sermons in the first volume, thirteen in the second and twelve in the third and, as was the convention of the time, the Gaelic font was employed throughout.

Each volume is prefaced by a one-page introduction which provides an insight into the work involved, the challenges encountered by the students and some idea as to their motivation and approach. For instance, the students' original intention was to publish the first volume in the summer of 1905, but publication was delayed for unspecified reasons. It is possible that the slow and tedious nature of the transcription involved was one of the root causes. More interestingly, the students stated in the preface that they did not expect to have to shoulder the burden of copy-editing the volume, having already transcribed the text from the manuscripts. They also made the decision not to include a glossary, as it was felt (probably quite sensibly) that there were few words or terms in the text that were not to be found in Fr Patrick Dinneen's newly-published *Irish-English Dictionary* (1904). These challenges negotiated, the students succeeded in producing in printed form from handwritten manuscript sources almost forty sermons in the course of three years.

The seminarians' endeavour had the financial support of the Maynooth Union.

The union subsidised the Maynooth Manuscripts Publication Committee, which was active between 1906 and 1915 but which ceased to meet after June 1915 for no apparent reason. In the introduction to the third volume, the editors indicated that they had plans to publish a fourth volume in which the text of eight more sermons would be included, along with brief accounts of the authors which, one assumes, meant the scribes who copied the original manuscript texts. In the true spirit of the crowd-sourcing approach they admitted: 'We would need help from anyone who knows about their lives and work. We shall be grateful for any assistance, no matter how small, that might be provided to us.' Events intervened, however, and, for reasons that cannot be established, the fourth volume appeared in 1911 but not in the form they anticipated. The volume was given over instead to the presentation of a new edition of the eighteenth-century Irish sermons of Bishop James Gallagher, two of which had appeared in the previous volumes of *Seanmóirí Muighe Nuadhad*. This volume was edited and prepared for publication by Fr Paul Walsh, the renowned Celtic Studies scholar.

The sermons published by the students span the years 1724 to 1844, and the list of scribes of the various manuscripts from which they derive reads like a 'Who's Who' of those who were actively engaged in this activity at the time. The two most prolific were Micheál Óg Ó Longáin (fourteen sermons) and Seán Ó hÚghbhair (ten sermons). Ó Longáin (1766–1837) was one of the most productive scribes and translators operating in eighteenth-century Ireland. In his comprehensive description of scribal activity, Breandán Ó Conchúir listed over 150 manuscripts known to have been written in part or in whole by Ó Longáin, and a further fifty or so to which he contributed in a lesser way. Others involved in transcribing the manuscripts in *Seanmóirí Muighe Nuadhad* were Seán Ó Conaire, Seán Ó Muláin and Seán Ó Murchú na Ráithíneach. The subjects of the sermons were those commonly addressed by Catholic sermon-writers of the time and include such matters as the Mass, eternal life, temptation, sin, penitence, the sacraments, heaven, purgatory and hell, the passion of Christ, and devotion to various saints (e.g. Patrick and Columbanus).

These manuscript sermons were written as part of a tradition of preserving and disseminating devotional material in Irish that extended back to the work of the Irish Franciscans, who were based at Louvain in the early seventeenth century. The students' idea of producing printed material from the native corpus of manuscripts was doubtless influenced by the contemporary revival movement about which they were already aware. As priests in the making, these clerical students experienced their formation in a college that was imbued with the potential for change in the early years of the twentieth century. In 1903, for example, the seminary authorities allowed the students access to Catholic periodicals in English, French, German and Italian. Their exposure to the writings of Catholic authors in European languages may have encouraged them to pay more heed to what was now identified as their native language and it is likely, therefore, that they saw themselves as contributing to its revival. In October 1898, the seminary trustees sanctioned the establishment of a student society whose aim was to foster among students an appreciation for the cause of religion, the national literature and its language, as well as history, hagiography and archaeology. The society became known as Cuallacht Cholm Cille, a society that still exists in Maynooth. With the prevailing sense of revival in the language nationally, conditions were ripe for projects such as the one in hand. In referring to their work in the introduction to the first volume, the editors stated: 'We hope that it will benefit those who desire to preach the Word of God in Irish.' Furthermore, in keeping with the enthusiasm for the promotion of the language associated with the early decades of the twentieth century, the editors commented: 'Anyone who reads these sermons will observe the excellence of the Irish in them and how unspoilt and how vibrant the language was when they were written' (volume 2), and that: 'The Irish in this book is an eloquent, elegant Irish. We do not contend that it is without flaw but let it be understood, nevertheless, that it is the speech of the authors themselves and that we neither added to it nor detracted from it save on occasion here and there' (volume 3).

In producing *Seanmóirí Muighe Nuadhad*, the students who participated saw themselves as making a contribution to the advancement of the Irish language in the revival era, especially in the context of the Catholic Church and religious practice. By so doing, they provided to the Irish-reading public examples of the best devotional writing of previous centuries, indicating to them simultaneously the richness of the library holdings in the college. Their efforts illustrated their enthusiasm and sense of purpose. They also contributed to the promotion of a tradition of literary and scholarly activity in Maynooth College, which has remained part of the college's tradition to this day.

Further Reading

Patrick J. Corish, *Maynooth College, 1795–1995* (Dublin: Gill & Macmillan, 1994).
Breandán Ó Conchúir, *Scríobhaithe Chorcaí, 1700–1850* (Dublin, 1982).
Meidhbhín Ní Úrdail, *The Scribe in Eighteenth- and Nineteenth-Century Ireland* (Münster: Nodus, 2000).

In Memory of Maynooth
FR DREA'S DRAWINGS

David Bracken

n Limerick Diocesan Archives, among the collected papers of Dr Jeremiah Newman, President of Maynooth (1968–74), is a curious volume entitled 'Drea Drawings'. A graphic diary of sorts, largely completed by September 1913, it documents the ministry of the newly ordained Fr Martin Drea (1888–1965). Following ordination in Maynooth for the diocese of Ossory in June 1911, Fr Drea was appointed to Hexham and Newcastle diocese, where he served in St Michael's Parish, Eshlaude, County Durham, and from 1912 ministered in the outlying All Saints Church, Lanchester.

Ostensibly a collection of humorous pen and ink cartoons, the 114-page diary (22 x 18.5 cm) is a remarkable window on the work of an Irish priest in England at the beginning of the second decade of the twentieth century. Of particular interest, however, are reminiscences of student days in Maynooth from 1904 to 1911, twenty-four pages in all, recalled from the distance of the English mission. Drea paints an evocative picture of St Patrick's College, with character studies of students and staff, together with observations on discipline and the rule. Staples of seminary life, including sports and recreation, student theatre, the rhythm of chapel and class hall, punctuated regularly by exams, all feature in this unique record. A talented cartoonist, three of his drawings were published in Patrick Corish's *Maynooth College, 1795–1995* but incorrectly attributed to James Cassin, also of Ossory diocese.

Drea recalls freshmen from city and country – 'cool', 'dead solid', 'not a stayer!' – encountering the assembled Maynooth professors during entrance week. 'All seemed at least six feet seven! Fearfully black!! Awfully severe!!! Oppressively dignified.' He charts the good student's 'pilgrim progress' from first year 'chub' to 'old fourth', quoting from Shakespeare's *Julius Caesar*, 'O what a fall was there, my countrymen!'. In contrast with the rake who, once 'drawn and quartered', left the college, 'unwept, unmourned, and unsung'. The voice of the bell, voice of God, rings constantly and the omnipresent figure of the dean, enforcer of the rule, shadows the pages. Vice-President Dr Gil[martin], 'sometimes came during drill to show us how to walk'. The round of classes, *De Deo uno*, St Thomas cheek by jowl with Darwin. 'The V.P. (Dr Gil) gives a lantern lecture.' Professor of Philosophy Peter Coffey 'calls' a student in criteriology: his contemporary, the philosopher [Maurice] de Wulf literally astride the page, 'De Wulf goes for a train'. 'Expedients in Gregorian chant' for the benefit of the 'flying Dutchman', Heinrich Bewerunge, Professor of Church Chant and Organ. 'Oh for shame Bev!' The 'foretaste of purgatory' that was the oral exam and the '*non-intelligo!*' of the student before his inquisitor.

In counterpoint to the strictness of the seminary regimen there is a sense of camaraderie and levity among the student body. As in the case of a seminarian judged by fellow students to have '"made a howl" in some department', hoisted shoulder high and unceremoniously dumped on the cloister to be discovered by the dean. Games also provided release. Lawn tennis for the more refined. Gaelic football, soccer, rugby and hurling – which 'cannot be done justice to on paper' – were all played in shorts above the knee in relaxation of former practice. A series of twenty-two miniature character studies, entitled 'Recollections of some of the Maynooth plays', depict cast members in various theatrical productions mounted by students. These include *King Lear* and one of the four Shakespearean plays featuring Falstaff, with James Bonnar, a Derry student ordained in 1915 in the comic role. In fact, eleven student actors are named by Drea and most are identifiable, including Christy Flynn as the eponymous Lear.[1] Fr James Christopher O'Flynn, ordained for Cork and Ross in 1909, founded the Cork Shakespearean Company and later came to prominence for his ground-breaking work in speech therapy. Other plays presented to the student body included *Richelieu*, likely the 1839 play by Edward Bulwer-Lytton, and one of the plays based on the Irish mythological figure, Deirdre.

---

1   Student actors with diocese and date of ordination: either [Michael or James] Cashman, 'as Cordelia' (Cork and Ross, 1914 and 1915 respectively); P[eter] Connolly, 'as the King in *Deirdre*' (Clogher, 1915); Tom Doyle (Derry, 1910); [Patrick] Gaynor, 'as Rich[e]lieu' (Killaloe, 1911); [Michael] Grogan (Galway, 1913); J[ohn] Henaghan (Tuam, 1909); Mick Kirwan, 'as the Jester' (Waterford, 1912); [Joseph] McGonigal, 'in *Rich[e]lieu*' (Raphoe, 1915); either M[ichael or Martin] Murray, 'as Deirdre' (Waterford, 1911 and Killaloe, 1914 respectively).

Drea Sketches

Drea Sketches

In March 1905 the Daughters of Charity of St Vincent de Paul took charge of the Senior Infirmary. Their work is recalled in a plate entitled, 'Undergoing an operation in Maynooth (from life!)'. The procedure is conducted by two frightening surgeons, assisted by an anaesthetist, pocket watch in hand, and one of the sisters. Overhead, a picture of the sacrifice of Isaac by his father Abraham! An aside subtitled, 'An unexpected operation on the part of the patient' sees the patient rise up mid operation fists flying!

In the Lanchester drawings a similarly vivid portrait emerges of his parishioners, many of whom were Irish emigrants working in the Durham pits. The sketches also capture glimpses of the domestic life of the community, with additional references to education, sport, the emerging scouting movement and the novelty of the cinematograph. Beneath the playful whimsy of many of the pieces, which betray a keen eye for detail, is a perceptive commentary on the life of a young Irish migrant priest. A particularly poignant self-portrait, 'Thinking of old times', head buried in his sketchbook, hand clutching desk, conveys something of the loneliness and isolation of the young priest and the difficult experience of transitioning from seminary to parish ministry.

The volume is dedicated to Dr Daniel Mannix (1864–1963), coadjutor Archbishop of Melbourne and formerly president of St Patrick's College, Maynooth. The dedication reads, 'Never having had any training in the art of drawing, the curate in charge on the English mission who perpetrated these sketches makes no apology for their artistic defects. His sole object in filling this little book was to give a little memento to the late president of Maynooth (under whom he spent seven happy years)'. A letter of thanks from Mannix acknowledging receipt of the volume in July 1914 mentions a levy duty on works of art coming into Australia. 'The authorities opened the album … and it took them two weeks to decide whether the album was liable to duty, and how much.' He thanks Drea for 'a gift that cost you so much, and so much appeals to me'. A treasured memento from a former student, it was removed from the archbishop's papers after his death in 1963. While on holiday in Ireland during the summer of 1965, a Kilkenny priest based in the diocese of Melbourne, a Fr Duggan, gave the book on loan to Fr W. O'Keefe, parish priest of Castlecomer. Fr O'Keefe in turn sent it to Dr Jeremiah Newman, then on the staff of Maynooth College and later Bishop of Limerick, where the drawings ended their peripatetic journey in the diocesan archives.

Fr Drea returned to Ireland in 1920 and was appointed curate in Thomastown, County Kilkenny, later serving in various positions in the diocese of Ossory before returning to Thomastown as parish priest in 1943. He died there on 23 April 1965.

A Time and Motion Study
A REMINISCENCE OF WALTER McDONALD

Thomas O'Loughlin

In early 1990s the Jesuit Library in Milltown was being catalogued on computer. In the process many lost items were found, duplicates and dross eliminated, and much merriment caused at morning coffee by some of the older titles or the curious decisions of earlier librarians as to where books belong. It was while the librarians were working through the Eucharist section that one day it was remarked that among works on Eucharistic controversies they found a book on physics! How could such a blunder have occurred? Someone expressed the opinion that Homer nods and another a sigh of simple disbelief. 'Yes,' replied the librarian, 'it was there indeed: a book on motion and kinetic energy!' I was not taking much part in the conversation having just come from class, but at the word 'motion' my ears pricked up: could it be? Surely not, they were all destroyed! At once I checked that the book had not been binned and asked to see it. Five minutes later I held in my hands a copy of *Motion: its Origin and Conservation*, published in Dublin in 1898 by Walter McDonald, a Maynooth professor. I realised at once that that the older librarian had *not* erred: this was a book that was shelved correctly and it should be returned to its place or, more properly, placed in the strong room with other precious or unique items. Why such excitement?

When McDonald died in 1920 he knew that this book – his magnum opus – had been condemned by an unpublished decree of the Holy See as dangerous heresy and was convinced that every copy had been consigned to the flames. After a judicial process it was decreed that not only was it to disappear completely, but even the memory of the fact that a Maynooth professor had strayed into heresy was to be obliterated.

However, McDonald was dauntless and had written an autobiography of sorts, his *Reminiscences of a Maynooth Professor*, which set out his side of the story, all the secret decrees, and a summary of his position and arguments. Moreover, he had arranged that Denis Gwynn, an Anglican, would carry out his wishes and have *Reminiscences* published posthumously. He had asked an Anglican to do this for him because, as such, he was a not a canonical subject and

Rev. Prof. Walter
McDonald

so could not be prevented in the task *sub poena peccati* (for heretical disobedience) nor by excommunication *latae sententiae* (for uttering secret documents of the Holy See). McDonald himself could not be punished as he also was, by then, no longer a subject of canon law (due to death) and this was his last chance to vent his theological vision. In the pages dealing with motion (pp. 111–66) there is a note of bitter sadness that not only did those around him – all the way to Rome – not understand what he was trying to do, but that even if they banished his work, that one day, some day, his work would be vindicated. Just as Galileo had replied to his tormentors: 'but it still moves!'; so McDonald knew every time he heard the whistle of a steam train passing Maynooth that the kinetic theory of motion was a cornerstone of modern physics, no matter what Roman congregrations decreed.

But what is the problem? Today we cannot even fathom the assumptions of the paradigm within which McDonald lived, taught and was condemned. Put simply, if one starts from an assumption that all 'change' (e.g. from Fido alive to dead) and all 'motion' (e.g. from being here to being there) are linked to so-called Aristotelian 'substances' (not what we mean by 'substance' in everyday life), then change and motion (to add confusion, both words are usually rendered as '*motio*' in Latin) must behave in parallel ways. But modern physics thinks of energy being transferred from mass to mass without an Aristotelian 'agent' (who brings the motion into existence), and so eventually Einstein could conclude $E=mc^2$. But what about the Eucharist, when there is a change with one 'substance' becoming another – without energy being transferred (for that would mean that wine had a natural potency to become a divine substance) – and this motion was caused by an agent (the priest) who had the potency to truly and really cause the change (and metaphysical '*potentia*' is almost the opposite of physical 'energy')? Since this latter motion was certain (defined by Trent, however it be labelled), and this change took place in the real world of things (e.g. the wafer on the paten), it had to conform to the laws of physics. If the students of physics (e.g. the scientists whom McDonald was reading) could not explain this *motio* during Mass within their theory, then they must be the wrong-headed followers of a corrupt modern theory. Consequently, any theologian who took them seriously – as distinct from the Neo-Scholastic theories just then being brought back into fashion – must be guilty of error.

The reason we today cannot enter this debate, except as curious travellers back in time, is that we recognise that both McDonald and his opponents assumed that theological explanation – which is, after all, seeking to express a mystery in words – is a *different kind of pursuit* from that which underlies empirical science. Moreover, we realise that taking any statement of a religious truth and expecting that it behave as an axiom across the board is the very kernel of fundamentalism. Catholics often snigger on hearing of nineteenth-century Protestants using the book of Genesis to counter the evidence of geologists that there was no Flood, or using the book of Ezekiel to calculate the end of the world, but McDonald and his critics were engaged in a struggle with exactly the same epistemological parameters. If one cannot ask the weight of a human soul nor measure with a theodolite the depth of someone's love, then one cannot address the Eucharistic mystery with a physics of change: even if this had been done for centuries. McDonald was condemned as the outsider, but reading *Motion* today we can see that he was as much locked within this univocal system as those who silenced him.

So was McDonald an original theologian? A paradigm is only replaced when the contrary evidence becomes so overwhelming that is it seen to be absurd. In a world of theological repetition, Walter McDonald had the energy, insight and courage to bring the problem to a head. This fearless confrontation of problems is McDonald's claim to be the only original theologian Maynooth produced in its first century. *Sacrosanctum Concilium*, the Second Vatican Council's constitution on the liturgy, would not appear until forty-two years after his death.

The crisis over *Motion* rattled on with occasional articles for nearly a decade, and though he remained a teacher in Maynooth and made other contributions to research, notably *Some Ethical Questions on War and Peace*, McDonald was a man under a cloud. He tells us that he wrote other theological textbooks but they were not passed by the censor, and that he had deposited them for safe keeping in the hope of future publication in more open times. Where are they now? Perhaps we will get some nice surprises one day!

He died, according to his grave marker, on the feast of St Athanasius, 2 May 1920. How appropriate for a theologian who in his own time was *contra mundum*.

GUNN, GUN OR CEASEFIRE?
A Maynooth College Naming (and Shaming) Saga

Denis Bergin

ven if your current acquaintance with Maynooth is confined to a nostalgic nod as you traverse the M4 motorway that bypasses the town, you cannot but be impressed that despite all the machinations of modern infrastructural development, the spire of the College Chapel still dominates the landscape.

This is the landmark of which a local newspaper remarked, during the final stages of its construction in the early 1900s, that 'when the edifice is completed 116 feet of it will be composed of white stone, which will make the memorial strikingly conspicuous at a distance of many miles and effectually locate the famous college to travellers passing within its view'.

Even though it has been a feature of the college's architecture for only a little more than half of its lifespan, the chapel's iconic status has been bolstered by a distinctive appellation: The Gun. Or, indeed, The Gunn.

In the annals of higher learning the naming of academic buildings for benefactors or notables is so common as to be unremarkable – until, as happened some time ago with the Rhodes Building and its statue of the eponymous Cecil at Oxford's Oriel College, somebody creates a fuss and demands a public shaming and precipitate de-naming.

However, sometimes the accepted name of a prominent building can languish and die for no good reason other, perhaps, than the fact that no one can remember who the honoured one was, why he or she was being commemorated in the first place, or even if they ever existed. The corporate mind is uneasy about the possible ramifications of such tenuous situations, and so it is often tempted to resolve them by official forgetfulness.

The publication in 2018 of a short official illustrated history of the College Chapel at Maynooth by Pat Watson therefore brought an end, it would seem, to its popular appellation among staff, students and the wider world.

There is no reference in the publication to any connection of the chapel, in its foundation, funding or use, with any named person or weapon. An official

College Chapel

pronouncement by the college authorities that all future references should be to 'the College Chapel', may have hastened the disposal of the hallowed designation.

The South Campus of Maynooth's combined institutions (Pontifical University, National Seminary and Maynooth University) does not have much in the way of exotic or imaginative building nomenclature, particularly of the honorific variety. New House, for instance, is called that because it was new in the early nineteenth century, and indeed new again upon its rebuilding following a disastrous fire in the 1940s.

Loftus, whether in its singular or plural form as one hall or many, top or bottom, is named for an unremarkable Dublin-born civil servant who moved to England on promotion. Michael Loftus died in retirement in Bournemouth in 1929 and left the equivalent (in today's money) of €1.75 million to the college, with the provision that the early annual income from it be applied to modernising the college library.

The modernising implemented by the college authorities involved the takeover by the library of the floor area below it, previously used as classrooms, and the construction of a two-storey add-on that would become the new theology halls, as indeed they still are; the name of the generous donor remains resolutely attached.

In more recent times the dedication of a new library to Pope John Paul II and the naming of spaces and facilities on the South Campus for the architect Pugin and College Presidents Renehan and Russell, have been joined by the designation of the former Senior Infirmary, now the nerve-centre of Irish ecclesiastical administration, as the Columba Centre, a gesture to a distinguished saint who died twelve hundred years before the college was founded.

There are a few signature buildings on the North Campus that are named for people like John and Pat Hume, or concepts like Iontas, but, generally speaking, and apart from a few soaring vistas for the greater glory of God, modesty is the theme of the built environment on both sides of the Kilcock Road.

The word that sounds like 'gun', however spelt or capitalised, was traditionally used in common Maynooth parlance to refer to excellence in personal achievement or artistic presentation. An ordnance-based derivation of the term was credible because the impact of the person, event or object referred to in those terms could easily be related to the impact, and sometimes the sound, of the weapon's purpose or firing.

A 'gun' was a person of academic note; a 'gun' or even 'gunny' practice sermon had serious complimentary overtones; the appellation 'the gun chapel' was, by implication, an indication of a striking architectural statement, both inside and out, as the College Chapel undoubtedly is.

The question of what came first, the concept of 'gunniness' that was then applied to the new building, or the completion of the College Chapel that then inspired it, is at the heart of this seminal issue in the college's history.

Some commentators have connected the use of the patronymic, as opposed to the ordnance, version of the word to a Junior Dean named John Gunn, an Elphin priest who had a brief and unremarkable career in the college in the 1840s. In fact, so unremarkable and ill-received was Gunn's deanship (according to Patrick Corish's bicentenary history) that to be called a 'gunn' might be regarded as a form of insult.

When he died in retirement in a Dún Laoghaire hotel in 1893, 'Dean Gunn', as he seemingly chose to be known, left an estate of £210, or about €30,000 in present-day value. The dean, who had written a fond reminiscence of Maynooth, which was published in the *Irish Ecclesiastical Record* in the 1880s, may indeed have made a gesture of financial support to his alma mater from this or a previous munificence.

The president of the college for much of Gunn's short tenure as dean was a man who had spent his entire adult life, as student, professor and administrator, at Maynooth from its establishment in 1795. He was a Tyrone-born priest named Michael Montague. The planning of the College Chapel began shortly after his death in 1845 and would continue for six decades until the completion of the spire (while some references suggest 1902 as the date of completion, others do not fix the execution of the finishing touches until 1911). Along the way it engaged (and sometimes disposed of) the talents of four architects, beginning with the notable Mr Pugin.

Fr Montague had a nephew named James McMahon, who attended Maynooth in the early years of his uncle's presidency, graduating to the Dunboyne Institute before embarking on a mission first as a Sulpician student, priest and professor in Paris and then Montreal, and finally as a pastor in a number of New York City parishes.

Using a small legacy and carefully managed donations, McMahon built up a fund so large that he became known as America's richest priest (his *New York Times* obituary called him a 'frocked Croesus'). In 1892, he retired to quarters on the campus of the Catholic University of America (CUA) in Washington DC, to which he promptly gave $400,000, or about €10 million in present-day value, to fund an academic building to be known as McMahon Hall, a name it still bears.

Aula Maxima (before buttresses were added)

When the Maynooth authorities heard of this, they wrote to him seeking assistance with the costs of completing the College Chapel and a nearby assembly hall or Aula Maxima. He sent $3000, worth about €75,000 in today's money, and this was applied mainly to the hall, which was, like its Washington counterpart, to be known as McMahon Hall.

Sadly, the McMahon luck did not rub off on the plain little building. Within a quarter of a century its physical state was such that it had to be repaired at a cost exceeding what had been expended on the original construction. It remains today much as it has been since that rebuilding: large, functional and relatively unmodernised. Nor did the naming plan work: it is still known, as it has been for almost all of its 120 years, as the 'Aula Maxima'.

McMahon had a fellow-Irishman as a colleague at CUA: a young Marist priest, also from Tyrone, who had just arrived in the US after spells of learning and teaching in Dundalk, London and Rome. Then, and later as a parish priest in Atlanta and a Bishop in Mississippi, he showed an extraordinary interest in church building and organ construction. His name was John Gunn. Perhaps from his own resources, or with some assistance from McMahon, Bishop Gunn gave some money for the completion of the College Chapel and it was named, formally or informally, in his honour.

If this was indeed so, the name stuck to the sponsored building in a way denied to the nearby structure supported by his rich friend. In recent times, for instance, the Gunn appellation has been used in the title frame of a US Catholic television programme broadcast from 'The Gunn Chapel, Maynooth'; a report in a Catholic journal about the conferring at Maynooth of an African priest with a degree in theology, which took place in 'The Gunn Chapel'; and the parking instructions for Maynooth parishioners whose church was under reconstruction, in recent years, and who were allowed to use the facilities of the 'College Chapel (Gunn Chapel)'.

As further evidence that old habits continue to die hard, the official Pontifical University/Seminary website carried a report on a graduation ceremony held in November 2019 in 'the Gunn Chapel'.

Some time ago, when I addressed a Maynooth alumnus and senior staff member of the secular university as a former 'gun' (though gunmanship may, of course, be a lifelong attribute), he corrected me severely, and said that everybody knew the correct term was 'Gunn', in memory of Canon Gunn, who was a Senior Dean when the chapel was built (factually at least, he is wrong on two, and possibly all three counts).

Meanwhile, another relative of both Msgr McMahon and his uncle, Fr Montague, had chosen a different route to fame or notoriety. Francis Montague entered the college alongside McMahon during the elder Montague's presidency; he was ordained from there in 1842, served in various Armagh parishes and eventually was appointed to Drogheda. There he fell in love, eloped secretly to England and got married. He returned to Ireland some time later and was appointed parish priest of Cookstown. But his double life was detected, and he returned to England, where his growing family soon began to show signs of spectacular potential.

One son became a respected historian and Oxford don (coincidentally, at the aforementioned Oriel College); another became Chief Medical Officer of Fiji; a third, Charles Edward Montague, married the daughter of the *Manchester Guardian*'s C. P. Scott and became, in effect, editor of that paper during fallow periods of his father-in-law's sixty-year tenure.

After the priestly Francis Montague died in England in 1893, leaving a widow, four grown offspring and several grandchildren, nine of his nieces and nephews in Tyrone, including a priest, petitioned the courts for a declaration that he had no immediate family and that they should be allowed to administer his estate. Their petition was granted.

College Cemetery

If Ireland ever wanted to right that particular wrong, it could do worse than consider the achievement of Charles Edward Montague's son, and Fr Francis Montague's grandson, Evelyn Aubrey Montague. Like his father, he would become a notable writer and war correspondent before his early death at age forty-eight. In 1924 he ran in the Paris Olympics, training and competing in so remarkable a manner that his story was dramatised in the 1981 film *Chariots of Fire*. He could, in many respects, be called 'a gun'.

It may be that Maynooth is not the place for a monument to the Montague family or their connections (though the Montague priestly tradition continues down to the present day in Armagh, and living memories remain of a Fr Gerard Montague's term as dean in Maynooth in the 1940s and 1950s and later as pastor in Belfast during the early Troubles).

The strange unwinding of the Montague and McMahon sagas, and their overtones of spectacular wealth and contorted legalities, surely deserve at least a thought as one observes the unusual gravesite of Michael Montague, the College President, in the Pioneers' Plot of Maynooth College Cemetery. For whatever reason, it is the only one completely enclosed by an unscalable iron railing.

Canopy of Yew Trees approaching the College Cemetery

TEETOTALLERS' REBELLION IN THE PROFESSORS' DINING ROOM

Michael Mullaney

To read the history of Maynooth College, it would sometimes appear that its past is constituted of long periods of somnolence punctuated by brief interludes of passionate, even explosive, tension. One such interlude might easily be assumed to reflect and participate in the rise of national enthusiasms that manifested themselves at the cusp of the nineteenth and twentieth centuries. This was, after all, the period that saw such bursts of raw energy as created the Father Mathew temperance movement or the Gaelic League and was a prelude to the decade of the 1916 Rising and the War of Independence.

These movements had widespread spin-offs in society generally and, in spite of its enclosed nature, the college was not immune from parallel enthusiasms, often with unusual preoccupations and unpredictable outcomes. One episode that might be included in such a category was an odd, not to say comic, moment from the early years of the twentieth century that amounted to a rebellion of the teetotallers in the Professors' Dining Room. The incident is recorded in detail in correspondence found among the papers of a recently deceased colleague.

These years witnessed a process of what used to be called 'tightening up' in the organisation and discipline of the seminary after the long presidency of the elderly Denis Gargan. He died at the age of eighty-three after spending himself in the effort to build and pay for the spire that marked the centenary of the college in 1895 and still marks the Maynooth skyline.

He was succeeded by the towering figure of Daniel Mannix, who would later, as Archbishop of Melbourne, dominate the Catholic Church in Australia for half a century. It was clear even at the time that this authoritarian cleric had been appointed to 'tighten things up'. He had been unkindly described by a visitor to the college as 'a consecrated ramrod in a purple cassock'.

No one had any doubt that the seminary needed a thorough reform and, as happens in such circumstances, it was probably equally clear that there would be restiveness from students and staff. Few, though, could have foreseen the explosive outcome of the National University agitation and the Michael O'Hickey case from 1909 to 1911.[1]

In the midst of all this drama, a number of these reforms, as well as the enthusiasms of the time, all well-meaning, seemed to come into headlong collision, in a fashion that produced a somewhat farcical backdrop to the greater issues.

At the October (1909) meeting of the Episcopal Trustees of Maynooth College, at the height of the impassioned debates over the role of Irish in the National University and the pending dismissal of Michael O'Hickey, Professor of Irish in the college, amid all the sound and fury, a request appeared on the agenda of 'Their Lordships' which must have set many of them, beset as they were, clucking with impatience. As had so often happened in the long history of the institution, it was the result of an internal row among the teaching staff.

As part of the 'tightening-up process' conducted by President Mannix, the trustees had been persuaded to create a new entity within the college: 'The Cellar'. Very likely the brainchild of Mannix himself, who had of course been a member of the staff since 1891, it would appear to have been an ingenious method of, if not control, at least surveillance, of the drinking habits of its members.

Briefly, a common stock of wines and whiskies was to be laid down in the handsome stone vaults of the cellar immediately under the Professors' Dining Room. The capital for this was to be constituted by each member of staff contributing an equal share at the beginning of each year. Each member in turn then took charge of the key so that all should have access to wine or spirits, either for an occasion at the common table or for after-dinner guest entertainment. The attraction for this was the monetary advantage to the members of bulk-buying and, for the authorities, a certain discreet supervision of drinking habits.

This should have been fairly foolproof, but it had not taken account of the

1 Fr Michael O'Hickey (1860–1916) was appointed Professor of Irish at Maynooth in 1896, succeeding Fr Eugene O'Growney, and vigorously promoted the language once there. In 1897, Eugene O'Growney wrote from Arizona that, in place of only four or five ardent students of Irish, there were now over 200, thanks to O'Hickey's efforts, despite his being renowned as a rather dull teacher. In 1908 the Gaelic League demanded that Irish should be considered an essential subject for matriculation in the newly founded National University, established under the Universities Act of that same year. This was opposed by Fr William Delany SJ, President of the Catholic University, and himself also a Gaelic Leaguer. Although he had recently resigned from the Gaelic League for other reasons, Michael O'Hickey weighed in on the controversy in favour of making Irish mandatory for matriculation. He took aim at the senate of the new university, which was comprised, among other notable Catholics, of two archbishops and the President of Maynooth, asking how 'any body of responsible Irish ecclesiastics could embark upon a more foolish or reckless course than to take sides in this instance with the enemies of Ireland'. The conflict escalated, culminating in O'Hickey being asked to resign his chair at Maynooth and, having refused to do so, he was dismissed from his post. A subsequent appeal to Rome found no traction. O'Hickey died in Portlaw, County Waterford, in 1916. See Leon Ó Broin, 'The Gaelic League and the Chair of Irish in Maynooth', in *Studies: an Irish Quarterly Review* 52:208 (winter, 1963), pp. 348–62.

new enthusiasms of the moment. There was by this time a sizeable minority of total abstainers on the staff (eleven of them, claims the correspondence to the bishops), no doubt as a result of what that correspondence also refers to as 'the healthier attitude in public opinion in regard to drinking', perhaps an early fruit of the Pioneer Total Abstinence Association, founded in 1898.

The teetotallers therefore petitioned the bishops to authorise them to set up their own exclusive common stock. They demonstrated by a long and closely reasoned calculation that they, the teetotallers, were, by the current regulations, being 'taxed' to support the drinking of the non-abstainers, and so being forced to act against their principles. This, they represented, involved their lordships in an arrangement inimical to the campaign to promote total abstinence in the country as well as being a monetary injustice to the non-drinkers. They rejected entirely what were clearly the arguments of the drinkers, namely that the arrangement that obtained had always been customary, that any society needs to have 'give and take', that the injustice to the teetotallers was minimal (*parvulum pro nihilo sumitur*, 'a little is counted as nothing') and so on. One suspects here not only argument but also personal intrigue on the part of the

Fireplace designed by Pugin

drinkers, but the argumentation bore the clear imprint of minds with a lifetime's experience of dialectic.

The copious correspondence went on until 1910 in the teeth of the national drama being played out *extra muros* and to the exasperation of the bishops. It was largely sustained by Peter Coffey, priest of the diocese of Meath, internationally known luminary of Neo-Scholasticism, enthusiastic revivalist of the Irish language, and lifelong proponent of total abstinence, typically a fine example of his time. The letters and the arguments went back and forth, getting ever more pernickety, until the affair was ended by a curt letter from the secretary to the trustees dated June 1910, putting paid to it all and enforcing the status quo ante.

The common stock arrangement subsisted in essence until recently, though with decreasing relevance to current circumstances. The college cellar is still carefully secured and tightly monitored by its stewards in the vaults beneath the Professors' Dining Room.

As a final irony, the correspondence detailing this brief, intense internal revolt turned up in the papers of the late Ronan Drury, himself a priest of the diocese of Meath and a lifelong teetotaller. He was also, perhaps, one of the last members of the Father Mathew Union, an association of clerical abstainers whose rules were somewhat less rigorous than those of the Pioneers. They permitted drinking wine abroad, for example, and were stoutly promoted by the Vice-President of Maynooth, Msgr P. J. Hamill, an inveterate traveller. His contemporaries used to tease Ronan Drury for his fidelity to the union by claiming that the laxity of its central rule meant that its members were permitted to drink alcohol 'only when they felt like it'.

The letters have now been deposited in the college archives.

SEAN O'RIORDAN CSSR (1916–1998) AND *THE FURROW*

Brendan McConvery

Sean O'Riordan CSsR

Sean O'Riordan would never have been a student in Maynooth had it not been for the Second World War. The war made it impossible for prospective postgraduate students in theology to travel to the continent, where most Irish religious orders sent their students for degrees that would enable them to teach in their seminaries or houses of study scattered throughout Ireland. Many opted to send their students to 'the Dunboyne' – the postgraduate department of the Maynooth Faculty of Theology. The Dunboyne was bursting at the seams with Irish, Scots and English students, religious and diocesan, who were unable to get to the continent during the war and some years subsequent to it. The Redemptorists sent three promising students – Fr Antony McHugh to take a degree in canon law, Fr Gerald Crotty to specialise in moral theology, and Fr Sean O'Riordan in dogmatic theology. The regime in the college was spartan: wartime rations were thin and the high ceilings and long corridors of the college buildings were virtually impossible to heat with the limited amount of fuel available, particularly in the memorably cold winter of 1947. The members of the religious orders, including the Redemptorists, were spared some of its rigours by spending the weekends with their communities and returning to Maynooth on Monday morning.

O'Riordan was regarded as something of a prodigy in his own community. Born in Tralee on 18 October 1916, his father Michael was a national school teacher who was hungry for knowledge. He introduced Sean to Latin at the age of six and to French a few years later. He studied privately for the BA of the University of London, graduating in 1924 in Latin and geology, gaining such distinction in his examinations that he was elected a fellow of the Royal Geographical Society on the strength of his results. Sean's mother had died earlier that year and Michael brought the boy to London for his final examinations: late in life, Sean remembered the impression of awe and mystery that the Wembley Exhibition made on him.

Sean went to the Redemptorist College in Limerick for his secondary education. Being too young to go to the novitiate, he sat the Leaving Certificate twice. The first time, he got first place in Ireland in English, and on the second occasion, got high distinction in his remaining subjects.

After his profession as a Redemptorist in 1935, he began the study of philosophy in the Redemptorists' student house in Athenry, County Galway. The full range of philosophical and theological subjects was taught to thirty-seven students by a staff of five who served as lectors in the main subjects (moral, dogma, Scripture, philosophy, Church history) and shared out the minor ones between them. The course, aimed at the lowest common denominator of student, did little to tax young O'Riordan's brain power. The director of students gave him the run of the library, with permission to read as much as he wanted, and when Esker's limited store of German books ran out, arranged for him to have access to the library at University College Galway. The only condition attached to this privilege was that Sean was not to spread too many new ideas around among his fellow students!

After ordination, there followed a BA in History and Classics at University College Galway, and after a year teaching in his old alma mater in Limerick, he was sent to Maynooth to take the licentiate and doctorate in theology.

Sean O'Riordan found Maynooth congenial. More gregarious than his Redemptorist companions, he enjoyed the company of his Kerry co-diocesans particularly. He took part in many of the student activities and met a man who was to become a life-long friend, John Hennig, a German refugee and authority on the medieval Irish Church who had found a niche teaching German in Maynooth. By birth a Lutheran, Hennig's marriage to a Jewish woman, Kläre Meyer, made it impossible for him to remain in Germany. In 1936, he converted to Catholicism, followed shortly afterwards by Kläre. A Jesuit friend found him a place teaching in Belvedere College in Dublin, from where he found part-time teaching in Maynooth. The Hennigs' circle of friends included other Germans in the Dublin academic world like Erwin Schrödinger, Nobel prize-winner for physics, and the scholar of Old Irish, Ludwig Bieler. After the war, economic conditions forced Hennig to take a job with the recently founded Bord na Móna, and later with the ESB, combining work with his study of medieval religious texts. A large number of his articles were collected and published as *Medieval Ireland, Saints and Martyrologies*.[1]

Sean wrote his doctoral thesis on 'The Figure of Wisdom in the Old Testament' under the direction of John O'Flynn, professor of New Testament, and the College *Kalendarium* of 1947 records that he was granted the doctorate in divinity. The choice of topic meant he was embarking on a career as a lector in Scripture in Cluain Mhuire, the newly founded Redemptorist house of studies in Galway city. His name duly appears in this capacity in the class lists of 1946. Sean was never textbook driven. Teaching basic Hebrew to students, he sometimes resorted to using poems by modern Hebrew poets to teach a grammatical point.

During his time in Maynooth, Sean O'Riordan had made the acquaintance of a small group of Maynooth colleagues and friends who conceived and brought to birth *The Furrow*.[2] It probably owes its name to Sean who was a reader of an Austrian Catholic pastoral journal of the same name (*Die Fürche*), which had been founded in Vienna immediately after the war as a liberal Catholic weekly for society, politics, culture, religion and the economy. O'Riordan first got the smell of newsprint in his nostrils at the age of fifteen when he wrote an article on the Eucharistic Congress of 1932 for *The Kerryman*.[3] With J. G. McGarry as editor, Sean and Ronan Drury as assistant editors, and Michael Mooney as treasurer, they scraped together enough money to launch it in 1950. Sean was a regular contributor, writing articles ranging from 'The Assumption in Irish Tradition' (1950), or 'The Cult of St Brigid' (1951), to one introducing the still largely unknown Alcoholics Anonymous to the Irish public.[4] Sean's main contribution in the early years was to comb the continental theological and pastoral journals for items of interest to the Irish clerical public, and to write book reviews.

During a short study visit to Rome, O'Riordan was asked if he would be willing to come to teach at the Alphonsian Academy, which had been recognised by the Holy See in 1957 as 'a public internal institute', under the care of the

---

1   John Hennig, *Medieval Ireland: Saints and Martyrologies*, ed. Michael Richter (Northampton: Variorum Reprints, 1989.

2   His own reminiscences of his links with the journal can be found in 'The Furrow: 1950–1990: A Personal Review of "A Varied Programme"', in *The Furrow*, vol. 41, no. 2 (February 1990), pp. 71–80.

3   'The Congress: A Kerry Student's Impressions of a Memorable Visit'.

4   'Grace Is Sufficient – Why Alcoholics Anonymous?', in *The Furrow*, January 1951. It was frequently reprinted by the AA as a handout to enquirers.

Redemptorists, but open to external students. He was duly appointed in July 1958, and for a few years divided his time between Ireland and Rome. In 1960, he became an 'extraordinary professor' when the academy was affiliated to the Lateran University with the power to confer the doctorate degree. Later he would be appointed 'ordinarius' and serve as first vice-president of the academy from 1973 until 1983.

O'Riordan's arrival in Rome coincided with the summoning of the Second Vatican Council. Ireland expected little from the council. The wave of new theological thinking Sean had been exploring in his *Furrow* surveys of the German and French reviews had not broken on the Emerald Isle. Rome in those days was an exciting place to be. Theologians who were media-friendly were popular, and Sean's natural ease of manner and willingness to put complex topics into non-technical language won him many friends among the English-language correspondents covering the council. Among his colleagues in the Redemptorist community house were Francis X. Murphy CSsR who, apart from teaching patrology in the academy, was an 'insider commentator' on the council under the pseudonym of Xavier Rynne,[1] and Bernhard Häring, moral theologian and council *peritus*.

Sean contributed a series of articles to *The Furrow* detailing the work of the council and the conversation (and occasionally gossip) that surrounded it.[2] It was a task he continued through the series of synods that followed the council.[3]

Sean celebrated his seventieth birthday in 1986 with a colloquium that brought to Dublin some of his peers and former pupils like Bernhard Häring, Charles Curran, Joseph Fuchs, Kevin Kelly, Raphael Gallagher and others to present papers in his honour. A few more years of shuttling back to Rome remained until he finally retired from the academy. He delivered his last lecture on his eightieth birthday, 18 October 1996, and his last doctoral student defended in December of that year. Failing sight made it impossible to do any further writing, and he died peacefully on 26 January 1998.

---

1   His books include *Letters from Vatican City: Vatican Council II, first session; background and debates* (1963); *The second session; the debates and decrees of Vatican Council II, September 29 to December 4, 1963* (1964); *The third session; the debates and decrees of Vatican Council II, September 14 to November 21, 1964* (1965); *The fourth session; the debates and decrees of Vatican Council II, September 14 to December 8, 1965* (1966).
2   For example, 'The Second Vatican Council: The End of the Second Session', in *The Furrow* vol. 15, no. 1 (January 1964), pp. 14–21; 'The New Theology', in *The Furrow* vol. 17, no. 2 (February 1966), pp. 67–72; 'The Second Vatican Council: The Pope, the Curia and the Bishops', in *The Furrow* Vol. 14, No. 12 (December 1963), pp. 735–43.
3   For example, 'The Synod of Bishops: A Theological Event',in *The Furrow*, vol. 18, no. 10 (October 1967), pp. 565–72.

TWO CONCERTS IN THE 1940s REMEMBERED

James Good
(Background by Penelope Woods)

most unusual letter arrived in the college post room for the Russell Library. It had come from Lodwar, a desert town west of Lake Turkana, in Kenya. The letterhead showed a simple line map of the region, and the paper was tissue thin. Dated 3 March 1994, the letter was sent to me by the late Fr James Good who was then a missionary in Lodwar. He wrote in response to a request in *The Furrow* for information. Fr Good had thought back to his days as a seminarian, between 1941 and 1950, had sat down at his typewriter and, with a clear memory and delightful turn of phrase, had written about two musical events that had been arranged for the students by the College President, Msgr Edward Kissane, described later by Msgr Patrick J. Corish, then still a student himself, as genial by temperament, large-minded and a lover of the arts. He had become president in 1942. The first event was a performance by a piano quartet, the Quatuor Belge, and the second was one by the world-famous Hungarian violinist, Jelly d'Arányi. The first was to have a dramatic impact on the second.

The four distinguished musicians who came together to form the Quatuor Belge in 1941 had fled Belgium, probably in May 1940 when the country was invaded. The only performances in Ireland traced in the newspapers took place in 1943. The quartet gave concerts in the Aberdeen Hall of Dublin's Gresham Hotel in March and April 1943. Was this the time when they were invited to perform at Maynooth?

There were three sisters d'Arányi, grand-nieces of renowned Hungarian violinist Josef Joachim. All three were musicians and had left their native Budapest in 1909 to visit England, and there they had remained. The two youngest, Adila and Jelly, were famous as concert violinists. Jelly regularly played with Ethel Hobday as her accompanist. Ethel was originally from Dublin and together they gave several concerts in Ireland. Jelly played to great acclaim in the Royal Dublin Society on at least three visits in the late 1920s. She was hailed as one of the finest female violinists in the world. In 1937 Ethel Hobday had started a subscription to present Jelly with a Stradivarius violin: £1,400 was raised. In those days a Stradivarius cost £3,000. Jelly paid the difference herself, saying that she had bought the body of the Strad and her friends and admirers its soul. Her biographer, Joseph MacLeod, based *The Sisters d'Arányi* (1969) on the long conversations he had with Jelly shortly before her death in 1966.

Jelly had performed with the Radio Éireann Symphony Orchestra at the Capitol Theatre in Dublin on 12 December 1943. She paid another visit to the city in 1945. Moved by the destitution and misery that she saw on the streets she arranged on both visits to play for the Legion of Mary. During the 1945 visit, while shopping with Mrs W. B. Yeats's coupons, she received an invitation to meet the Taoiseach, Éamon de Valera. According to Jelly's own recollection, the concert at Maynooth took place on the same tour. She was very definitely a performer of the highest calibre. On 5 February 1945, she gave a concert in the Gresham Hotel with Kitty O'Callaghan as accompanist. The Maynooth concert perhaps took place at about the same time.

Fr Good wrote:

> Not many seminarians in Maynooth during my years were involved in music. The then president, Rt Rev. Mons. Edward Kissane (distinguished scriptural scholar), tried his best to educate the students in fine arts and invited some distinguished musicians to perform in the College Aula Maxima. The Quatre Belges [recte Quatuor Belge], an ensemble of four, performed about 1942. When they came on stage to prepare their instruments before their formal entry, the students applauded and the four almost panicked at the noise.
>
> Jelly d'Arányi, Hungarian violinist, performed about the same time. The student body was solemnly warned not to make the slightest sound during the performance. They obeyed so totally that at the end the artiste declared that she was so overcome by the silence that she almost smashed her Stradivarius off the ground with tension. At the end of the performance a memorable event occurred which also revealed her tension. The President, a magnificent figure in flowing gown, marched up on to the stage to congratulate the lady on her performance, whereupon, much to the delight of the 600 students, she attempted to throw her arms around his neck, getting what was probably the most vociferous applause of her career for this very special performance.

Now, Jelly had a reputation for 'gypsy fire' and for being 'vivacious and passionate' on the stage, so when the students sat completely silent, as bid, after their noisy faux pas at the earlier concert, it was no wonder Jelly became utterly frustrated. Poor Jelly. However, she did get a thundering accolade in the end when, instead of exchanging courtesies with the president, she made to fall on his neck with what must have been mixed anguish and exasperation. That was it for the boys, imagine the hoots and cheers! The college was an enclosed world at that time: the Daughters of Charity in their white starched cornettes had charge of the infirmaries, refectories and sacristies; but otherwise women were rarely permitted inside, so the impact made by Jelly d'Arányi must have been extraordinary. There was yet more to make the occasion memorable. It was usual to hold concerts in the mid-afternoon. Jelly had apparently been invited to lunch beforehand. According to MacLeod, after lunch she asked to rest in the artists' room, and found it filled with smoke because a cleaner, thinking the fire was out, had put the cinders in a bucket with some amateur costumes on top. Subsequent reports compared Jelly to Joan of Arc at the stake. This is the only part of the Maynooth visit mentioned in the book!

These concerts took place during 'the emergency' of the Second World War. It was a time of austerity – shortages made conditions difficult and demanded ingenuity and self-sufficiency. In 1945, there were 573 young men to be housed and fed. In bread alone, they ate their way daily through a loaf apiece, each two pounds in weight. The college owned a thousand acres of agricultural land apart from the College Park, and a new farmyard with a granary had been recently built. The bursar, Daniel Hourihane, kept a diary and accounts which show him as much a farmer as anything else: making weekly calculations of livestock, pricing sheep dip, selling wool and buying seed for turnips, cabbages, kale and onions. Good coal for the boilers was not to be had, and turf was needed for generating college electricity. The buildings were bitterly cold and damp, particularly in February, the presumed time of the d'Aranyi concert. It was even worse that particular year, for the boiler in the Aula Maxima had broken down at the end of January …

A concert would raise morale. What fee had to be paid to have an internationally famous violinist perform for the college at that time? When Jelly had played with the Radio Éireann Orchestra in 1936, the fee of £10 was the highest ever paid by the state.[4] That turned out to have been a very special rate, reduced on account of her friendship with Thomas J. Kiernan and his wife, Delia Murphy, the ballad singer. Kiernan had been secretary to the Irish High Commission in London between 1924 and 1935 and subsequently director of Radio Éireann. He returned

---

4   My thanks to Dr Joseph Kehoe for this information.

Jelly d'Arányi – signed portrait of the Hungarian violinist

to the diplomatic service in 1941 and for five years was minister plenipotentiary to the Holy See, in close contact with the Irish religious communities in Rome and at home. Was it through him that the concert in Maynooth was arranged? To date, no details have been found in the college archives. Fr Good concluded his account with the sting in the tail:

> We were told later that she sent a bill to the College for £100, which was a massive sum in those days.

If true, it was indeed.

DEBATING CINEMA AND CENSORSHIP IN MID–1940s' MAYNOOTH — WITH A TWIST

Salvador Ryan

t the Catholic Truth Society of Ireland (CTSI) conference in 1923, its vice-president, Sir Joseph Glynn, encouraged Irish Catholics to build the state along Catholic lines and to 'restore to their public life the Catholic atmosphere it once possessed'. He also referenced the poor level of organisation among the Irish Catholic laity, especially when compared to their counterparts in the rest of Europe.[1] His rallying cry was a call to Catholic Action. To some extent this had been already happening since the early years of the twentieth century when vigilantism and nationalism, in Maurice Curtis's words, became 'strange bedfellows', as campaigns emerged to combat the sale of English Sunday newspapers and other immoral literature.[2] Through the 1920s it was not unusual for groups with names such as the Angelic Warfare Association to hold up trains and sequester any newspapers they found morally objectionable and, indeed, to boycott any shops that were content to sell them.

By the 1930s and 1940s there was a new threat to the preservation of good morals: motion pictures. In 1934 the League of Decency was founded in the US to ensure that the censorship process for Hollywood films was sufficiently rigorous. This was soon followed by the establishment by Will Hays of the Production Code Administration (PCA). The PCA pledged to first refer all prospective film scripts to the League of Decency for assessment, and there was a heavy fine ($25,000) for any film that was found to be without official PCA approval at the end of the process.[3]

The League of Decency won the admiration of Pope Pius XI. In the introduction to *Vigilanti Cura*, a 1936 encyclical letter addressing the US

---

1   Maurice Curtis, *The Splendid Cause: the Catholic Action Movement in Ireland in the Twentieth Century* (Dublin: Original Writing, 2008), p. 61.
2   Ibid., p. 49. Moreover, just two years before Glynn made his speech, Frank Duff had founded the Legion of Mary, which would go on to become one of the most successful forms of the lay Catholic apostolate in the world.
3   Alexander McGregor, *The Shaping of Popular Consent: a Comparative Study of the Soviet Union and the United States, 1929–1941* (Youngstown, NY: Cambria Press, 2007), p. 250.

hierarchy, he spoke of a 'holy crusade against the abuses of the motion pictures'.[4] Calling the motion picture 'a school of corruption', he referred approvingly to the 'millions of American Catholics signed the pledge of the *"Legion of Decency"*, binding themselves not to attend any motion picture which was offensive to Catholic moral principles or proper standards of living.'[5] Asking that the motion picture be 'transformed into an effectual instrument for the education and the elevation of mankind', he highlighted the role of Catholic Action in doing this:

> In this as in every other field of the apostolate, Pastors of souls will surely find their best fellow workers in those who fight in the ranks of Catholic Action, and in this letter We cannot refrain from addressing to them a warm appeal that they give to this cause their full contribution and their unwearying and unfailing activity.[6]

The following year The Knights of Columbanus endowed a Chair of Sociology and Catholic Action at Maynooth College and Fr Peter McKevitt was its first incumbent. He would hold the position until 1953, when he was succeeded by Jeremiah Newman.[7] In 1939, at Maynooth, the Irish Catholic bishops considered the broad area of Catholic Action, assisted by *A Report on Catholic Action* drawn up by Professor McKevitt. There was some disquiet regarding some of the movement's more radical elements and a pledge that the hierarchy and the clergy more generally would keep a tighter rein on its activities.[8]

Fears that the film industry was corrupting the morals of Americans in the 1930s were replicated in Ireland in the 1940s. Shortly after his retirement in 1941, Ireland's first film censor, James Montgomery, made his views on the destructive potential of motion pictures clear when he wrote an article for *Studies* magazine, entitled 'The Menace of Hollywood'. In this article he revealed that the code by which he had made decisions as censor was simply the Ten Commandments.[9] All fictional representations of divorce on screen, for instance, were prohibited by Montgomery, and his successor as censor, Richard Hayes (who held the position until 1953), ordered the distributor of Paramount Pictures' 1940 release to change the title *I Want a Divorce* to *The Tragedy of Divorce*, in order that the Irish public might not be inadvertently encouraged to regard divorce with the slightest of wishful favour. Equally, Hayes judged *The Postman Always Rings Twice* (1946) a 'base, sordid picture into which moral

---

4 *Vigilanti Cura*, Encyclical Letter of Pope Pius XI on the Motion Picture, 22 June 1936.
5 *Vigilanti Cura*, II and III.
6 *Vigilanti Cura*, II.
7 Hilary Tovey and Penny Share, *A Sociology of Ireland* (Dublin: Gill & Macmillan, 2nd ed., 2003), p.29.
8 Maurice Curtis, '"Miraculous Meddlers": the Catholic Action Movement', in *History Ireland* 18:5 (October, 2010).
9 Kevin Rockett, 'Protecting the Family and the Nation: the Official Censorship of American Cinema in Ireland, 1923–1954', in *Historical Journal of Film, Radio and Television* 20:3 (2010), pp. 283, 285.

considerations of any kind do not even faintly enter'.[10] And other voices also expressed their concern regarding the corrosive influence of the film industry. Professor William Magennis (1867–1946), professor of philosophy at Carysfort College and chair of metaphysics at University College Dublin, while a member of the Irish Seanad, also published an article in *Studies* magazine in March 1944 which, referencing its 'portentous range of influence', declared that it had become a 'sinister rival of the Universal [Roman Catholic] Church'.[11] An especially heightened degree of vigilance can be seen in the CTSI periodical *Up and Doing* which, at one point, went so far as to warn that approval of a film by the American Legion of Decency, was no guarantee that the film censor would agree to its ever being shown here.[12] Meanwhile, when the National Film Institute of Ireland (NFI) was founded in 1943 and officially incorporated on 2 June 1945, 'it took as its terms of reference the principles underpinning *Vigilanti Cura*'.[13] In the same year, The Catholic Stage Guild was founded (its first president was Jimmy O'Dea). Eamon Andrews, another member, was a little bemused by its very existence, quipping at one point, 'I always felt a Catholic Stage Guild in Dublin was like forming a league of decency in a convent'.[14] 'But it was not just the censor who played a significant role in monitoring what films were shown. Catholic Action continued to play its part well into the 1960s. In his memoir, *A Great Feast of Light: Growing up Irish in the Television Age*, television critic John Doyle remarks how 'some people said that the Legion of Mary could stop a film from being shown at the cinema in Nenagh if they didn't like the sound of it'.[15]

Maynooth College was not immune from the wider culture of debate surrounding the influence of motion pictures. On a recent visit to the college archives, I stumbled upon a set of minutes of the English Debating Society of Junior House from the mid-1940s. Among the many issues that were debated

10 Ibid., pp. 287, 295.
11 Ibid., p. 294.
12 Curtis, *The Splendid Cause*.
13 Kevin Rockett 'Protectionism and Catholic Film Policy in Twentieth-Century Ireland', in *Moralizing Cinema: Film, Catholicism and Power*, ed. Daniel Biltereyst and Daniella Treveri Gennari (London: Routledge, 2014), p. 196. A decision was made in 1982 to delete all references to *Vigilanti Cura* from the articles of association to better reflect the secular nature of the institute, which was also renamed the Irish Film Institute (IFI). See https://ifi.ie/about/history/ (accessed 15 June 2020).
14 For more on this see Alex Cahill, *The Formation, Existence and Deconstruction of the Catholic Stage Guild of Ireland* (Cambridge: Cambridge Scholars Press, 2017).
15 John Doyle, *A Great Feast of Light: Growing up Irish in the Television Age* (New York: Carroll and Graf, 2007), p. 52. I subsequently used this reference to convince the director of the 2011 film *Stella Days*, starring Martin Sheen (about the opening of a cinema in a small Tipperary town in 1957), to change one scene in the film. A meeting of a local group of parishioners descends into lively debate about the questionable morals of American films. Originally this group was designated as a meeting of the ICA. Far more effective, I argued, would be to make this a local meeting of the Legion of Mary (and I quoted the above reference in support of my argument). My decision was taken on board and the scene was rewritten to that effect, complete with the requisite Legion of Mary props which I subsequently obtained for use. See elsewhere in the volume for a more complete account of my experience of working on *Stella Days*.

by first- and second-year seminarians who were members of the society, the following two entries are of special interest:

> Minutes of the Meeting held on Sunday 3rd Dec. 1944.
> A competitive debate for prizes was held on the motion that 'The cinema is radically wrong in Ireland to-day'. Rev. Mr P. Corish[16] (Ferns) was the adjudicator, Mr. McNally (Raphoe) proposed the motion, which was seconded by Mr McNamee (Limerick). Mr Moran (Tuam) and Mr Arthure (Waterford) also spoke for the motion. Mr Morris (Clogher) proposed an amendment which was seconded by Mr Murphy (Killaloe). Mr Kiely (Cork) and Mr Feehan (Cashel) also spoke in favour of the amendment.
> The arguments for the motion were based mainly on the amorality of those in charge of the film industry, and the fact that it was a financial concern, and therefore was not concerned with the religious, educational, or cultural progress of the people. The opposition spoke of the social value of the Cinema and its potentialities for good and stressed the need for entertainment in the country.
> The team which proposed the motion were declared victors and the prize, for the single best speech of the debate went to Mr. McNally (Raphoe). A note of thanks to the adjudicator was proposed and passed unanimously.
>
> Signed:- W. Hyland (Secretary) 23rd January 1945
> John J. Leonard (Chairman) 23rd January 1945

The following year, this time under the presidency of Raymond McAnally, the society debated the merits of the cinema once more.

> Minutes of the Meeting held on Sunday, October 14th 1945.
> The motion 'That Catholics as such should boycott the Cinema with a view to counteracting its influence' was proposed by Mr Connolly[17] (Meath) and seconded by Mr Finnegan[18] (Elphin). An amendment 'That boycott was too radical a measure to use against the Cinema'

16 Later Professor of Ecclesiastical History, and subsequently Professor of Modern History at Maynooth.
17 Peter Connolly, whose later career as Professor of English at Maynooth is covered by Michael Conway elsewhere in this volume.
18 Thomas Finnegan later served as Junior Dean in Maynooth College from 1960 to 1966 and in 1998 was appointed Bishop of Killala, where he served until his retirement in 2002.

Minutes of the meeting held on Sunday, October 14th 1945.

The motion "That catholics as such should boycott the cinema with a view to counteracting its influence" was proposed by Mr Connolly (Meath) and seconded by Mr. Finnegan (Elphin). An amendment "That boycott was too radical a measure to use against the Cinema" was proposed by Mr Fenton (Kerry) and seconded by Mr Keohan (Cork). Others who favoured the motion were Mr. Markey (blgbr) and Mr O'Connor (Waterford) while Mr Ferguson (blgbr) supported the amendment.

Boycott, it was claimed, was justified by the failure of all other methods hitherto tried, + by the fact that boycott had succeeded to a great extent already in America (the Hayes Board). Censorship is inadequate + cannot really deal with the problem.

The speakers for the amendment stressed the fact that boycott was too radical. It would deprive our own people of a cheap form of recreation, it would stifle our own film industry, stop up a flow of culture since general boycott cannot differentiate between the good and bad films. The attitude of Ireland would not affect Hollywood. The real solution was a creation of a censorship board from the religious and educational personel of the country.

The amendment was carried by a large majority.

Signed:- Raymond McAnally. : Peter Connolly. (Chairman).
(Secretary) 4/11/'45.   4/11/'45

Minutes of the English Debating Society of Junior House, 1945

was proposed by Mr Fenton[19] (Kerry) and seconded by Mr Keohan (Cork). Others who favoured the motion were Mr Markey (Clogher) and Mr O'Connor[20] (Waterford) while Mr Ferguson (Clogher) supported the amendment.

Boycott, it was claimed, was justified by the failure of all other methods hitherto tried, & by the fact that boycott had succeeded to a great extent already in America (the Hayes[21] Board). Censorship is inadequate & cannot really deal with the problem.

The speakers for the amendment stressed the fact that boycott was too radical. It would deprive our own people of a cheap form of recreation, it would stifle our own film industry, stop up a flow of culture since general boycott cannot differentiate the good and bad films. The attitude of Ireland could not affect Hollywood. The real solution was the creation of a censorship board from the religious and educational personel [sic] of the country.

The amendment was carried by a large majority.

Signed:- Raymond McAnally (Secretary) 4/11/'45
          Peter Connolly (Chairman) 4/11/'45

The 'twist' in this account, of course, concerns one of the names that features prominently in both sets of minutes; in the first as proposer of the motion that 'The Cinema is radically wrong in Ireland to-day', and in the second as that year's president of the society, but also in this instance as secretary, recording a debate on whether Catholics should boycott the cinema with a view to counteracting its influence. That individual is Raymond (Ray) McAnally (1926–1989), a native of Buncrana and a seminarian for the diocese of Raphoe, who would choose to leave Maynooth College shortly afterwards. Having debated the evils of the cinema in his student days, he would go on to enjoy a hugely successful career on stage and screen, winning four BAFTA awards in the 1980s, twice for best actor and twice for best supporting actor. He is probably best remembered for playing Cardinal Altamirano in *The Mission* (1986) and the father of Christy Brown in *My Left Foot* (1989). McAnally was scheduled to play the 'Bull McCabe' in *The Field* (1990), but died before he could assume the role, the part eventually going to Richard Harris who received an Oscar nomination for his performance.

But that is not all. The student who proposed the motion 'That Catholics as such should boycott the Cinema with a view to counteracting its influence'

19 Pádraig Ó Fiannachta, whose career as a professor in Maynooth is discussed by Pádraig Ó Héalaí elsewhere in this volume.
20 Daniel (Danny) O'Connor would later teach Scripture at Maynooth College.
21 Note the more typical Irish spelling of Hayes (rather than Hays) here.

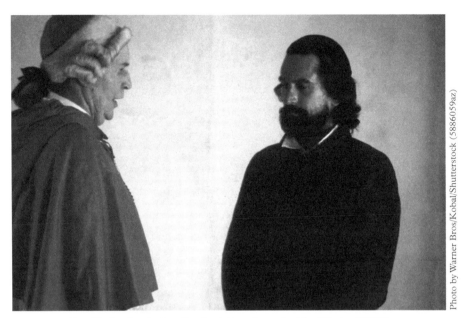

Ray McAnally playing Cardinal Altamirano in *The Mission* (1986),
with Robert de Niro as Br. Rodrigo Mendoza

was Peter Connolly of Meath diocese who, as detailed in the contributions of
Denis Bergin and Michael Conway respectively, went on to become Professor
of English at Maynooth, and spent his academic career as a firm opponent of
literary censorship. His interest in the world of film was a constant, and he
served on the jury of the Cork Film Festival and was film critic for *The Furrow*
from 1957–60. He was succeeded in this role by Fr John C. Kelly SJ, Professor
of Communications in Milltown Park. Writing of the development of film in
Ireland, Ruth Barton has observed of the latter:

> Paradoxically, much of the credit for the emergence of a film culture
> in Ireland must go to the educated, often middle-class clergy. In the
> pages of *The Furrow*, Fr Kelly's film criticism was required reading for
> anyone with an interest that went beyond plot and stars.[22]

The first- and second-year students who gathered in Maynooth College on
a Sunday in the mid-1940s to debate various motions, including that of the
influence of the motion picture on Irish society, could have little knowledge of
where their later lives would take them. In the case of one of their number, at
least, that life took him into the very heart of the world of theatre and film, a
world he would make his own over four decades.

22   Ruth Barton, *Irish National Cinema* (London: Routledge, 2004), p. 66.

A SURVEY OF SPORT
AND ITS PRACTITIONERS
IN MAYNOOTH COLLEGE

Stephen Farragher

For much of its 225-year history, St Patrick's College Maynooth was a self-contained unit, a closed system cut off from the outside world. From the outset it was a highly regimented institution and remained so for many years to come. Students returned to the college at the beginning of September and had little or no contact with the outside world during term, and even newspapers were forbidden. On specific days of the week traders set up stalls within the grounds of the college and sold shoes, umbrellas, boots, sportswear and sundry items to the students. The seminary was divided into three distinct divisions: St Columba's, St Joseph's and St Mary's, known to the students as Junior, Middle and Senior divisions respectively. Rigorous segregation of these divisions was in place until 1902 when the rule of division between Senior and Middle was relaxed. Junior House was to remain a self-contained unit for years to come, with its own sporting and cultural events.

The earliest reference to sport in the college, as far as can be ascertained, is contained in *Mo Scéal Féin*, by the renowned Irish writer of the early Gaelic revival period, an t-Athair Peadar Ó Laoghaire, who was a student in Maynooth from 1861 to 1867. Recalling his early years as a seminarian, he refers to a group of students playing handball. Handball had a long tradition going back centuries in Ireland. The town statutes of Galway in 1527 contain a rule forbidding the playing of ball games against the walls of the town. At one point there were four sets of handball alleys in the college. It is not exactly clear when they were erected, probably at some time in the early to mid-nineteenth century. Two sets of those alleys remain standing, and two have been demolished.

In his book *Reminiscences of a Maynooth Professor*, Walter McDonald mentions that during his student days in Senior House (1872–74) a football was introduced in St Mary's Division and a subsequent 'kick around' created quite a stir among the students. The college authorities, regarding football as a dangerous innovation, promptly confiscated it. The hour had not yet come for

Cahir   Roche.   Vaughan   Connolly   D   O'B   Coolahan

This is the oldest photo of a Maynooth team with is known to exist. It was taken in 1902 and shows a team of hurlers from St Mary's Division. Prior to 1902, when the Administrative Council relaxed the rule of division between St Mary's and St Joseph's, there were very strict segregation between all three Divisions. This decision meant that it was now possible to have inter-divisional sports and more competitive leagues than was hitherto possible
The Team, Front Row (L–R): John Hegney (Clonfert), Joseph Guinan (Ossory).
Seated (L–R): Michael Grace (Killaloe), John Smyth (Killaloe), John Moloney (Galway), Thomas Hogan (Killaloe), James Russell (Cashel), James Wall (Limerick), Patrick Sterling (Tuam).
Back Row (L–R) Standing: James Cahir (Galway), John Roche (Killaloe), Edward Vaughan (Killaloe), Michael Connolly (Clonfert), Jeremiah Dooley (Cashel), Patrick O'Brien (Cashel), John Coolahan (Tuam), Jeremiah Casey (Kerry)

football in Maynooth. The authorities preferred the students to take part in the more sedate and gentlemanly sports of cricket and handball.

The GAA was founded in 1884 and it received much support from the Catholic hierarchy and clergy. There was a renewed interest in sport among the students and this is reflected in the minutes of the seminary administrative council where occasionally requests from the students concerning sporting matters were considered. The authorities, at least initially, were cautious in their attitude to sports. At its meeting of 31 April 1888 there is reference to 'Arrangements for cricketing to be considered'. At their meeting in March 1895 the council refused permission to introduce tennis in Senior House. At the same

Ball Alleys, St Patrick's College, Maynooth. Photo taken early in the twentieth century showing ball alleys that were subsequently demolished. Handball is the earliest recorded sport in the college. Note the different colour stone of the spire of the college chapel which was completed in 1902

meeting a request for inter-divisional sports was refused. In 1898 an application from St Mary's to play a cricket match with St Joseph's was refused. At the same meeting the council discussed whether to forbid athletic sports due to some abuses. What the exact nature of those abuses were is not clear. The support of the Catholic hierarchy and clergy for the newly founded GAA meant that Gaelic games and athletics became very popular among the student body at Maynooth. At the start of the twentieth century a more open and tolerant attitude towards sport is evident. At their meeting of 28 January 1902 the members of the council decided that 'hurling is to be allowed in the different divisions (see the image of St Mary's Division Hurling Team 1901). The minutes of a meeting of the college authorities record the first mention of athletics in the college when, in March 1895, they considered and refused an application for inter-divisional sports. It seems reasonable to conclude that, prior to this, students were taking part in athletic activities within their respective divisions. The authorities finally relaxed the rule of division between Senior and Middle House in 1902. It was in the aftermath of this decision that the college sports, held during Easter week, became the high point of the college's sporting calendar and this situation lasted until the 1960s.

Rhetoric Pitch with ball alleys, 1920s: Rhetoric Pitch was where Junior House students took part in a variety of sports. The ball alleys in this photo were demolished sometime in around 1938. The photo shows the presence of a number of improvised lawn tennis courts, whlle the lanes marked in the background were probably for the Junior House sports that took place in Easter week

In 1901 the GAA introduced the infamous 'ban', or Rule 27, forbidding its members from taking part in 'foreign' or non-national games. This rule remained in the GAA constitution and was officially removed only in 1971. One of the other seminaries training priests for the English-speaking mission and for the diocese of Ossory was St Kieran's, Kilkenny. It seems that at some time in 1905 there was some tension between advocates of Gaelic games and those of the so-called 'foreign games'. The President of St Kieran's, Fr John Doody, wrote to the President of Maynooth, Dr Daniel Mannix (later to become the celebrated Archbishop of Melbourne), to inquire about the various sporting activities of the students and how they were regulated. In his reply to Doody, dated 9 September 1905, Mannix was able to report a wide variety of games within the college:

> They play handball, football; Association and Gaelic – hurling, cricket, lawn tennis and if I mistake not I have seen them try baseball occasionally. They also indulge in weight throwing, jumping, running and possibly, in other minor games that do not now occur to me.

Dr Mannix also added that at all times a watchful eye was kept by the authorities who would deal with any abuse that would arise in connection with the games permitted.

Andy Heaney (Tuam) winds the 220 yards in the College Sports, Easter 1914. Heaney won three gold medals at the National Athletics Championship in Mallow in 1914

Apparently one such abuse did arise in 1906. At their meeting of 30 March 1906, the authorities felt it necessary to specify the type of dress that students were expected to wear on sporting occasions. They also specified types of dress that were unacceptable. The minutes of that meeting read:

Agreed to prohibit the students from appearing in the following articles of dress:

1. Drawers
2. White or striped jerseys.
3. White or coloured hats. Dark coloured jerseys and trousers cut short to be allowed.

At the turn of the nineteenth century the GAA nationally concerned itself with the organisation of athletics, along with football and hurling. One of the outstanding hurlers of this era was Mick O'Dwyer from Holycross (later Fr Michael O'Dwyer, Superior General of the Columban Fathers from 1924 to 1947), who was the star of Tipperary's triumph over Dublin in the replayed All-Ireland final of 1908, played in Athy in 1909. During the summer holidays of 1910 he was a member of the Tipperary team that toured Belgium as part of a pan-Celtic series of games played in Brussels and on the battlefields of Fontenoy.

During the first two decades of the twentieth century Maynooth had a number of athletes who were outstanding by national and international standards. One such was Andy Heaney, a student for the archdiocese of Tuam who entered Maynooth in 1909 and was ordained in 1916 (see the photo of Heaney winning the 220 yards at the college sports and the photo of Heaney, Curley and Finn, wearing the prescribed black sports gear). By that time Gaelic football, hurling, rugby and soccer were being played by the students and Heaney proved to be adept at all of them. The first opportunity for him to prove his ability as an

Fourth Divines, winners of the Class Championship 1927
Back row (L–R): Tommy Burns (Cashel), Pat Dunne (Meath), Paddy Browne (Kerry),
Mike Rhatigan (Elphin), Jack Clery (Killaloe), Ned Flanagan (Clogher).
Middle row, seated (L–R): Stephen Roland (Tuam), Mark Kilbride (Elphin), Peter Fagan (Meath),
Jack Lane (Kerry, dean in Maynooth from 1928–1949), Larry Marron (Clogher),
James P. Prendergast (Tuam).
Front row (L–R): Michael McLaughlin (Ardagh), Tommy Doherty (Raphoe), Jimmy Tully (Elphin)

Second Divinity Class Team 1934, Class champions.
Back row (L–R): Jack Quirke (Killaloe), Frank McFadden, (Armagh), Eamonn Devlin (Armagh),
Frank O'Reilly (Ardagh), Frank McGirr (Armagh), Paddy Tuohy (Dublin).
Middle row (L–R): James Horan (Galway), Joe Dunphy (Ossory), Bob Walsh (Dublin),
Dan O'Connell (Cloyne), Gerry Gunn (Clogher), Charlie McAvinchey (Armagh),
Christy Flood (Meath), Mike Egan (Ardagh), Tom Cruise (Tuam).
Seated (L–R): Frank Little (Clogher), Michael Casey (Kerry), Shane Cullen (Armagh),
Frank Cremin, captain, (Kerry), Ned McEllin (Tuam), Tom Murphy (Clogher),
Hugh McKeague (Derry)

athlete presented itself at the Junior House sports in 1910 when he came first in the 100 yards, 440 yards and the 28 lbs throw, and second in the hop, skip and jump. Students were allowed to participate in athletics, hurling and football during the holidays but usually under assumed names. During the summer holidays of 1912, on 3 August, Heaney was at the centre of controversy when, along with Martin McHale, a student at All Hallows College in Drumcondra, he took part in the prestigious Rangers' Sports in Glasgow, running under the assumed name of J. Wickhame of Donore Harriers. That particular controversy is beyond the scope of this article. On 9 July 1914 Andy Heaney won three gold medals at the National Athletics Championships in Mallow. On that occasion he ran under the assumed name of J. Burke. Heaney continued to dominate athletics in Maynooth right up until his ordination. Other outstanding athletes in the college at that time were James Nangle (Meath diocese) and Eugene Fynn (Limerick diocese). During his years as a student, Heaney kept a diary of all his various conquests, the sports meetings he attended, the medals he won. The final entry in that diary was a very poignant one: On 2 May 1916, shortly before his ordination on 10 June, he wrote 'Goodbye athletics, A. Heaney, 2nd May, 1916'. From now on he would be forbidden, by ecclesiastical sanction, from taking part in competitive sports.

For many years to come seminarians continued to play for club and county during their summer holidays but were forbidden to leave the college once they returned in September. The hurlers had a distinct advantage in that the All-Ireland hurling final was played the Sunday prior to the return after the summer holidays. There are numerous stories of footballers who played minor and senior football for their counties during the holidays but, having returned to the enclosed life of the college, missed out on the opportunity of winning an All-Ireland medal for their county. One has only to think of John Kennedy of Galway, Donie O'Sullivan of Kerry, Sean Freyne of Mayo, all of whom missed out on the opportunity of lining out for their counties on All-Ireland football Sunday. The one exception to this was John Wilson, a member of the ordination class of 1949 (which boasted no fewer than seven county footballers within its ranks), who played in an All-Ireland final while a seminarian in the college. According to Msgr P. F. Cremin, who was Professor of Canon Law at the time, he took responsibility for having Wilson back in the college in time for Evening Prayer that day. Not long after that event, John Wilson left Maynooth and went on to have a distinguished career in politics, serving as minister in various Fianna Fáil governments.

Throughout the 1930s and 1940s the list of inter-county footballers in

Maynooth included Martin Hannon (Mayo), Kevin Connolly (Louth) and Frank McCorry (Antrim), while the list of hurlers included Dr Jim Young and Fr Bobby Dineen, both of whom made their All-Ireland debut on the team captained by Jack Lynch (Taoiseach, 1966–73). In the 1940s the outstanding hurlers included Tommy Maher of Kilkenny (trainer of Kilkenny senior hurling teams from 1957–78), Martin O'Connor and Paddy Tully of Galway. In the 1950s it was Limerick's turn to provide the most talented hurlers in the persons of Liam Ryan (Professor of Sociology at Maynooth from 1969–2000), who captained a Limerick hurling team to an All-Ireland final in 1955. He was supported by his brother Seamus at centre half back. The outstanding athlete and footballer of the 1940s was Kevin Connolly, a student for the archdiocese of Armagh, who won the 300 and 440 yards at the National Athletics Championships in 1947. He was ordained priest in 1949 and was introduced as a substitute for Louth against Kerry in the All-Ireland semi-final of 1953, under the assumed name of Kevin McArdle. His introduction almost saved the day for the 'wee' county and many were at a loss to understand why he hadn't been introduced earlier.

In an effort to promote fraternity and cohesion in the college, each diocese was allocated a particular space for the playing of football, croquet and tennis, and the diocese was expected to provide its own posts, nets, hoops and balls.

One of the main obstacles to the playing of a good standard of Gaelic football and hurling in the college was the relatively small size of the pitches. Both codes were played on what are now the soccer pitches opposite the entrance to the college cemetery. Furthermore, the football pitch was shared with the rugby players, which meant that it was often very muddy. It came as a welcome breakthrough, therefore, when, in 1938, it was announced that a rather reluctant bursar had agreed to hand over the present High Field as a playing field. Apparently there had been repeated requests from the students prior to this decision and the reason for the reluctance on the part of the bursar was that it meant the loss of a sizeable portion of good pasture land.

1956 is the next significant date in the annals of Maynooth GAA history. In that year, Jack Mahon, of Galway football fame, approached the Senior Dean, Dr Montague, with a view to inaugurating an annual Past vs Present competition in football. At that time Maynooth had a strong and active past pupils' union, Vexilla Regis, made up of laymen like Mahon himself, who had spent a number of years in Maynooth. After giving the matter careful consideration, Dr Montague agreed that it was a good idea, so Easter 1956 saw the commencement of the annual Vexilla Regis (Past vs Present) competition which lasted until the 1990s. A beautiful trophy was donated for the competition by Dr Eamonn O'Sullivan (well-known trainer of Kerry teams), who was also a past pupil. It was an historic occasion because it was the first time that a Maynooth team played a team from outside the college with the full approval of the authorities. It also paved the way for Maynooth's eventual entry to the newly formed Higher Education League in 1968. In the 1960s and 1970s Maynooth had within its walls footballers and hurlers of the highest calibre. The first-year class (chubs) of 1962 had a thirteen-a-side team made up of footballers, all of whom had played minor for their counties and included young men such as Oliver Hughes (Galway) and John Cleary (Mayo).

The decision of the Irish bishops to open the college to lay students in 1968 meant that Maynooth students were finally given the opportunity to take part in external competitions.

From the outset, Maynooth teams showed themselves capable of competing at the highest level. A Maynooth team that included county players such as Tom Colleary (Sligo), Jackie Fitzsimons (Down) and J. J. Cribbin (Mayo) won the inter-faculty cup, an inter-varsity competition in 1970. Entry into the higher education competitions brought with it the logistical challenge of fundraising and all the associated responsibilities involved in training teams, sponsorship etc. Initially the hurling and football clubs came under the one umbrella, mainly for the purposes of obtaining better capitation grants from the college. Men such as Aidan Fox (Meath diocese) and others rose to the organisational challenges involved in fielding teams in external competitions. Writing in the *Gaelic Weekly News* in November 1969, in an article titled 'Winds of Change', Jack Mahon commenced by stating 'The new University League has already become a major GAA talking point. Hardly had the fixtures been made when Maynooth handed out a drubbing to UCG in very wet conditions at Maynooth.' Mahon summed up the mood of many Maynooth students, past and present, when he went on to say 'Apart altogether from the GAA side of things, what a wonderful aid this will be to clerical-lay relations in the future. For far too long Irish seminarians have been hemmed inside closed bars almost, living in a world of their own being prepared theoretically for a life they would be thrown into after ordination.' He then went on to paint a picture of life in Maynooth during his seminary years, when eating chocolate or smuggling in newspapers were regarded as serious transgressions. He welcomed the recent more open attitude of the Church and college authorities.

The 1970s was a decade when Maynooth teams excelled in intervarsity competitions. In 1973 and 1974 the hurlers won the Fitzgibbon Cup for hurling with stars that included Willie and Paudie Fitzmaurice of Limerick, and the

Maynooth Fitzgibbon Cup Winners 1973
Back row (L–R): Fr Gerry Meagher, Paddy Bollard, Aidan Kerrigan, Michael Brennan,
Dick Browne, Paddy Barry, Andy Fenton, Pat Gough, Joe Clarke
Front row (L–R): Sean Silke, Ollie Perkins, Gus O Driscoll, Liam Everard, Joe Condon,
Henry Gough, Iggy Clarke

Maynooth Fitzgibbon Cup Winners 1974
Back row (L–R): Fr Gerry Meagher, Martin Downey, Pat Goff, Christy Kennedy, Victor Blake,
Iggy Clarke, Dick Browne, Sean Stack, Andy Fenton, John Martin, Willie Dillon, Ollie Perkins,
Fachtna O Driscoll, Joe Condon, Mickey Brennan.
Front row (L–R): Tony Kelly, Joe Clarke, Gus O'Driscoll, Paddy Bollard, Paudie Fitzmaurice,
Paddy Barry (capt.), Harry Goff, Sean Silke, Liam Everard, Seamus Fitzgerald

Galway trio of Sean Silke and Joe and Iggy Clarke. In 1976 Maynooth won its only Sigerson Cup, captained by Dan O'Mahony of Mayo. Camogie was introduced to the college in this decade and Maynooth contested two Ashbourne Cup finals. The team included the two Kilkenny stars and sisters, Ann and Angela Downey. Fr Gerard Meagher, who was Professor of Scripture until his death in 1982, was a great nurturer of camogie.

For many years after entering external competitions in Gaelic football and soccer, Maynooth teams were backboned by seminarians. Internal competitions in all codes were very vibrant until the 1990s. The class championship in Gaelic football continued to be played. The inter-provincial competition was played in the last term and the final always attracted a large number of spectators to High Field. The Soccer Club organised a lot of internal leagues that involved hundreds of students, lay and clerical. The majority of the members of the executives of the various clubs were still seminarians. All of this began to change towards the end of the 1990s as the number of vocations to the priesthood began to decline. During my years on the staff of St Patrick's College Maynooth (1994–2001), a full-time sports officer, Paul Davis, and a full-time GAA officer, Tom Maher, were appointed by the NUI. This took a huge burden of organisational responsibility off the students. In 1995–96, I was approached by two lay students, Brid Canny from Kilrush, County Clare, and Mary Ryan from Cashel, County Tipperary, asking for my assistance in setting up a Ladies' Gaelic Football Club. And, so it was that Maynooth fielded its first Ladies' Gaelic Football team that year, trained by James Keating from Tipperary. Furthermore, the sporting facilities for all codes were greatly improved with the introduction of all-weather and floodlit pitches.

Students today are free to participate in a wide variety of sports and competitions never dreamt of by students of an earlier era, particularly those students for the priesthood who were excluded by ecclesiastical sanction from taking part in external competitions until the college opened its gates to lay students in the late 1960s.

REMEMBERING FR JOHN BRADY
(1905–1963)

Paul Connell

Fr John Brady

he library of the diocese of Meath, based in St Finian's College, Mullingar, contains a large and very fine history collection spanning the nineteenth and twentieth centuries. The quality and range of the material is due particularly to three individuals. Thomas Mulvany, Bishop of Meath from 1929 until 1943, left his books to the collection. The collection of Maynooth College professor and noted Gaelic scholar and historian, Fr Paul Walsh, was purchased by the priests of the diocese after his death and deposited in St Finian's in the mid-1940s. Fr John Brady, who was the official Meath diocesan historian from 1936 until his untimely death in 1963, also had a wide-ranging history collection and his books and papers were gifted to the library after his death. Thomas Mulvany is best known for the building of the new Cathedral of Christ the King in Mullingar. The range and quality of Fr Paul Walsh's historical publications are well known and have been brought together in recent years through the excellent work of Nollaig Ó Muraíle.[1] Fr John Brady, however, has almost been forgotten in recent years, due to the passage of time and the death of his contemporaries. What these three men have in common, apart from their common Meath diocesan heritage, is that they are all past students of Maynooth College. This contribution is designed to shed light once again on the work of John Brady and also on his contribution to the history of Maynooth College.

John Joseph Brady was born on 29 July 1905 to William and Frances Brady

---

1   Paul Walsh, *Irish Leaders and Learning Though the Ages*, ed. Nollaig Ó Muraíle (Dublin: Four Courts Press, 2003).

in Dunboyne, County Meath, and was baptised on 1 August 1905, by Fr Peter Cantwell, a nephew of the famous John Cantwell, Bishop of Meath from 1830 until 1866. He had five siblings, a brother William and four sisters, Lena, Moira, Rosaleen and Sheila. Educated in Dunboyne, Belvedere College and St Finian's College, Mullingar, he entered Maynooth College in 1925. The evidence of the college *Kalendarii* indicates that he was a bright student. He achieved a second-class honours in his English language and literature BA examinations in 1928 and three years later he showed his keen interest in history with a very good result in ecclesiastical history. However, the real sense of his intellectual ability emerged only later, as indicated by the range of his scholarship and writings. Following his ordination in Maynooth College on 5 June 1932, Brady was sent on loan to the diocese of Southwark in London where he remained for three years. Upon his return to Meath in 1936 he was appointed to the dual roles of diocesan catechist and diocesan historian. His next appointment was in 1948 when he was made chaplain to the Butlin's holiday camp in Mosney, County Meath. There he succeeded in building a church for the many visitors. Appointed to parish ministry in 1961 as administrator of the parish of Drumraney, near Athlone in County Westmeath, he became its parish priest in February 1963. It was while ministering there in 1963 that he died suddenly in Longford, while attending a wedding reception on 30 September of that year.

What all these appointments had in common was the way they assisted him in terms of time and access to the necessary historical research that enabled him to flourish as a historian. He made very good use of his three years in Southwark, scouring the British Library and the English National Archives, then based in Chancery Lane, London, for material relating to the diocese.[2] Following his return to Ireland, Bishop Mulvany, by appointing him diocesan catechist, gave him a reason to visit every corner of the diocese and thus access to a myriad source materials, enabling him to carry out his first great task, that of updating the monumental work of Anthony Cogan on the history of the diocese published in the 1860s.[3] This was duly published in pamphlet form, parish by parish, throughout the late 1930s and 1940s. It was not published in book form at that point due to the shortage of paper during the war years.[4] In 1995, when a further update commissioned by Bishop Michael Smith[5] was published, it incorporated the full text of Brady's pamphlets and included five that had not previously been

---

2   Aubrey Gwynn, 'Father John Brady', in *Ríocht na Midhe* Vol. III, No. 2, (1964), p. 87.
3   Anthony Cogan, *A History of the Diocese of Meath*, 3 vols. (published 1862; reissued 1993, ed. Alfred P. Smyth. Dublin: Four Courts Press).
4   John Brady, *A Short History of the Parishes of the Diocese of Meath, 1867–1937* (Navan: Meath Chronicle Printing Works, 1937).
5   Olive Curran (ed.), *History of the Diocese of Meath 1860–1993.* (Mullingar: 1995).

published. His appointment to Mosney in 1948 gave him easy access to the archives and libraries in Dublin. In addition, as his reputation as a fine historian grew, he carried on an extensive correspondence with many scholars of history both at home and abroad.[6]

From a bibliography of Brady's work, down to 1959, which was published in *Riocht na Midhe* in 1960, we get a real understanding of the depth and breadth of his output.[7] During this period, he contributed to publications as wide and varied as *The Irish Ecclesiastical Record, Archivium Hibernicum, Irish Historical Studies, Irish Book Lover, Studies, Reportorium Novum, Riocht na Midhe, Clogher Record, The Furrow, Irish Independent, Meath Chronicle* and a number of others. In the words of one of his contemporaries, Aubrey Gwynn, they were each packed with 'accurate biographical or bibliographical matter'.[8] Articles on figures like Laurence O'Connor, a Meath schoolmaster;[9] Fr Paul Walsh,[10] Fr Christopher Cusack, the Irish College Douai[11] and Daniel Arthur, St Oliver Plunkett's London agent, to name but a few.[12] He was renowned for his work on Oliver Plunkett and also for his study of the medieval Irish Church. In the words of Aubrey Gwynn again: 'What was especially noticeable was his grasp of the main developments in Irish and Anglo-Norman history, combined with the accurate knowledge of local history and topography'.[13] His work for *Archivium Hibernicum* was particularly rich. Here he published the text of hitherto unknown documents, not only concerning the Irish dioceses, especially Meath, but also the Irish colleges abroad.[14] To *Archivium* he also gave his crowning achievement, his publication concerning Catholics and Catholicism in the eighteenth-century press, first published in a number of the volumes and later as a stand-alone publication.[15]

Brady did not neglect the study of his alma mater. In total he published five articles concerning the history of Maynooth College. In 1942 he began what was to become a series of three articles on the history of the lay college in Maynooth. It has not often been appreciated that, from its beginning in 1795, the Royal Catholic College of Maynooth had a lay college attached to it, which survived until 1817. Brady's first article appeared in 1942 and outlined the history of the lay college. The second article, which followed in 1943, concerned its staff. The final article, published in 1950, focused on the student body. All these appeared

6   See his correspondence in the archive of St Finian's College, Mullingar, SF/B/0037–0425.
7   *Riocht na Midhe,* Vol. II, no. 2 (1960), pp. 64–6.
8   Aubrey Gwynn, op cit.
9   John Brady in *Irish Ecclesiastical Record,* March 1937;
10   John Brady in *Irish Ecclesiastical Record,* LVIIII, (1941) pp. 413–23.
11   John Brady, *Measgra I gCuimhne Mhicil Uí Clérigh.*
12   John Brady in *The Irish Independent,* 17 September 1953.
13   Aubrey Gwynn, op cit.
14   See, for example, *Archivium Hibernicum,* Vol. 8, pp. 203–43; Vol. 13, pp. 45–66; Vol. 14, pp. 66–91.
15   John Brady, *Catholics and Catholicism in the 18th-Century Press* (Maynooth, 1965).

in the *Irish Ecclesiastical Record*.[16] In addition to these articles, in December 1945 he also penned a piece in *Studies* on the origins of Maynooth College. This highlighted how the foundation of Maynooth College broke an intimate bond of contact with the continent of Europe that had lasted for two and a half centuries in terms of the links that the Irish Church had with many of the continental colleges.[17] Finally, in 1960 he published a truly fascinating article in the *Irish Ecclesiastical Record* on the oath of allegiance to the House of Hanover that had to be taken by every student and member of staff of Maynooth College. The wording of the oath was, in Brady's words, 'striking proof of the power of anti-Catholic propaganda and of the deeply rooted prejudice against, and ignorance of, Catholic teaching'. It included a specific renunciation of allegiance to the then pretender Charles III, and a declaration rejecting any authority to depose princes excommunicated by the pope.[18]

Given the fact that John Brady died at what would now be considered a relatively young age, his contribution to Irish ecclesiastical history, both at a local and national level, was immense, if unfortunately, nowadays somewhat forgotten. Following his death, many tributes were paid to him by friends, colleagues and acquaintances. Despite what was described as his shy and diffident nature, his courtesy and generosity in terms of his scholarship was one of the hallmarks of his character that was much remarked upon. Perhaps it is fitting to leave the last words to one of his great friends and contemporaries and, indeed, a giant of historical scholarship from the Maynooth College stable, Msgr Patrick J. Corish:

> He had an extraordinary knowledge of the Irish Catholic past, the fruit, not merely of a lifetime's reading, but of what seemed some special gift of memory, of having everything he had read always at hand. There can be few students of Irish history who cannot recall saying, when searching some particularly obscure corner: *I must drop a line to Father John Brady* ... He knew Irish Catholic history well enough to appreciate all our faults and foibles. He could chuckle over the foibles, and as for the faults, his quiet priestly humanity was keenly aware of how many good Christian lives leave little record that the historian can trace, and how evil and the indictment of evil has always been news. There will be little in his indictment.[19]

16 John Brady, 'The Lay College, Maynooth I', in *Irish Ecclesiastical Record*, LXI (1942), pp. 385–8; 'The Lay College, Maynooth II', in *Irish Ecclesiastical Record*, August 1943, pp. 94–7; 'The Lay College, Maynooth III', *Irish Ecclesiastical Record*, September 1950, pp. 201–06.
17 John Brady, 'Origins of Maynooth College', in *Studies,* December 1945, pp. 511–14.
18 John Brady, 'The Oath of Allegiance at Maynooth', in *Irish Ecclesiastical Record,* September 1960, pp. 129–35.
19 *Westmeath Examiner,* 12 October 1963.

'GILES'
PE Instructor for Generations

Tom Looney

'Giles' – Mr James Gillespie

For generations, soutaned undergraduates tramped along the concrete floor of Junior House Handball Alley to the command 'Left, Right, Left, Right'. The commander was Donegal native James Gillespie, fondly known to us all as 'Giles'. That nickname comes from the Irish words *Giolla Íosa*, or servant of Jesus. We were told he came of Quaker stock. My memories of the early 1960s tell of a college campus lacking any facilities for indoor sporting activities excepting the swimming pool and billiard tables. Junior House students spent one class per week parading in the Alley, where he taught us some physical

Athletics in the early 1900s

exercises that were intended to keep us all physically fit into the future. Breaking with the given Maynooth tradition and practice of the day, Giles never addressed us as 'Mister', but in his Donegal brogue as 'Shonny'.

I asked Donie O'Sullivan, former All-Ireland winning Kerry captain, about memories of his late 1950s Maynooth PE classes. 'I can still faintly recall cold winter mornings being put through our paces by a former British Army Officer dressed in tweeds spouting orders to mere Irish country boys ... I cannot recall a mention of Gaelic games or for that matter anything Gaelic.' As Kerry's first All-Star, Donie went on to win many sporting accolades, including four senior All-Ireland Celtic Crosses in Croke Park. We were told that our PE instructor resigned his British Army commission shortly before the infamous Curragh Mutiny of 1914, which was linked with the formation in 1913 of The Ulster Volunteers and impending partition of our country.

During the spring of 1963 I asked Giles to pose for a photograph. I invited our octogenarian PE instructor to stand near his ultra-sporty Triumph Herald. My black-and-white portrait took first prize in the Junior House Photographic Competition that year. Given the green-leaved rose bush in the background, I titled my study 'Evergreen'.

REMEMBERING MAYNOOTH

Rev. Prof.
Enda
McDonagh

Enda McDonagh

came in as a student to Maynooth College in September 1948. I have been formally attached to the college as student or staff member, active or retired, ever since. On retirement, at the regulation age of sixty-five in 1995, the trustees, composed of the Irish bishops, approved my continuing residence in the college. In those seventy-plus years there have been extraordinary changes in the college, its buildings, its programme of studies and its diversity of teaching and student population. While it had been a Recognised College of the National University of Ireland from 1910, with power to grant degrees of that university under the supervision of UCD, the range of degree subjects on offer at that time was extremely limited as the only students were seminarians who had to qualify in philosophy if they were to continue their studies into theology. This applied to students such as myself taking a science degree, who had to complete their philosophy studies in that time. It was not a particularly satisfactory arrangement for students taking philosophy in this adjunct way or for their teachers.

After my studies at Maynooth, despite encouragement from Professor James

McConnell, probably the best professor I had in all my student days, I was given a year off by my archbishop (of Tuam) and advised to go to Rome, where I concentrated on philosophy at the Angelicum (Dominican) University, although I was free to move around to take other advanced courses. In September of the next year (1958) I was, with Denis O'Callaghan of Cloyne diocese, who had just completed his doctorate in divinity at Maynooth, appointed Professor of Moral Theology and Canon Law. This was the custom at the time in many Catholic institutions. It had inevitably distorting effects, particularly on moral theology, which had become a legal tract as revealed by most of its presentation manuals such as Noldin, a primary text in places like Maynooth for so long. So, in our initial years of teaching we were meeting challenges we had not been anticipating.

The interaction between the strictly personal, the social in community relations, and the structural in buildings is critical to the understanding of the historical development of a complex institution like Maynooth College. Some of that development took place during my student years (1948–57) and still more during my teaching years (1960–95). Not that I was involved, except in some narrower academic pursuits and then in some extra-curricular activities such as sport, student magazines and student theatre. Happily, in this period, the extra-curricular was in a healthy state, if not always as attractive as it might have been. In all this, football and hurling in the High Field, with their intense inter-class matches, were particularly notable. A well-known county player of that era remarked that he would feel safer in an inter-county or inter-club game at home during the summer than at many an inter-class game in Maynooth. I recall one particular incident when a very accomplished inter-county player from Ulster, dismayed at his classmate's performance upfront, called out from his full-back position, 'Will yiz play like Catholics?' The faith of the one true Church was the standard to be applied in Gaelic games also.

I have, perhaps, over-emphasised the lighter and largely secular dimension of Maynooth life, if only to stress my favourite title for the priesthood for which we were being prepared, as secular priests. We were to be priests in the world, discerning the Creator and Saving God in all our activities, and communicating that effectively to our, or more profoundly, to God's people, all God's people. Thus all human, indeed all created reality, was a revelation of God's work and, above all, of his Word, which was made flesh and dwelt among us.

Dwelling among us was the critical and creative dimension, not only of the Incarnate Son of God, but also of his followers or disciples as members of his community or Church, in a more revealing and disturbing image still, as members of the Body of the Christ. If it took seven years at Maynooth to achieve that to the satisfaction of our mentors, who were we, as mere beginners in face of such mysteries, to complain? Complain many of us did, from time to time, but not to the extent that our mentors, our friends or ourselves were led to the conclusion this was not the life for us. Some of our directors encouraged us occasionally, or even frequently, to take another hard look at ourselves or at class photographs of our predecessors in search of who might have fallen out after ordination. This was treated as a recurrent, if rather sick joke, coming from the pulpit. The announcement of a lot of new jobs opening up in Bord na Móna comes to mind from the 1950s.

Such complaints as there were had more to do with poor physical facilities in our early years than with staff failures. There were surely some of these in teaching, discipline and spiritual direction, which we may have been too immature enough to notice or too kind to mention. Unlikely, says my memory of student gossiping.

Of course, Maynooth as an institution was never simply confined to educational-spiritual work. In sometimes controversial situations, the Irish Conference of Catholic Bishops held their meetings here. The most controversial in my experience was in the early 1950s, dealing with the Mother and Child Bill introduced by then Minister for Health Dr Noel Browne. As the government fell, a columnist in the *Irish Times*, Myles na Gopaleen, I believe, posed himself the question: Q. 'Can an Irish Government introduce whatever legislation it wishes?' A. 'It may or it May-nooth'. A sign of a growing anti-Catholicism, at least among a certain class. How far it developed subsequently may be difficult to estimate, but it almost certainly has not disappeared or even stood still.

Maynooth has not stood still either. The late 1960s, the 1970s and the 1980s were its periods of most radical change in academic staff and disciplines and in student composition, with the decline of students for the priesthood to its present tens replacing its earlier hundreds, while staff and students have moved into the hundreds and thousands. This ushered in the recognition of lay disciplines and staff receiving recognition as an independent Maynooth University in the Universities Act of 1997, while theology and philosophy, in its continuing dual affiliation, continued with their pontifical recognition from Rome. The recent appointment of a rector of the seminary, as distinct from president of St Patrick's College, is at such an early stage that it is too difficult for this, or perhaps any observer-participant, to foresee what may be the next moves. They will certainly go much beyond my early experiences of an all-male, clerical institution, much as I enjoyed those years and still cherish their memory.

MAYNOOTH IN THE 1950s

Joseph Duffy

In the 1950s Maynooth College was still exclusively a major seminary, a third-level centre reserved for clerical students. Apart from the few who graduated elsewhere before coming here, and the annual summer and Christmas holidays, students lived in with full accommodation for the long stretch of seven consecutive years. The academic curriculum was concurrent: three years of philosophy with a degree course in either arts or science, leading to four years of theology.

With more than seventy other young men, aged seventeen or eighteen, from all parts of the country, I checked in to Maynooth in September 1951. We were each given a room in one of the three buildings of Junior House with their – to us – strange names of Logic, Rhetoric and Humanity. Meanwhile, we were made most welcome by five final-year students who were to be our monitors. A kindly serenity prevailed on those momentous first days, replaced in the darkness of night by an isolating silence. I can still hear the jackdaws in the trees outside my window in Top Logic; no other sound. When the second years joined us a few days later, they lost no time telling us of the famous Ghost Room in Rhetoric House. A more lasting experience was the mundane process of getting used to having the same companions every day at prayer, dining table and in the various class halls. By the time ordination came round, seven years later, we had certainly got to know our different mannerisms and had learned to live with them.

From day one, the unremitting focus on priesthood set out to convert rules and formalities into a committed way of life. The pressure was intense but never unrelieved. There was always the personal encouragement and ready wit of companions. There was also the shared enrichment of talents, be it on the stage, the sports field, the class hall, or simply in the casual exchanges of conversation. One day, out of the blue, we were told that an unobtrusive Killala student, afterwards an esteemed Ancient Classics professor in Maynooth, the late Tom Finan, had been awarded a European prize for a Latin essay, much to the pride

Msgr. Edward Kissane, President 1942–1959

of the President, Edward Kissane, himself a widely respected biblical scholar.

The only private area, strictly kept out of sight, was our personal vocation to priesthood; this was left to the patient care and wisdom of the two spiritual directors. About half of our initial class were ordained; the others left at all stages along the way, right into the final year, when the high emotion of ordination was already in the air.

As it had been for generations, Maynooth in the 1950s was a fortress-style, carefully regimented institution, far removed from the intimacy of home and family, but also from the stress of earning one's own bread in hard times. The daily timetable, from the rising bell at six o'clock until the solemn silence after Night Prayer, rarely changed; the spiritual exercises got priority time and were never stinted. There was, for example, prayer on the way to meals from the chapel and public spiritual reading during meals. In spite of the prevailing scarcity of supplies, the food was always on the table, plain but adequate, the hot porridge welcome, especially on cold mornings. Keeping warm in the winter months usually meant wearing an overcoat over the standard soutane when out of doors. Outside the college and during holidays the normal dress in public was a black suit. A black hat was also prescribed but seldom worn.

Boundaries were strictly observed. There was no entry into another's room, no leaving the premises without express permission and reporting on return, minimal tolerance of visitors, no easy access to teaching staff. I often thought it fitting that the man who broke the mould here later became the leader of the Irish Church. He was the gregarious and informal Tomás Ó Fiaich, the Armagh man who came to live in Long Corridor in 1954 and got to know every student by name in a matter of months. In those years we were all, of course, proud of Maynooth and its well-merited reputation, but in the post-war world the urgent need of renewal was being openly expressed. For all its apparent efficiency, the tightly insulated system was already dépassé. There was no radio, no secular reading material, no telephone access; television had not yet arrived, but was on its way. In 1956 a minor revolution occurred when a single copy of the daily *Irish Independent* and *Irish Press* began to be left in a reading room allocated to each division. The sports page was always the most in demand, GAA news in particular.

Within priesthood our common vocation was diocesan ministry. It was only in Maynooth that we became aware of belonging to a diocese, many of which had evocative medieval names. If the class bond grew out of the routine of the chapel and the class hall, the diocesan bond in Maynooth blossomed in recreation time. Each diocesan group had a spot designated by tradition for meeting after meals for general conversation and news from home. Larger dioceses welcomed the smaller ones into their soccer teams, tennis and croquet games, the latter a curious relic of sedate Victoriana. But the diocesan unit was supreme, claiming and winning total loyalty. Occasionally, we got a glimpse of the more disturbing and more challenging future ahead of us. I have vivid memories of a get-together of our Clogher group behind the old handball alley in Senior House on Ordination Day 1957. Our deacons were being ordained at home in the diocese on that day and we had, therefore, time on our hands. The ordination ceremony in the college that morning provoked an unplanned discussion. One of our men, who left the fold later, confronted us with his growing disillusionment, not with priesthood but with our prospective diocesan mission as he saw it. To his credit, he forced us to articulate honestly our own experience and our own convictions.

In the late 1950s the drama of the Second Vatican Council was still well beyond our horizons. In the meantime, a less rigid regime was slowly becoming more acceptable to the administration. In our more generous moments, we appreciated that the three deans worked hard to manage the preparation of some 500 young men for priesthood. We knew that, in addition to their daily routine, men like Gerry Montague and Michael Harty went the extra mile to foster all kinds of special interest groups among students. These catered for

Gerard Montague, Josef Jungmann the Jesuit Scholar and Liturgist, J.G. McGarry and Michael Harty

music and drama, regular debates chaired by staff and occasional addresses by celebrities like Frank Sheed, the Hyde Park apologist, Canon Hayes of Muintir na Tíre, or Din Joe O'Mahony, the comedian from Cork. I remember personally inviting Joseph Svoffierfy, an international folklorist and former secretary of the Hungarian Cardinal Mindszenty, living in exile in Dublin at the time, to a regular meeting of Cuallacht Cholm Cille, the Irish language society. The evening he came coincided, by accident, with the doomed anti-communist rising of autumn 1956. Fortunately, our distinguished guest had the language as well as the passion to rise to the occasion.

Neo-Thomism and canon law, with standard textbooks in Latin, were still securely in place during my years of theology. They were totally consistent with the overall rigid structure and cast-iron discipline of the place. Personally, I found coming to theology from Celtic studies an uneasy transition. Having attended his classes for three years, I found the Irish Professor, Donnchadh Ó Floinn, the outstanding personality of the Maynooth staff; what he imparted remained. Inevitably, there were widely different reactions to his embryonic and highly original vision for the Irish Church, based on reconnecting with the Christian heritage enshrined in the Irish language. However, he certainly made his mark. A similar spark was missing in theology, even though we knew it was our specific professional business. The lectures, on the whole, were reasonably lucid and methodical; short-term motivation and memory were enhanced by dint of regular examinations and repetition of basic principles. However, examinations were quickly forgotten and repetition had the ultimate effect, on me at any rate, of closing down the subject from real-life application or the curiosity of further exploration. As a preparation for preaching in later life, it is hardly an exaggeration to say that our mainstream theology added little to the Maynooth catechism we learned at national school. Sacred Scripture and Church history were, on the whole, welcome exceptions, and did much to restore interest and flexibility of thought.

Finally, a word of appreciation for a new Maynooth publication of my time which endeavoured to break new ground, as its title declared. *The Furrow* was a monthly journal (still thriving), founded and edited by J. G. McGarry in 1950. His idea was to identify the fault lines and pastoral needs of the Irish Church, targeting issues peculiar to the time like the care of emigrants in England, seeking inspiration from the wider Church, including the other Christian communities. Dr McGarry was our Professor of Sacred Eloquence, less formally, Director of Preaching; a task he carried out with unrelenting rigour and dedication, listening critically every year to hundreds of students' sermons (the homily was not yet in vogue). He came across as a serious, formal, rather severe person who chose his words with ponderous precision. He amused us greatly one day when we heard that he had dismissed his dog from his room when a student arrived at his door for Confession. *The Furrow*, which became his life's work, was aimed at the younger generation of clergy and educated laity: it took on the enormous challenge of being critical of Church management from within the fold without being less than dignified and diplomatic. An example was the stimulation of priests' councils throughout the country by simply publishing a list of those already working. The journal excelled especially in treating of the Liturgical Revival, promoting aspects of the reforms that later came into current use with the Second Vatican Council. I recall Dr McGarry, in class one day, making the case in his laconic way for the Old Testament, which had been more or less neglected up to then in Church worship. Another day, he spoke of the Resurrection: 'The Son of Man must be lifted up' (John 3:14).

FOUNDING A DEPARTMENT OF
FRENCH IN MAYNOOTH[1]

Brendan Devlin

In the late 1940s, two clerical students for the diocese of Derry, myself and Ignatius McQuillen (subsequently monsignor and vicar-general of the diocese), applied, on the instructions of our diocesan authorities, to take French as a degree subject in Maynooth. French, we were abruptly told, was not on offer. Things normally would have rested so. In those days, you registered or tried to register for your subject, and the registrar, having told us that it wasn't on, would have thought no more about it. However, diocesan colleges in the Six Counties were short of priests who were qualified to teach French and all I can assume is that the request must have gone up the line and been duly communicated to the President, Msgr Edward Kissane. It was a very small administration in those days, quite unlike the plethoric modern university. In any case, I duly found myself summoned to the presidential presence to make my case, an intimidating matter in those days of hierarchical distance.

What I did not know was that it was a cherished project of Edward Kissane's to have the teaching of French restored in Maynooth after the ten-year gap caused by the Second World War. He himself was a noted Francophile, having lectured in French Canada, and his outstanding scriptural scholarship was heavily influenced by French writing. I discovered subsequently that, having learned that there were two students who wanted to do French, he insisted that they be accommodated, seizing at once the opportunity to cater for an

---

1   This is a reworked extract from of an interview given to Denis Bergin in 2016.

increasing demand and remedy what he saw as a major lacuna in the Maynooth curriculum.

In point of actual fact, Maynooth had had the oldest chair of French in these islands, founded in 1801, ten years before Trinity College Dublin and fifty years before Oxford or Cambridge, which didn't teach modern languages until the 1850s. Circumstances in the twentieth century conspired to have a negative effect on the department, however. Firstly, the general abandonment of French by the diocesan colleges in the Republic after independence cut off three quarters of the possible supply of prospective students, these coming from then on only from three diocesan colleges in the Six Counties. Secondly, the onset of the Second World War finally disrupted the teaching of French at Maynooth; when the war broke out the Professor of French (who was from southern France) went home and was not replaced.

Now, while faced with an opportunity, Kissane had also to provide a teacher at very short notice. He communicated with the Professor of French at UCD, a friend of his, and asked him to recommend a promising young student with a degree who would be capable of initiating the teaching of French here for just two students. In due course a young man came down; he was a law student in UCD, but he had got first-class honours in French in his BA degree. He began teaching by simply taking the UCD curriculum and repeating it here. Six years later, when I was studying theology in Rome, I met him again, he now studying canon law as a member of Opus Dei.

He taught us for two years, by which time Kissane had got a real Frenchman, a priest, Hubert Schild, who came here in 1951, taking up his post at the beginning of our third year. Unfortunately, he was by no means the ideal choice. First of all, he was a native speaker of German, not French, although as an Alsatian his educational formation was French. His command of English was sketchy, but of course this had the advantage of his communicating with us exclusively in French. It also meant that he never really fitted into Irish ways and had a touch of that annoying French prejudice of looking down on other traditions. He had just completed his term of military service in the Algerian war and was something of a supernumerary in the Institut Catholique de Paris.

The fact that he had come to Ireland was largely a matter of chance. Msgr Kissane had, via the Department of Foreign Affairs, contacted the French embassy with a view to finding a French priest to restore the teaching of French in Maynooth College. As often happens in such cases, the French Embassy contacted Foreign Affairs in the Quai d'Orsay in Paris. The Quai d'Orsay, aware of the ecclesiastical background, consulted the Institut Catholique and the Institut Catholique probably looked around for a suitable and available candidate and thus Fr Schild was chosen.

It would have been better if a more serious process of head-hunting had been followed, particularly since the plan then, I have been told, was to work towards a university department of French culture in Maynooth. Edward Kissane envisaged such a creation, through which a dedicated academic might have had a real influence on the Irish clergy and on the contacts of the Irish with the French Church.

Admittedly there were only half a dozen of us studying French at that stage, but the haphazard process and the lack of clear direction meant that we got no real overview of French culture or French literature at all. We were from Derry, Armagh and Dromore, all dioceses of Northern Ireland (Down and Connor didn't come here for university studies), so that there was no possibility of influence on the diocesan colleges of the Republic and no provision for providing an introduction to the French language for those students who had had no opportunity of that sort in their secondary education.

Fr Schild remained in Maynooth for about five years. When he decided to return to France, my bishop, Dr Neil Farren, recalled me from Rome, where I was completing a doctorate in ecclesiastical history and directed me to enrol for an MA degree course in French in UCD. Naturally, in those days, nobody thought to inform me as to what the purpose of this sudden change might be. My professor in UCD, however, Dr Louis Roche, was later able to inform me that he knew from Msgr Kissane that Fr Schild was planning to return to France and Msgr Kissane wanted to have a candidate ready to take his place.

For this purpose, my bishop then informed me that I must have my MA in place by the end of one academic year. Dr Roche nearly had a seizure; the MA was a two-year course! After much negotiation, it was agreed between the two that I would be awarded an MA if I presented an accceptable thesis within one year and if the bishop undertook to have me spend the second year in France. It was with some perplexity that, having successfully presented my thesis at the autumn exam session, I found myself appointed to a remote curacy on a County Derry mountaintop in the month of November.

The year rolled on until some time in spring I received an episcopal one-liner:

> Dear Fr Devlin, Apply immediately to the President of Maynooth
> College for the Chair of Modern Languages. Signed Neil Farren.

I didn't know there was a vacancy in Maynooth until I got that letter. Long afterwards I found out the explanation of my rushed MA. My bishop wanted at all costs to have a priest of his diocese appointed to Maynooth and some busybody had (quite falsely) alerted him that the Archbishop of Dublin already had a priest with a degree in French and was planning to steal a march. Hence the panic. In fact, it was a case of mistaken identity; the man with the degree in French was in fact the venerable parish priest (at the time) of Swords, who had no intention of giving up his pastoral cure.

Anyhow, I duly wrote my application for the June meeting of the episcopal trustees and, on being appointed, my first care was to contact again my former professor, Dr Roche. When he heard the story of my spending my second MA year on a mountain in County Derry, he was absolutely furious, but when he calmed down he realised it was not my fault and sympathised with me at my being so scurvily treated. He was now stuck with me as a future colleague, and he became, from then on, a tower of strength to me.

A tower of strength was what I was going to need in my new predicament. Having been appointed Professor of Modern Languages, I was supposed to be able to teach French, Italian and German. Now I knew Italian well, but my French was very rusty after four years in Italy, and I could barely read academic German. I would have to go to Germany to learn enough to teach at elementary level; although, as it turned out, I never got past more than a few weeks in a Goethe Institut.

On going back to Msgr Kissane, who was, fortunately, still President, he agreed with me that for one person to teach three languages at university level was ridiculous and we found a lecturer to give courses in Italian – not at university level, just basic Italian – and the same in due time for German. However, he insisted that I teach French to university level, in other words initially at least a full undergraduate course. Now it must be remembered I had no formal training whatever. My last contact with French, apart from writing that rushed thesis for an MA, was my undergraduate course seven years before, which in fact had not given me any profound acquaintance with French literature or French culture. I had only ever spent six weeks in France in my life, and here I was, confronted with building a French Department from nothing and without direction, because the French professor had gone home and had left nothing in the way of an academic structure behind.

When I took over, I went to the library to see what I had inherited in the line of books. There was only one book that had been published in the twentieth century, although there was a fine collection of early editions of the French *philosophes* of the eighteenth century, clearly the *nachlass* of the Sorbonne men who were the first professors of theology in Maynooth. The annual grant for books in the library was £5. French was regarded among the general student

·body as not a serious subject, fit only for convent girls and boys who couldn't play football. I had no training. I didn't know how to conceive of a course or what a university course should be. I didn't even speak good French any more – I spoke much better Italian. I was really in a difficult situation. Fortunately, my opposite number in UCD, Louis Roche, was, as I have said, very understanding and kind to me, and he did all he could to help me avoid the worst blunders.

University gossip in Dublin made a story out of this. Dr Roche's wife was a strikingly handsome lady from County Tyrone whose surname happened to be Devlin, no connection of mine whatever, but of course all university circles in Dublin concluded that Roche had got a job (the Maynooth job) for the wife's nephew – me!

I had to teach the whole three-year curriculum, mark all university essays, do oral and written French single-handed, working fifty hours a week and unable to keep up with it. The level of serious interest in French among the student population was low. The students of university standard were all from the Six Counties, so thankfully there were only small classes in each year at the start. The first year I had two students, the second year I had three students, and the third year I might have had four, I don't remember, but fewer than the fingers of one hand. As well as that level, I was obliged to teach French at elementary level to any student who enrolled for it. It was even obligatory to do so for students in the science departments. The result was classes twice a week of up to a hundred in number, and very low motivation on their part. I solved this by implementing reasonable standards in the class examinations, which produced a failure rate of about fifty per cent. This reduced class sizes to manageable proportions.

In the pecking order of the Maynooth teaching staff I just didn't rate. French was something of a joke subject compared with the serious things like Classics or English, or of course theology, the queen of the sciences; French was at best a social adornment. That order of importance was even observed in our dining arrangements; we even sat at table in that order ... President, Vice-President, Deans, Spiritual Directors, Professors of Canon Law, then Professors of Theology, then members of the Theology Faculty who were professing things like history, Scripture and so on, and then arts, and finally science. In the arts pecking order, I came in last. It was organised first of all by subject and secondly within the subject by seniority, so that you would have moved up maybe two or three places in a lifetime, but not much more.

Frankly, I didn't know what to do. I had the support and good will of Edward Kissane and Louis Roche, but in the extraordinary financial stringency of that time there was little practical help they could give me. There were only two permanent members in the Department of French in UCD, so one could hope for little from there except good will. Nor could I look in the direction of Trinity College. Archbishop McQuaid would have seen to it that any cooperation with Trinity would have been more than my pathetic career was worth. Anyway, Trinity was in no better case than UCD. Nobody took modern languages seriously in the Republic of Ireland, and I came to realise that in everything, methodology, coursework, not to mention finance, the system was seriously out of date.

So I had to begin at rock bottom and that meant first of all with myself. I had to find some sort of training, if only to find out what I was supposed to be doing. With no possible support in the universities, the only other option was the French embassy. It was not contemplated in those days that an insignificant priest should take it upon himself to contact the rarefied world of a diplomatic mission, but I had no other choice and with some trepidation I rang the French embassy and asked for an interview with one of their staff.

It would not be unfair to say that back then the Quai d'Orsay did not take Ireland seriously – it was just an odd if endearing little country, probably a kind of English province, since they all spoke English anyway. One advantage that the country had was that it was superbly good for equestrian pursuits and the embassy was often graced by younger sons of the French nobility who wanted to ride to hounds. The gentleman who met me was a baron, no less. His knowledge of French literature, though, was shaky. He tried to impress me by throwing out a quotation prefaced by 'As Voltaire says … '. I said to myself, 'No, it's Montaigne', but I thought it better to let it pass.

His courtesy was impeccable, but it became clear that I didn't fit easily into any of his parameters. We're talking now about 1963 and by complete coincidence in that year the powers that be in the Quai d'Orsay decided to appoint a cultural counsellor to their embassy in Dublin and to initiate a more active cultural policy. Up to then, that policy had hardly amounted to any more than a modest annual subsidy to a well-meaning Franco-Irish friendship committee, comprised for the most part of respectable Anglo-Irish notables and whose activities ran largely to cheese and wine parties.

As soon as I found out that this cultural counsellor was in residence, I contacted him and invited him to lunch in Maynooth, a thing unheard of in those days in that straight-laced dining room. I had a couple of hours with him, described my situation to him and showed him the pathetic library we had. I outlined to him what role Maynooth played in the life of the country and the possibilities it offered from his point of view as the National Seminary and a way into the Catholic clergy. The argument that possibly did most to

Brendan Devlin (seated) with John Hume(left)
and Ciaran Devlin (the author's brother, right), 1958

convince him was my pointing out that the German embassy had just set up a lavish scholarship programme to educate our professors of theology in German universities. I claimed with some truth that they were turning Maynooth away from its traditional French origins, over to German influence. As a matter of fact, in the wake of the Vatican Council, promising young professors of theology such as Kevin McNamara, Enda McDonagh and Donal Flanagan were already studying in Germany on lavish German scholarships. In this way the Germans shifted the theological emphasis here at relatively little expense to themselves.

It was to be expected that the French would not like that. Unfortunately, the restrictions of *laïcité* meant that they could not work as openly with a religious institution as the Germans. Nonetheless the cultural counsellor, M. Arbelot, secured for me, provided I could get a sabbatical year, a place in an institute in the Sorbonne that specialised in training third-level teachers of French literature in foreign countries. My mentor could only get me a one-year scholarship, which was not long enough to do a doctorate, and I should have had a doctorate to teach in university. I felt, however, that what was on offer was better than nothing. And so I got my one year's study in France, which was the only training I ever got and the only time I ever lived in France for more than a few weeks all my life. Just that once ...

My tribulations were still not over. I wasn't due a sabbatical year for seven years and I had been only five years in Maynooth at that point. This meant convincing the episcopal trustees to make an exception for me in this case. I decided to approach the archiepiscopal chairman to request his support. This would normally have been the Archbishop of Armagh, Cardinal Dalton. Unfortunately, he was ill and incapacitated, and I was left with the prospect of an interview with his replacement, the redoubtable Archbishop McQuaid of Dublin.

Still, there was nothing for it, and so, at the appointed time, I presented myself at the archiepiscopal residence in Drumcondra. After an appreciable wait in an anteroom where the atmosphere was dominated by a pink carpet and wallpaper, where there was no furniture other than a circular table in the precise middle of the room, and by it a single chair, a soft-voiced ecclesiastic entered to call me to the presence.

I honoured the extended archiepiscopal ring and was invited to sit in a low-slung armchair to the right of the archiepiscopal desk, inundated by the morning sun. I stated my business and, to my astonishment, after a few brief questions I was promised the support I needed. A protracted silence ensued and, feeling uneasy, I rose to take my leave. But His Grace would have none of it. He assured me that I was not abusing his time and he waved me back to my position. Whereupon he turned to the bookshelves behind his desk and from them took a handsomely bound volume which he handed to me. 'What do you think of that, Father?' he enquired. It was a French translation of the *Imitation of Christ*. I could only mumble something complimentary about the quality of the binding, whereupon he invited me to look at the flyleaf. I did so. It was signed *Daniel O'Connell*. 'Yes, Father,' he said. 'That book belonged to the great Liberator.' He took it from me to replace it on his shelves and suddenly said to me over his shoulder: 'Of course, Father, you do not like the *Imitation of Christ*, do you?' I recalled that I had indeed expressed some reserve, in a review in *The Furrow* of a recent Opus Dei publication, *The Way*, with regard to volumes of spiritual maxims. I maintained my reservations and extended them to the *devotio moderna* in general.

After another silent interlude, he asked me what my favourite spiritual reading was. Feeling that this was getting beyond his jurisdiction, I replied that I read the

Fathers of the Church. 'And which Father in particular, Father?' 'Leo the Great,' I replied, 'for his Latinity. I regret to say that my Greek is weak.' 'Have you read St Ambrose?' he enquired. 'A very great Father'. I replied that I had done a two-year study of his work in Rome. While this brought the subject of spiritual reading to a close, it did not end an interview, or rather an interrogation, which lasted for another half hour, ranging from university teaching to the French *philosophes,* to James Joyce, to the role of priesthood in the modern world. In order to interrupt yet another of these embarrassing silences, I made so bold as to enquire of His Grace whether he had any guiding principle to offer me for my life in the priesthood. Reflecting a moment with pursed lips, he articulated in a soft voice: 'Yes: "*Qui me confessus fuerit coram hominibus* ... ". That has been my guiding principle and I recommend it to you'.

When eventually he rose to signal my dismissal, he graciously accompanied me from his office to the front hallway. As I rose to my feet from my genuflection, he said, looking at the empty hallstand: 'Where is your hat, Father?' – an essential article of clerical attire in the archdiocese of the time. 'Your Grace,' I replied, 'I was so nervous coming in here that I felt it safer to leave it in the car.' He smiled thinly, wished me well and I escaped down the steps, my mission accomplished.

After the June meeting of the trustees, the College President, Msgr Mitchell, informed me that I had indeed been granted my year's leave. I would of course have to pay my replacement myself and, since this would necessarily be a lay person, it would constitute a serious burden on my finances, already stretched since I was too old to benefit from student subsidies in the French university system. However, none of that mattered since I had an academic year to educate myself in Paris. I had hoped to solve my accommodation problems by finding a lodging in the Irish College there, only to find myself turned away on the excuse that it was fully occupied by Poles. This disappointment was to open another and completely different chapter in my life, the recovery for the Irish of that historic institution. I eventually found shelter in a clerical community run by Pax Christi, in the excellent company of three French-Canadians, two Catalan monks, an Irish-American and a Brazilian. All of which was an education in itself and only twenty minutes' walk from the Sorbonne.

When I returned to Maynooth I was determined to put my own seal on the French Department in the light of my new experience. I got copies of all the university courses in Ireland in French and compared them. I found that they were all carbon copies the one of the other, and they were all very much out of date. Few of them had any writing more recent than the Romantics. Trinity, presuming itself, as usual, to be the most up to date, had audaciously come as far as Maurice Barrès. I therefore drafted what I believed to be a more representative curriculum.

Here there was another snag. To appear in the Maynooth *Kalendarium*, it had to be presented to the board of studies of the National University of Ireland and passed as adequate, which meant of course that it was submitted to all the French Departments in the country. And being a suspicious northerner, I said to myself, 'My colleagues will have the opportunity to block it, or to cherry-pick it.' So I'm afraid I completely forgot to submit my proposed curriculum to the board of studies at all, I just published it in the *Kalendarium*. Nobody questioned it. The board of studies never challenged it, and I got a precious two- or three-year start.

It was not, of course, undisturbed! On my first year back, I received a *latitat* from Bishop Michael John Browne of Galway for having Voltaire on my curriculum. 'Voltaire, Father,' he trumpeted, 'is dynamite!' The text in question was only the well-known novella *Candide*. I was itching to point out to him, but lacked the nerve, that he himself had unwittingly been quoting Rousseau's *Nouvelle Héloïse* at a prize-giving in St Mary's College, Galway, the month before, when he remarked that the mountainous parts of his diocese produced the brainiest students. The next thunderbolt from the same quarter was an objection to Baudelaire's *Fleurs du Mal*, which, it was pointed out, even a French court had pronounced to be obscene. Being somewhat tired of this, I decided to try an experiment. I put on the third-year course Choderlos de Laclos's erotic masterpiece *Les Liaisons Dangereuses* and waited. No voice in condemnation was raised, probably because no one had ever heard of it. And that was the end of that.

I felt by that year of 1965 that I had my small department at cruising speed and could have some confidence in achieving what I was charged to do. Unfortunately, in that very year the trustees decided to open Maynooth to all students, and what had been a limited enterprise now found itself faced with the prospect of growing rapidly into a fully fledged university department. Having begun with just two students in 1958, I was to see at my retirement thirty-eight years later over 250 undergraduates in the French Department. More dramatically still, three years later, 1968 was to see universities around the world shaken by student revolt, Maynooth being no exception. The college was launched into a process that was ultimately to spell the end of the ecclesiastical institution in which and for which I had initially worked.

But that, as they say, is another story.

COLLEGE BUTLER
AND PRESIDENT'S MAN:
MICHAEL O'RIORDAN REMEMBERS

Interview with Salvador Ryan[1]

Old Long Corridor before the reconstruction

 hat were your first impressions in 1954 when you walked in the college gates?

The first person I met was Fr Dan Hourihane, the bursar. He was very welcoming. I was a Cork man and he was a fellow Cork man. Also the copper trees. I had never seen a copper tree until I came to Maynooth. They weren't down our neck of the woods (Kildorrery, County Cork).

The size of the place. I just could not get over the size of Maynooth College. And when it lit up at night, I was stunned; that was my immediate reaction.

1   This is the abridged text of an interview with Salvador Ryan on 22 January 2020.

I had come from a country parish and had never seen anything like it. Not even in Cork city was there anything quite like Maynooth.

And you were appointed as a housekeeper in Dunboyne House?
Yes, I started as a housekeeper in Dunboyne House, and that was my job from 1954 to 1958. My duty was to serve the Dunboyne priests; they were postgraduate students, but known as 'the Dunboyne priests', and they were very highly thought of. Everything was done for them. Their meals were served. You cleaned up after them. Their beds were made. Their rooms were cleaned. The handbasins were washed. You cleaned the corridors; cleaned the toilets. Everything was done [for them]. It was not an easy job.
The first year wasn't too bad; there was about eighteen in the postgrad. But then, two years later, the year that Ronnie Delaney won (1956) there were twenty-seven in the Dunboyne Establishment, and the Junior Infirmary was brought into play. Some stayed over there, but the majority stayed in Dunboyne House. I remember Long Corridor being built from the floor up, there was only two stories on it, and they were just knocking it down in 1954, and they rebuilt it.

Where did they eat their meals?
In the Senior Ref; at the top of the Senior Ref [Pugin Hall today]. The tables went the opposite direction, right across. The top of the Ref was their place and they were served; they were well looked after. They had their breakfast; they had their lunch (I think the dinner was served at lunchtime) and then there was supper in the evening. There was nothing in between for them.

What was a typical breakfast or lunch?
There would be porridge available. There might be … might be, a boiled egg; toast and brown bread or white bread. But in those days it was miserable; absolutely awful; really, the food was so scarce. The quality was not what we are used to today.
   It was my job to serve them; I brought the food up; and, in fairness to them, they would help; if you brought the dish up to them, they would serve it themselves: they were very helpful.
   Of course, I wasn't on my own totally in the Ref. There was a lady there, Mrs Malone, Maureen Malone. She was like a mother to me. She didn't have children herself, but she was like a mother to me. When I came, I was only sixteen. She was in her late thirties. And I learned the hard way from her (her mother worked here as well). And if you didn't do what she said … there was no messing.

Were those meals eaten in silence?

Yes, the whole Ref was silent for dinner. And there was a reader. And the Senior Dean at the time (Dr Montague from Belfast) could be hot tempered. But, having said that, he was a genuinely decent man and a decent priest. He stood up for us on the staff; he was our advocate.

Tell us about Ronnie Delaney winning gold in 1956 and what that meant for the students and staff in Maynooth?

That morning we all knew he was going to be on the radio at a particular time. One person had a radio: one out of twenty-seven; an Offaly student. Everybody that was interested in the Olympics assembled in the Junior Infirmary. And, oh, the excitement! It was just fabulous. The whole country was buzzing!

American students

In 1957, there were three American postgrads who couldn't understand why you weren't allowed to have a car on campus. Fr Quill was one of them; he was the one that stands out as he was very talkative; he'd want to find out what your side of life was. He'd want to know where you were from, how you grew up and so on. He was very affable. He had great empathy. But they couldn't understand why there was no cars. Then the next year, Tommy Meagher, who was doing education at the time in the Dunboyne (and was the great trainer of the Kilkenny hurling team later on), he got an employee to mind his car, and if he wanted to go to Dublin he'd go out to him and get his car and off he'd go. But he couldn't have it within the walls of the college.

Servants

From June 1954 to April 1958 I was living with the servants.

The servants lived near where the Maynooth University bursar's office is now. There's an underground building and a building on top of that. And the offices there, off the President's Office, were all bedrooms, upstairs and downstairs. And they were the servants' living quarters. Mr Downey was living at the bottom of the stairs in one of them. He was an old man and had a room for himself. He was the telephonist, who took over from Tommy Farrell who was the original telephonist. Tommy had a uniform and everything and worked at the lodge. You knew who he was by the way he was dressed, that he was someone of importance. But Ned [Downey] was different. One time someone came in to the college to break into the place, so Ned locked the gates to keep him in. Ned Downey is buried in the college graveyard, and so is Tommy Farrell, his predecessor.

As servants, we went to the Bakehouse to get our food (that's where the delivery store is now, facing Loftus). There was a character there; he was around my age, and we played some horrible tricks on him. The butter was rationed; everything was rationed. We got a square of white turnip; took his butter and left the turnip there instead and skedaddled.

All the servants ate together. And I remember the time going out and picking mushrooms to fry them up and cook them. But weren't they the wrong ones? Oh my God, we got so sick. We couldn't say what we'd done. It took us two weeks to get over it, you know.

The same kitchen staff provided our meals. There were about six in the main dining room and, after that, a couple of servants. But women were mostly in the background; they were never put forward. But the ice was broken in 1966 when the college started to accept lay students. They brought women supervisors, etc. The whole thing changed. Everything changed.

Servants had to be in their beds by ten o'clock; no ifs or buts about it. But somebody that was on the ground floor could get out the window and buzz off, even though the gates would be locked. They'd climb the wall; they'd do anything, those who were courting.

There was one servant whose job was simply fires and shoes: he cleaned the fire for the professors; he left fuel out for them; and he also polished their shoes. You'd leave them out for him. It was looked upon as a very good job as you were well looked after.

If staff wanted washing done, there was a laundry at the top of the town, where the Presentation School is now. There were baskets everywhere. You left out your bag and they would take the bags of washing up to the laundry. And a house, or maybe two houses, had particular days for the laundry going out and coming back the next morning. It gave great employment.

When I was about nineteen, I got ideas about going out to see a girl. There'd be nights when I'd climb the gate and the night watchman would say, when he'd see me coming in, 'If I catch you doing that again, you know the result!' Well there was one winter and the snow was absolutely shambolic, so we decided, 'this fellow, we'll get him!'. He was in bed and he never locked his door, but we quietly opened it. And then they came with a bucket of snowballs, and absolutely destroyed him! The following night he said 'I'll get you fellows' and he got a bucket of snowballs, but he put a lump of anthracite in them. But the mistake he made was he didn't get us, but we got the snow and the anthracite! They're the happy times!

What happened during the summer months?

When the summer came, and the students were gone, either you were able to paint or you would be gone yourself. Fortunately, for me, that was the main reason I came in the first place. My uncles were great at painting and I'd be dabbling along. Those that were left, we'd have a football match at break time, and it was hell for leather. And then I remember [Msgr] Frankie Cremin coming out in the evenings when the whole day was finished, a long summer's evening, in his soutane, kicking football with you. They just loved him. They loved Frankie; he was a real granddad to them! And I must agree with them. He was very grandfatherly.

And you'd make a line to attend his Mass on a Sunday. Ten minutes. When I moved on from the Dunboyne Institute, I used to get Mass at the side altars along the corridor (of the College Chapel). The Mass for the students was at ten o'clock and the altar Masses were at ten o'clock as well. And they were all individual Masses. So the students were at Mass inside the College Chapel and there might be four or five priests saying Mass outside the College Chapel on the side altars. But we'd always make a beeline for Frankie. Ten minutes. But, after Vatican II, that became thirty to thirty-five minutes.

Over where the President's Office is now, in Riverstown House, there was an oratory for the servants, and the bursar would say Mass there. And you had to be there. You'd no choice. You could fit thirty to forty people in it. And the bursar, Fr Dan Hourihane, would know his numbers, and who was or wasn't there. And especially during Lent; ye'd be expected to go to Mass every morning during Lent.

And you became the president's man in 1958. How did that come about?

The President was Msgr Kissane. I didn't apply for it but was earmarked for it. He was terrific.

At the President's Arch, on the right-hand side, in the tower, there's a toilet on one side, but on the other, that was my bedroom. I slept there. Msgr Kissane's bedroom was directly over me.

My duties were to be always available when needed; to be a chauffeur at a moment's notice (I could be asked to go anywhere for the president, or to take the president anywhere). Then you served him his breakfast and you served him his lunch in the Professors' Dining Room (you were totally responsible for him). You looked after the president full stop. That was your job.

I remember, for instance, picking up Professor Pádraig Ó Fiannachta, just arrived back to Ireland from Wales to take up his position at Maynooth. I remember going in to the boat in Mitchell's car to pick him up, and all he had was a tea chest, nothing else.

Michael Nevin was the butler in the dining room at that time. He was from Maynooth and had a son a priest.

I would be waiting for the president to come in to the dining room and, once I'd get him his breakfast, I'd go upstairs. He would sit at the top of the table. On his right would be the vice-president; on his left, the Senior Dean. But that was for more formal dinners and it didn't arise for breakfast. If you had a [news] paper you could go in and sit where you wanted. But I looked after the president; even if he sat at the very bottom of the table. That was my job. And if he wanted anything – another newspaper – whatever, he would ask, 'Could you get me this, could you get me that?'

And another thing was, if a student was being reprimanded, you had the job of going to such and such a number, and such and such a house, and tell him to come to the President's Office at a particular time. That was a horrible job because you knew what the ultimate result was going to be – he was going to get his P45! And I felt so sorry for them; I walked up with some of them, knowing their fate. But that was another part of the job.

And then, on the eve of ordinations in 1958, there was an accident in the pool. A guy jumped off the first level where the showers were and broke his neck. The eve of the ordinations – what turmoil! He would have been due to be ordained the next year.

And then KLM did a big flight around the world, and the President, Msgr Kissane, was invited to join the flight. And he did. And he came back before Christmas and never got over it. He got ill and never came out of the illness. He died in the spring of 1959. And a huge crowd for the funeral, including Charlie Haughey, who stands out in my mind.

And Msgr Mitchell became president after Msgr Kissane?
He was appointed in June 1959. But in the intervening period between February and June there was a difficulty; I didn't have a job as such because Msgr Kissane was gone. So I was in limbo. So I went up to Msgr Mitchell who lived in Dunboyne House and I knocked on his door and he said 'Come in', and I told him my dilemma. And he said 'Michael, you look after me the same way as you looked after Msgr Kissane … '.

So when June came and he did become president we helped move him up to the president's rooms. He had beautiful furniture, but it hadn't been looked after. He had a beautiful bookcase that I cleaned – pure mahogany – and when

Funeral Procession of Msgr Kissane, 1959

his sister visited she said 'Michael, how did you manage it or what did you do?' I said I just polished it and I cleaned it (I wouldn't tell her how I did it – that would be wrong – it was my secret!). 'But just tell me the ingredients you used,' she said, so I gave her that and she went home happy!

In that period of time I was courting – the same girl I married fifty-five years ago. And I just got fed up of this thing of having to climb the gate. But Msgr Mitchell said, 'Leave it to me'. James Cosgrove was bursar at the time. He had moved from being Middle Dean. Msgr Mitchell said to me, 'I'll look after it; I'll get you a key.' And he said to Cos[grove] 'I need a key for the gate; not for myself (I have my own), but I need it for Michael, and I want it at tea time.' Myself and Cos got on great.

There was another occasion under Msgr Mitchell's time when Galway got into the All-Ireland and one of the students had played in the quarter-finals and the semi-finals, but when it came to the final, they wouldn't be let out. However, Msgr Mitchell said, 'I'm not saying anything, and I won't say anything.' And the student got to play; although under another name.

How did it come about that you became butler in 1963?
My predecessor Michael Nevin had had enough, and there was a finance council meeting; and they were the people who dictated everything (they were the bond of the whole college). So the decision came up as to who was going to become butler. Maurice Dunne was the other candidate. He was in the parlour at the time as one of the waiters. And Cos made the decision to swap Maurice to president's man and to take me as butler.

I had absolutely no idea this was happening. The finance council meeting took place – I didn't even know there was a meeting taking place – and Cos rings me to bring over a cup of coffee and a biscuit. He took out a cigarette and I was wondering 'What is he up to here?' and he said to me that there was a finance council meeting earlier this morning and it was decided that you're going to be the next butler. 'Oh sweet Jesus,' I said to myself, 'how did this come about?'. 'The fact is that you're the best man for the job and when it was put the way it was put, everyone agreed. But Maurice will be the president's man and you'll help him.' 'But,' he says, 'have a cigarette and we'll talk about it.' 'And,' he said, 'before you go now, Michael, you go into Dublin and into Clery's this afternoon, and you get a tuxedo suit made; white shirts and bow (or two); and, from the time you start, that's your gear.' And that's how it all came about.

So, what were your duties from early morning until late in the evening?
Normally, six-thirty or seven o'clock you would come in. Sometimes the heating wouldn't work. In the wintertime it would be a scourge. Then in the summertime it would be too hot and the sun would blazing in on the dining room. You would rectify all those things – or you'd try.

You'd come in and open up. They wouldn't open up the door until a quarter to eight. You'd prepare everything – put out butter, milk, sugar, marmalade, fresh bread. The fresh bread used to be brought in (it was made outside), but there was fresh bread every morning. You'd the option of a boiled egg, scrambled egg or a rasher, if you so desired; porridge; there were flakes then; but it was all served from the kitchen. You'd ask the professor, 'What are you having this morning, Father?'; you'd greet him and he'd say, 'Good morning' (if he didn't, it was too bad). This particular morning this young fellow went up and said (in a jocund voice) 'Good morning Father! What are you having this morning?' The reply: 'I'll have what I have every other morning: a boiled egg and tea and toast!'

You were expected to know what each professor had, but if there was any doubt you might ask if it was all right to give him what he had the previous morning. That was totally different to asking 'What are you having?', but the poor young lad couldn't see it. I think that might have been McGarry, actually, the founder and editor of *The Furrow*.

Breakfast would go on until ten o'clock. Then you'd clean down after breakfast. There'd be a cup of coffee around midday because the dinner wasn't until a quarter to four in the day; that was served. There was a choice of soups and a choice of meat (roast beef, roast lamb, or chicken and ham; maybe fish on the appropriate days). Top grade. If you were to have wine you had to be a member of the cellar; and being a member of the cellar wasn't always helpful. There was one particular story told: there was a guy who did not like the steward of the cellar and he walked out of it. So the steward of the cellar says to me, 'There's wine on St Patrick's night, and remember N does *not* get wine'. The wine was being served that night and N put his glass out for wine and I had to say, 'I'm awful sorry, you're not a member of the cellar any more; you can't have it'. Well, he absolutely let fly. And I said, 'Hold on a minute, I'm just telling you the regulations; I can give you a box of wine, no problem, but these are the regulations and I have to abide by them.' In order to be a member of the cellar, you had to pay into it – it was a quarterly fee and you could get what you wanted.

Supper was from seven till nine. You could get a cold meat salad; a rasher and an egg; and if you wanted quality you came in early. And then there were fellows who wouldn't bother coming early and then might kick up an almighty row when they came in.

For the main meal of the day, seating was by seniority. I would prepare the table, lay out the serviettes, and you would know where you were sitting. If you weren't for lunch you informed me as butler. It was ordered as follows: President, Vice-President, Senior Dean, Middle Dean, Junior Dean, spiritual fathers; and on down along in terms of seniority of staff. Seniority worked by when you were appointed. There was one long table that would seat thirty-six. Then, when the college expanded, we had to take down the partition and extend the table.

The fire in the dining room wasn't lit during my time. There was a woeful chimney fire on Christmas in my first year and it was never lit again.

Tell us about some of the protocols that needed to be observed in the Professors' Dining Room.

Well, that reminds me of the Bishop of Galway, Michael Browne, who was here as a professor just before my time. Anyway, this particular evening, he was full of chat; and he said to me: 'Michael, sit down, sit down!' He took to me like I don't know what. But, anyway, he said, 'Sit down!', and I said, 'I can't; it's not in my jurisdiction to sit down; I'd love to.' 'Well, sit down!' he insisted. I said, 'No, but, do you know what, I'll go the opposite side of the table to you and talk to you face to face. But please understand that I can't sit down; now you understand what protocol is.' And I think that made me more understanding of protocol. And then the bottle of wine at dinnertime; he loved his glass of red wine. And when he'd ask for a glass of wine, Cosgrove would say to me, 'There's a big meeting this afternoon – make sure to give him plenty; he'll snore his head off!'

Were there newspapers available in the dining room?

In the morning the postman (the person responsible for collecting the post) would bring in the newspapers. Tom Flood (Maria's father) was in charge of the post at that time. And he would write the names on the papers. Whoever got a paper, their name was written on it and it was left in the dining room and they would pick it up on the way in.

There's a great story told about Frankie [Cremin]. On Sunday there was a paper left in (and, of course, Frankie wouldn't get a paper on a Sunday, but he started reading it). And then the guy whose paper it was came in, and of course there was no paper; but Frankie was reading it. I think it might have been Donnchadh Ó Floinn. And he said out loud, 'God, you'd think these fellows would buy their own paper.' And, of course, Frankie didn't budge. And he said it again. He knew right well that Frankie had his paper. And he almost had his breakfast finished when he said it again and Frankie thought to himself that he'd better close the paper. And he said, 'Oh my God, Donnchadh, I had your paper – I'm so sorry.' It wasn't unusual to have several people reading papers over breakfast.

Tell us about the postbox in the dining room.

There was a little postbox at the end of the dining room. You came in and put your letters in there. It was locked and the postman, Tom Flood, would come around three o'clock or a quarter past three. And he would check it all out, that there was stamps on it, and everything. And the professor would come to him at the end of the week and ask, 'What do I owe you?'. That was the system.

And then the delivery of the post: whoever was looking after the rooms, say, one section of St Pat's, he'd bring up the post and deliver it to the rooms. And he'd be responsible for their rooms, their corridors, their toilets, the whole lot.

Tell us about some of the memorable visitors to the college during your time as butler.
Those that stand out are Princess Grace and Prince Rainier. They were in Ireland for three weeks in August 1963, and they stayed in Carton House. And Msgr Hamell would bring them to Mass every Sunday morning. They were beautiful people. And the children were young at the time and they came in for breakfast after Mass; top table in the Professors' Dining Room, you had a table reserved every Sunday morning. And I served them. There were no added protocols whatsoever; they were just like ourselves; having a chat.

I also remember Montini [the future Pope Paul VI] who came in for tea one Sunday evening. He just appeared out of nowhere. Nobody knew anything about it. He just arrived in Maynooth. His English wasn't bad. And I got in touch with one of the deans to inform him that he had arrived and was asking whether it was possible to have supper. 'Oh, I'll be down immediately,' was the reply.

Then, much later, in 1979, we had Pope John Paul II, the infamous morning of the fog; he couldn't take off. Eventually around midday he landed, four hours late. Everybody worked together 110 per cent to get everything ready for him. I actually didn't serve him that day; he was in a hurry to get away again (he was going to Knock). He didn't even have time to have a cup of tea before he'd go. He had to be on the altar in Knock at two o'clock. It was all a rush job. Lasted about twenty minutes.

I remember the visit of the King and Queen of Spain, too, on 2 July 1986. I looked after them in their own suite upstairs. He was around for a weekend.

And Mother Teresa's visit in 1993. She was an absolute dote, if I may use that expression. She came in and she was brought up to the cardinal's rooms. It was the only room available off the president's suite. When she arrived, the cardinal wasn't available; he wasn't around. But she met people in his rooms. I was looking after her. Oh, her humility seeped through her. All she would have is a cup of tea. Nothing else. Not even a bottle of water. So she didn't take any meal in the Professors' Dining Room.

You got involved in the fire department at one point …
I did, in 1969. First of all, I got married in 1965, that was the beginning of it all. I got married in 1965 and the bursar at the time, 'The Cos', as I call him, we got a house on the Kilcock Road, rented from the college. We got it in October 1964

Fire in New House, 29th March 1940

and I decorated the whole thing and presented herself to it and we got married on 4 January 1965 in the depths of snow and came back to it, and we were there for five years and then I bought a site in the meantime and the house we built, we're still living in it, almost fifty years later.

Tom Flood was in the fire brigade, you see, and he was the head buck of the fire brigade and Cos says, 'Will you join the fire brigade? Just, you know, there'll come a time when there's three or four that's in the college will no longer be in the fire brigade, their time will come, so would you mind joining?' So I says, 'OK, if you think I'm up to it.' So I joined.

I did my time in the fire service and then I became station officer in 1983.

The fire broke out in Dr Cremin's, in Frankie's rooms. Let me see, I retired out of it twenty-six years, I'd say thirty years ago, maybe more. He had a chimney fire.

We got a call because it was serious. It was right beside the Gunn. Right beside it, you know. So, I went up and of course, Frankie saw me, and he said,

'My God, Michael, I've somebody I can talk to, that I know, what it's about.' I said, 'Look, if you do me a favour, you've got to get out of here, you've got to, we can't have you here, for your own health and safety, if nothing else, please.' So, in the meantime, Pádraig Ó Fiannachta appeared and took him down to the Professors' Reading Room and we got on with it, but we had to draw a line in the carpet and take it from there and I'm sure there was money, cheques and everything …

Drew a line in the carpet?
For putting the fire out inside and outside, there's a line you have to draw … we'd six guys up on the roof outside and the frost, it was freezing, minus eight degrees, and I says to the lads, 'Tie one another will you, for God's sake, will you, you know, don't be silly.' I was down below, but I had a vice, sub-officer upstairs as well. That was his job, his brief. I looked after Frankie's room below and we drew a line and from there on in, everything was pushed in and, if we found a cheque, fine, but if we didn't, too bad, it went in and everything was mustered around that and contained as fire, so that was it. It was put out and was history, thanks be to God … on my watch it would have killed me if the Gunn had gone. It would have killed me, really.

Frankie, in fairness, wrote me the most beautiful letter (I have it somewhere), still have it, I can't find it, and he was very gracious in his comments and he said, there's twenty pounds in this, so much for yourself and he wrote it down, the number of guys, it probably came to about a pound each! How lucky he was. But there was never a fire lit in it since, bolted up, and never will be. That was the closest thing to the college collapsing during my time, right beside the Gunn. My God. It would have killed me, on my watch, you know … to be associated with it.

Any concluding remarks?
Those years at Maynooth were very tough but, having said that, there was great loyalty on both sides. I built my own home, we had five children, now have twelve grandchildren. I owe Maynooth College a debt of gratitude for making me the strong person I turned out to be. I say this with a sincere 'Thank you'.

PÁDRAIG Ó FIANNACHTA

Oide agus Comhghleacaí

Pádraig Ó Héalaí

IbhFeabhra na bliana 1959, le linn dó bheith ag saothrú i bparóiste sa Bhreatain Bheag, fuair an sagart scolártha, Pádraig Ó Fiannachta, sreangscéal ó údaráis Choláiste Phádraig, Maigh Nuad — *Veni statim; classes te expectant* — ag iarraidh air glacadh láithreach le post mar Léachtóir le Sean- is Meán-Ghaeilge agus Breatnais sa Choláiste. Bhí gaoth an fhocail faoina theacht faighte ag an mbaicle beag againn a bheadh ag plé leis na hábhair sin i gcúrsa an BA, agus ba ghearr go raibh fiosruithe á ndéanamh againn faoin léachtóir nua a bhí chugainn. Thug na scéalta a bhí ag teacht ar ais le fios go raibh fear neamhghnách chugainn gan cheist, fear fíoréirimiúil, 'gunna mór' i mbéarlagar an Choláiste, fear a bhí scafa chun oibre, é lán d'fhuinneamh agus de cheol, agus fear a bhainfeadh siúl asainn.

Ní bréag a rá go rabhamar ag breith chugainn féin, agus nuair a tháinig sé os ár gcomhair níor mhaolaigh ár n-imní láithreach, mar bhí sé soiléir uaidh ón tús gur éiligh sé iomlán dúthrachta óna mhic léinn agus nach mbeadh aon ghlacadh le siléig ná sleamchúis. De réir a chéile, áfach, nochtadh dúinn taobh eile den sagart óg dúthrachtach seo – bhriseadh racht gáirí air ó am go chéile sa rang agus léirigh *obiter dicta* uaidh an daonnacht a bhí ann. Thuigeamar uaidh gur spéis leis cás gach duine againn, spéis ar chuir sé friotal fileata air níos déanaí ina dhánta nuair a shamhlaigh sé sinn lena chuid gearrcach agus é féin ina mháthair áil againn.

Dlúthaíodh le chéile sinn mar bhuíon nuair a d'eagraigh sé tréimhse dúinn ag foghlaim Breatnaise ar Oileán Móna – sinn ar lóistín le chéile, agus eisean ina threoraí againn ar dhúchas agus ar fhoinsí na teanga sin. Ba é buaic an turais ná an 'rang teagaisc' a shocraigh sé dúinn i seomra ranga i measc na leanaí i mbunscoil sa cheantar. Anseo ba é Pádraig, an fear grinn é, agus geáitsí linbh á gcur aige air féin i gclós na scoile. Ní mór eile go mbeadh an caipiteal sóisialta agus cultúrtha acu a cheadódh dóibh a leithéid a dhéanamh!

Tharla blianta beaga ina dhiaidh sin gur fógraíodh ócáid seoidh ar pháirc Reitrice – cluiche peile idir an fhoireann teagaisc agus mic léinn Theach na

An t-Ath. Pádraig Ó Fiannachta

Sóisear. B'ábhar spraoi agus cainte an cluiche seo sa chomhluadar beag dúnta sin, agus ar ndóigh, bhí flosc ar Phádraig a chumas féin ar pháirc na himeartha a léiriú. Tá cuimhne na hócáide sin buanaithe in aigne chuid againn, ar aon nós, ag an dán magúil a scríobh sé faoin ngortú a bhain dó san imirt, agus go sonrach, an chomhairle nathach ann: 'Géill d'*Anno Domini* – bí feasta id sheanduine.'

Comhghleacaí groí ab ea é nach mbíodh i bhfad ag baint suaitheadh as pé comhluadar ina gcasfaí é. Bhíodh a gháire le clos go minic i seomra bia na foirne, é ag beannú do chách agus é ag cur tharais go tiubh. Is iomaí rúideog ghéar agus sáiteán cruinn a scaoil sé síos is suas an bord uaidh. Is cinnte nach mbeadh sé ann i ngan fhios agus ní bheadh aon cheilt aige ar aon eachtra a raibh sé féin chun tosaigh ann. Ag siúl na cearnóige le baicle beag dá chairde, ba mhinic, go mbainfeadh a gháire, nuair a bhuaileadh an riastradh é, macalla as na fallaí mórthimpeall.

Ba bhunchloch ina fhealsúnacht phearsanta an tuiscint gur obair aspalachta *par excellence* ag sagart Éireannach é saothrú an léinn dúchais, agus thug sé faoin obair sin le flosc agus le cumas. Is mór go deo an chomaoin a chuir toradh a shaothair ar scoláireacht na Gaeilge, go háirithe maidir le foclóireacht, clárú lámhscríbhinní, scagadh ar an litríocht agus fiú soláthar lámhleabhair 'shimplí' gramadaí. Bhí sceitimíní áthais air nuair a d'aimsigh sé leagan de *Táin Bó Cuailnge* i lámhscríbhinn na leabharlainne i Maigh Nuad agus is é féin a réitigh an chéad eagrán den téacs seo maille le nótaí ortagrafaíochta agus teanga. Téacs tábhachtach den Táin é seo ar bhaist cuid dá chomhghleacaithe go ceanúil *Táin Bó Fiannachta* air!

Cuid eile den chomaoin atá curtha aige ar léann na Gaeilge is ea an deis a chuir sé ar fáil do scoláirí eile toradh a gcuid taighde a chur i láthair faoi inphrionta An Sagart, an comhlacht foilsitheoireachta a bhunaigh sé féin. Faoin inphrionta sin d'fhoilsigh Pádraig irisí a raibh sé féin ina eagarthóir orthu, leithéidí *Léachtaí Cholm Cille* agus *Irisleabhar Mhá Nuad*, agus chuir sé amach sraitheanna d'imleabhair léannta mar *Maynooth Monographs* agus *Dán agus Tallann.*

B'éasca leis ceangal docht a dhéanamh idir dúchas agus creideamh; bhí an dá rud fite fuaite ina chéile ina chuid smaointeoireachta agus is dócha gurb é an léiriú is coincréartí ar sin ná an foras a bhunaigh sé sa Daingean níos déanaí ina shaol, An Díseart, a bhí tiomnaithe aige do chur chun cinn na spioradáltachta agus an léinn dhúchais. Tá friotal álainn ar an nasc idir dúchas is creideamh ina aiste fhileata, *Léim an Dá Mhíle,* mar a dtuairiscíonn sé Críost ina bheatha shaolta ar camhchuaird i gCorca Dhuibhne. Ba mhisinéir dúthrachtach é ag cur an chultúir Ghaelaigh chun cinn agus thóg sé ar láimh stiúrthóireacht chomórtas Ghlór na nGael ar feadh na mblianta, comórtas a bhí thar a bheith éifeachtach ag an am ag díriú airde ar an nGaeilge i mbailte beaga agus móra na tíre seo. As na nithe go léir a spreag Glór na nGael bhí gean faoi leith ag Pádraig ar an Ollscoil Scairte – cineál daonscoile a d'eagraíodh sé i gceantair éagsúla de réir mar a d'fhaigheadh sé cuireadh **ón** bpobal chuige. Ba dheacair cuimhneamh ar aon ghníomhaíocht eile is fearr a d'oir **dá** phearsantacht spleodrach ná an Ollscoil Scairte. Thug an cúram seo i measc na ndaoine é, rud ba gheal lena chroí, agus níos tábhachtaí fós, thug sé caoi dó tarraingt ar a chuid léinn chun an obair ba phráinní, dar leis, ó thaobh fhoilsiú na hoidhreachta dúchais a chur i gcrích. Ba é sin, a dtraidisiún liteartha agus béaloidis féin a chur i láthair an phobail logánta go tuisceanach agus go báúil, ionas go méadódh a meas air.

Ach nuair a smaoinítear ar éachtaí Phádraig Uí Fhiannachta, déarfadh a lán daoine go bhfuil tús áite dlite dá mhórshaothar i soláthar an Bhíobla Naofa i nGaeilge na linne seo. Ba eisean an rúnaí ar an gcoiste a bhunaigh an Cliarlathas chun tabhairt faoin obair seo agus chiallaigh sin, ar ndóigh, gurbh eisean capall na hoibre sa chúram. Is air siúd, cuid mhór, a thit sé an mheitheal aistriúcháin a chur le chéile agus a bhainistiú, toradh a saothair a chur tríd an gcló, agus de bhreis ar an méid sin, d'aistrigh sé féin deich gcinn fhichead de leabhair an Bhíobla. Is maith a thuig an Cairdinéal Tomás Ó Fiaich agus Brollach á scríobh aige leis an *Bíobla Naofa* a foilsíodh in 1981, cad é mar éacht a bhí curtha i gcrích ag Pádraig:

> Is gá agus is ceart a rá go hoscailte, nach mbeadh Bíobla Mhaigh Nuad ann san aois seo ar chor ar bith murach dúthracht dhochloíte agus acmhainn mhillteanach oibre an Athar Pádraig Ó Fiannachta. Faoi mar a thugtar Bíobla Bhedell ar aistriúchán Gaeilge ón 17ú haois, measaimid nach mbeadh sé mí-oiriúnach Bíobla Uí Fhiannachta a thabhairt ar leagan an 20ú haois.

Ba mhinic le Pádraig a rá, i dtreo dheireadh a shaoil, gur chruthúnas dó féin é ar Dhia bheith ann, an áilleacht go léir atá sa dúlra. Bhí daingniú ar an dtuiscint sin le fáil aige in *Laudato Si*, Aitheasc Aspalta an Phápa Proinsias, a d'aistrigh sé go Gaeilge. Ba é seo an saothar liteartha deireanach dá chuid, agus in ainneoin nár mhair sé féin lena fheisicnt i gcló, is oiriúnach anois mar bhuanchuimhniúchán ar Phádraig dúinn é, tar éis a bháis in 2016.

Níl aon duine eile a bhí suas lena linn is mó, is leanúnaí agus is díograisí a thug léiriú ar a ndúchas do phobal na tíre seo ná Pádraig Ó Fiannachta. Fathach fir a bhí ann maidir le foilsiú ár n-oidhreachta cultúrtha is spioradáltachta, agus is cuí mar chlabhsúr anseo an ghuí thraidisiúnta, 'Méadú ar a ghlóire!' a chur lena anam.

Not Such a Dark Age
MAYNOOTH COLLEGE, 1961

Richard Watson

n 1961 the Faculty of Science in Maynooth had four professors in charge of four departments: Michael Casey (Chemistry), James McConnell (Mathematical Physics), Gerry McGreevy (Experimental Physics), and J. J. McMahon (Mathematics). The Department Of Experimental Physics had laboratories in the basement of Stoyte House. The Department Of Chemistry had its laboratories on the ground floor of Logic House, with one laboratory assistant, Michael O'Riordan, later to become college butler. Lectures in all the science departments were delivered in the Physics Hall or in class halls in Logic House. And that was that! There were no other lecturers to share the burden of enlightening the minds of the students, there were no tutors to help with teaching, there were no departmental offices and there were no executive assistants to provide administrative support for staff and students.

It is not surprising then that some of the staff appointed in the 1970s and 1980s, particularly in the experimental subjects, regarded the Science Faculty of the 1960s as existing in a dark age, and, presumably in the hope of encouraging improvements and preventing a return to a dark age, continued to point this out at every available opportunity. Certainly, there was a gender imbalance, which was remedied by the admission of lay students in the late 1960s, and there were other shortcomings (mentioned below); yet I think that, while it was not a golden age, it was not as dark as sometimes depicted.

The curious thing is that some of the good features and some of the shortcomings of the faculty at that time sprang from the same source, namely, the small numbers of students and staff. In terms of one of the current metrics used by those who assess the quality of third-level institutions and love to use the best jargon, preferably with lots of acronyms, the FTE student:academic staff ratios were very good. (For those who have had a sheltered upbringing, I should explain that FTE stands for full-time equivalent). The student numbers were small: in 1961, fourteen students, all seminarians, began to study science at Maynooth. I know this because I was one of them. With similar numbers in

1955 Science Faculty, L-R: Rev. Prof. J.J. McMahon, Mathematics; Rev. Prof. P.J. McLaughlin, Experimental Physics, Vice President; Rev. Prof. J.R. McConnell, Mathematical Physics; Rev. Prof. M.T. Casey O.P. General Science, later Prof. of Chemistry 1957

second and third years, the student:academic staff ratio in the Science Faculty must have been less than 10:1. This compares favourably with the present ratio of 25:1 over all faculties in Maynooth University, whose Science Faculty has evolved (metamorphosed?) from the 1960s one.

I hardly need to list the benefits of small class sizes for students and staff. For students, there is individual attention, closer collaboration with classmates, better communication in and outside the lecture hall or laboratory, and continuous pressure to keep abreast. For staff, small classes are generally not demanding, there is no need for crowd control and much less time is required for marking. There are things of benefit to both students and staff: there is no place for a student to hide, lack of engagement is easily detected, and more work is demanded from even the most dilatory student. A possibly apocryphal statement attributed to James McConnell was his admonition to students of mathematical physics: 'No plays, no films, no sport. Spirituality is occasionally tolerated.' One of my fellow students, weary of the constant pressure to study, held out a vision of things to come: 'Lads, it will be great when we get up to theology: we can sit looking at the wall all night!' His vision, alas, was not realised: the study of theology proved to be quite demanding, though it was easier to hide in larger classes.

Of course, there were downsides to the smallness of the whole operation. After a common first year taking all four subjects, the students had a very limited choice in second and third year. We could aim for an honours degree in mathematical science, taking mathematics and mathematical physics, or we could go for a general degree involving three subjects. In addition, the lectures in mathematics and mathematical physics in second and third year were delivered in a two-year cycle. This resulted in pedagogical problems in such cumulative subjects: for example, every second year some unfortunate students had to face the intellectual challenges of relativity and quantum theory before acquiring much knowledge of the classical pre-1900 mechanics.

Whatever the student experience, it was a very challenging task that faced each professor: how can one person attempt to cover what might be considered the major components of an undergraduate course in any discipline, given that no one is an expert in every aspect of any subject? This, no doubt, was one of the thoughts supporting the view that the 1960s faculty belonged in a dark age. It is true that there were lacunae in the courses delivered. But lacunae can be filled, and due credit must be given to the four professors in the Faculty of Science for what they achieved despite the lack of support, the scarcity of resources, the difficulty of conducting research, and all the other obstacles they faced. The quality of their teaching deserves recognition, for they continued a long tradition in Maynooth of inspiring and enabling students to explore their academic disciplines as far as they wished to go, in arts, science or theology.

The Faculty of Science had some illustrious members of staff, such as Nicholas Callan and Pádraig de Brun, and had produced some remarkable scholars in the first 150 years of the college's existence. More recently, in the 1940s, it produced at least one famous philosopher, Ernan McMullin; in the 1950s it produced great mathematical physicists like Ciaran Ryan and Joe Spelman, among others; and it continued to equip students of the 1960s for further study. Apart from the content of the courses, what was imparted to me, and lots of other science students in the 1960s, was an intellectual curiosity as to what happens next and a desire to find out more. Is not this one of the great benefits of a university education?

The strength of the scientific formation provided is evidenced by the subsequent careers pursued by the graduates, particularly folk like myself who decided eventually that they were not destined for priesthood and so did not have to follow paths chosen by their bishops. I mention only three, in consecutive years. Kieran Murphy graduated in 1963, was awarded a NUI travelling studentship in 1964 and later went to Berkeley, California, while flower power was still flourishing. I graduated in 1964 and, courtesy of a Northern Ireland scholarship, found myself in the University of Warwick as the Swinging Sixties swung tiredly to an end. Michael Murtagh graduated in 1965, used a NUI travelling studentship to go to Harvard, and with his PhD from there enjoyed a stellar career in Brookhaven National Laboratory, while no doubt occasionally seeing the bright lights of New York. We had our professors to thank for enabling us to progress from not such a dark place to postgraduate study in other, perhaps more exotic, centres of learning.

I was very happy to be appointed to the staff in the Faculty of Science in 1973, not least because of the challenge it offered to continue the good work of former professors, some of whom were now my colleagues, but also because of the opportunity it provided to try to make some return for the benefits I had received. As they used to say in Belfast, *pro tanto quid retribuamus*.

A SURE BET
(1962)

Eugene McGee

I was a Clogher chub in the spring of 1962, a happy student in Junior House. My brother Gerard was still a final-year student in Armagh. He was then, and remains to this day, very interested in the bloodstock industry. It was the opening of the flat racing season in England and Ireland.

Gerard gave me a tip for a horse running in the Lincolnshire Handicap and, of course, he had no idea that a Maynooth student would not have access to the bookies to have a bet on this horse. Hill Royal was the horse. That evening I consulted my co-diocesans at the Pose and an experienced Clogher log took up the challenge and told me he knew the navs and could arrange to have the bet placed. This log, who is happily still a prominent Clogher priest, seemed to have

College Graduation, 1950s

done this sort of thing before and, to the best of my knowledge, still enjoys an occasional flutter on the gee-gees.

We agreed that we would have ten shillings each way on Hill Royal. It still strikes me that one old pound was a huge amount of money for a student in 1962 (a packet of cigarettes, which I frequently bought, was about three shillings, say six packs for the pound) and a pint of Guinness, which I had never bought, was about two shillings and six pence (eight pints for a pound).

I have no recollection of how we got the result of the race, probably via the afore-mentioned navs, but good old Hill Royal won the Lincoln at a whopping price of 28/1 and the Clogher log and I pocketed the princely sum of seventeen pounds ten shillings. That was a lot of money. I hope my log friend shared some of our good fortune with the nav in question. Word spread all round Junior House that we had won and I gather due to logs and bas meeting for lectures in Callan Hall the following morning the news that a Clogher chub and a Clogher log had had such great luck spread all the way through Senior House. We were the talk of the college and had acquired fame and a reputation that we didn't seek – and could have done without.

Rev. Dr Thomas Finnegan DD was the gentle Junior Dean and it was his custom to address the entire house from the tub in Junior Chapel once a week during the time normally devoted to spiritual reading. His talks were a mixture of spiritual guidance, etiquette, instruction etc. On the evening in question I happily skipped into my allotted seat towards the back of the chapel. Tommy Finnegan began quietly referring to the parable of the wheat and the thorns. I didn't flinch till he upped the tempo by getting to the bit where the seed might fall among thorns but the sower couldn't do much about it for fear of damaging the wheat by pulling up the thorns, but that eventually the thorns would have to be plucked out; 'plucked out', he repeated, and I could just about see his delicately manicured forefinger and thumb plucking at the holy air around the tub. I cast my eyes to my left to catch a glimpse of the Clogher log, seated absolutely expressionless in the very front stall of the chapel. I felt the eyes of 200 fellow students trying to look my way without turning to identify me with their eyes.

I couldn't wait for the end of supper to get to the Clogher Pose to have a serious consultation with the entire first- and second-year student group in serious whispered analysis of our situation. It was finally unanimously decided that the two successful gamblers should go to the dean during the following study period and own up. Tommy Finnegan lived in Rhetoric House, and he had a double door arrangement whereby we had to open a green baize outer door before the timid knock on his door. It was opened by the inquisitive, arched-eyebrowed face of the dean. 'Gentlemen, how I can help you?' By arrangement, the experienced log did the talking. 'We realise, Doctor, that you were probably referring to us when you spoke in the chapel last evening. We regret what has happened, it was an innocent action on our part as we come from schools where betting on big horse races was common activity, we didn't think etc. etc.' The dean, who, incidentally, never invited us to come into his room (this all took place at his door), thanked us for coming to see him. He didn't know who the students were who had asked for money to be wagered in a turf accountant's (like hell, I thought); that it was against the rules; but his greatest shock and issue was that in doing this we had scandalised the servants. Imagine in 2020: 'scandalised the servants'.

Even then I thought the archaic terminology was the oddest way of expressing his view. He said that in response to our honesty in coming forward he would not at this stage take any further action. Neither of us made the orders list on Black Friday in June that year! We kept quiet afterwards, but I am still amazed that he never spoke of the amount of money involved; he made no suggestion as to what we should do with the money, no suggestion that we should give it back or donate it to charity; his only issue was the scandal and the servants.

MAYNOOTH, SEPTEMBER 1963
First and Lasting Impressions

Michael Mullins

On 20 September 1963 I entered the National Seminary at Maynooth as a student for the diocese of Waterford and Lismore. It was a time when the Catholic Church was enjoying a great sense of renewal. The five-year papacy of Pope John XXIII had seen a much-loved charismatic leader universally respected throughout the world. His calling of the Vatican Council had raised great hopes of renewal and updating. *Aggiornamento* was the 'in word' for his vision. His death in June brought widespread sadness and raised hopes that his successor would continue the work of the council. Giovanni Battista Montini appeared on the balcony of St Peter's with outstretched gesturing arms of welcome to the world, taking the name of the great apostolic missionary, Paul. On that very day I had an interview with the diocesan authorities about final arrangements for going to Maynooth.

In the world of politics and international affairs Catholics held their heads high as America boasted its first Catholic president, John F. Kennedy. He was universally respected as a champion of civil rights and a fearless opponent of Russian nuclear aggression, as evidenced in the Cuban Missile Crisis of 1961. His recent visit to Ireland, with special focus on his ancestral home near New Ross, reawakened our pride in the success of all the emigrants who left Ireland during and after the Famine and made such a huge contribution to society and the Church in America. It was a proud time to be Catholic and going for the priesthood was very special. In the climate of the time, it was a source of pride to family and friends, and of prayers and good wishes from everyone in the parish.

I had heard so much about Maynooth that I approached the college on that day with a sense of entering into a very historic tradition stretching back to the time when the Church emerged like a phoenix from the ashes of the Penal Days. My first impressions on entering the college were those of encountering history in the very architecture and layout of the buildings. The beauty of the grounds enhanced the historical site as the college was truly in its autumn glory, with the Virginia creeper gilding the walls and autumn colours turning every leaf into a flower in St Joseph's Square. That evening in the Junior Oratory the dean, Dr Finnegan, mounted the pulpit, and I can still see and hear him saying with a smile: 'You are welcome to Maynooth'.

Over the next few days, I met those who would be my classmates, especially those who had been at St Kieran's College in Kilkenny with me. What struck me forcefully was the wide variety of accents from the different parts of Ireland. Television was in its infancy and many of us did not have a television at home, so we did not have much exposure to such a variety of accents. I was fascinated by the accents and soon began testing to see if I could identify them. In those first few days we got to know our class and then the other seminarians arrived. Everything seemed rosy in the garden.

Not so rosy, however, was the experience of hearing the rules read by the Senior Dean when the administrative council presided over an assembly of the students in the oratory. In solemn tones we were told what was required of 'aspirants to the sanctuary'. Silence was to be observed at all times except when speaking was permitted, and speaking was permitted only at recreation times after meals. No newspapers were allowed except one placed in the common room. No radios, no food or lemonade, were allowed in rooms. No leaving of the college boundaries; and food parcels on the occasion of a visit were to be given up for the poor of the parish etc. Conformity in dress and decorum were required and the great crime, apparently, was 'singularity'. The *aggiornamento* of Pope John and the Vatican Council had not yet taken hold, but our generation saw it arrive, gently at first, with the liturgical reforms, and then gather speed. The eight-year period I spent in the college (1963–71) must surely be one of the most interesting in its long history. It saw the transition from a closed monastic-style, all-male institution to the beginnings of an open university.

The high point of my coming to Maynooth came when we began the history course for First Arts. The professor, an tAthair Tomás Ó Fiaich, brought to life in his lectures the events, scenes and personalities of the past. In our first year we studied Irish and European history from the French Revolution to the First World War. His enthusiasm for the subject, combined with his friendly, outgoing personality, created an atmosphere in the classroom as we stormed the Bastille, set the heather blazing in Boolavogue, joined the Monster meetings with Daniel O'Connell, suffered the agonies of hunger and emigration during the Great Famine, and saw the disastrous outcome of the wrong turn that led to the Archduke Ferdinand's assassination in Sarajevo. That first year was a foretaste of the two years to follow in which we came to appreciate the great works of the Renaissance, the excitement of the voyages of discovery into the New World and

(L–R): Timothy Crowley, John O'Flynn, Jeremiah Newman, Cardinal Montini (later Pope Paul VI), Patrick Muldoon and J.G. McGarry (August 1961)

the drama of the Reformation. Throughout those three years I looked forward, from class to class, and when the degree course was complete we were well prepared to enter the lectures of another giant of historical studies, another outstanding teacher, Professor Patrick Corish.

As we lived through the great changes in the college, during and after the Second Vatican Council, we experienced history in the making and saw it in the light of the ongoing history of the Church in which we were so well instructed by those two wonderful history professors. When I remember Maynooth they are indelibly imprinted among the best memories of my student days.

I returned to a very changed Maynooth in 1998 to teach in the Scripture Department of the Theology Faculty from 1998 to 2009. Instead of lecture halls full of seminarians in soutanes, the mixed group of young men and women, clerical and lay, that filled the halls showed clearly that the seeds of change sown in the 1960s had come to fruition. The sacred sciences were no longer the preserve of the clergy. As the individual backgrounds and future aspirations of the students brought a new challenge to the teacher I could look back with confidence and draw inspiration from those teachers who had loomed so large in my earlier experience in Maynooth. To them I shall be eternally grateful.

'I Wonder Who's Ratzinger Now?'
MAYNOOTH, 1961–65

Eddie Finnegan

aynooth's Junior House of early 1963 was an info-lite zone. Rhetoric House's Ground Zero summed it up. The under-nourished Junior Library on the eastern corner matched the under-nourishing Junior Refectory to the west, sandwiching Tom Flood's tuck shop and the recreation room, dating from the winter of 1947, with two morning copies of the *Press* and *Independent* for our communal consumption. *Pabulum mentis cum pabulo ventris* it was not – yet better than the pre-1957 newspaper famine, an 'anti-Modernist' hangover from early in the century. Entering Tom Flood's narrow emporium was about as easy as eyeing a column-inch or two of a sports page next door when 200 locust-like logs and chubs were seized by a simultaneous consuming passion. One needed to be robust to go a-foraging in either room.

True, we had gleaned enough from the *Press* and *Independent* to make us all *periti* on the nuclear winter threatened earlier by Fidel and Nikita. Our missile expertise did not extend to *Missale Romanum* schemes or dogmatic schemata erupting that same October from San Pietro siloes, yet even without John Horgan's *Irish Times* daily feedback some enlightened logs in smoke-filled Munster Shed caucuses were soon name-dropping Ottaviani, Bea, Frings, Suenens, as glibly as Kennedy, Khruschev, Gromyko, McNamara.

Early January saw the original Beast from the East bring us a loin-girding winter, concentrating our minds on our own extremities and nether regions. Our era pre-dated the advent of Damart thermal underwear; Clery's soutanes were thin indeed, with battered old birettas our only headgear and sole concession to 'singularity of dress'. That mini-Ice Age saw brisker business for our Saturday mart's haberdashers and cobblers – healing soles, heels and uppers against frost and slush – than for Charles Davis's or Hans Küng's progressive paperbacks from Gill & Son's Wednesday afternoon visits. Just as Lá 'le Bhríde greeted spring with worse blizzards than 1947, we Armagh lads lost our bishop, Cardinal John D'Alton, with just one council session under his sash. Fittingly, our primate, ex-Maynooth President and Classics Professor (*Horace and His Age*, 1917) was

Detail at St Mary's Oratory

escorted back to Armagh by two successors-to-be, Tomás Ó Fiaich and Gerry Watson.

Easter's April showers brought flowers even to the desert, the trill of birdsong returned to Johnny D'Alton's garden, and by May Day the voice of a German progressive theologian was heard in our land. Not Gregory Baum, the German-Canadian who came at the end of 1963, and to whom Archbishop McQuaid took strong exception as an 'alien, stranger-priest'; though he could not ban him from Maynooth once President Mitchell had given Enda the green light. What John Charles made of the account of the Second Vatican Council's opening session by another alien progressive *peritus* in *The Furrow*, May 1963, history does not record. Our Greek Professor, Fr Bill Meany of Ossory, had translated the January lecture by Fr Joseph Ratzinger, *peritus* to Cardinal Frings of Cologne. An excellent translation, insofar as I could judge then or now; an advancement of learning for information-starved clerics-in-embryo, or even for a few Irish council fathers who had been there. A belated thanks to *The Furrow*'s founding editor, Fr Gerry McGarry, for that 'Council Issue', and to Bill Meany for his very readable rendering. But whatever, I wonder, became of the young Joseph Ratzinger?

> It would be too early yet to attempt either a theological or historical appraisal of the Second Vatican Council. Its work is still far from complete, and no one can say at this moment exactly what its precise results will be.

A mere month after Session One, Fr Ratzinger must have grinned knowingly with his Bonn audience as they recalled that Trent had wound up just 400 years earlier after twenty-five sessions over eighteen years and three popes. Yet, even today, his opener rings true: It would still be too early. Another Vatican council to match Trent's remaining twenty-one sessions might be useful. Pending which, shades of more progressive Manutiani haunting Junior House's Munster or Ulster Sheds would appreciate a Ratzinger sequel, if he finds the council's work by now more complete, and if the *Furrow*'s present editor can track him down. Of course Cardinal Frings's thirty-five-year-old *peritus* of 1962/63 must be well into his nineties, pastor emeritus with the smell of the sheep about him in some remote Bavarian parish, having resisted all temptations to ascend the rungs of Rome's ancient *cursus honorum*, but clear as ever that a pastoral council

> should rather be defined in the context of a positive concern for the needs of modern man [*sic*]. He has had to listen long enough to being told what is wrong, what he may not do. He wants to hear the truth, though he has heard far too little of this, and what positive message the faith can offer to our time.

For this lowly Junior House log, aware that not every Maynooth generation could hope to experience the novelty of an ecumenical council, Fr Ratzinger's lecture brought insights and surprises that even my namesake, Junior Dean Tommy Finnegan, later Bishop of Killala, never broached. In mentioning the dynamism that emerged from the council's early paralysis, Ratzinger says: 'We may ask which groups of bishops were chiefly responsible for this new dynamism. One can straightaway name three groups: the Central European episcopate (Germany, France, Holland, Belgium); the South American; and the missionary bishops.' He adds that, while the Spanish episcopate showed interest in 'the new questions', the English language group (England, Ireland, US) remained strongly conservative, even if not quite so 'curially' conservative as Ottaviani's Italians.

Fifty years later, on a hot June day in 2013, just months after a papal resignation, I fled the selfie-stick tourist hordes in St Peter's Basilica and propped myself at the base of one of the portico columns to slake my thirst. I hadn't noticed the floor memorial to the Second Vatican Council's inauguration when last there in June 1969; much harder to miss the names of hundreds of bishops engraved on tablets of stone soaring up the portico's walls and columns, yet lacking all the art of Horace's *monumentum aere perennius*. Risking a crick in my neck, I traced our local 'adsistentes' at Pius XII's Definition of the Dogma of Our Lady's Assumption, November 1950: D'Alton, Kyne, McQuaid, Walsh, Browne, Fergus, Farren, Lucey, Quinn and a score of others. A mix of remote, bumptious, kindly, familiar yet *rarae aves* seasonally glimpsed around Joe's Square or the Dunboyne, half of them back in Rome for the council's 1962 opening. 'Local Ordinaries have gone; ordinary locals are left' (*Silhouette* Diary, Ourselves).

Re-reading between young Fr Ratzinger's lines, I wonder whether ageing devotees of infallibly dogmatic old questions at the start of one decade could be open to tackling 'the new questions', even with the lubricant of Papa Roncalli's 'balm of mercy' at the beginning of the next. Fatigued and baffled by endless bog-or-better-Latin interventions led by the 'big boys', many must have found their names chiselled on those Holy Year stone tablets a source of soothing balm and reassuring identity as they adapted to their future default mode of 'steep learning curve'. Yet far ahead of that curve till 3 June 1963 was the ageing, ailing Angelo Roncalli.

A RUMBLE OF THUNDER IN 1965

Patrick Hannon

In the forenoon on a Thursday in November 1965, Msgr P. F. Cremin, the Senior Professor of Moral Theology, was late for a postgraduate seminar in the common room in Dunboyne House. Participants were due to discuss a chapter from *Marriage Questions*, the second volume of Ford and Kelly's *Contemporary Moral Theology*; instead we listened as the professor recounted what had happened in the class period immediately before. What happened was that students had interrupted the lecture to complain about the content of the courses, the core of their claim being that he showed no awareness of the 'renewal' of moral theology in train for more than a decade. We were as astonished as he was; criticism of mentors was a staple of conversation but, except for an occasional careful airing in student magazines and debates, we generally kept it to ourselves. In the distance there was a rumble of thunder.

The renewal in question was in response to a critique of the manuals of moral theology, textbooks used in training for the priesthood following reforms ordered by the Council of Trent. Trent also laid down requirements regarding the Sacrament of Penance, and education in moral theology was envisaged as a training of confessors. The focus was on sin rather than on virtue, 'thou shalt not' rather than 'thou shalt', and the picture of morality that these books conveyed was negative and legalistic. The renewal was rooted in studies published during previous decades, which presented the moral life of a Christian as a following or imitation of Christ, and which emphasised the primacy of the love-commandment, but it took time for these to enter the mainstream. A key figure was Redemptorist Bernard Häring, whose work was beginning to be available in English, and whose three-volume *Law of Christ* aimed to provide a more positive account, grounded in the Scriptures and engaging with personalist and existentialist currents in philosophy.

Frank Cremin was the Irish bishops' *peritus* or expert at the Second Vatican Council, which would close a few weeks later on 8 December. He was not at all unaware of what Häring and others were saying, but he remained an unrepentant exponent of the moral theology of the manuals. He was taken aback by the student protest but by no means daunted. Kindly and fair-minded, he wasn't

Painting of professors at the college gates by Fr Jack P. Hanlon (1913–1968)

a man for reprisals. Even as he spoke he found excuses for those misguided youths as he saw them; and an old-fashioned loyalty prevented his voicing an obvious subtext, criticism of his junior colleagues Enda McDonagh and Denis O'Callaghan for exposing their charges to the new thinking. The session in the common room inevitably went into extra time, and we were very late for lunch.

The protest on that November day turned out to be the first of many, which in due course included two or three student strikes; Maynooth had its own version of *les événements*. The college was shortly to admit lay students in arts and science, and soon a students' union was founded, and it's noteworthy that among the founders, and for many years among the leaders, were numbered 'clerics', as students for the priesthood were commonly called. The clerics in theology had some specific gripes, starting with a truly oppressive lecture load. They were obliged to attend five lectures a day from Monday to Friday, three or four on Saturdays: five a week in dogma, four in moral, and four in Scripture, to mention only what were known as the major subjects. Terms ran from mid-September to mid-December, mid-January to Easter, and Easter to mid-May, when a ten-day revision period was followed by examinations. There were no tutorials and little in the way of written work, and BD oral and written examinations were in Latin. The outcome of persistent student pressure was a radical reform of the theology curriculum, completed in 1971, with the introduction of tutorials and seminars and the appointment of five extra staff.

However, student dissatisfaction was not just with the theology programme. The college followed what seemed like ageless ways, and the mien it presented was bleak. A small thin black book, given to each freshman, contained rules meant to shape our lives. Much was forbidden, and it seemed easy to err. Some of the rules rang strange: silence was the rule 'except when speaking is permitted', we were not to be 'familiar with the servants', nor to engage in 'feasting' in our rooms. College life was not in fact as miserable as all of this portended: there were the usual sports, drama and cinema in the Aula, regular visits by leading

musicians and the two Radio Éireann orchestras, and a kind of counter-culture that was healthy. Healthy too and inspirational was the influence of individual members of the staff in both the Pontifical University and the Recognised College, antecedent of Maynooth University. But the regime could and did stunt growth, it didn't fit students for ministry in a new Ireland and it was high time for a change.

It's not too much to say that when I joined the staff in 1971, the place was scarcely recognisable as that which I'd left just four years earlier. In theology there was the changed curriculum: two lectures a week in subjects in which formerly there were four or five, far fewer lectures in the day, group work, essays and other written exercises; importantly, a director of pastoral training and the first serious attempts at providing opportunities for experience of work in the field; in general a broadening of horizons. Importantly, too, the regime was less constricting, there was more freedom to come and go, and there was a call on the personal responsibility of students, thought to be more conducive to maturity. The opening of theology to lay students was still in the offing, but already there was a significant lay presence as a new campus fused with the old. *Pastores Dabo Vobis,* when it came in 1992, found ground already tilled.

What emerged wasn't perfect, of course, and in time there was room for critique and reform again, and there always is. For those of us who were young then, the papacy of Francis is evoking memories and hopes of the council time. Things are different now, in Church and country and world, in ways that were unimaginable then. But what happened then was unimaginable in 1795, or when Healy wrote his history a hundred years later. Who knows what St Patrick's College Maynooth is to become? What we do know is that the Gospel is the same as it was in the beginning, and it is a message of hope.

Facing page: Painting of seminarians at St Mary's by Fr Jack P. Hanlon (1913–1968)

Suspended Between Two Worlds
THE CLASS OF 1966

Brendan Hoban

I t was the best of times. It was the worst of times. And it took us a bit of time to realise that, as with life, it was both. On that September day, eighty-four of us comprised the Maynooth class of 1966. A dean, who walked as if on castors, glided into view in Callan Hall and informed us that his job was to get rid of at least half of us. 'Inauspicious' could hardly describe the welcome.

As the autumn days passed into our first Maynooth winter, we found ourselves suspended between two worlds. Like chicks trying to break an already shattering shell – despite constant efforts to plaster over every crack that emerged. Like deep-sea divers coming up occasionally for air, like people watching a demented garda at a busy intersection offering contradictory signals to oncoming motorists, we weren't quite sure where we were going. Or, indeed, what was happening.

John McMackin, Senior Professor of English, resting languidly in the seventeenth century in the company of his literary hero, John Dryden, continually commended Dryden's enduring thesis that everything had a beginning, a middle and an end – in that order. Sitting serenely on his lectern, and dressed in soutane, overcoat, galoshes and biretta, he represented the solidity and stability of an enduring, unchanging world.

On the other hand, the Junior Professor of English, Peter Connolly, bobbing up and down on the same lectern and bristling with ideas, more than hinted that the future might well comprise, in Philip Larkin's line, keeping 'a few cathedrals chronically on show'.

In Maynooth, though we didn't quite realise it then, we were between worlds, swathed in ankle-length soutanes representing the traditions of the past, while a generation of female students strolled through the college gates in that enduring 1966 invention, the miniskirt. In the same year, the Bishop of Clonfert protested over the contents of an RTÉ *Late Late Show* after Gay Byrne asked an inappropriate question about night attire, and Minister for Education Donogh O'Malley announced details of a new free secondary education scheme.

St Mary's Oratory before and after reordering

Ireland, not just the hallowed cloisters of Maynooth, was suspended between two worlds, yet with the unmistakable feeling that change was the order of the day.

A plethora of revolutionary documents overwhelmingly voted through the Second Vatican Council had thrown a grenade into Maynooth, where J. G. McGarry's *The Furrow* had voyaged carefully but effectively around the menacing promontory that was Archbishop John Charles McQuaid. But now, with the streets of New York and Chicago full of protesters objecting to a war involving half a million US soldiers in Vietnam, revolution was in the air, and the class of 1966 seemed ready for the challenge of dragging Maynooth into the twentieth century, though in retrospect it was more a version of Peter Hebblethwaite's comment about 'giving a haircut to a drowsy lion'.

A classmate approached the College President for permission to organise a mixed-sex swimming competition in the college pool even though the timetable for using the pool was carefully monitored between the sexes. The request was turned down. Students togging out for attritional inter-class GAA battles were cautioned to wear their soutanes over their jerseys to High Field (and back) in deference to the sensibilities of the burgeoning female student population. Rag weeks, an invention, not part of the Maynooth tradition but copied from other universities, witnessed an *Urbi et Orbi* moment when a youthful Pope Innocent XXI addressed the faithful from a window in St Joseph's Square and, announced, in his new encyclical, *Non Sacerdotalis Caelibatus,* that the traditional vow of celibacy would be forthwith abandoned, to the delight of (most of) the gathering.

Inevitably, students found other fish to fry. Unease with the content of the theology course, and the quality of some of the lecturing, generated a lively correspondence between the students' representative council and the Faculty of Theology but no meeting of minds, even though both were agreed that the number of lecturers should be increased.

A robust student gathering in Callan Hall came to a series of unusual and unprecedented decisions in the wake of an emotional and tendentious meeting: that a student strike should be called for a specified day; a student action committee elected; and the bishops informed of the development.

A whiff of revolution – some would say a whiff of cordite or even sulphur – was in the air as the great day dawned. Letters had been despatched to the lecturers that morning to spare their blushes on arriving at empty lecture-halls. Paddy Corcoran, a Marist priest (who was filling in for a lecturer on a sabbatical), wryly informed a student of his relief on discovering that the strike didn't just apply to him.

The day of the Maynooth Spring of 1971 came and went, though it hadn't the feel of a triumph. Clearly, the bishops were entrusting the college authorities to handle the contretemps in house, as an altercation on the field of play might be deemed merely the business of a football manager. The heavy hitters were kept hovering in the background, like Soviet tanks massing on the outskirts of Prague a year or two earlier.

Suddenly, as if to bring the situation to another level, a heading in the *Evening Herald* informed the nation that Maynooth students were on strike and wondered what the response of the Irish Episcopal Conference might be now that their students had, metaphorically, 'thrown down the gauntlet'. Apparently, the story was the result of a furtive phone call made from the precincts of Loftus Hall.

Maynooth College, possibly even Christendom (we imagined), held a collective breath. The curt response from the bishops was that all students would be sent home and Maynooth College closed unless the strike was called off. A crisis meeting of the committee ensued with just one item on the agenda and one inevitable decision.

The bishops arrived in Maynooth for their spring meeting and letters were despatched to each of them withdrawing the strike. It felt like the beginning of the end of something, but it turned out to be the end of the beginning. A five-member delegation of bishops met the students for a clearing-of-the-air session and declared that while they were unhappy with the strike they were prepared to listen to students' concerns and to respond.

The following June at their summer meeting the bishops appointed five new lecturers to the Theology Faculty and a system of tutorials was introduced the following September, thereby effectively accepting and validating student demands.

Professor Patrick Corish, the distinguished historian, in an atypical rewriting of the facts of history, warned us at a subsequent lecture not to imagine that it was through our influence that the bishops had moved to appoint new lecturers and to order an effective re-vamping of the Theology Faculty. The lecturers were appointed, he assured us, because the Faculty of Theology had already applied for them. It took some time before the jeering subsided and Professor Corish retreated to the nineteenth century and the riveting question of the abolition of tithes.

Maynooth had taken in its stride the later unease with the revolutionary fervour sweeping Europe that had spooked Church leaders like the later Pope Benedict XVI. For Maynooth, life went on, as one student commented, 'here today and here tomorrow'.

The soothing sounds of Leonard Cohen's 'Marianne' wafted along the corridors of St Mary's while, in the coffee room, the discussion raged on whether the words 'Mother Mary' in the Beatles' hit, 'Let it Be', referred to Our Lady or, more prosaically, to marijuana.

Let it be. Indeed.

HOW I REMEMBER MAYNOOTH,
1967–68

Nollaig Ó Muraíle

When I came to Maynooth just over fifty-two years ago, I had no idea that the college – then reputed to be the largest seminary in the Catholic world – was about to undergo a more radical change than any in its 172-year history. I was about to experience the last year of the *ancien régime* and the beginning of a phase in its story that its founders could surely never have envisaged.

My first encounter with the college could be said to have begun even before I reached Maynooth. Some weeks earlier, I had to travel by train from Ballyhaunis to Clery's department store on O'Connell Street, Dublin, to be fitted out with clerical garb that consisted of a suit, overcoat and hat, all in black, plus a black soutane, white surplice, biretta (a piece of headgear with which nobody under the age of forty is likely to be familiar), a Roman collar that seemed to be made of plastic, and some shirts (collarless, to accomodate the aforementioned 'dog collar', as some of the more irreverent called it).

Of all these items, what seemed to me the strangest was the large black hat; it looked like the one my grandfather – who had died almost a decade earlier – used to wear. I don't think I ever actually wore it, for, shortly after arriving to Maynooth, we learned from the older students that the only reason it was still deemed obligatory was that the formidable archishop of Dublin, John Charles McQuaid, insisted that no clerical student was to be seen walking bareheaded within the archdiocese. That included Maynooth, although the feeling within the college walls was that the writ of John Charles did not run there; instead, the college was under the supervision of the trustees, who included not just McQuaid but all four Irish archbishops and thirteen of the twenty or so bishops. Several years later, when the Professor of History, Tomás Ó Fiaich (or Tom Fee, as he was known to the students), was Archbishop of Armagh, he revealed in a radio interview that he thought his hat was ludicrous and wondered how he might get rid of it. Eventually, on his way to the Gaeltacht in Rann na Feirste, west Donegal, on a rather slow train – it was during the Second World War

Midsummer Glory by Sara Kyne

and the train was fuelled by turf – he put on the hat and stuck his head out the window of the train. Shortly afterwards, a gust of wind whipped the hat off his head and the last he saw of it was as it was blown along across the heather. And the remarkable thing, he added, was that nobody in the college ever afterwards remarked on his lack of a hat! As for my hat, I brought it home at Christmas and gave it to an elderly neighbour. He was delighted with it, and soon afterwards I saw him wearing it while he was haymaking.

Maynooth in 1967 had over 600 clerical students, the vast majority of whom belonged to the twenty-six Irish dioceses – although Dublin students were notable by their absence from the first three years (when studies for NUI degrees were undertaken); Dublin BA and BSc students attended UCD, after which a selection of them were sent to Maynooth to study theology. (Another reflection of John Charles McQuaid's deep and abiding hostility to Maynooth.) Our first-year class had 112 students, a number that would decline steadily over the years – of these, less than a third were ordained in 1974. The practice of dropping out (or 'cutting', as was the in-house slang) began early. After breakfast on our very first morning in Maynooth, we were astonished to hear that one of our number had already left! Scarcely anyone, apart from his 'co-diocesans', even knew what he looked like.

We soon learned that we were never to go outside the college gates without express permission, which was not granted easily. If, in an emergency, one were allowed to go into Dublin (on the number 66 bus), it was made clear that under no circumstances could one enter any shop or other house in Maynooth village. College folklore told that this ban had its roots in an incident that occurred sometime in the 1830s, when a member of staff converted to Anglicanism and was appointed a Church of Ireland minister in or near Kilcock. This seems to have been accepted with equanimity in the college, and when he was due to take up residence in his new parish, a number of senior students were permitted to help him move his furniture, books etc. Having done their good deed, the students were caught in a heavy downpour as they made their way back to Maynooth, so they repaired to a hostelry in the village and drank rather more alcohol than was wise. On returning to the college, they entered the refectory where staff and students were dining together (apparently the practice at the time). They became rather obstreperous and, when reprimanded, they reputedly overturned the table at which the professors were seated.

As a result of this incident, students were henceforth forbidden to enter a public house, or any other house, in the village. Moreover, the practice of giving each student a mug of beer for breakfast was discontinued; instead, they were given butter for their bread. (The beer had been brewed in the college and, when the practice ended, the brewery became the Junior Infirmary – known to students as the 'Junior List'. According to Patrick Corish's *Maynooth College 1795–1995*, pp. 65–6, that building, still standing behind Logic House, dates from around 1836.)

In my first year, exiting the college without permission was still deemed such a grievous offence, and the rule interpreted so literally, that even if one were to do so accidentally, you were deemed to have been expelled – or expelled oneself – and had to apply to the college authorities to be readmitted. I recall on some Sunday afternoons, when nothing much was happening in the college, some of us would gather at the front gate and tempt fate by gingerly stretching one foot over the imaginary line that marked the 'frontier' with the outside world. One foot over the line was considered permissible, but if one of your mates ungallantly shouldered you out, even for a second, then you were (at least theoretically) 'expelled'.

This narrowly legalistic attitude to 'the rules' may be compared to the even more draconian penalty for removing a book from the library (known in college

Detail from the ceiling of the Lady Chapel, College Chapel

slang as 'the Gun library'). As stated by a typed notice in Latin in a glass frame outside the upstairs door of the library, such a heinous deed incurred the sentence of excommunication. I remember a senior student – perhaps one of the monitors – remarking that it was a sign of the Church's waning authority when it was deemed necessary to back up the typed notice with a burglar alarm. (It may, in fact, have been a fire alarm.)

A more extreme example of narrow legalism was reflected in a notorious anecdote with which we were regaled shortly after arriving in Maynooth. This told of how the much-feared Middle Dean, Paddy Muldoon (a priest of the diocese of Raphoe), had, some time before, expelled a student for the crime of 'secret feasting' (i.e. eating a sweet, or perhaps just a square of a bar of chocolate, in his room); the sole incriminating evidence for this misdemeanour was a tiny piece of silver paper found on the floor under the student's bed. It could only have been found if the dean had lain down on the floor to look under the bed, and that is presumably what he did.

Among other aspects of college life that cannot be treated of here was the way each member of each year/class was assigned a number that we were told we kept for life. I was No. 7 and my 'immediates' – the lads numbered 6 and 8 – always sat on either side of me at breakfast (in the Junior Refectory in Bottom Rhetoric), and likewise in the Junior Oratory at morning Mass or evening prayers. The Junior Dean, Michael Olden, once told us – perhaps semi-jocosely – that the theory was that if two immediates were, many years hence, being considered for appointment as bishops, and both were deemed to be equally suitable, preference would have to be given to the one with the higher number (e.g. 4 rather than 5).

Another aspect was the strictly formal relationship between staff and students. On the rare occasion a member of staff (all referred to as 'Professor' and always wearing the black Maynooth toga) might speak to a student, he would address him as 'Mr X' (using the English form of his surname). It was suggested by some that the use of such English name-forms – even for noted Irish scholars (Tom Fee, Paddy Fenton, Charlie Hanley, Paddy Healy, for Tomás Ó Fiaich, Pádraig Ó Fiannachta, Cathal Ó Háinle, Pádraig Ó Héalaí) – may have had its roots in the role of the British government in the founding of Maynooth in 1795. (Incidentally, the great exception to this stiff formality was Tomás Ó Fiaich – it was said 'Tom Fee speaks to everybody', and, not alone that, but he would always address them by their first name; indeed, it was no idle boast of his that, in the days before the college 'opened up', he knew every single one of the 600 or so students by name, where they came from, and various other details. There were many anecdotes of Tom meeting former students, long after they had left Maynooth, perhaps in a foreign land, and being able to greet them immediately by name.)

On the basis of this brief account, it might appear that the Maynooth of 1967–68 was a particularly harsh and unfriendly place, but this is not how I remember it. Yes, there were some archaic rules that had obviously outlived their usefulness, and a very occasional staff member with a large bee in his bonnet, but overall I recall Maynooth as a place of considerable freedom – certainly by comparison with the secondary boarding school in Ballaghaderreen that I had attended for five years prior to coming to Maynooth. For example, most of us had a room to ourselves, in which we could have a transistor radio and a bookcase full of books. We also had access to newspapers, and to a reading room in Bottom Rhetoric as well as the nearby Junior Library. There was a record player in a room in Bottom Logic, with a selection of 'serious' LPs, and in another room there was a television (although, to the best of my recollection, it could only be turned on for a short while each evening).

When we returned to Maynooth after the summer holidays in 1968, it was to a college that, outwardly, seemed the same, but in fact was dramatically different. It had had begun to open up and was about to take a momentous leap into the later twentieth century, but that is another story …

Change in the Air
CONFERRING DAY, NOVEMBER 1967

R. V. Comerford

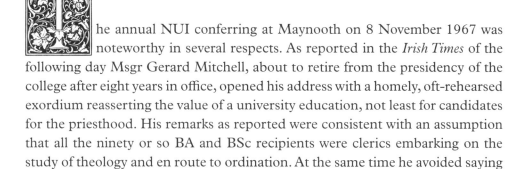he annual NUI conferring at Maynooth on 8 November 1967 was noteworthy in several respects. As reported in the *Irish Times* of the following day Msgr Gerard Mitchell, about to retire from the presidency of the college after eight years in office, opened his address with a homely, oft-rehearsed exordium reasserting the value of a university education, not least for candidates for the priesthood. His remarks as reported were consistent with an assumption that all the ninety or so BA and BSc recipients were clerics embarking on the study of theology and en route to ordination. At the same time he avoided saying anything that might discommode the considerable proportion of the graduating class that had in fact already departed the clerical state.

The most striking aspect of the conferring list was not that it had a large minority of former clerical students, but that some women were included. They were not recipients of the BA or BSc but belonged to the first Higher [postgraduate] Diploma in Education (HDipEd) class at Maynooth that was open to lay people. Its inauguration in October 1966 was the first substantial practical outcome of the decision taken in June of that year that Maynooth should become 'an open centre of higher studies'. The HDipEd, directed from 1966 to 1986 by Dr Séamus Ó Súilleabháin CSC (Professor of Education from 1968), was to have an incalculable impact on the growth of Maynooth as a university institution. However, initially it had the perceived advantage of making minimal inroads on the conventional life of the college. The classes were held in the evening in Callan Hall, near the front gate, after undergraduate teaching had ended for the day. At this stage the notion of disrupting the regular tenor of college organisation so as to provide refreshments or other social facilities for non-resident students would have seemed uncalled for. That would change in subsequent years.

The twelve women among the more than fifty recipients of the HDipEd on 8 November (many of them conferred *in absentia*) were the first females to receive academic awards at Maynooth. They included Mary O'Rourke who, twenty years later, became minister for education. The first women admitted to degree programmes in Maynooth were religious sisters who matriculated in 1967. The first admissions of lay people, men and women, to BA and BSc courses came in 1968.

The *Irish Times* has no mention of what if anything the monsignor had to say about such developments, although the opening up of the HDipEd had been an initiative of his presidency. As it happened, Maynooth's tentative plans had been overshadowed by major developments in government policy that had profound and uncertain implications all around. The dramatic uncertainty of the situation is caught in this statement by Msgr Mitchell: 'This may very well be, if not the last, very nearly the last conferring of degrees of the National University of Ireland in Maynooth'.

What was afoot? March 1967 had seen the publication of the long-awaited recommendations of the Commission on Higher Education. The most striking of these was the dissolution of the NUI and the raising of its constituent colleges in Dublin, Cork and Galway to the status of independent universities. Since 1910 Maynooth had been a 'Recognised College' of the NUI, with its arts and science programmes approved by the NUI and the relevant examinations conducted (at Maynooth) by the NUI. However, the charter of the university provided that a Recognised College would be under the tutelage of one of the constituent colleges, and in the case of Maynooth that was UCD. In the proposed new order Maynooth could continue as a Recognised College of the upgraded UCD with very little disruption of existing arrangements. Or it might seek independent status. A month later the minister for education, Donogh O'Malley, threw the entire university sector into turmoil with the announcement that he was not accepting the recommendations of the commission's report but had decided on a merger of UCD with Trinity College into a single Dublin university. This created much uncertainty in Dublin, but also for Maynooth. Would the college have the option of becoming a subsidiary of the new university? Would Maynooth be part of whatever arrangements UCC and UCG might make under the new order? Or would Maynooth face the daunting challenge of becoming a fully independent institution?

That was the background against which, seven months later, Msgr Mitchell was predicting the early demise of the NUI degree at Maynooth. He expatiated in a low key: 'But there will still be university degrees conferred in Maynooth. There is, I believe, general agreement that within the new university framework there will be a place for Maynooth and that it will continue to retain its university status.' This conveys a tone of 'demob' relief on the part of someone who, as

Detail from the ceiling of the Lady Chapel, College Chapel

president, had dealt with emerging challenges for a period of eight years. The burden of converting vaguely positive 'general agreement' about the future status of Maynooth into some concrete reality would now fall on his successors as president, initially Patrick J. Corish (from November 1967 to May 1968) and then Jeremiah Newman (from 1968 to 1974).

The turmoil created by the 'merger' policy was exacerbated in March 1968 when Donogh O'Malley died suddenly. His deservedly heroic status as the initiator of free education at second level meant that for several years following his death all his projects were beyond public criticism, even in a rapidly changing third-level environment in which the rationale for the Dublin amalgamation soon lost much of its force. The 'merger' was finally abandoned only in the mid-1970s. In the event new legislation for the universities would not be enacted until 1997.

The Universities Act of that year transformed the former constituent colleges of the NUI into constituent universities and gave the same status to the NUI sector of Maynooth, thereby creating a new institution – NUI Maynooth – which chose for overwhelming practical reasons to locate itself alongside St Patrick's College on the historic campus. Long before 1997 the sometimes painful transition from an entirely clerical institution with an annual first-year intake of about a hundred to a university college participating fully in the national expansion of third-level provision for all was achieved at Maynooth, and it was done within the pre-existing legislative and institutional framework, and with the indispensable support of the Higher Education Authority. The creation of NUI Maynooth in 1997 was not an act of legislative benevolence, but the overdue recognition of three decades of achievement. To think of 1997 as a beginning (other than in a technical sense) is to risk discarding the contribution of generations of scholars and teachers going back to 1795 and, more importantly, to risk undervaluing the confidence reposed in the NUI sector of St Patrick's College Maynooth by thousands of students and their families in the thirty years preceding 1997. Their wagers are the foundation stones of NUI Maynooth.

The 1967 prediction of the imminent disappearance of NUI degrees from Maynooth was wide of the mark, and by much more than thirty years. While the 1997 act empowers all four constituent NUI universities to award degrees, it also specifies that all awards of any of the four are also awards of the NUI and are to be so described. This provision still holds and is the basis on which graduates of the four constituent universities qualify for inclusion on the Seanad Éireann electoral list.

REMEMBERING
AN BRÁTHAIR Ó SÚILLEABHÁIN

Mary O'Rourke[1]

An Br Séamus
Ó Súilleabháin

He died many years ago, but I have never forgotten him and, on the occasion of the 225th anniversary of St Patrick's College, I have the opportunity once again to express my gratitude to him for being my mentor at an important time in my life. The man of whom I speak is an Bráthair Séamus Ó Súilleabháin.

I often meet young people in the course of my day and, indeed, I have grandchildren, and I'm always reminded how essential guidance is to them; they are at a time of great change in their lives and often a helpful word or piece of advice can mean so much. Perhaps they might be a bit lost or wondering where to go next in life, and having someone older and more experienced, who has 'seen it all', can set them on the right road. He was that person for me.

Let me go back to one spring morning in 1966. I was a young mother at home with my elder son, Feargal, who was two at the time, when there was a knock at the door. I opened it to find my father standing there, a copy of the *Irish Times* under his elbow. He often stopped by when he was in town and I was delighted to see him.

He was in a state of great excitement and he exclaimed, 'Have you read the paper yet?'

1   This is a slightly adapted version of a piece originally published in Mary O'Rourke, *Letters of My Life* (Dublin: Gill, 2016). With kind permission.

'No,' I replied, 'I was going to push Feargal up in his buggy to the shops to get it later.'

'Well,' he said, opening the paper and pointing to a big ad, 'Look at this.'

The ad was on the front page of the newspaper, and it announced that from now on, Maynooth College, as it was known then, was no longer to be exclusively for the education of seminarians, but was to open up to lay students also. One of the first qualifications they were offering was the HDipEd for current or mature students.

I couldn't think what the ad had to do with me, but my father said, 'You should consider doing that.'

I was a bit taken aback. I had finished my BA degree in 1957 and had worked at the hotel before I got married, as well as doing the books for my brother Paddy's haulage business, but teaching had never been on my 'to-do list'. When I had finished my degree, I had flirted with the idea of doing law, which you could do at that time with a one-year LLB course added on to your primary degree. I suppose I was influenced here by my brother Brian, who had so successfully studied law, but in my heart of hearts, I had a yearning to do journalism. I had always loved the news and news stories, but in Ireland in 1957, there was no history at all of any college offering courses in journalism. More to the point, there were no female journalists that I knew of; journalism at the time was very much a man's world, and whilst I've never let that stop me, I couldn't see how I could go about learning to do that job. So, I tucked that desire to the back of my mind. Of course, life was to come full circle and I would return to journalism many years later, but that's another story.

So, my father was standing there, in the living room, newspaper in hand. 'You should consider going,' he insisted. 'Look, it says it's on Monday, Tuesday, Wednesday and Thursday for two hours a night.'

'But how on earth would I go?' I protested. 'Who would mind my lovely Feargal?'

'I have it all worked out,' he insisted. 'I'll pay for a woman to come in and mind Feargal while you go to college, and I'll put petrol in that old black jalopy you have,' he said, referring to the Wolesley car that Enda and I owned at the time. 'I think you should give it serious consideration.'

Now, times were very different then, and I dare say that my father was offering me this opportunity because he felt a bit guilty. When I had come home to Athlone with my newly minted BA ten years earlier, my father had asked me if I would stay to help out at the hotel for a while; my sister Anne had moved to Galway, Brian was in Dublin and Paddy was in England, so there was only me, and, ever the dutiful daughter, I agreed. In fact, I was only too delighted, because I'd lit my eye at this stage on one Enda O'Rourke, whom I'd met the year before playing tennis at the Hodson Bay. We'd hit it off, and I was already madly in love with him. Why would I be haring off to Dublin, I reasoned? So, I stayed at home, working in the hotel and doing the books for Paddy. They both paid me and I was set fair in work and in love. I worked during the day and off I flew every night with Enda in his little black Ford Prefect. Halcyon days.

The point of my story is that I needed my father's encouragement to start out on this new road. This might seem very old-fashioned to modern women, but in my day, your parents made a lot of decisions for you, and you did what you were told. I was fortunate in that my father was very forward-thinking. I think he knew that I would need to have my mind enlarged and this was his way of doing it. I think he sensed that I was not going to be happy sitting at home with baby number one, and possibly, baby number two – the dutiful wife and dutiful mother living in suburban Athlone – but I needed his help to see it. I also needed Enda's support, which he gave willingly: when I discussed the idea with him, he was very enthusiastic about it and fully behind me.

This is where an Bráthair Ó Súilleabháin came in. I enrolled on the HDip course in Maynooth, which at the time was quite a distance away – this was long before the lovely motorway – and I put an ad in the local paper for others to share the car journey with me there and back. Before too long, there were four of us: Sister Christopher, a young nun in La Sainte Union in Our Lady's Bower convent; a man called Louis Walsh (not the boy band manager!); Beda Heavey, who wanted to add the HDip to her BComm, and yours truly. It was agreed that we'd each take turns to do the journey. It was just fifty-five miles, but on a narrow road through towns and villages that would become so familiar to us over the year: Moate, Horseleap, Kilbeggan, with the whiskey distillery, the lovely plantation town of Tyrellspass, then on to Rochfortbridge, Milltownpass, Kinnegad, Enfield and on to Maynooth.

Every single weeknight, except Fridays, off we'd go. I can still remember Feargal swinging on the gate in front of the house, back and forth, proclaiming, 'My mammy's goin' a gool'. He was very happy with Mary Flood, a lovely young woman who'd come to mind him while I went off on my great adventure. Because he was happy, I was happy too. This is one of the big lessons that I've learned from being a working mother, and one I hope will be useful to others: whatever you decide is best for yourself will be best for your child. Of course, we all struggle with feelings of guilt, asking ourselves if we are spreading ourselves too thinly, if we can really 'have it all', as they say nowadays. We can't, of course, but we can make our accommodations with whatever it is we've chosen.

So, on that first night, as sixty-seven of us gathered in Maynooth, I felt such a sense of history and learning in this lovely old building, and in the mature grounds. I could imagine all the hundreds – thousands – who had gone before me, who had spent many years studying theology in this wonderful place. I felt such an affinity for Maynooth; much more than for my alma mater, UCD. In fact, many years later, I was delighted to receive an award from the university at a dinner called 'Maynooth Made Me', along with a number of others who had benefited from an education there. Of course, Maynooth did make me, and in so many ways.

Anyway, there he was, an Bráthair Ó Súilleabháin, on our very first night, a big, dark-haired, swarthy Kerryman, full of energy and vigour, ready to instil learning in a rum lot. And instil he did. He taught everything on the HDip course. If our lecture was psychology, or comparative education, or methodology, there he'd be at the top of the class, giving us the benefit of his learning. As Plutarch said, 'Education is the kindling of a flame, not the filling of a vessel', and he was very progressive in this way, encouraging and supporting our learning, inspiring confidence in us that we could do it – we could teach and teach well. I can still remember his maxim:

> Never fear to overstretch a student's mind. They can take it. They are forever reaching for more information, and if it is above their reach at that time, it will always come back into their minds, so always remember that you can never overcrowd your students' minds.

What he meant by this, I think, was that we should always assume that our students were capable of more, and that lesson has stayed with me always.

When it came time to practise everything we'd learned in the classroom, he also supervised every single student's teaching practice. I can still remember him coming down to Athlone to watch me teach a class of lively teenagers in St Peter's School. He stayed overnight in the Prince of Wales Hotel and off he went with Enda to the Green Olive, the local pub, for a few pints! I was scared, of course, because I wanted to impart knowledge, but also to keep control of the class, which contained a few livewires. I'd told them that he was coming in, and most of them behaved. Somehow I managed to teach them Latin for the allotted class, trying to remember everything he'd taught me, and, at the end, I learned that I'd passed. I'm not sure if this was down to my teaching skills or abilities or the fact that I'd persevered and had come the long distance every night. I can still remember that every time he'd see the four of us – Louis, Sister Christopher, Beda and myself – he would joke, 'I'll have to pass the four of you for sheer effort.'

I can honestly say that an Bráthair Ó Súilleabháin changed my life. Suddenly, I was in love with teaching. Not fearful of it, not wary of it, but delighting in it. During the five years that I would spend in the classroom, I found that I had an affinity with it, with the pupils and with the subjects of English, history and Latin. I loved my students, I loved the fact that they were growing in body and mind before my very eyes. I have always thought that that is wonderful – the transformation in the young person – and because I was still quite young myself, only thirty at this stage, I was still young enough to enjoy their company, to understand what they were reaching for and to be a part of it all. All of this I owe to him. I feel strongly that if he had not happened to be the person in charge of the HDip at Maynooth, I would not have taken so readily to teaching.

Thanks to him, I was able to use my skills as a teacher in my later career as a politician. If you have ever stood in a classroom of young girls and boys and talked with them, brought them with you on the road of learning, enjoyed their company and sometimes faced them down, you can deal with anything. Because of teaching, I was never afraid of speaking up. I had learned how to express myself clearly and strongly and this was all thanks to him. Being a teacher opened up my life and taught me such valuable lessons and gave me the skills to do my best in what would become my favourite job, that of minister for education. If I could leave readers with one message, it would be always to be willing to take the next step, and not to be content to rest on your laurels.

Writing this piece has brought me back to that day in 1966 and to the memory of my father, his face alight, newspaper under his arm. He always spoke quickly and forcefully in his Clare accent and he was full of excitement about the new opportunity he had presented to me. He was giving me the chance to continue my education, but also alerting me to what life could still have to offer me, in the academic sense, and, later on, in a political sense. In this great new adventure of mine, my father was my first mentor and an Bráthair Ó Súilleabháin was my second. I hope that readers of this tribute will admire him as much as I did, but will also know that, with a little bit of encouragement, they, too, can achieve anything.

ENTERING FIRST SCIENCE, 1968

Mary (Burke) McQuinn

he 1960s saw many changes in the world, in the Roman Catholic Church and in Ireland. In that decade St Patrick's College Maynooth admitted lay students to study for the HDipEd. During the year 1967–68 my father, Lieutenant Colonel Denis Burke OC Artillery Barracks, Kildare, wrote to College President Msgr Jeremiah Newman, enquiring if it intended admitting girls to study for degrees. A correspondence ensued, in which Newman finally wrote that the bishops had decided to admit girls as undergraduates.

September 1968 was the month in which eleven girls, some boys, religious sisters and brothers commenced study in St Patrick's College Maynooth. Margaret Horan, Emer McDermott, Liz Higgins, Rose Hyland, Patsy Lynch, Frances Doyle, Betty Gorey, Anne Whelan, Margaret Walsh and Margaret Sheridan enrolled in First Arts and I, Mary Burke, enrolled in First Science. My class had twenty students, among whom was Sister Dolores (Frances) Crowe, with whom I have had a lifelong friendship. Three of us, Margaret, Emer and I, had studied together in the Presentation College of Our Lady of Victories, Mountmellick – a school renowned for its teaching. Several other girls had also been taught by Presentation Sisters in various schools.

Those of us in science very quickly realised what a full timetable we had, with lectures early in the day and laboratory practicals in the evening. Our subjects in first science were chemistry with Rev. Professor Michael T. Casey OP, physics with Rev. Professor Gerry McGreevy, mathematics with Rev. Professor J. J. McMahon, and biology with Eamon Duke, Declan Murray and Brother McCullough. Our science professors always addressed me as Miss Burke, never as Mary! Our practical notebooks, where we recorded our experiments, were meticulously kept, and were marked by the professors as part of our examinations. Laboratory protocol was taught – and adhered to. Safety procedures, as laid down, were followed.

Our Chemistry Professor, Rev. Michael T. Casey OP, had worked as the state analyst in Dublin. As a practical analytical chemist, he often interspersed the laboratory practical classes with anecdotes from his professional experience. His method of teaching was to use an antique lantern with which he projected

First Science Class 1968–9
Back row (L–R): Br John Mullan, Br Gerry Gordon, Dermot Bennett, Aidan T. Mullan, Noel Keating, Nicholas A. P. Slavin, Br Abraham Huggard, Michael McGrath, Jimmy Duffy.
Front row (L–R): Joe Devine, Sr Joseph, Sr Catherine, Mary Burke, Br Ignatius, Br Frank Lynch, Sr Benedicta, John Lawless, Kevin O'Brien, Sr Paul, Sr Dolores

handwritten notes and chemical formulae and equations on a screen – advanced high-tech visual aids! As a Dominican priest, he always wore the cream-coloured habit of the order. He proudly identified the various small stains on the habit by their chemical names and formulae!

Rev. Professor Gerry McGreevy held lectures in the Physics Hall, using 'talk and chalk' on the long blackboard. The experimental classes took place in the physics laboratory. Before class he always said a prayer to the Holy Spirit in Latin. Several experiments were carried out in small laboratories downstairs in Stoyte House. I remember the absolute darkness in the black room for the light experiments – Newton's rings in particular.

Rev. Professor J. J. McMahon held his mathematics classes in the Physics Hall. He often came round to us to explain the topic, and to make sure we understood. Rev. Professor Joe Spellman lectured in mathematical physics; about five students took this subject. Biology lectures, with Eamon Duke, Declan Murray and Brother McCullough, were held in a lecture hall beside the chemistry laboratory in Logic House. Practicals were held there too, as the benches were flat and facilitated microscope work and dissections. These experiments instilled very careful laboratory skills, which I have kept for life. At that time in St Patrick's College, biology was taught in first year only.

First-year science class was held on its own, while second- and third-year classes were taught together, with a rotating curriculum. Between lectures we studied in the Junior Library, now the Geography Department in Rhetoric House. This was ideal due to its proximity to Logic House and to the Junior Garden. The Junior Garden provided a welcome respite from a very busy schedule. Students often made speeches to their colleagues from the circular seat around the central tree! The swimming pool, known as 'The Plunge', had a designated time in the evenings for the female students.

Walks 'Up Graf' in springtime were delightful, when the fresh foliage burst forth on the beech trees. We sometimes studied in the college library, now the Russell Library. I loved the ambience of the library and the sense of history there. This was a time of transition in the church after the Second Vatican Council. We often attended Mass in St Mary's. The altar had been changed from under the beautiful stained-glass windows (where it is now) to the right-hand side to facilitate the new form of liturgy which was now said in English, with participation in the readings by members of the congregation. I can recall that the first time I read at Mass was in St Joseph's Chapel.

As well as formal classes and laboratory workshops, we had activities outside the lecture halls. Debates in English and Irish were contested. Drama productions were staged in the Aula Maxima. I recall a staging of John B. Keane's play, *The Field*, by the students. The RTÉ Symphony Orchestra performed Beethoven's Fifth Symphony. In preparation for this performance some of the music students gave a class in the appreciation of this classic piece in the music hall. Seating in the Aula Maxima was as follows: clerical students downstairs, staff and lay students on the balcony.

Christmas 1969 saw the performance of the first carol service in the College Chapel, sung by a mixed choir under the direction of Rev. Noel Watson, Music Professor, with Fergus Clarke on organ. The organ console was under the gallery then. The carol service was recorded and broadcast by RTÉ television. The choral group travelled to the hospice at Harold's Cross, Dublin, to sing Christmas carols for the patients. I met an old lady there who told me that her grandfather had worked on the carving of the stalls in the College Chapel in Maynooth.

During the month of May, evening devotions were held in the College Chapel. The great doors were opened, and the sun streamed into this beautiful chapel. The clerics, in their soutanes, surplices and birettas, filled the stalls, while the priests of the college celebrated benediction. I can still see and smell the incense in the evening sunlight.

The clerical students always wore their soutanes to class. Black suits were worn by the students if they were going out to the town or to Dublin. (The number 66 bus took us to the capital). Students wore a black stock over collarless shirts. A fellow science student had a beautifully crocheted stock, handmade for him by an aunt in the convent. Many students had relations in the priesthood or religious life.

FORM B

Dear *Colonel Burke,*

I have much pleasure in according provisional acceptance to your application on behalf of *Mary T. Burke* as a student in the Faculty of ~~Arts or~~ Science at Maynooth during the coming year.

Please send on to me the necessary Matriculation Certificate as soon as possible. A testimonial of good character and two recent photographs (passport size) will also be required.

All applicants will be expected to present themselves at the Matriculation and Selection Board (meeting in the Callan Hall, Maynooth, at 11 am. on Wednesday, 25th September next).

Classes will begin on Thursday 26th September.

Yours sincerely,

Jeremiah Newman

(Rev.Jeremiah Newman)
Registrar for Extern Students

P.S. I understand that the Presentation Sisters' Class can secure suitable accommodation & transport for your daughter. Hope to hear from you soon.

A letter from College President, Rev. Prof. Jeremiah Newman to Mary Burke's father in 1968

Professors often walked four abreast from their dining room, through St Joseph's Square, out the front gate, down the town, and back again after their lunch. They wore soutanes, with long black velvet-trimmed clerical togas – quite an impressive sight!

I subsequently studied for the HDipEd, M.Ed, and Diploma in Arts (Church Music) in Maynooth. I have attended lectures, events and music recitals in the college, and have always received warm hospitality.

I have given my college notes, which were written in hardback foolscap notebooks, to the archives in the college library. I also donated my student card and my scarf. The college scarf, woven in wool, has black, green and white stripes on one side for the lay students, with black and white stripes on the reverse for the clerics.

I appreciate and am grateful to St Patrick's College Maynooth for my education and for the very fulfilling career I have had in science teaching.

THE 1960s SEE THE FIRST
FEMALE LECTURERS

Mary Cullen talks to Vincent Comerford

hen you and your family came to live on the Main Street in Maynooth in *1964, what impressions did you get of the college?*

St Patrick's College loomed large in the consciousness of the town, but direct contact was very limited. Like any Big House the college was surrounded by high walls with a front gate entrance that at night was locked and controlled by a watchman. I don't remember seeing the students at all. We understood they were forbidden to come into the town. I learned later that the college statutes prohibited them from entering any house in the town, and that included shops, pubs and restaurants.

How visible were the professors?

That was another story. There were about thirty professors and deans. We regularly saw groups of about four to seven walking up the Main Street. They walked shoulder-to-shoulder on the broad pavement on the north side of the street, passing the house where I lived. They were dressed in black, with the Roman collar and wearing academic gowns, which I later learned to be distinctive Maynooth clerical togas. They were an impressive sight.

How did your connection with the college begin?

My late husband, John, knew Dr Donal Flanagan, who was one of the Professors of Dogmatic Theology. It was the era of the new theology and the papal encyclical *Humanae Vitae*, and there was quite an amount of discussion between theologians and lay people about moral issues. Donal visited us from time to time, and we had many lively discussions. He introduced us to Dr Kevin McNamara, Professor of Moral Theology, who also visited us every so often. From 1966 there was much talk of the expected admission of lay students to St Patrick's College with a consequent expansion of staff. I had an MA in history from UCD and saw an opportunity. One evening, as Kevin was leaving the house, I plucked up my courage and said I supposed I would soon be coming

Footbridge to the North Campus (1976)

in to teach in the college. Kevin at once turned back and asked if I would be interested and said he knew that the Professor of Modern History, Fr Tom Fee (Tomás Ó Fiaich) was looking for someone. At that time Tomás, distinguished Irish scholar that he was, had not yet changed to the Irish form of his name. A few days later Kevin brought Tomás up to our house, and he immediately began discussing how he and I might divide the courses. I remember he asked me if I would prefer to take the Renaissance or the Reformation and I said the Renaissance. He later told me that afterwards he regretted giving me the choice, but he gallantly stood by the division.

Was there a general sense of the great significance of the changes under way when you were appointed in 1968?
Yes, and I gathered that Cardinal Conway took a personal interest in the new appointments. Tomás told me that he told the cardinal about me and I suspected that he would have been reassured by the knowledge that the woman proposed for modern history was married with a family.

What were your first impressions of the college when you started?
I did not know what to expect when I ventured into the college and was very

J.G. McGarry, Éamon de Valera and Tomás Ó Fiaich

pleasantly surprised at how friendly people were. Of course the 1960s saw the Second Vatican Council, liberation theology, student movements, second-wave feminism and civil rights organisations, and I should not have been surprised that all these had reached St Patrick's College, especially as I already knew Donal Flanagan and Kevin McNamara, and had had many lively discussions with both. I used to have coffee with the resident staff. The atmosphere was always lively, open to all sorts of ideas, full of banter and laughter, and I got to know many of the professors.

I was known to be a feminist and Gerry McGarry, Professor of Pastoral Theology, who had founded the journal *The Furrow* in 1950, aiming at an 'exchange of views on new pastoral methods', invited me to write an article on women and the Church, which he published in *The Furrow* in 1971.

How did you find working in the Department of Modern History?
It was a very positive experience. Of course I was fortunate in the professor I worked with. Tomás was a great character. He was warm and friendly and very

popular with his students, all of whom he seemed to know by name. He was very easy and supportive to work with. We introduced tutorials on the model I was used to in UCD. History students did a research project as part of their BA. Tomás told me that he had introduced this when all the students were seminarians and his aim was that later as parish priests they would conduct local history research. I remember bringing groups of students to Dublin on visits to the Public Records Office at the Four Courts and the State Paper Office in Dublin Castle. This was in the days before the opening of the National Archives on Bishop Street. Tomás used to visit our house, and John and I particularly looked forward to his visits in the summer after he had been on his annual trip to France. We would get out the atlas and follow his train journeys, which always ended in some destination that had a connection to an Irish saint or pilgrim. He also came with us to one of the 'medieval banquets' in Maynooth Castle organised by the Maynooth Development Association and enjoyed it immensely.

The students were very friendly too. At first the majority were seminarians and I remember some of them telling me that in the days before they were allowed to go into houses, shops, pubs and restaurants in the town they felt that Maynooth was an unfriendly place and how pleasantly surprised they were to find that this was far from the case. They also taught me a very useful lesson on the occasion of my first lecture. I don't remember what the subject was, but I do remember my preparation. I was very nervous and sure that the students would know at least as much as I did, if not more. So I concentrated on gathering as many different interpretations as I could find without including any initial summary of the actual sequence of events. I gave the lecture and they listened in silence. I felt that all had gone well until Tomás came to me the following day to report: they had said they did not understand a word of what I had said. As I waited for the axe to fall on a brief career, Tomás began to laugh and discuss the following week's programme. So I survived and learned a valuable lesson, that for fruitful interaction between speaker and listener, analysis and interpretation of events in history needed to be based on some shared information on the events to be analysed and interpreted.

Were there further changes afoot regarding external staff?
Yes, for one thing, I did not remain the only woman on the teaching staff for long. In 1969, the year after my appointment, Angela Lucas joined the English Department, and when full-time permanent positions were established more women began to arrive. The first appointments of external staff were part-time and temporary and in 1971 these were replaced by full-time permanent

appointments via the Higher Education Authority. The positions were advertised for public competition and part-timers had to apply like everyone else. Both Angela and I were fortunate enough to come through and continue in our posts. In all there were twelve new permanent appointments, mostly of lay people. These included Paddy Duffy as lecturer in geography, charged with establishing this as a new subject in Maynooth. We were allocated a room where we could meet for coffee. This was very interesting and enjoyable, and we all got to know what was going on in other departments.

What recollections do you have of Msgr Jeremiah Newman as College President?
Mgr Newman had many important developments to make decisions about and to supervise, among them the acquisition of the Lanigan O'Keefe property on the north side of the Galway Road to allow for the expansion of the college. This involved the construction of a footbridge across the road and I remember some people referred to it as Newman's Folly. As a junior member of staff, I had little contact with the president's decision-making. However, I always enjoy remembering one decision which I did observe him make. It was on the occasion of the first graduation ball organised by the college. It was held in a hotel in Dublin. Tomás and I were there and sat at the president's table. A deputation arrived from some of the other tables to ask a very important question. Could the clerical professors dance with the female students? Jeremiah considered this for a moment and then came up with his answer; Irish dances would be acceptable. Not surprisingly, we had lots of Irish dances for the rest of the night and a good time was had by all.

'MAYNOOTH IS ITS STUDENTS'

Tadhg Ó Dúshláine

ince the foundation of the Royal Catholic College at Maynooth in 1795, the British government's policy of keeping Irish clerics free from revolutionary ideas, by having them trained at home in a college under their own jurisdiction, was only partly successful. Nor did the establishment of Maynooth, 'for the education of those of the Popish persuasion', put an end entirely to the Irish continental movement, with Irish clerical students studying at Salamanca until 1954 and those at Maynooth and Clonliffe availing of bursaries, until the 1980s, to broaden their cultural and theological horizons by following summer courses at the Institut Catholique in Paris, while residing at the Irish College on rue des Irlandais.

The summer of 1968 proved a hot one in Paris, with Daniel Cohn Bendt, Danny the Red, replacing Che Guevara as student idol, and the six Maynooth clerics who studied that summer at the Institut Catholique passed by the Sorbonne, the epicentre of the troubles, daily. Two of these students, both from dioceses in the North of Ireland, exchanged their beginners' French for an apprenticeship of protest in tearing up cobblestones and manning barricades. On their return to Maynooth that September they were to lead the challenge to the vow of blind obedience by establishing the Student Representative Council (SRC), and the results of the honours BA autumn examinations became their Burntollet. One of the 'heavier guns', a student of English and history, received the expected first-class honours in history, but the Professor of English would agree to the award of third-class honours only. The SRC convened an emergency meeting and declared that a gross injustice had been perpetrated. The Professor of English claimed that he had been libelled and threatened, in the words of the Professor of History, 'to take his case to the highest court in the land'. The students lobbied the academic staff for support, but when one of the more understanding professors remarked that he thought the students had a reasonable case, the Professor of English countered, 'That's nonsense and coming from a professor it's dangerous nonsense', and was supported by a colleague who claimed that he 'had been physically assaulted before Mass in the sacristy that morning and that this rebellion had to be nipped in the bud'. The instigators were 'catted', and the two leaders were withdrawn from Maynooth and sent to Rome to read theology.

But student unrest continued to rumble and by the summer of 1969 the authorities sought to appease matters by agreeing to participate in a Theology Think-In, organised by the SRC, on the question: 'What does it mean to be a Christian in Ireland today?' The address by the Bishop of Ossory, Dr Peter Birch, entitled 'Religion in the New Ireland', proved as much an incitement to student protest as did that of Pádraig Pearse at the grave of O'Donovan Rossa:

> The nearest thing we have to the pilgrimage today is the protest march, organised to contest indifference, privilege, injustice. The young who take part in such marches may be doing great good most of the time … Perhaps this may look a bit lawless, too uncontrolled at times – but then there was not too much control apparent in the Sermon on the Mount.

President Jeremiah Newman's opening address was buoyant with hippie enthusiasm and naivety:

> This is a time of 'Train-Ins', and 'Sit-Ins', and 'Teach-Ins', 'Live-Ins' … I may be wrong in this, but I believe that the Maynooth students have come up with this one first of all, namely, the THINK-IN, and it is not insignificant that it has that admirable quality about it of abstaining from teaching others. So many of the other 'Teach-Ins' are for the purpose of teaching the teachers, that it is indeed healthy to find students thinking … Maynooth is many things. Maynooth is magnificent buildings, some of the finest in the world. Maynooth is its professorial staff of which we have just reason to be proud, but I firmly believe that Maynooth is nothing if it is not its students and it is for this reason that I regard any development among the student body as a sign of encouragement, as something which should definitely be underlined.

When the final panel discussion threatened to get out of hand, the newly appointed Professor of Sociology, Fr Liam Ryan, brought proceedings to a close on a cautionary note, remarking that in the light of twenty years of pastoral work, part of the real challenge of a priest's life – as of everybody's – was to learn to cope with frustration when the world showed itself indifferent to youthful idealism and to come to terms with the limitations of one's own talent, personality and charism. This could mean allowing God to make a different kind of saint of you from the one you had planned.

Unfortunately, like Eoin MacNeill's plea on the night before the Easter Rising in 1916, Fr Ryan's call for moderation came too late for the second divinity class. They had begun to read moral theology and canon Law, expecting to treat such lofty questions as the idea of freedom, justice, and equality, and were treated to frustrating legal cavilling by a professor who presented them with nothing but legal teasers, such as that of the rabbit caught in the snare. Who owns the rabbit? The catcher, the owner of the snare, or the landowner? The Professor of History professed a certain sympathy for the students who, instead of exploring the profundities of morality, found themselves 'confronted by a fecking rabbit catcher'. Said professor called for an enquiry and encouraged all to speak their minds openly. The students agreed. The theology staff did not. The students countered by staying away from class en bloc, calling a general meeting in Callan Hall and issuing the following statement:

> This document embodies the main reasons for the action taken by Second Divinity Class on Monday, 15 February. Although it is by no means a blue-print, it does provide information on how we envisage a revised theology program in the light of the Second Vatican Council.
>
> The Christian adequately trained in theology believes and lives the word of God and is able to communicate this word to all men. In order to become a mature person capable of communicating the Christian Message to the Modern World, one must have an adequate personal formation. This formation depends on two central factors. Firstly, that all theological studies are related directly to living, and to one's future pastoral ministry. Secondly, that one be constantly in intimate contact with one's director. In this way it will be ensured that 'information' will be seen in its proper context, this is, in the context of formation.
>
> We would also envisage a radical overhauling of the present curriculum both in content and methodology. In fact we believe that there should be a shift in emphasis from the lecture to the working-group. The number of lectures should be reduced to one concentrated lecture per subject per week. These lectures should be seen as the spring-board and stimulus for discussion, and should be complemented by group study and by typed notes.
>
> Finally, we feel that students should have some consultative right in determining courses and in the communication of these courses. This is recognised in all truly responsible Universities and seminaries today.
>
> To sum up, then, we feel that there must be an immediate and radical change in the system of lecturing in Maynooth.

This was a bold attempt by the students, with a little help from their academic friends, to have the *Decree on Priestly Formation* of the Second Vatican Council implemented. The hierarchy, however, were not impressed. 'This is mutiny,' declared Cardinal Conway, who, in no uncertain terms, advised the president to get his act together or else …

And so, by a combination of threats of caveats and promises of expansion in the Theology Faculty, President Jeremiah Newman just about saved his dream of one Catholic university, clerical and lay, at Maynooth, just as it was about to get off the ground. For us 'chubs' it was a baptism of fire and a lesson in the triumph of failure, and those footfalls of protest that echo in the memory are only slightly tinged with regret, and we still retain those ideals of social justice that continue to energise and cocoon us against the vacuous spin of PR that now infects our third-level institutions. On a secular campus festooned with clapboards of high achievers proclaiming 'I am Maynooth', the underlying heroic subtext of 'I am Spartacus' has been ousted from the student curriculum by 'I am Billy Murphy'. The proclamations of our generation were more inclusive and a little less ostentatious: 'Maynooth is its students'; even rebellious: 'Educated [comma] not in Maynooth [comma] but in spite of it'. The attraction, the call, the vocation of Maynooth, was originally to serve the One who declares 'I Am Who Am'. Over the fifty years of my engagement with the institution, interpretations of the Maynooth call have changed, the concept of 'vocation' been replaced by the commercial term 'brand', but, through it all, the timeless, authentic Maynooth stamp of dedication to the notion of the common good has prevailed, fuelled by the prerogative of youth, namely, a healthy disrespect for authority and a courage to react against the despotism of fact. In his futuristic novel *A.D. 2016*, written in 1988, an tAthair Pádraig Standún portrays two old Maynooth priests, of that ordination class of 1971, reflecting on their academic formation and their lives since. For all their learning and experience there is a profound Maynooth simplicity in their conclusion:

> ' … *Céard faoi a bhfuil sé, dáiríre?*'
> '*Faoi ghrá Dé.*'
> '*Chomh simplí leis sin?*'
> '*Chomh simplí leis sin*'.

> ('…What's it all about, really?'
> 'It's about God's love.'
> 'As simple as that?'
> 'As simple as that.')

THINK-IN '69 MAYNOOTH

Bishop Peter Birch,
Ossory, who was invited
to deliver the keynote
address at Think-In '69

MAYNOOTH COLLEGE
IN THE LATE 1960s

D. V. Twomey

he anarchy and violence of Paris in May 1968 hit the headlines all over the world. I, and my fellow students in Maynooth, could not but admire the French students' passion for justice in a corrupt world marked by inequality, famine (widespread in Africa at the time) and modern weapons of mass destruction (the Vietnam War). We were all infected by the Zeitgeist.

That universal 'spirit of the times' became localised, indeed painfully palpable for us, thanks to our fellow-seminarians from the Northern dioceses. Many of their families were dramatically caught up in what was the beginning of the so-called Troubles – a civil war that itself was sparked off by the 1968 ecumenically minded student protests (Belfast and Derry mostly) for the rights of the Catholic minority.

But I had my own concerns: namely about the state of the Irish Church.

As a late vocation, I was acutely aware in the course of the six years I spent working and socialising in Cork city after the Leaving Cert (but not having the finances to go to university) that, to use the image of Matthew Arnold, the tide of faith was slowly but surely ebbing out. When we (some thirty-four novices, the biggest SVD – Divine Word Missionaries – intake ever in Ireland) entered the novitiate in Donamon in 1963, the Second Vatican Council was about to start its second session. It was an exciting time. Our theological and philosophical studies in Roscommon were stimulating. We were full of hope for the Church's future. I still remember the winter evening early in the year 1966 when Fr Paddy McHale, SVD, Prefect of Scholastics, called us together to hand out to each one of us Fr Austin P. Flannery OP's translation of the Documents of Vatican II. To us it was manna from heaven.

Then came our transfer to our SVD house in Dublin (first in Hume Street, Dublin, then in Booterstown and, finally, in an empty hotel in Bray!) to attend theology lectures at the National Seminary and Pontifical University of Maynooth. Our expectations were high – Maynooth, after all, had a solid reputation for scholarship.

Top Loftus class hall with Prof. Donal Flanagan

At the time, there were some 500 diocesan seminarians, who, like the professors and deans, were mostly of rural provenance. Thanks to the initiative of the provincial superior of the Divine Word Missionaries, Fr John Lynch SVD, we were the first non-diocesans to be admitted to the epicentre of Irish Catholicism on a full-time, non-residential basis.[1] The first Divine Word Missionary students entered in 1965; my class the following year. We were a shock to the system. But Maynooth was also a shock to us.

Gone was the excitement of the philosophy, theology, literature and anthropology we enjoyed in Donamon. Gone was the sense of excitement at the new opportunities for the Church opened up by the Second Vatican Council. However, for me, what was most perplexing was that even the best Maynooth theologians seemed to me (in hindsight, probably unfairly) to be out of touch at the time with what was actually happening in Irish society and its underlying cultural transformation. Irish urban society in the late 1950s/early 1960s was,

1   The Irish bishops had for some time previously, been toying with the idea of admitting non-diocesan, residential seminarians (see Patrick J. Corish, *Maynooth College, 1795–1995* (Dublin: Gill & Macmillan, 1995), p. 342.

generally speaking, Catholic only in external conformity.[2] The rest of the country would inevitably follow suit to a larger or lesser degree.

Something had to be done. One of my first attempts to open a window on to the outside world (and to what was in fact happening in Irish society) was to resuscitate the defunct Literary and Debating Society with the help of my classmate, Denis Bergin of Ossory. We brought in speakers from outside Maynooth. Maynooth seminarians engaged in intervarsity debating – right up to the Irish Times Debating Tournament.

In the autumn of 1968, I wrote an article for an in-house student magazine criticising the fact that, while earlier that year other universities were having their sit-ins to change the world, Maynooth was disgracefully inert. I suggested that we in Maynooth should make up for this inaction – and go one better – by holding a 'Teach-in'. At a subsequent meeting of the organisers [see below], it was decided to substitute 'Think-In' for 'Teach-in'. It was agreed that we should attempt to reflect collectively on the situation of the Church in Ireland as a kind of 'wake-up' call.

My proposal found an echo in the student population. A classmate, Jim Lynch of Meath, encouraged by two young postgraduate priests, Frs Walter Forde and Micheál Ledwith, both of Ferns, persuaded me to help organise what became Think-In '69. Despite strong opposition from Cardinal William Conway, Archbishop of Armagh at the time, and so chairman of the trustees, the President of Maynooth, Jeremiah Newman, could not but give permission, once he perceived the enthusiasm the idea had created among the seminarians. The cardinal agreed, but only on one condition: that we would invite a bishop to give the keynote address. We invited Bishop Peter Birch of Ossory, known for his 'forward thinking' at the time.[3]

The theme of Think-In '69 was 'Being a Christian In Ireland Today'. The organising committee was made up of Lynch, Forde, Ledwith and myself. I chaired the network of some forty committees needed to run the event, including an advisory policy commission, as it were, made up mostly of postgrads and sympathetic professors like Fr Peter Connolly and Fr Donal Flanagan. If anything went wrong, I could take the full brunt of the blame, protected as I was by living outside the college under the sympathetic attitude of my immediate SVD superiors.

Think-In '69 would bring to Maynooth student representatives from all the Irish universities and seminaries to listen to well-known speakers on public

2 See my analysis of the situation of the contemporary Church: *The End of Irish Catholicism?* (Dublin, 2007).
3 When, after joining the Maynooth staff in 1983, I met the former president, then the Bishop of Limerick, in the Professors' Dining Room, he roared at me with a mischievous twinkle in his eye: 'You almost had me fired!'

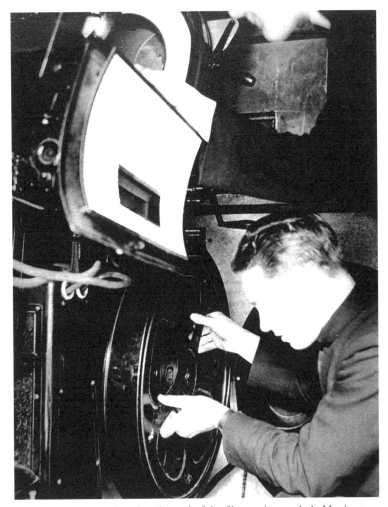

Tommy Maher changing the reel of the film projector, Aula Maxima

life from Ireland and Britain discussing the state of faith and politics. It was held during the first half of Holy Week 1969. The newly opened SVD House in Maynooth became the hub of the event.

Near Maynooth's Aula Maxima, Raidió Éireann set up an outside broadcasting unit to report on the event. Journalists from the national newspapers flocked to the press conferences. The event got front-page coverage each day as well as being covered as part of the national news on Raidio Éireann. Stimulating papers were read by a host of academics, journalists, politicians, historians and theologians. They produced lively discussions in highly organised seminars and workshops.[4]

4   Too highly organised for some participants, one of whom protested vociferously at one of the plenary sessions!

These in turn fed into plenary sessions held in a packed Aula Maxima.

Seminarians and professors, speakers, journalists, Irish university students and other participants mixed freely during the breaks and took part in the discussions. One Fourth Divine came up to me afterwards to thank me: in all his seven years in Maynooth, he confessed, he never thought he would see the day when a usually revered professor (most of whom behaved like distant deities) would pour a cup of tea for him in the students' refectory.

Humanitas and hope broke into our lives like a ray of sunshine on a rainy day. We experienced something of the revolutionary atmosphere of May '68, which echoed William Wordsworth's reaction to the French Revolution two centuries earlier:

> Oh! pleasant exercise of hope and joy! ...
> Bliss was it in that dawn to be alive,
> But to be young was very heaven! ('The Prelude')[5]

Sit-ins are now but a vague memory. In Ireland, the term 'think-in' entered everyday language; it is now [mis]used by political parties for their annual get-togethers to debate the affairs of state (i.e. their own political opportunities) – and so has been robbed of its original meaning.

The opening up of Maynooth, first to SVDs and then, in time, to other religious congregations and, finally, to the laity, would lead to a radical transformation of the nature of the Royal Catholic College of Maynooth, culminating in the separation of the University of Maynooth from the original Royal College of St Patrick. Think-in '69 was but a harbinger of what was to come. Some seasoned staff members never forgot – or forgave us SVDs, as I discovered to my cost, when I joined the staff in 1983 as a lecturer in moral theology. In retrospect, I now have a better understanding of their viewpoint, since in many ways, thanks to the historic decision by the trustees to admit SVD seminarians to study theology at Maynooth as non-resident students, all had changed, changed utterly.

---

5   He soon changed his tune when he went over to France and saw the terror it had unleashed. It took a bit longer for this writer to see the light. That occurred when I went to Germany for postgraduate studies and witnessed the effects on the German universities of the 1968 students' revolt (coupled with the anarchic 'spirit of Vatican II'), not least in the theology faculties. Two years after Think-In '69, Maynooth students went on strike for some five days. Though not the leader, John Feighery SVD was a spokesperson for it because, like this writer, he too had the advantage of being a non-resident student. The strike was entirely about the deplorable level of teaching.

1969: THE GENESIS OF
THE GERMAN DEPARTMENT

Pat Russell

When I google the German Department of Maynooth University with its highly accomplished staff and splendid array of courses, scholarships, foreign contacts etc., I have to marvel that the frail sapling that I planted in September 1969 has grown to be such a sturdy oak. Maynooth had become a constituent college of the National University only a few short years before.

I came to Maynooth with no teaching experience or qualifications and started with a First Arts class of four students – one seminarian and three lay people, two boys and two girls. We had a small stock of books sourced by the genial college librarian of that time, Fr John Corkery of the diocese of Ardagh.

I had ideas of teaching the great German classics, Goethe and Schiller and so on, but a visiting German student roundly scolded me for teaching such '*alte Museumstücke*', old museum pieces. It was no use arguing that Shakespeare could be regarded as a museum piece. Good old Günther – I hope you are alive and well and still laying down the law to your German parishioners!

Written work was conscientiously done but the conversation classes that I had set my heart on trickled into the sand. No Irish student was going to make a show of him- or herself by trying to speak German. It was a three-year course and Erasmus courses in a German-speaking country were far in the future.

I was also required to take an elementary German class for all comers and to do some work in German with the postgraduate students. One of these students, Vincent Twomey, went on to become a very distinguished theologian and later studied under Josef Ratzinger at the University of Regensburg. I have that much in common with the future pope.

Things improved a bit in the second year with the arrival of an energetic young lecturer, a modest intake of new students and the establishment of a new language laboratory. However, the best thing I ever did for German in Maynooth was to leave in 1972 to prepare the way for Ireland's entry into the European Economic Community, as it was still known at that time.

Statue of Johann Wolfgang von Goethe, Berlin Tiergarten Park

What I chiefly remember from that time was the great sense of adventure and excitement that prevailed across the entire campus. It was the voyage of the *Mayflower* all over again, launching into uncharted seas with a vaguely glimpsed distant destination. There was a very healthy mingling of seminarians and lay students in classroom and campus and on playing fields. Worthy divines must have been spinning in their graves in the college cemetery to see the appearance of young women on Maynooth's playing fields and on stage in the Aula Maxima. New clubs and societies appeared regularly. I became president of the chess club and played many memorable games during those years.

> Bliss it was in that dawn to be alive,
> But to be young was very heaven. (Wordsworth, 'The Prelude')

Of course it was a new beginning for the town of Maynooth too. The college gates, previously opened only on Ordination Sunday, were now thrown open to the public to the great benefit of both sides. It was a shot in the arm for shops, restaurants, pubs and many other businesses. Barton buses ferried students all over the country at weekends and to various sporting and cultural intervarsity events far and near. I was a bystander one summer Sunday when the Dublin-Galway road of the time was closed and a bridge thrown across it to link the northern and southern sides of the campus. The splendid new John Paul II Library near that bridge would not come for a further ten years.

As it enters on its second half-century, I wish the German Department of Maynooth University every success and blessing. *Ad multos annos!*

ON FIRST MOVING IN
TO MAYNOOTH, 1969

Peter McCawille, SMA

hen to the sessions of sweet silent thought I summon up remembrance of things past', several memorable snippets spring to mind from my days in Maynooth College (1969–76). Though I have since spent forty-three fairly feverish years sweating my life away under West Africa's boiling sun in Nigeria, many moments from those distant days in Maynooth still figure prominently as I take this leisurely stroll down the corridors of recollection. I had already spent two years as a SMA (Society of African Missions) seminarian when the SMA administration decided that from September 1969 we should dip our African missionary toes into Irish diocesan waters. When we heard the news, it was like being told we were moving from the Brandywell to the Bernabéu!

During our first few days I think our diocesan counterparts may have felt we had already spent some time 'out foreign' and were reluctant to risk contracting a tropical malady by getting too close to us. It was only when I assured a few of my new-found diocesan friends that I had never been to West Cork, never mind to West Africa, that they began to feel a bit more comfortable with us! If it happened today, we might well find ourselves in Direct Provision!

On that first evening we spent a few hours wandering around Joe's Square admiring the manicured lawns as the number of 'chubs' arriving began to swell. After supper on the second evening we were summoned to Callan Hall to be addressed by Fr Bill Cosgrave, the Junior Dean, who outlined for us in great detail the myriad rules and regulations contained within the statutes of Maynooth that suitably subservient students of St Patrick's College Maynooth were expected to acknowledge and obey. I think it was the only occasion in my seven years there that I was moved to ask a question, prompted by a growing sense of great unease at what I was hearing from the lips of Fr Cosgrave. I ventured to ask: 'Father, can you please tell us what part tradition had to play in the formulation of these rules to the exclusion of common sense?' Fifty years later I stand aghast at my then juvenile impudence.

In that same Callan Hall over the next seven years we chuckled heartily during debates at the razor-sharp wit of Pat Connaughton, whose incisive put-downs and timely ripostes often brought a shuddering halt to displays of high-flown rhetoric or high-falutin language. Nor can we ever forget the mammoth six-hour session that took place there on the Monday evening after the dreadful events of Bloody Sunday in Derry on 30 January 1972. Since the news broke late the previous evening, emotions had been running high throughout the day. It was standing room only as a huge crowd of staff and students converged on Callan Hall to discuss ways of registering our disgust at the barbaric behaviour of the British Parachute Regiment in murdering fourteen innocent civilians the previous day. I can still remember the calm and assured control with which the chairperson, Donal Moloney from Donegal, somehow managed to keep a tight rein on an increasingly seething audience. After many hours of heated exchanges, it was decided by staff and students to register our disgust by marching the thirty kilometres from Maynooth to the British Embassy in Dublin the following Wednesday. On reaching the embassy, we were somehow moved at the sight of the Union flag flying at half mast, thinking that maybe it signalled a more sympathetic change of heart on the part of the British authorities at what had happened. Our hopes were quickly shattered, however, when we were told that it was the death of the King of Nepal, not the murder of fourteen civilians on the streets of Derry, which caused the flag to be flown at half mast! Early the following Sunday morning, a busload of us headed for Newry to join in what turned out to be the last meeting of the Civil Rights Movement.

The year before we reached the college a gap of nearly 150 years had been bridged when lay students were re-admitted to Maynooth and within ten years outnumbered clerical students. What had been regarded by many as a bastion of male clerical exclusivity re-opened its doors to lay male and female students, thereby becoming one of only two institutions worldwide that housed both a seminary and a university on the same campus. I remember it as a warm and welcoming place where the atmosphere was free and easy without being easy and free.

It may seem hardly credible today but in those pre-*Prime Time* days an opportunity to visit Maynooth College was highly coveted by the great and the good of Irish society. It was while I was there that I saw Peter Sellers, who had recently taken up residence in nearby Carton House after divorcing Britt Ekland, being conducted around the college by a future Archbishop of Dublin, Kevin McNamara; that I engaged in an impromptu kick around on Highfield one Saturday afternoon with the already legendary Mick O'Connell, and later in the week thrilled to the sound of Andy Irvine, Christy Moore and Planxty as they topped the bill in the Aula Maxima.

What made our days in Maynooth College especially rewarding, however, were the enduring relationships we built up with the non-academic staff working within the college and with several influential personalities who lived outside its gates. Prominent among the non-academic staff was the evergreen head gardener, Bart Redmond, a native of Ballygarret, near Gorey, County Wexford, whose nimble green fingers cultivated such exquisite floral landscapes and encouraged us to admire and appreciate such beauty with fresh eyes; the unflappable Patsy Malone, who spent half a century keeping the home fires burning in the college furnace and once performed creditably in the heats of the annual Maynooth Song Contest, all the while doing a more than passable imitation of Gene Autry singing 'South of the Border;' the ex-soldier and now college janitor Mick Grant, with whom we struck up a profitable friendship, and who was regularly invited to join a group of us for elevenses during our BA days on Long Corridor. Being a Kildare native, Mick had an understandable devotion to the sport of kings and supplied us on occasions with a few hot tips, which yielded sufficient dividends to keep the larder well stocked with ample quantities of PG Tips and Jacob's Milk Chocolate Goldgrain.

It was the same Mick Grant who was once captured in an iconic photo that adorned the front page of the *Irish Press* during a bishops' meeting in March, 1972. Bucket and mop in hand, Mick was on his way to Senior House to resume his afternoon duties when he came face to face with Cardinal Bill Conway and Archbishop Dermot Ryan at the top of Joe's Square. They were heading for a casual stroll after lunch. Wily opportunist that he was, Mick seized the moment, switched the bucket and mop to his left hand and with his right reverentially doffed his hat in the direction of the two episcopal heavyweights. It is a picture that still speaks volumes today, and if we had been prescient enough at the time it might have even provided us with some helpful insights into the future direction of church-state relations in Ireland. As one of our revered professors at the time, Msgr Frankie Cremin, frequently commented, 'Wouldn't life be so much easier if we had afterthoughts beforehand!'

Throughout our time in Maynooth, soaring head and shoulders above the celebrated 'personalities' with whom we associated was Kevy Mac, a noble son of Leitrim, and his wife Peggy, who lived a mere stone's throw from the college. For years Kevy had his finger on the pulse and the pockets of both staff and students. Kevy Mac's shop was a social vortex that attracted a wide range of disparate customers who revelled in animated light banter with its garrulous and far from genteel proprietor. Any attempt at political correctness or solemnity got short shrift in Kevy Mac's company and loud laughter was the predominant sound when Kevy was in full flow. Media practitioners in today's image-fixated age would have struggled to take issue with Kevy's utter disregard for the kind of phoniness and shallowness that are such a drearily predictable feature of so much modern media coverage.

As I draw a reluctant veil over this most fertile and fruitful period of my life, I conclude my recollections in a tone of wistful reverie. On the college's 225th anniversary and forty-four years after I left, my thoughts are punctuated by poignant reminders of all those who have gone before us marked with the sign of faith, and I utter a silent prayer for them. I remember them all with deep gratitude as I invoke the comforting words of William Butler Yeats:

> Think where man's glory most begins and ends,
> And say my glory was I had such friends.
> ('The Municipal Gallery Revisited')

MEMORIES OF SOME
MAYNOOTH TEACHERS

Nollaig Ó Muraíle

It is a sobering thought that all but three or four of my teachers when I was an undergraduate in Maynooth from 1967 to 1970 are now dead. To spare the blushes of the survivors (almost all, as it happens, in Roinn na Gaeilge, and two of them contributors to this volume), I will omit them from the following brief reminiscences – except to say that I have particularly happy memories of the classes of Cathal Ó Háinle and Pádraig Ó Héalaí. Apart from being very nice men, very approachable and with a good sense of humour – and excellent teachers – it also helped that they were they were the members of staff who were closest in age to me and my classmates. (In later years, I was to have close contact, especially in academic matters, with both of them, as well as with Breandán Ó Doibhlin, while Pádraig and I ended up as colleagues for some years in NUI Galway.)

The member of staff with whom I became particularly friendly, and who was to greatly influence my career, was the man known to all in Maynooth as Tom Fee. However, having written in some detail on my memories of him in *Seanchas Ard Mhacha*, 2017,[1] I will omit that remarkable man from the following pages. Another of my Maynooth teachers to whom I am greatly indebted – although our relationship could at times be a little stormy – was the mercurial Pádraig Ó Fiannachta (or, as he was known to the students, Paddy Fenton). As an undergrad, I would have hesitated to use the anglicised form of his name when speaking to him, but I recall on one occasion telling him that I had heard the Limerick writer Críostóir Ó Floinn, during a radio talk on publications in Irish, refer to the magazine *An Sagart*, which Pádraig edited. Críostóir was most complimentary of the fact that Pádraig brought the little publication out without fail four times a year. Noting that the editor had often also to be the main contributor, he commented that *An Sagart* deserved to be known as 'Fenton's Quarterly'. Rather than being offended, Pádraig was absolutely delighted by this remark, and recalled it from time to time afterwards. As other contributors will

---

1 Nollaig Ó Muraíle, 'Tomás Ó Fiaich as Scholar, Teacher, Mentor and Friend', in *Seanchas Ard Mhacha* 26:2 (2017), pp. 1–36.

mention Pádraig in these pages, I will now pass on to a few memories of other members of staff in the late 1960s.

One man who did not teach me, but to whom I continue to be indebted, was the vice-president in my first year, 'Joey' Hamell. He was a kindly white-haired man whom we considered to be quite ancient – in fact, he was in his late fifties! My only dealings with him involved serving Mass for him on one occasion, after which he presented me with a Catholic Truth Society booklet he had written, *The Eastern Catholic Churches*. (I still have that eighteen-page work, in mint condition.) When I later mentioned in the Ref that I had served Mass for Joey, a cynical – more senior – fellow student asked if I had been given a copy of the 'magnum opus', and when I answered in the affirmative, he proceeded to tell all in earshot that Joey had a few thousand copies of the slim booklet in his room, because nobody had ever actually bought one! Ignoring that slander, which was not malicious – I never heard anyone say a bad word about Joey – I have frequently had cause to be grateful to the late Msgr Hamell for two substantial volumes, meticulous listings of students and ordinations, which he published in the early 1980s, *Maynooth Students and Ordinations, 1798–1895* and *1895–1984*, respectively. Scarcely a month goes by that I do not consult the latter volume, in particular, to check the year of ordination, the diocese or the class photograph of a Maynooth priest, particularly one who was a student in my time there.

I will recall briefly some vignettes of those who taught us in the following areas: Latin, philosophy, English, and a subject with the wonderful title of 'sacred eloquence'. Latin was compulsory for everyone, so the class hall in Logic was always packed, with perhaps a hundred students, the majority of whom were not particularly interested in the language and culture of ancient Rome and could, therefore, be quite rowdy. The subject was taught by Tom Finan and Joe Coulter. The latter had the misfortune to have had a younger brother who had composed 'Puppet on a String', the song that, the previous year, won the Eurovision Contest for the UK. Yes, Phil Coulter. Each day as Joe came into the hall, he was invariably greeted by a couple of fellows who thought it was the height of hilarity to hum the air of the song Sandie Shaw had sung. I felt sorry for Joe, who must have been heartily sick of hearing that tune, but he would merely remark: 'Yes, gentlemen, I *have* heard it before.' (One day, a lad in the class, a member of the photographic society, met Joe and Phil coming out of Rhetoric House, and, as he was carrying his camera, he asked their permission to take a photograph. They agreed and I recall seeing various copies of that pleasant photo – I wonder if any survive.)

Tom Finan we considered an enigma. He would throw out Latin phrases

Pádraig Ó Fiannachta, Cathal Ó Háinle, Críostóir Ó Floinn and Tomás Ó Fiaich

without elaboration – a particular favourite was '*Carpe diem*'. I fear that I added very little to my knowledge of Latin in that year. Years later when I got to know Tom (and found him delightful company), he said that all he felt able to do with the general Latin class in first year was to prevent cannibalism! It was only in second and third year that he could impart some of his vast knowledge of the Classics to students who had a genuine interest in the subject. I recall, however, our surprise when, one day, Tom devoted a whole class to a riveting exposition of Patrick Kavanagh's poem 'The Great Hunger'. We were amazed, and quite impressed, that he obviously had interests outside of what we considered the 'boring Latin class'.

In English we had John McMackin (known as Johnny Mac) and Pete Connolly – who struck us as polar opposites. Pete's classes were memorable and enlivened by his sharp wit; I can still recall some of his acute insights into Emily Brontë's *Wuthering Heights*, Dickens's *Hard Times* and Shakespeare's *Othello*. (It was in his class that I first heard the word 'elemental' – as in 'elemental passions' –

and had no idea what it meant.) If Connolly was modern, Johnny Mac was determinedly of the old school. In the course of the year, we made our way, *very slowly*, through about a third of Newman's *Idea of a University*, as well as dipping into the first chapter (eleven pages, entitled 'What is a university?') of *University Sketches*, a collection of essays by the same author. Johnny liked to read extracts from the two books, with exquisite diction, but I do not think he explained very much. At this remove, at least, I cannot remember a single one of Newman's arguments, and it was only long after I left Maynooth that I could bring myself to read anything by, or even about, the great John Henry. (In my copy of the *Idea* – Doubleday, New York, 1959 – I see that I have corrected an introductory note which states that Paul Cullen, who brought Newman to Dublin, and later caused him to leave, became 'Cardinal Archbishop of Drogheda'!)

In philosophy we had three very different lecturers. Matt O'Donnell's lectures in logic were scintillating. Even though he was desperately shy, and the subject appeared rather abstruse – some of it reminding me of honours maths, a subject that gave me nightmares in secondary school – he was able to link it with ease to current topics. I remember him once doing a dissection of Chairman Mao's *Little Red Book*, which was then very much in the news. Then we had Timmy Crowley who, inter alia, went carefully through Thomas Aquinas's 'Five Proofs' for the existence of God. A Corkman with a mordant wit, Timmy seemed to us to be rather elderly – he was, in fact, not quite fifty! He read out his notes methodically and gave the impression that he had been reading them, unchanged, for the previous twenty years. He was quite imperturbable. Some of the lads would try to prod him into an argument over the ideas of Teilhard de Chardin, the French Jesuit palaeontologist whose books were all the rage at the time. Timmy resisted the bait for a long time, but one day replied in some exasperation: 'But that man is not a philosopher. He's only a poet!'

By way of contrast, P. J. McGrath was a breath of fresh air – modern (if not modernist!) and clued in to the latest thinking in philosophy. I remember him citing the likes of A. J. Ayer and Anthony Flew – of whom we had never heard – and he effectively demolished the 'Five Proofs', one by one. This led one of the class to ask worriedly what we should do when answering Professor Crowley's exam questions on this topic. P. J. replied with disarming honesty: 'If you want to get good marks from Professor Crowley, you should stick to what you have in the notes from his class. Your answers to my questions will be judged on their merits.'

In the space remaining I can mention only one other of my undergraduate teachers: the great, unforgettable Ronan Drury, who passed away a couple of years ago at the age of ninety-three, having worked to the very end on *The Furrow*, which he had edited for forty years. He it was who had the task of teaching us 'sacred eloquence' or, in more prosaic terms, elocution. He was famous for his wit; it could be sharp, but also very funny. (I recall him trying, with some difficulty, to impress on us the difference in pronunciation between 'dew', or 'due', and 'Jew', and attempting to banish various other mispronunciations.) My most abiding memory of him is of a day I was rushing to his class in Callan Hall, having been delayed in the class immediately preceding. I dropped the books from that class in my room, and, as I was dashing out, suddenly remembered that Ron, as we called him, had told us to bring a book with us from which to read a passage that he would then critique. Lying on my desk I saw Tom Barry's *Guerilla Days in Ireland* but, on second thoughts, decided that this might not be the most appropriate work for this occasion. Then my eye fell on a small book (or, rather, booklet) I had recently bought – the encyclical *Populorum Progessio*, 'On the Development of Peoples', by Pope Paul VI (1967).

As I awaited my turn in class, I chose what I thought was a suitable paragraph, and, when called, began to read. I had gone no further than the second sentence when I was halted in my tracks. 'Where did you get that rubbish you are reading?' asked Ron. Taken aback by this astonishing attack on the words of the Holy Father himself, I replied lamely (albeit with a slight feeling of having the power of the papacy to back me up): 'It is a papal encyclical.' 'I thought as much,' he replied, and then proceeded to explain that this was not the kind of literary masterpiece he was expecting us to read from. This was, he explained, but a slab of lifeless prose cobbled together in Latin by a Vatican bureaucrat (probably from an original draft in Italian) and then translated, badly, into English by another bureaucrat – and, just because Papa Montini had put his name to it, it had not thereby been turned into good English prose!

LEABHAIR LÉINN GHAEILGE
NA MBALL FOIRNE
c.1940–c.1973

Cathal Ó Háinle

eapadh An tAthair Donnchadh Ó Floinn (1902–1968) ina Ollamh le Gaeilge i gColáiste Phádraig sa bhliain 1940 agus sa bhliain 1973 chuir an tAthair Pádraig Ó Fiannachta (1927–2016) bailchríoch ar chlár lámhscríbhinní Gaeilge an Choláiste. Idir an dá linn foilsíodh mórán saothar léinn a bhí scríofa i nGaeilge ag baill d'fhoireann teagaisc an Choláiste Ollscoile. Bhí mé féin i mo mhac léinn (1958–61) ag an mbeirt atá luaite agam cheana, agus ag an triúr údar eile a mbeidh saothair dá gcuid faoi chaibidil agam anseo, mar atá, Pádraig Ó Súilleabháin OFM (1912–1975), Tomás Ó Fiaich (1923–1990) agus Colmán Ó hUallacháin OFM (1922–1979).

I bhfad sular ceapadh Donnchadh Ó Floinn ina Ollamh i Maigh Nuad, ba nós leis cuairt a thabhairt ar Oileán Chléire gach bliain agus is tigh Chonchobhair Uí Shíothcháin a bhíodh sé ar lóistín. Ón gcéad bhliain (1929) ar aghaidh bhí sé ag bailiú bhéaloideas an oileáin agus d'fhoilsigh sé trí chnuasach de bhéaloideas ó Chléire (1929, 1935, 1941). Mar sin, nuair a dheachtaigh Conchobhar ábhar an leabhair *Seanchas Chléire* (1940) agus nuair a chuir a bheirt mhac, Ciarán agus Micheál, i scríbhinn é, ba é Donnchadh a rinne eagarthóireacht air (1936). Is é atá ann cumasc de chuimhní cinn agus de sheanchas, agus véarsaíocht, logainmneacha agus seanfhocail mar anlann leo. Bhí an leabhar sin ar na leabhair a bhí le léamh againn mar chuid de chúrsa na céime sa Ghaeilge.

Sa bhliain 1945 chuir an Cliarlathas coimisiún ar bun chun leagan nua Gaeilge den Tiomna Nua, agus é arna aistriú ón mbun-Ghréigis, a chur ar fáil. B'iad Donnchadh, an tAthair Seán Ó Floinn agus an Moinsíneoir Éamonn Ó Cíosáin baill an choimisiúin. Níor foilsíodh aon leabhar go dtí 1964. Ní leisce ná siléig ba chionsiocair leis sin, áfach, ach ómós do bhriathar Dé. An té a thuigfeadh an tóir a bhí ag Donnchadh ar uaisleacht na Gaeilge clasaicí, thuigfeadh sé nach mbeadh sé sásta le rud ar bith faoina bun sin mar aistriúchán ar Ghréigis an Tiomna Nua. Foilsíodh an leagan Gaeilge de Shoiscéal Lúcáis a rinne Donnchadh i gcomhar le Seán Ó Floinn, *Soiscéal Naofa Íosa Críost de réir Lúcáis*, sa bhliain 1964. Tamall ina dhiaidh sin dúirt Donnchadh go raibh Soiscéal Mhatha aistrithe ceithre huaire aige sula raibh sé sásta go raibh a leagan Gaeilge dílis ar fad don bhunsaothar. Foilsíodh *Soiscéal Naofa Íosa Críost de réir Mhatha*, sa bhliain 1966. D'aistrigh sé na hocht gcaibidil thosaigh de Shoiscéal Mharcais freisin.

Ceapadh an tAthair Pádraig Ó Súilleabháin OFM ina léachtóir i Roinn na Gaeilge sa bhliain 1954 agus d'fhan sé i mbun an phoist sin go dtí 1965. Cuid mhór dá shaothar saoil ab ea an eagarthóireacht a rinne sé ar scríbhinní cráifeacha Gaeilge ón 17ú agus ón 18ú céad: *An tAithríoch Ríoga* (1952) a bhí bunaithe ar an scrioptúr agus ar scríbhinní N. Aibhistín agus a d'aistrigh Seán Ó Neachtain go Gaeilge uair éigin i ndiaidh 1659; agus na scríbhinní Proinsiasacha, *Rialachas San Froinsias* (1953), *Beatha San Froinsias* (1957), *Beatha Naoimh Antoine ó Phadua* (1957) a d'aistrigh Tadhg Ó Neachtain sa bhliain 1717 nó tamall roimhe sin, *Lucerna Fidelium* (1962) a d'fhoilsigh Froinsias Ó Maolmhuaidh OFM sa Róimh sa bhliain 1676 agus *Buaidh na Naomhchroiche* (1972) le Ieróm Savanarola a d'aistrigh Bonaveantúr Ó Conchúir OFM go Gaeilge sa bhliain 1650. Foilsíodh ceithre cinn de na scríbhinní Proinsiasacha sin sa tsraith Scríbhinní Gaeilge na mBráthar Mionúr de chuid Institiúid Ard-léinn Bhaile Átha Cliath agus is leabhar eile sa tsraith sin a chuir Cainneach Ó Maonaigh OFM in eagar, mar atá, *Scáthán shacramuinte na haithridhe* (1952) le hAodh Mac Aingil (Lováin, 1618) a chuir Pádraig mar théacsleabhar ar chúrsa na céime onóraí sa Ghaeilge, tráth a raibh mé féin i mo mhac léinn dá chuid.

Bhí an Cairdinéal Tomás Ó Fiaich ar dhuine de na chéad mhic léinn a bhí ag Donnchadh Ó Floinn agus bhí sé ina chomhghleacaí dá chuid ón uair a ceapadh ina Léachtóir le stair sa bhliain 1953 é. Fuair sé ardú go céim an Ollaimh sa bhliain 1959, post a bhí aige go dtí gur ceapadh ina Uachtarán ar an gColáiste sa bhliain 1974 é.

Ba é *Gaelscrínte i gCéin* (1960) an chéad leabhar a d'fhoilsigh sé. Tráchtann sé ann ar an saothar a rinne manaigh na hÉireann chun teachtaireacht an tSoiscéil a scaipeadh i dtíortha na hEorpa agus ar na mainistreacha a chuir siad ar bun. Tá gné eile de theagmháil na nGael leis an Eoraip faoi chaibidil aige in *Imeacht na nIarlaí* (1972, i gcomhar le Pádraig de Barra) inar sholáthair sé réamhrá agus tráchtaireacht eolgaiseach a shoilsíonn an cuntas a scríobh Tadhg Ó Cianáin ar imeacht Aodha Uí Néill agus Ruairí Uí Dhónaill agus a muintir is a lucht leanúna as Éirinn go dtí an Eoraip sa bhliain 1607. In *Má Nuad* (1972) chuir sé cuntas áisiúil ar stair Choláiste Phádraig ar fáil. Sna 1970í d'fhoilsigh Tomás eagráin d'fhilíocht beirt d'fhilí Oiriall, an ceantar lenar bhain sé féin ó dhúchas: *Art Mac Cumhaigh* [c. 1738–73]: *dánta* (1973) agus *Art Mac Bionaid* [1793–

1879]: *dánta* (1979, i gcomhar le Liam Ó Caithnia.

Duine de cheannairí ghluaiseacht athbheochan na Gaeilge sa dara leath den fhichiú céad ab ea Tomás Ó Fiaich, agus dlúthchara dá chuid agus comhoibrí leis sa ghluaiseacht chéanna sin ab ea an tAthair Colmán Ó hUallacháin OFM. Ar feadh tréimhse gairide (1956–61) bhí seisean ina Ollamh le Loighic agus le hEitic i gColáiste Phádraig, agus sa bhliain 1958 d'fhoilsigh sé *Foclóir Fealsaimh* ina bhfuil snasadh agus eagrú déanta aige ar théarmaíocht Ghaeilge na fealsúnachta, na téarmaí Gaeilge mínithe agus a gcomhthéarmaí sa Ghearmáinis, sa Bhéarla, sa Fhraincis agus sa Laidin tugtha.

Duine eile d'iar-mhic léinn Dhonnchadh Uí Fhloinn ab ea Pádraig Ó Fiannachta. Tar éis dó tréimhse a chaitheamh ina shagart cúnta i bparóistí éagsúla sa Bhreatain Bheag (1953–59) ceapadh é ina léachtóir le Sean- agus Meán-Ghaeilge agus le Breatnais agus sa bhliain 1960 rinneadh Ollamh de. Is sa bhliain 1957 a d'fhoilsigh sé a chéad leabhar, *An chomharsa choimhthíoch* ina bhfuil tuairisc tugtha aige ar mhuintir agus ar shaol na Breataine Bige mar ab eol dó iad.

Tugadh cuireadh do Phádraig sa bhliain 1961 páirt a ghlacadh in obair na meithle a bhí ag ullmhú ábhair le foilsiú sa *Dictionary of the Irish Language* de chuid Acadamh Ríoga na hÉireann, agus tá a ainm mar eagarthóir leis na fascúil L (1966), C1 (1968), C2 (1970) agus C3 (1974).

Bhíothas tar éis 'Part 1' de *Catalogue of Irish manuscripts in Maynooth College Library* leis an Athair Pól Breatnach (1885–1941) a fhoilsiú sa bhliain 1943. Is é atá sa leabhar sin an cur síos a rinne Pól ar dheich gcinn de na lámhscríbhinní. Bhí clárú déanta aige ar 48 lámhscríbhinn eile agus ag an Athair P. Iognáid Ó Maoileachlainn ar 57 gcinn eile fós, ach ní raibh aon chuid den saothar sin foilsithe go dtí go ndeachaigh Pádraig i mbun oibre agus gur fhoilsigh sé seacht bhfascúl eile: 2 (1965), 3 (1966), 4 (1967), 5 (i bpáirt le hIognáid Ó Maoileachainn, 1968), 6 (1969), 7 (1972), 8 (1973).

Is é atá i gceann de na lámhscríbhinní a chláraigh Pádraig i bhfascúl 5 den chatalóg ná cóip de chuid mhór de Leagan 1 de *Táin bó Cuailnge* a bhreac Iollann Buidhe Ó Maolchonaire sa bhliain 1587. Spreag an tOllamh Maolmhuire Díolún Pádraig le tabhairt faoi eagrán den téacs sin a réiteach, rud a rinne sé. D'fhoilsigh Institiúid Ard-Léinn Bhaile Átha Cliath an t-eagrán sin sa bhliain 1966.

An bhliain chéanna sin chuir an Cliarlathas coiste nua ar bun le leagan Gaeilge den Bhíobla iomlán a chur ar fáil. Ceapadh Pádraig mar rúnaí ar an gcoiste sin agus leagadh cúram an fhoilsithe air. I gcomhar leis an Athair Wilfrid Ó hUrdail OP bhí sé tar éis aistriúchán ar dhá leabhar den Sean-Tiomna a fhoilsiú cheana féin, mar atá, 'Leabhar Ióna' (in *Irisleabhar Muighe Nuadhat*, 1962) agus *Leabhar Dhainéil* (1963).

Bhí Pádraig tar éis a bheith ina eagarthóir ar an irisleabhar *An Sagart* ó 1962. Tamall éigin ina dhiaidh sin bhí aistriúchán ar leabhair 1–10 d'Fhaoistiní Naomh Agaistín réitithe ag an scoláire Sasanach Seoirse Mac Tomáis (George Thomson) agus ag Pádraig féin faoin teideal *Mise Agaistín*, agus, i ngeall ar a mhíshásta a bhí Pádraig le moilleadóireacht an fhoilsitheora phroifisiúnta a bhí lena fhoilsiú, chinn sé ar an leabhar a fhoilsiú é féin faoi inphrionta An Sagart (1967). Bhí sé ar sheol na braiche anois. Is faoin inphrionta sin a foilsíodh bunáite leabhair an Bhíobla feasta agus ba é Pádraig féin a d'aistrigh a bhformhór. *Apacailipsis Eoin* (1969), *Soiscéal Naofa Íosa Críost de réir Eoin* (1970) agus *An Pentatúc* (1971) ba thúisce a foilsíodh. Shlánaigh sé an t-aistriúchán ar an dara Soiscéal agus foilsíodh é sin, *Soiscéal naofa* Íosa Críost *de réir Mharcais*, sa bhliain 1972 agus foilsíodh a aistriúchán ar dhíolaimí leabhar eile de chuid an dá Thiomna go luath ina dhiaidh sin, mar atá, *Na leabhair staire 1* (1974), *Na leabhair staire 2* (1976), *Leabhair na hEagna* (1976) agus *Gníomhartha na nAspal agus litreacha Aspal* áirithe (1977).

Faoin mbliain sin 1977 bhí Gaeilge curtha ar leabhair uile an Bhíobla agus ba é Pádraig eagarthóir *An Bíobla Naofa* a foilsíodh sa bhliain 1981 faoi inphrionta An Sagart.

Tá mé tar éis dul lasmuigh de na blianta 1940–73 scaití le trácht a dhéanamh ar shaothair a bhain le sraitheanna ar cuireadh tús leo le linn an ama sin. Sa tréimhse sin féin is dochreidte an saothar a rinne Pádraig Ó Fiannachta agus, nuair a chuirtear san áireamh a laghad ball foirne a bhí i ranna Choláiste Phádraig agus an t-ualach oibre a bhí orthu an t-am sin, is rí-shuntasach an líon leabhar tábhachtach léinn a d'fhoilsigh an ceathrar scoláire eile a raibh a saothar faoi chaibidil agam.

LÉACHTAÍ CHOLM CILLE

Caoga Bliain Faoi Bhláth

Tracey Ní Mhaonaigh

Déardaoin an tríú lá déag de mhí Dheireadh Fómhair 1898, ag cruinniú de chuid Iontaobhaithe Choláiste Phádraig, Maigh Nuad, socraíodh go dtabharfaí cead do mhic léinn an choláiste cumann Gaeilge a bhunú, agus tá Cuallacht Cholm Cille ar an bhfód ó shin. Shocraigh mic léinn na Cuallachta gur cheart dóibh taifead a choinneáil ar a gcuid imeachtaí agus cuireadh tús, dá bharr, leis an *Record of the League of St Columba*, a tháinig in inmhe i 1907 nuair a tosaíodh á chur amach faoin teideal *Irisleabhar Muighe Nuadhad*. Bheadh baint ag an gCuallacht le scata foilseachán eile thar na blianta, *Seanmóirí Mhuighe Nuadhat I–III*, *Seanmóirí Easbuig Uí Ghallchobhair*, Éigse *Suadh agus Seanchaidh*, agus *Mil na mBeach* ina measc. Ach ba sa bhliain acadúil 1969–70 a thabharfaí an chéad chaint riamh i sraith léachtaí poiblí a bheartaigh an Chuallacht a reáchtáil gach earrach sa Choláiste, agus tá Léachtaí Cholm Cille, mar shraith cainteanna agus mar shaothar clóite, á n-eagrú agus á gcur amach ó shin. Tá an leathchéad á chomóradh, mar sin, in eagrán na bliana seo, 2020.

Thar dheireadh seachtaine gar d'aimsir na Cásca a thionóltar na léachtaí anois, ach ní mar sin a bhí nuair a cuireadh tús leo. Thar scata seachtainí, léacht in aghaidh na seachtaine, a tugadh iad ar dtús le linn an Charghais. Míníonn Pádraig Ó Fiannachta, a bhí ina eagarthóir ar an gcéad eagrán clóite, ag tosach an eagráin sin go bhfuil sé 'beartaithe ag Cuallacht Cholm Cille i gColáiste Phádraig Má Nuad, i gcomhar le Dámh an Léinn Cheiltigh, sraith léachtaí poiblí a reachtáil gach Earrach sa Choláiste'.[1] Míníonn sé cuspóir na sraithe mar seo a leanas: 'Pléifidh na léachtaí aon ghné amháin den tsaíocht dhúchais gach bliain. … le súil go mbeidh siad ina gcabhair don mhuintir uile ar spéis leo an éigse dhúchais, mar gur dhóigh linn go léiríonn siad beagán dá stair, dá tréithe, dá nádúr agus dá saibhreas – agus dá bhfuil fós le déanamh'.[2] 'Litríocht na Gaeilge' a roghnaíodh mar théama na chéad sraithe, agus thar thréimhse sé seachtaine, tugadh trí léacht i nGaeilge agus trí cinn i mBéarla. Breandán Ó Doibhlin a

---

1 Pádraig Ó Fiannachta, 'Focal ón bhFear Eagair' *Léachtaí Cholm Cille I: Litríocht na Gaeilge* (Maigh Nuad: An Sagart, 1970), lch 4.
2 Ibid.

thug an chéad léacht ar fad, dar teideal 'Irish Literature in the Contemporary Situation'. Ba iad an Fiannachtach féin, Tomás Ó Fiaich, Pádraig Ó Héalaí, Maolmhaodhóg Ó Ruairc agus Cathal Ó Háinle a thug na cúig léacht eile, agus léargas tugtha acu ar an aoir fhileata, ar fhilí Uladh, ar an mbeathaisnéis, ar Art Ó Maolfabhail agus ar ghearrscéalta Mháirtín Uí Chadhain faoi seach. Ní haon iontas é, i bhfianaise na léachtaí agus na léachtóirí seo, go maireann an tsraith i gcónaí agus bonn breá láidir curtha fúithi ina bliain tionscnaimh.

Cé go bhfuil athrú tagtha ar sceidealú na léachtaí, agus iad á dtabhairt anois i bhfoirm comhdhála thar dheireadh seachtaine, tá an bunchuspóir céanna leo i gcónaí—an taighde agus an scoláireacht atá ar siúl i léann na Gaeilge, idir shean agus nua, a thaispeáint, a dháileadh, a chíoradh agus a chur chun cinn. Thar thréimhse saoil na léachtaí go dtí seo, mar sin, tá tobar saibhir, doimhin, luachmhar eolais curtha ar fáil.

Ach cad é go díreach atá sa tobar seo?[3] Sna deich mbliana tosaigh, breathnaíodh ar litríocht an 18ú, an 19ú agus an 20ú haois, ar an ngrá agus ar an gceol i litríocht na Gaeilge, ar theagasc na Gaeilge, agus ar ár ndúchas creidimh. Díríodh sna hochtóidí, ansin, ar an dúlra sa litríocht, ar na mná sa litríocht, ar ár scéalaíocht agus ár naomhsheanchas, ar léann na cléire, ar an nuafhilíocht, ar an aoir agus ar litríocht na Gaeltachta. Sna nóchaidí, caitheadh súil ar an mBíobla in Éirinn, ar an úrscéal Gaeilge, ar oidhreacht na n-oileán, ar Mhaigh Nuad agus an Ghaeilge, ar an dán díreach, ar an bhFiannaíocht, ar scoláirí Gaeilge, ar iriseoireacht na Gaeilge agus ar thraidisiún na hamhránaíochta. Le casadh na mílaoise breathnaíodh arís eile ar an dúchas spioradálta, agus ina dhiaidh sin ar cheist na teanga, ar churaclam na Gaeilge, ar Chearbhall Ó Dálaigh, ar oidhreacht na lámhscríbhinní, ar scoláirí léinn, ar an bprós comhaimseartha, ar shaothar Mháirtín Uí Chadhain, ar oidhreacht an 17ú haois, agus ar chúrsaí sochtheangeolaíochta na Gaeilge. Agus, le deich mbliana anuas, pléadh traidisiún an cheoil, filí INNTI, teagasc na litríochta ar an tríú leibhéal, scoláirí thíortha na Gearmáinise agus an Léann Ceilteach, oidhreacht Eoghain Uí Ghramhnaigh agus an Athar Peadar, an scríbhneoir Gaeilge, an éiceolaíocht i dtraidisiún na Gaeilge agus saol agus saothar mhuintir Nualláin.

Tuilleann eagrán amháin de na cinn dheireanacha ábhairín níos mó airde, creidim. I mí Iúil na bliana 2016 cailleadh Pádraig Ó Fiannachta. Bhí an Fiannachtach an-dílis riamh do Mhaigh Nuad agus d'oidhreacht na Gaeilge agus an léinn dúchais anseo, agus fiú agus é ina sheanaois, thagadh sé chuig na léachtaí gach aon bhliain agus idir chaipín an fhoilsitheora (é i gceannas ar An Sagart) agus chaipín an tacadóra air. I ndiaidh a bháis, socraíodh gur cheart

---

3   Faightear mionchur síos ar na léachtaí a tugadh le caoga bliain anuas, mar aon leis na daoine a thug iad, san innéacs atá curtha i gcló in eagrán na bliana seo, 2020, de *Léachtaí Cholm Cille*.

an t-ómós a bhí tuillte aige a thabhairt dó agus cad eile a dhéanfaí ach sraith a dhíriú air agus a thionól in An Díseart sa Daingean, áit a raibh na blianta deireanacha caite aige. I measc na n-ábhar a pléadh an deireadh seachtaine úd bhí a dhúchas Duibhneach, na blianta a chaith sé mar mhac léinn i Maigh Nuad agus mar Ollamh le Sean-Ghaeilge ina dhiaidh sin, an obair mhór a rinne sé ar an mBíobla Naofa, a chuid oibre le Glór na nGael, a chuid oibre mar fhoilsitheoir agus Pádraig an scríbhneoir.

Tugann sé sin muid go dtí uimhir a caoga i stair na léachtaí. Bíonn sé tábhachtach i gcónaí ceiliúradh cuí a dhéanamh agus sprioc mhór bainte amach – ar aon dul leis an gcnuasach seo mar chomóradh 225 bliain ar bhunú Choláiste Phádraig – agus beartaíodh, dá bharr, agus réimse an chaogadú heagrán á roghnú, gur cheart súil a chaitheamh romhainn ar thodhchaí na scoláireachta Gaeilge. 'Téamaí agus Tionscadail Taighde' an teideal a roghnaíodh, agus tugadh léargas don lucht éisteachta ar roinnt de na tionscadail sin a bhfuil maoiniú mór faighte acu chun dianstaidéar a dhéanamh ar ghnéithe éagsúla de léann na Gaeilge, idir shean agus nua.

Bhí na léachtaí féin ina dtionscnamh taighde nuair a cuireadh ar bun iad. Ina shaothar mór téagartha, *Maynooth College 1795–1995*, tagraíonn Patrick J. Corish dóibh agus é ag labhairt faoi thionscnaimh éagsúla ar cuireadh tús leo ag deireadh na seascaidí/tús na seachtóidí – tréimhse i stair an choláiste nuair a tháinig scata mór athruithe ar a fhoireann, ar a struchtúr agus ar a chló:

The most enduring initiative, however, came from the Faculty of Celtic Studies, beginning in February 1971 and long continuing. The lectures were published annually as *Léachtaí Cholm Cille*.[4]

In aitheasc chomhdháil na bliana 1993, labhair an t-eagraí, Pádraig Ó Fiannachta, faoi thábhacht na Gaeilge mar eochair a thugann dúinn 'tuiscint ar dhúchas, ar smaointe, ar ealaín, agus ar mheon ár muintire'.[5] D'iarr sé ar mhuintir na Gaeilge seasamh 'ar ár gcosa féin ar ár slí dhúchasach Chríostaí féin'[6] agus eolas a chur ar ár ndúchas. Ach an t-eolas seo a bheith againn bheadh saoirse aigne is chultúir againn, a mhaígh sé, saoirse atá níos tábhachtaí ná saoirse pholaitiúil ná saoirse eacnamaíoch de chineál ar bith. Tá tábhacht ag baint le teachtaireacht seo na hoidhreachta i gcónaí – do phobal na Gaeilge, cinnte, ach do phobal na hÉireann i gcoitinne leis. I ré seo an domhain bhig agus na

4   Patrick J. Corish, *Maynooth College 1795–1995* (Dublin: Gill & Macmillan,1995), lgh. 433–4. 1971 atá ag Corish anseo ach is botún é sin.
5   Pádraig Ó Fiannachta, 'Aitheasc na Comhdhála' in *Léachtaí Cholm Cille XXIII: Maigh Nuad agus an Ghaeilge* (Maigh Nuad: An Sagart, 1993). lch 5.
6   Ibid., lch 6.

Dr Damien Ó Muirí and Póilín Ní Thuile, with Dr Máire Ní Annracháin in the background

Dr Mary Leenane and Dr Muireann Ní Bhrolcháin

teicneolaíochta, le bagairt na bréagréaltachta thart timpeall orainn, tá géarghá, níos mó ná riamh, le braistint na féiniúlachta. Tá an fhéiniúlacht dhúchasach sin á caomhnú agus á cur chun cinn i gcónaí ar fhearann an choláiste i Má Nuad, ag *Léachtaí Cholm Cille* agus *Irisleabhar Mhá Nuad* araon. Téann an dá fhoilseachán seo le chéile toisc gur tháinig moladh inspioráideach a mbunaithe ó Chuallacht Cholm Cille an chéad lá riamh. D'aithin baill na Cuallachta na bearnaí a bhí le líonadh; thug siad aghaidh ar na dúshláin a bhí rompu agus níor leasc leo na deiseanna ag éirí as Dara Comhairle na Vatacáine a thapú. Ní áibhéil a rá go bhfuilimid ar thairseach ré dhúshlánach ar leibhéal domhanda sa lá atá inniu ann agus tuigtear dúinn, agus na hirisí seo á múnlú agus á gcur in oiriúint againn don phobal comhaimseartha, go gcaithfear na forbairtí nua teicneolaíochta a aclú i seachadadh na litríochta, agus bheith istigh agus tosaíocht a thabhairt dóibh, ach féachaint do dhínit an duine agus don chomhdhaonnacht faoi mar a bhí mar fheidhm agus mar chuspóir na Cuallachta. Gura fada buan *Léachtaí Cholm Cille* agus *Irisleabhar Mhá Nuad*.

A PAEAN — AND TWO POEMS — TO A TURBULENT PRIEST

Denis Bergin

In the 100-year history of Maynooth as a Recognised College of the National University, catering for a small but select group of clerical undergraduates, there was little opportunity or occasion for spectacular extramural academic achievement on the part of either professors or students. The rule of law and the odour of sanctity that prevailed in the hallowed halls discouraged exhibitionism or the flaunting of creative talent, even within that limited environment.

The world-class scientists (and there were a few) among the professors went about their work quietly and efficiently, teaching their small classes, doing their research, and mixing occasionally with their ilk at Dublin and international gatherings. The Irish scholars, too, were reticent in putting themselves forward, again keeping company, if they did at all, with the small circle of their colleagues from the other universities and (as with the scientists) the researchers at the Dublin Institute for Advanced Studies.

The classicists and the historians (such few of the latter as there were until the early 1950s, when the number doubled to two) were a little more convivial, particularly in their foreign travel and academic connections. But their concerns were not prone to controversy, until (in the Maynooth context, at least) the classicist Denis Meehan stunned colleagues and students by leaving the secular priesthood and the country to become a monk in California, writing a frank reminiscence of his former colleagues some years later to follow his more pedestrian *Window on Maynooth*. In the national context, the historian Tomás Ó Fiaich became a controversial figure as chairman of the Commission on the Irish Language (fate had other plans for him later).

The profession of English suffered no such dramatics. It found it hard to establish its identity and its relevance in the modern era as it faced the risk of profanity in the work of contemporary authors; the easiest solution was to ignore them. It also had to cope with its previous connections – English and French were once taught together in Maynooth, such was their symbiotic relationship

232

in the genesis of the National Seminary from the post-Revolutionary period onward. Even Neil Kevin's gentle and comforting *I Remember Maynooth*, first published in the 1930s under the pseudonym Don Boyne, and highly successful by the publishing standards of the day, did not disturb the scene, seeming strangely in keeping with the modest temper of the times.

But in the early 1950s, and following Fr Kevin's premature death, a young Meath priest named Peter Connolly was sent by his Bishop to Oxford to acquire some knowledge of the modern literary world. He came back to join John McMackin, the unobtrusive brother of a fiery if short-lived female Glasgow Labour MP, on the two-member faculty.

As if to revive the historic cultural pairing, four years later a young Tyrone priest named Brendan Devlin was appointed Professor of Modern Languages, the first such permanent appointment in decades. Brendan not only took his French brief seriously, but extended it to treat Irish (which he had learned properly only during his student days at Maynooth) as a thoroughly modern language, even if he had to partly invent that contemporaneous version himself, inserting it into a vibrant new literary mode that he also developed virtually single-handedly.

Peter Connolly came from that noble strain of levitical ancestry, the teacher/farmer father and the teacher mother, though in the case of the Connollys of Drumconrath in County Meath the extended family included four other teachers, and two other households, in addition to his parents'. There was a genuine sense of fun and worldly adventure among the Connolly siblings and their cousins, and Peter's vocation to the priesthood came as a surprise. However, throughout his life he maintained his devotional stance in the most traditional and faithful way, alongside a daring intellectual exploration of virtually every literary and moral trend in the universe.

Writing on the forms and media of creativity and their extremes and enemies (obscenity, censorship), he attracted the attention of everyone from Archbishop John Charles McQuaid to Peter Lennon, the Paris-based *Guardian* journalist and film-maker who included Connolly among the 'turbulent priests' documented in his print pieces on Ireland and later in his film *The Rocky Road to Dublin*. But it was Connolly's considered and conditional praise of the novelist Edna O'Brien at a Tuairim meeting in Limerick in 1966 that set the cat among the pigeons at every level in Irish Church and cultural circles, and it is notable that his career did not suffer in any significant way from the negative exposure the incident caused.

When the whole panorama of teaching English literature at Maynooth had changed decades later, he could look back with a certain nostalgia on those constrained years, where, in addition to dealing with the conservative mien of the Church fathers, his energies had been focused on preparing the callow youth of Ireland for a life of teaching or cultural mediation alongside their future priestly ministry.

Sometimes in those days his impatience showed, as the finer points of Jane Austen's chapter construction were missed or a Chaucerian play on words mangled in a student reading; sometimes he was able to take a small delight in an unexpected insight that appeared in a student's essay. However, he knew that a true literary genius would be less than likely to emerge from the ranks of his students, a fact that he persuaded his external examiners (which at one time included a certain J. R. R. Tolkien) to accept.

The best of his inculcatory vigour was reserved for the honours English class, where the fare was varied: Hemingway, the Eliots (George and Tom), Swift, Orwell, even the milder works of D. H. Lawrence (the students could order the books by mail from Blackwells in Oxford, who would send them in sealed packages addressed to the Rev. – , Maynooth, for what customs official would investigate material destined for such a respectable consignee?).

Connolly's small classes of two or three students delved deeper and deeper into English language and literature, often providing an enlightenment in the ways of the secular world that resulted in a decision not to pursue much further their studies for the priesthood. Thus, in the mid 1960s, he educated two future ambassadors, a future secretary of a government department and *chef de cabinet* to a European commissioner, a future chairman of the RTÉ Authority, and a future senior staff member of the American Overseas School in Rome.

It was in these classes that Peter Connolly found solace in what was otherwise an unforgiving task in an unforgiving time. There – gifted, irascible, sensitive to every machination and mood of the human spirit, open to all the cultural experiences the world had to offer – he was a revelation of the true mind and mode of the universal university professor who might have graced any educational environment of any denominational allegiance or of none at any stage in the twentieth century. The fact that he combined this with a deep faith and dedication to his priestly calling is one of the wonders of the age.

And then a wonderful thing happened. Having predicted the decline of the seminary system within which he had laboured for so many years, and reconciled himself perhaps to declining with it, a new and proper academic institution developed before his very eyes. Soon he was thriving in Maynooth's openness to lay and graduate students, and trading insights and enthusiasms with early

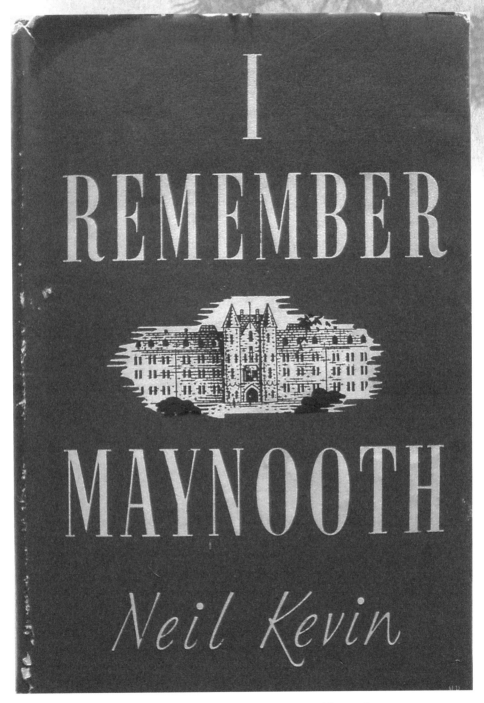

Cover of the 1945 edition of I Remember Maynooth

colleagues in the new dispensation like Barbara Hayley, a professor of Anglican background who came to live with her family in the former Church of Ireland rectory across Parson Street, and Peter Denman. Barbara Hayley's appointment as his successor upon his enforced retirement was a tribute to how much Peter Connolly had changed the literary environment at Maynooth, though he would surely be amazed at the present complement of senior faculty members in the Department of English, where women outnumber men among professorial and lecturer appointments by nine to seven.

However, the old ties still bound. One of Peter Connolly's regular visitors down through the years was a former student from Mullingar who went on to become a third-level teacher of English in Ireland and Canada before his death in 2013 at the age of sixty-six. Hugh O'Donnell was among the privileged who saw Peter Connolly at close quarters, sharing his enthusiasm for art, culture, bullfighting, Picasso and Edith Piaf, and being admitted to the inner sanctum of the book-lined room on middle Long Corridor.

When his mentor died in 1987 (fittingly after an energetic swimming session in Celbridge), three years after his retirement following an incapacitating stroke from which he had partially recovered, Hugh wrote this poem for the *Irish Review* (it was reprinted in *No Bland Facility*, a collection of Peter's writings compiled by James H. Murphy, one of his former students who became a member of the Vincentian order, and who at time of writing professes English at De Paul University, Chicago).[1]

The Sun also Rises
(*In memory of Peter R. Connolly*)

La muerta me esta miranda
Desde las torres de Cordoba
Death is watching me
From the towers of Cordoba
– Lorca

The number had been changed
No-one's there to answer; it's mid-term break.
I picture empty rooms and corridors
As if all have withdrawn with you,

---

1 T. H. O'Donnell, 'The Sun also Rises' (in memory of Peter R. Connolly), in *The Irish Review* 3 (1988), pp. 89–90. Reprinted with kind permission.

And behind the vested armchair. above the bookshelves –
The row of early dust-jacketed Faulkner –
See the storm clouds over El Greco's Toledo
Reach out again towards the visitor.

That first evening I sat across from you,
Our one-to-one Oxford-style tutorial at an end,
I hung on, curious, awkwardly asking questions,
We listened to 'Letter from Madrid',
To the cultured voice of the BBC's correspondent
Speculating on Franco's declining years,
Seeing the old dictator set up
For his last show, the ring master
Rehearsing his leap into eternity.
You asked if I knew Picasso's *Guernica*
Or the apocalyptic *Demoiselles d'Avignon*,
And talked of exploring Spain in the fifties,
Castile, Aragon, Andalusia,
Afternoons in the corrida, and once,
When the crowd on its excited feet, shouting,
The matador passed you, white-faced,
Wide-eyed and anxious, and very, very tired.

After I left, I'd keep coming back
If a year went by and I hadn't seen you,
I'd feel restless. Belfast, London, Limerick
Making the journey. The Gothic spire resting,
Rising into view. Expectations.
And then seeing you again. The charge
Of that energy. Liquid jazz pouring
Into the room. Billie Holliday's 'No Regrets'
What you'd been reading, Gabriel García Marquez's
One Hundred Years of Solitude, read and reread.
Gossiping about church politics
With Brechtian glee. And what you'd seen,
The laugh lifting through you, startling
The late-night cinema audience, not quite so quick
To see the joke, as the bishop raised

The double-barrelled shot-gun to blow
His just-absolved penitent's brains out.

I missed your going. You were already
In the ground when I went
To my neighbour's for the paper.
Coming away I saw the crocuses
Bunched hard and close under that moon
Where Lorca's rider saw death.
Now you lie in Drumconrath in Meath
While across from me the Clare hills look west
To the summer roads you cycled in your teens
When a crowd of you whooped your way
On Sunday evenings to the local flea-pit.
When the lights went down
For Warner Brothers, Paramount or MGM
And gangsters, whores and cops
To play their deadly game, your own eye
Read in the first image what was to come.

At about the same time, a former student who had entered a more secularly oriented Maynooth in the last year of Peter Connolly's tenure, and who went on to obtain a PhD in English, bought some books and teaching materials from among the late professor's effects. A decade later, and now a member of the college's administrative staff, he wrote a touching poem based on his experience of leafing through the heavily used and annotated volumes.

Recalling this connection, Bill Tinley (at the time of this writing the college's long-serving campus conference and accommodation manager) remembers: 'I attended Connolly's lectures on Joyce (*A Portrait of the Artist as a Young Man*) and Hopkins in my first year, but never exchanged more than a few words with him. I attended his funeral. The "penned-on paperbacks" refer to his habit of annotating (in scarcely legible hand) every book he had. His acetates for overhead projection were similarly scrawled on, to the extent one could hardly read what was shown'. The poem appeared in 1996 in *Agenda*, the international literary magazine founded in 1959 by Ezra Pound and William Cookson.

A Scattered Testament

On a book purchased from the library of the late Peter Connolly

Who considers in the musty days of labour,
On sunset afternoons or endless summer nights,
All quietness and rest, that what we must endure
And come to love can come to this? A desklamp lights
Some poems you have glossed, fingered by a stranger

Turning pages slowly in an unknown town,
The book you memorised returned to learning hands.
The dust from your estate of battered spines comes down
On empty shelves, penned-on paperbacks and seconds
Sold for next-to-nothing; and what was once your own

Becomes a scattered testament, a property
Dispersed like seeds to grow if chance ordains it so.
A lifetime's work conceives in death its legacy,
And even as the earth receives you, the shadow
Of your hand leaves dog-ears for a lost posterity.

FATHER PETER CONNOLLY (1927–1987)
From Dreaming Spires to Stern Reality

Michael Conway

orn in 1927 in Drumconrath, County Meath, Peter Connolly received his secondary education at St Finian's College, Mullingar. In 1944, sponsored by the Bishop of Meath as a seminarian for his diocese, he began studies for priesthood in Maynooth where he also commenced courses for a BA. English language and literature were his special interests and in 1947 he graduated with first-class honours in those fields. Ordained priest in 1951, he was selected by Bishop Kyne for higher studies with a view eventually to joining the Faculty of Arts in St Patrick's College Maynooth. The University of Oxford, in the fabled city of dreaming spires, became his post-graduate academic home for three years as he proceeded to an MA (Oxon). He described it to us, his students, as a campus very similar to our alma mater, only twenty times larger! In 1954 he returned as lecturer to his former seminary, where he eventually became Professor of English until early retirement due to ill-health in the early 1980s. Many of us who sat in his classes in those years would come to see him as one of the great lights of our undergraduate days.

My first encounter with him after I had elected to study English in First Arts was in Music Hall (now the admissions office for those seeking accommodation), opposite Callan Hall through the archway. This spacious lecture hall was the location for many of his lectures, the blackboard behind him decorated with musical notation. The timetable informed us that we would meet him five days a week. Eager students of English had to wait three days before he at last mounted the dais, carefully gathering his toga, and we got our first glimpse of him, a man of medium height with a receding hairline, viewing us quizzically through his glasses. Later we learned the reason for this delayed start. He had been busy in Cork city as a working member of the jury of the Cork Film Festival, then flourishing in the southern capital.

As freshmen (chubs) in St Patrick's College, we soon became aware of the pastoral magazine called *The Furrow*, published monthly under the editorship of Professor James G. McGarry. Founded in 1950, it was gaining an international

Rev. Prof. Peter Connolly

reputation for its thoughtful articles on various aspects of theology and Church life, plus its coverage of the arts in Ireland. Many of its topics were as yet way beyond the interests of young seminarians like ourselves. What did attract the attention of some of us were the reviews of new plays and just-released new films. The film reviewer was Peter Connolly! With each new issue we turned eagerly to his pages in the magazine. His thoughts on first-run films (rarely then called movies!) such as Fred Zinneman's *The Nun's Story* and Ingmar Bergman's *Wild Strawberries* conveyed insights that young film-goers like ourselves fell upon with pleasure as we dissected imagery and plot. His long review of George Morrison's *Mise Éire* reveals a profound understanding of modern Irish history as well as the art of documentary film-making, paying due tribute to the magnificence of Sean Ó Riada's musical score on the soundtrack.

Connolly's main business was to introduce us to the depth and the breadth of English literature. His enthusiasm for the contribution that this land has made to the literary culture of our nearest neighbour, even to the extent of adopting its language, ensured that Anglo-Irish letters would be no mere subset in his world-view. Early in his career, he had lectured international students gathered for the annual Yeats Summer School in Sligo. He was very insistent that we undergraduates pronounce the poet's name correctly – it rhymes with 'Yates', he told us firmly! The longer poems of this writer and their origins in the Celtic Twilight received due treatment. Shakespeare's plays and the English poets, Romantic and Augustan, were fully covered by him. He duly dealt with their use of sometimes complex imagery. Early in our time as undergraduates, he moved beyond the set curriculum to share with us in typed sheets the lectures he was giving on James Joyce to literary groups in various parts of Ireland, thus introducing us to perhaps our best-known writer at a time when that anti-clerical Dublin novelist was relatively unknown among us – although Connolly focused only on the accessible *Dubliners* and *Portrait of the Artist as a Young Man*.

He explored with us Jane Austen, especially her novel *Persuasion*, set in rural Hampshire, in depth. His underlining of her sense of irony and her understatement was for us, from another more open culture, a revelation, although he did warn us that several readings of her pages might be needed before we came to full appreciation of her literary skills. Long after his retirement, many television and big screen productions of her work have led to a minor industry based on this early nineteenth-century writer. Publication of her early novels had come slowly, *Persuasion* appearing only after her death in 1817. Some of us who sat at his feet in our student days, who were avid readers of his film reviews of yesteryear, would love to hear his critical assessment of those modern television and wide-screen adaptations.

The early roots of the English language that we now use are found in the Anglo-Saxon dialect that preceded Geoffrey Chaucer. Making use of Sweet's *Primer*, he read to us passages from the Gospel parables like the Good Shepherd, extracts in a developing tongue that would later evolve into the language we now use. His fluency in and mastery of that ancient tongue astonished us. As always, he was leading us through literature into an appreciation of a wider world.

Apart from his day job as a lecturer in English, Peter Connolly was also waging a quiet war on the literary censorship which, introduced by the new Irish Free State to curb pornography, came to be misused by zealots with a very narrow view of the canons of literary expression. By the 1950s, the Censorship of Publications Act had become a source of huge embarrassment when many serious works of literary value were being banned for the use of just a single word because an over-sensitive reader submitted a title to the Censorship Board. Its members then quite often supinely decreed it should be withdrawn from bookshelves. In 1966 in Limerick, he came to the public defence of Edna O'Brien, all of whose mildly titillating tales about young women living and working in Dublin, first published in the 1950s, were promptly denounced and banned. Before a sometimes hostile audience and sharing the same platform with her, he praised the 'high spirits and cheerful natural ribaldry in her writing'. She greatly appreciated his understanding of her literary intentions and skills, especially that at least one public intellectual understood what she was about. His contributions with others to this debate led eventually in the 1960s to much more realistic legislation. Connolly always spoke to us from a viewpoint of deep loyalty to and respect for the Church whose seminarians he was mentoring. That this open-minded debater in the public square on such a contentious issue was a priest-professor at Maynooth and our teacher in our undergraduate days became a source of deep satisfaction to his former students.

As a person, Connolly did not suffer fools gladly. Casual conversation with undergraduates on trivial topics was never his forte. Yet he was unfailingly polite and helpful in tutorials in his quarters when he came to read and evaluate our set exercises in English essay assignments, pointing out the deadness of cliché and the mangled sentence construction that leads to poor expression. In a corner of his spacious sitting room in the seminary, looking out on St Joseph's Square, could be seen a grand piano, catching our eye as we waited for his evaluation of our written pages. Students passing by his rooms in Long Corridor sometimes heard him tinkling the ivories.

Peter Connolly's keen and perceptive mind was focused on the English language as a means of expression. It is doubtful if he ever considered himself to be a prophet. Yet some thoughts he shared with Declan Kiberd in 1980, at a time when this priest-professor had become apprehensive about a newly emerging hedonistic Ireland, are sobering to read now. His words are indeed a shocking prediction:

> The Irish people are not sentimental. See how quickly they abandoned the Gaelic language in the early 19th century when they saw it as no longer of practical use. Religion will go in the next generation: and when it goes, it will go so fast that nobody will even know it is happening.

May he rest in peace in Drumconrath where, after taking early retirement from his Maynooth professorship, he was laid to rest beside his sister in 1987.

Frank McGuinness, poet and playwright

TRAVELLER

(In memory of Barbara Hayley[1])

Frank McGuinness

1. Japan

I heard the most wonderful story travelling in Japan.
It is quite true that they overwork you,
But they have strange ideas about time.
It took a horse in the Kabuki theatre an hour,
A solid hour to dance the stage, but that horse –
Its ribboned mane so beautifully stitched –
Where was I? The story that will interest you.

By pure accident I met a young woman,
Called McLaughlin. Your part of the country,
Inishowen, isn't that a tribal name?
There she was in Kyoto, their holy city,
More exotic than Knock, I can tell you,
Learning more about ceramics, she was a potter,
And working in a bar as a hostess –

Why do they so adore Western women, Japanese men?
She was quite lovely and told me this story,
Which is where I started. Have more coffee,
There's a good bottle of red wine buried in that press.
Open it, not for me, I'll pretend I'm Norwegian.
In Norway no one drinks and drives, so at dinner
They all bring a bottle to look at – God help us.

---

1   Barbara Hayley (1938–1991) was a renowned scholar of nineteenth-century Anglo-Irish literature, a literary
    critic and broadcaster, and Professor of English at St Patrick's College Maynooth until her tragic death
    following a car crash in 1991.

I was telling you of this Irishwoman in Japan,
And one day the woman who owned the bar,
Who by all accounts was usually so calm and kimonoed,
She gathered all her girls together and cried.
Not understanding a word, the Irishwoman listened
And though in her experience the Japanese never wept,
She knew this terrible grief was true.

The Japanese woman, the bar owner, they called her
Mother, she also ran a factory.
It employed those Japanese wounded in the war.
And she was crying because the factory was going under,
Bar profits kept it going, profits were failing,
And she could not fail, for she was Japanese.
She had decided to commit hara-kiri. She meant it.

The night of weeping was New Year's Eve.
The girls trooped in line from temple to temple,
Shinto, Buddhist, even the Catholic Church
In Kyoto, lighting candles to save her life.
They succeeded, she lived, and I like
To think of her life as candlelight.
I sometimes think, I cannot fail, I must not.

If I fail what will become of us all?
Take your time, you say. I will, if I may
Take my time to dance the stage like a strange, beautiful horse.
Yes, I liked Japan, even if they overwork you.
They believe the gods are beneath our feet.
This young woman called McLaughlin told me that.
She believed in such gods. So do I.

2. Caen

Do you remember a January day in Caen?
My birthday, and I was exhausted,
Having chaired a whole meeting in French?

We found a bar and I drank beer
And toasted our mutual health;
The beer you could buy for my gift –

I dislike birthdays and all they entail.
I was like women at the end of a war,
Tired and happy, at peace, in Caen.

3. Maynooth

Being an only child,
How I longed for a sister.
I am so glad I have two daughters.
Sophie and Celia,
How I love their names.
My close friend, Barbara Hardy,
Her name too I love,
Being like my own.
I instinctively trust anyone called Barbara.
That is vanity.
Forgivable vanity. Forgivable,
So much is forgivable.

This is the last day
I will spend on this earth,
This is the last day
I will spend in this college,
Yes, my last day,
Though I don't know it.
I will act as if I do.
I will tell, what?
Tell Maureen, my secretary,

How well she does her work.
Phone Frank and ask how was Brussels?

Did he and Philip behave themselves?
I hope not.
Ask Kevin and Aoife
To come see my new house.
Ask Peter – well named,
That man is a rock –
To do something, anything,
Knowing it will be done,
For into his good hands
I can entrust all things.
All these things I'd do
If I had time, but time is precious.

And life is fleeting as the wind …

There are days,
Yes, days,
I sit staring
At the white walls of my office.
The sun hits the self-same office
At an angle unbecoming to itself.
So one avoids the sun
And prefers to look instead at books,
I must return one borrowed from,
God, I've forgotten who –
I am growing confused
On the last day of my life.
I should ring Mariana
Gourlandris in London.
She would cheer me up
And order me to find
A good three-volume novel
And get back to the eighteenth century
Where I belong.
Oh Mariana, I wish I did.

Then I should die falling from my horse.
A carriage overturned.
But it will be in a car
Where coffee was spilt yesterday.
A riotous chocolate house.
I do not know it is the last day of my life
No more than I can know
That those who found me dying
Will tell what my last words were.
Am I dead? I asked.
I have always kept my manners.
I could see their distress.
I prepared them gently for my dying
By asking, am I dead?
So they could answer, no,
No, you'll be all right.
Kind,
Even though I knew,
They knew,
We all knew.
And I would weep this day
Buckets of tears
To know it is my last in this earth,
In this college,
But I don't know this,
So I'm damned if I'm going to weep.
I will get into my car,
I will drive and that is that.
That is how I want it, so
That is what I'll do.

And life is fleeting as the wind …

Prof. Barbara Hayley

Verissima Aestimatio:
RICHARD McCULLEN CM (1926–2015), VINCENTIAN AND MAYNOOTH MAN

Niall Ahern

he association between Irish Vincentians and Maynooth College is a venerable one and this year marks many milestones of this honourable connection. In fact, the Irish Vincentians had sprung from Maynooth in the mid-nineteenth century when a Maynooth dean of those days became so influenced by the work of St Vincent de Paul in Paris that he persuaded some newly ordained diocesan priests to join him in a new vision of priestly service. He resigned from St Patrick's College and they all moved to Castleknock, and by such origins began the tradition at Maynooth of Vincentian spiritual fathers. For so long as any living Maynooth man can remember, in his own spiritual shaping, some Vincentian priest would have played an intimate role.

In the context of the college's 225th anniversary of its foundation year, we recall that 475 years ago St Vincent de Paul established his congregation, and exactly 400 years after this foundation a young Armagh diocesan student left his studies at Maynooth to join the Vincentians. His name was Richard McCullen. He had his origins in County Meath and came from a levitical family. His doctorate *summa cum laude* was in canon law. However, some years after his ordination as a Vincentian, he returned to Maynooth in 1967 as spiritual director at the crucial time when the college was admitting its first lay students and the tenor of seminary life was undergoing change and adaptation in the light of the Second Vatican Council. He departed the college forty-five years ago to become provincial of his order. He was then elected superior general after some twenty years. On the eve of Christ's Nativity 2015, he died. He was on the cusp of his ninetieth birthday. He had become the paterfamilias of all Vincentians as they witnessed to their special charism of spiritual direction to students for the priesthood. He was a towering and lifelong influence on Irish diocesan seminarians during his Maynooth years and was, afterwards, amongst the worldwide Vincentian diaspora, a sure guide in turbulent times.

Richard was preeminent amongst those who gave many years of their lives to

the service of Maynooth College. He simply inhabited the Gospel. The Word was enfleshed in him. He was an anointed speaker. His spiritual conferences were beautifully crafted; they flowed from a well-furnished mind and contemplative spirit. Encouragments tripped off his tongue with great depths of sincerity since they were honed in his heart. His presence was benediction. Each time he spoke, and each time he preached, one was enveloped by his gentle humility.

He was shy regarding words about himself and would surely react coyly to this recollection. When, as Fourth Divines, we persuaded him to collate his student conferences for private circulation he remained reticent and introduced them with a favoured Julian of Norwich plea – 'I beg you all for God's sake, and advise you for your own, to stop thinking about the poor wretch who has shown you these things, and with all your strength, wisdom and humility look at God, that in His loving courtesy and eternal goodness, He may be willing to show all and sundry, to our own great comfort'. I also remember his inscription to me on the flyleaf of his treasury, *Deep Down Things*: 'To an earlier publisher from a still reluctant author!' I almost feel disobedient now! This compilation of his various conferences and addresses as superior general is never even faintly self-indulgent, but the soul and mind of the man come through.

The mind of Richard contained the heart and well-stocked memory of the inveterate reader, the reflective scholar and the Christian humanist who read everything from ancient Greece and Rome and the Church Fathers down to the latest European and American authors. And his personal musings range from ideals of education and the idea of a university to thoughts on the vocation to priesthood, and on death and dying and the *lacrimae rerum*, the final tears at the heart of things. He had a great store of epitaphs and the marmoreal poets' lines that crystallise those tears – from Horace or Virgil down to T. S. Eliot and, of course, his first favourite – G. M. Hopkins. His second great love was music and he once remarked to me that 'Mozart was the path to heaven but Bach was heaven itself'!

As fledgling students, we recognised great spiritual strength in the ascetic life of Richard McCullen and a certain *fama sanctitatis* attached itself to this quiet man. We reverenced him. He was distant but attentive; acute but gentle; cautious but encouraging. He inhabited that facility for intellectual apprehension and intuitive thought that the Greeks term *nous* and laid it before us as we discerned our way forward in Christ. His contributions as a participant at the synod in Rome that produced *Pastores Dabo Vobis*, the 1992 apostolic exhortation on the formation of priests, were widely acclaimed. When speaking of spiritual direction, his preference was for the more expressive title in old Irish – *Anam Cara*. He felt this term touched the very heart of the sacred encounter, for it throws into bold relief what must be the foundation of the relationship of any two disciples who, in the company of Christ, are fully intent, as he quoted, 'to bathe in his fall-gold mercies, to breathe in his all-fire glances' (Hopkins, *The Wreck of the Deutschland*). At the heart of this spiritual relationship and companionship is friendship, as it was between Christ and the two disciples on the road to Emmaus, and between Paul and Ananias. Richard raised to a new level the sanctity and centrality of this ministry while on the Maynooth staff. He evoked an unconscious admiration while underscoring the seriousness of the work to hand. And, in him, all that *gravitas* was leavened by a buoyant wit and quiet humour.

He had social graces, a gift for friendship, an interest in people and character – including character foibles and the general *comédie humaine*. And when, during in-house concerts, the students might affectionately mock his mannerisms, he would gently remind them that imitation is the greatest form of flattery. When one came to know him on mature terms as colleague, or one's former guide, there was no more entertaining and articulate raconteur, with the gift of total recall of characters and episodes. This we celebrated over later years when he would generously visit me in the west of Ireland and, as former students, we would gather round him and appreciate with new eyes this sage and aged man.

And age became him. Gratitude formed his signature tune in the spirit of St Vincent. His mantra was 'Thanks be to God, the source of all that is good, and who renders all manner of things well'. He didn't just live life, but rather, celebrated it at an extraordinary depth; and in all this he retained a calm vigour and youthful outlook. *'Non caligavit ocolus eius nec dentes illius moti sunt'* (Deuteronomy 34:7).

Richard directed us to the source. From the beginning was the Word. God alone remains permanent. Engraved on his Vincentian cross were two dates – that of his final profession and his first Holy Communion. He seldom shared

Detail – St Mary's Oratory

such intimacies, preferring to shy away from the limelight, and declined on several occasions to accept the students' choice of him for the annual class-piece. His was the hidden ministry of souls, and that was reward enough.

On that high, holy hill at Castleknock, where he awaits the Resurrection, one can hear the 'voices of the sweeter birds above the wailing of the rain'. And, delightfully too, the murmur of Hopkins – 'Send my roots rain'. Richard once wrote to me that after a shared retreat together in France these words kept reverberating through what he termed his 'praying soul'.

Now, Richard, we echo that cry to you who have shown us such love and nourishing. From heaven's home 'send our roots rain' as we continue in your spiritual accompaniment, and water with the wine of good judgement and future hope our shared alma mater, Maynooth, at this sacred time of remembrance. You, who on the eve of Christmas 2015, reached heaven's home, continue to birth Christ in us that we too might inhabit the Gospel. Towards you (having been called to sustain what St Paul so frequently refers to as the *pondus gloriae*), we continue to bend our ear for your word of mercy, and we hear that Marian assurance you so often murmured in your beloved rue du Bac in Paris:

> I say that we are wound;
> With mercy round and round;
> As if with air.
>
> – G. M. Hopkins
> ('The Blessed Virgin Compared to the Air We Breathe')

'Here to feed you not to fatten you!'
MEMORIES OF
MAYNOOTH COLLEGE CATERING

David J. Carbery

n 1968, I joined CERT (Council Education Recruitment Training for Hotel and Catering Industry) as catering instructor. Having left the plush carpeted surroundings of the grade A Royal Hibernian and Russell Hotels to arrive at the cold terrazzo floors of Maynooth College was a shock to the system to say the least! In 1970, I took over as director of the catering school and in 1973 was retained as catering manager by the President, Msgr Jeremiah Newman. My brief was to employ staff and set up an entire new catering department.

CERT had established a residential catering school in the college in September 1965. It was attended by 200 students from all over the country who were interested in pursuing a career in the catering industry. The college provided the residence and facilities to the right and left of Riverstown House. In return, the school placed their catering expertise at the service of 500 clerical students and staff of the college.

At that time we had four institutions within the walls of the college: National Seminary; Pontifical University; National University; and catering school. In 1973, after eight years in Maynooth, the catering school was transferred to a new, more suitable purpose-built building in the Regional Technical College (RTC) Galway.

This left a major problem for St Patrick's College Maynooth as they were now about to lose their catering department. It was decided to modernise the entire catering area.

At that time food had to be transported on trolleys from the old main kitchen through a tunnel that ran under Pugin Hall and exited into the pantry of the parlour dining room.

As far as food was concerned, the college was self-sufficient. It had its own adjoining farm, which provided vegetables, potatoes, milk and eggs. It also had its own abattoir which supplied all the meat.

The kitchens, which were built in 1845, were by 1968 antiquated and badly

Pugin Hall by Sara Kyne

in need of revamping. It was agreed to build a new kitchen that would service all dining rooms as well as a self-service unit for clerical students. This work was completed in 1973.

In the college dining room (later popularly known as the 'lay pros ref', to distinguish it from the parlour, or 'pros ref', where the clerical members of the teaching staff dined) was the original ceiling of the old kitchen, which gives you some idea of its height. The floor in the college dining room was put down when the old kitchens were being modified. The newly created room was used initially as a lecture hall and later converted to a 120-seater dining room for lay lecturers and staff, and had an adjoining separate private dining room and bar, which was reserved for use by the President of NUI Maynooth and others.

I was so proud of what we had made out of that 1845 kitchen. Sadly, the college dining room is no longer used as a dining room, which is a shame, as it had great potential.

Pugin Hall, then called the Senior Refectory, could seat 400. Each student had his own permanent place at the table which was allocated by his dean and they didn't dare sit anywhere else. Meals were taken in silence except for the evening meal at which students were allowed to speak.

From the pulpit, which was situated opposite the statue of Our Lady, spiritual readings and prayers were recited each day. I'm not sure if this was for guidance or in the hope that the chef might leave!

On one occasion when a student was celebrating his birthday, all 400 students gave a rendition of 'Happy Birthday'. Msgr Cremin, who was nearby, said to me:

'Do you hear that? You can do nothing about it; I can do nothing about it; and those who can, won't!' Frankie (as he was popularly known) was not happy!

The Junior Refectory in Rhetoric House, which is now occupied by the Geography Department, seated about 100 and all food had to be transported seventy yards across open space in hot trolleys. The Junior Ref, as it was called, was closed in 1973, after which all students dined in Pugin Hall.

During my time in Maynooth I came in contact with and catered for many dignitaries. Some famous, some later infamous. They included: Pope John Paul II; King Juan Carlos and Queen Sofia of Spain; the Count of Evora; King Gustaf of Sweden; Albert II Prince of Monaco; President Francesco Cossiga of Italy; Prime Minister Robert Mugabe of Zimbabwe; Mother Teresa; all the heads of European universities; Irish presidents and taoisigh.

Weeks before the papal visit in 1979, students were entertained by four helicopters landing and taking off on the pitches at the back of St Mary's. These were used to fly the pope and his entourage from Dublin to Maynooth and then on to Limerick. It was estimated that up to 50,000 people would attend the papal visit to Maynooth, but in fact, this number doubled on the morning itself. One of the reasons the pope was coming to Maynooth was to bless the foundation stone of the John Paul II Library.

On the morning of 1 October 1979 a thick blanket of fog hung over the entire area. It was not a widely known fact, but on the morning of the pope's arrival word had come from the papal nunciature that, owing to dense fog, the pilots would not be able to land and would instead fly on to Limerick. You can imagine the disappointment! Luckily the fog lifted sufficiently to allow the pope's helicopter to land while the remaining helicopters flew on to Limerick. His visit, although brief, was a truly memorable occasion and a personal highlight for me.

Following discussions with the then President, Msgr Tomas Ó Fiaich, we pursued the idea of the college becoming a venue for conventions and conferences, mostly of an ecclesiastical nature. The intention was to use this revenue stream to upgrade the rooms of the clerical students.

Catering Staff and David Carbery with HRH King Carl XVI Gustaf of Sweden, April 1992

Together with the late Liam Green, Maureen Dermody and I developed this idea as far as was possible at that time. Today that modest idea has grown into a substantial business under the skilful and poetic direction of Bill Tinley and his very capable staff.

Pugin Hall has now been beautifully restored with the oak tables brought back to their original state. Accommodation has been brought up to an acceptable standard and, with the suites in Stoyte House now at 5-star level, it leaves Maynooth suitably placed to attract prestigious conferences.

The college boasts beautiful heritage buildings, lovely walks and, of course, the rock garden, where the late Msgr Paddy Corish meticulously cultivated and transplanted the rare plants with such personal attention and skill. Now, in his absence, the seeds he lovingly sowed burst into bloom every year.

Before my retirement in 2002, we were providing 6,500 meals every day between the North and South Campus from six different outlets. Apart from Trinity College, we were the only 'in-house' catering unit in the university group. All others were franchised out.

None of this could have been achieved without the great commitment and dedication of the staff in my department.

Catering School students and staff, 1968.
Author standing extreme right at the end of the second row.

Many changes have taken place in Maynooth over the years, but it will always have a special place in my heart, especially knowing that my two daughters, Pauline and Orlagh, both graduated there, as did my son-in-law Paddy McGovern.

Pauline went on to set up the medical centre in the North Campus. Her nursing skills were also practised in St Patrick's College Infirmary where the students honoured her memory by including her in their 2017 class-piece. Sadly, we lost Pauline to cancer in October 2016. She would be so proud knowing that today her eldest son Evin is now studying law and business in her old alma mater, a place that she, like myself, loved and treasured so much.

Nowadays, no matter where I go in Ireland, chances are I will have crossed paths at some stage with the local bishop, parish priest, hotelier or maître d'hôtel – sure what more influence would a man want when away from home!

AN CHÉAD OLLAMH TUATA (1975)

Anthony G. O'Farrell

ome time ago I was invited by a former MSc student to attend his ordination to the priesthood. At one point in the ceremony, my man knelt before his seated bishop, and extended his arms with his palms pressed together, as you do when you pray. His lordship took the extended hands, and pressed his own palms around them, and then, looking into the young man's eyes he said: 'Do *you* promise to obey *me*?' My man responded as he was expected to, and the ceremony continued. I assume that this remarkable passage was not just a whim of this particular prelate, but a standard and ancient component of the ritual, mirroring the fealty to his lord required of every vassal in feudal times. Perhaps the promise has even more ancient provenance, dating back, like other elements of the Church's administration, to the practices of imperial Rome. A consequence is that a diocesan priest is as firmly bound to obey the instructions of his bishop as is a member of a religious order to obey his abbot. Therefore, if a senior cleric wants some priest to take up some job, then he *may* ask the priest, but he *must* ask his bishop or abbot. This creates a certain mindset in the hierarchy, a mindset having much in common with that of senior military officers.

I did not understand this in the spring of 1975, and so I met with some surprises as I acclimatised to Maynooth.

I was the first layman ever appointed to a chair at Maynooth. My appointment as Professor of Mathematics was approved at the June 1975 meeting of the trustees of St Patrick's College. The tradition in mathematics at Maynooth goes back to the very beginning, because at that time formation in mathematics and natural philosophy, as well as mental and moral philosophy, was regarded as essential in the preparation of candidates for the priesthood. Would that it were so today! The development of the 'two cultures', lamented by C. P. Snow, has brought us to the point where 'cultured' people are no longer ashamed to admit an inability to understand elementary mathematics or an ignorance of modern science.

The result has been that some people are deemed suitable for appointment to positions of influence who are poorly equipped to execute their duties. As someone who cares about the Church, I take comfort in the fact that the bench of bishops still includes a leavening of men with mathematical training, and I count my contribution to their formation among a few worthwhile achievements from my thirty-seven years in post at Maynooth. As someone who cares about mathematics, I take some satisfaction from the fact that at one point in my tenure over a quarter of the 5,000 (mostly lay) students in college were taking mathematics.

The historian Tomás Ó Fiaich was College President when I came to Maynooth, and had taken the trouble to examine the archives and tidy up the list of professors at the back of the annual *Kalendarium*. Perusing the list, I learned that just eight professors of mathematics spanned the 180 years from the foundation of the college until my appointment. This was encouraging. One could infer that the occupation was reasonably healthy. Mathematics is not the most important thing in life. I care more about love in all its forms, God, family, country, art and life itself. However, given that my main professional aim in life was (as it still remains) to advance and promote mathematics, it seemed likely that I had fallen on my feet.

I was in the US for the six years before my appointment to Maynooth. My peers were people around the world who cared mainly about developments at the moving frontier of known mathematics. Our science has enjoyed a golden age in my time, an age without precedent in the history of humanity. I wanted to come home and share my expertise and passion with my countrymen. I was coming, no matter what, and I refused all offers in America before coming for interview at Maynooth. (Decisions are made earlier in the academic year over there.) If all else failed, I was sure of a post-doctoral research position that would put food on the table until something better turned up.

I believe there was some reluctance to advertise the chair of mathematics. Maynooth had a couple of new departments (biology and geography) headed by laymen at the rank of Senior Lecturer, but up to that point professor meant priest, except for the fact that the Professor of Education, Séamas Ó Súilleabháin, was a Christian Brother. Indeed, for years afterwards, Maynooth's villagers used the two words as synonyms, so that priests holding the rank of lecturer were addressed as Professor, and academics who did not own a clerical collar were described as lecturers. There were other chairs in play at the time, but they were likely to be filled by clerics, and the headship of another new department (German) was advertised at Senior Lecturer level.

The appointment process looked quite normal to me, similar to the kind of thing I had experienced before. I was in California, working at UCLA. Kindly supporters (Trevor West, Dick Timoney, family) let me know about the public advertisement of the post and encouraged me to apply. In Timoney's case, he made it clear that I had no chance of appointment, but he said that if I were shortlisted it would put me in a good position for the next NUI statutory lectureship that came up. I sent in an application and was called to interview around Easter, 1975. I put on a suit and tie – the tie was yellow, definitely non-clerical – and I took the number 66 bus out to Maynooth. I was welcomed at the gate by Tom Finan, Professor of Latin and for that year secretary of the academic council, and he took me for tea in St Patrick's and then around for my first look at the place. I was an outsider to this clerical world. I considered joining a contemplative order before I fell in love with Lise Pothin, but was never attracted to the diocesan priesthood. Like any Irish person of my generation, I had some ideas about the importance and influence of Maynooth, and I was aware of some current staff who had national reputations, such as Msgr Ó Fiaich in history, Enda McDonagh in theology, Pádraig Ó Fiannachta in Irish and Gerard Watson in Ancient Classics, not to mention some greats of the past. But I had not been to the college, and its splendid Pugin-designed buildings and delightful setting made a favourable impression. I decided it would do, in the unlikely event that they chose me. (I should explain that the smart money was on other, more senior, candidates, and that, as far I as I was concerned, I was already very happy to have won a free trip home.)

The college had wrestled a bit about the best way to compose assessment boards for chairs, which would make a recommendation to faculties, councils and, eventually, trustees. They decided to have the College President, the Professors of Mathematical Physics and Experimental Physics, and two external assessors, John Lewis and David Simms. They also had a non-voting chairman, a truly silly idea that was abandoned not long afterwards. This was A. J. McConnell, then provost of Trinity College, Dublin, a very distinguished expert on relativity. I have to say that Dr McConnell's genial conduct of the business made it thoroughly enjoyable. He was impressed by the fact that I had burned my boats. The President made sure I spoke Irish. For the rest I took Trevor West's advice – he was a great all-round coach – to relax and have a conversation about my chosen profession.

I gave a colloquium in UCD the following day. David Simms took me aside and let me know (absolutely off the record) that they had recommended me for the job. I was beyond astonishment but decided not to count my chickens as yet. I went back to work at UCLA, and waited for the letter from Maynooth, good or bad. What's on paper is what counts.

The official word came in the most extraordinary way. In the second week of June, still in Los Angeles, I got a telegram from my mother that said:

CONGRATULATIONS, PROFESSOR!

I telephoned her, and she told me that my appointment to the chair had been reported in the *Irish Independent*. She read me the article. The headline was:

Bishops Act on Unmarried Mothers

There followed an article reporting on the outcome of the bishops' June meeting at Maynooth, mainly concerned with the setting up of what is now known as CURA, an agency that helps women who are in so-called crisis pregnancies. Then, in the last paragraph, it said that 'Anthony O'Farrell, a Dublin man, has been appointed to the chair of Mathematics'.

I rang the president, and Msgr Ó Fiaich (who understood perfectly well that this way of announcing the appointment was out of line with current academic norms) apologised, told me his own telegram was on its way, and explained that the bishops' spokesman had briefed the press as he saw fit, making a selection of matters to mention without regard to whether they arose in the meeting of the conference of the hierarchy (all the bishops, dealing with Church affairs) or the meeting of the trustees of St Patrick's College (seventeen of the bishops voting, with the rest possibly looking on). I assume that this spokesman assumed that since I was 'a Dublin man', and the Archbishop of Dublin had approved my appointment, my acceptance of it was not in question.

This little comedy was not the first hiccup in the evolution of the college from its traditional pre-conciliar state as the National Seminary to its modern state as a pair of sister universities, nor was it the last. It has, for the most part, been enjoyable, amusing and rewarding to observe (and occasionally influence) this evolution over the past forty-four years. I have seen eight presidents of SPCM and three of NUIM (now Maynooth University) come and go. All the other professors who sat round the table in Front Stoyte at my first academic council meeting and all the members of my assessment board have gone to join the majority, may they rest in peace. Maynooth endures.

SIGERSON CUP MEMORIES (1976)

Tom McGuire

At a time when 'diversity' is positively promoted as a twenty-first-century value in Irish society, it is probably closer to the truth to say that a diverse society evolves through each generation. In the case of St Patrick's College Maynooth, the years from the mid-1960s through the 1970s were a seminal period.

The admission of lay students to Maynooth College in 1968 was a significant change and heralded a campus with an enhanced culture emanating from the broad and varied interests of a student community that was more diverse than the college had ever experienced.

Over the next decade Maynooth experienced dramatic changes, which were supported and facilitated, for the large part, by both staff and students alike. As lay and clerical students shared lectures and leisure the emergence of a student representative council (later to be the students' union) and a corresponding growth in the number of clubs and societies and their membership led to a much broader cultural canvas on the campus.

In a short few years, the winds of change blew through the Aula Maxima and the goalposts of High Field; no longer did productions of the Drama Society need the imprimatur of the academic council nor were GAA matches confined to annual outings to other seminaries.

It was in 1968 that GAA teams were permitted to participate in external competition (higher education leagues) to be followed in 1972 by the admission of St Patrick's College Maynooth into the Inter-Varsity Championships, the Sigerson Cup in football and the Fitzgibbon Cup in hurling. Here was an opportunity for the fledgling teams to measure themselves against UCD, Trinity College, UCG, UCC and Queen's University, Belfast.

There was an almost immediate impact in hurling when Maynooth defeated UCG to claim the college's first Fitzgibbon title in Galway in 1973 and followed up with a second title in 1974 when victorious over UCD in Ballycastle, County Antrim.

From a football perspective, the prevailing political climate and the atrocity of Bloody Sunday in Derry in 1972 had echoes in Maynooth's debut in the

Sigerson Cup. The team that lost to UCC in the quarter final in Clonmel had, four days earlier, taken part in a mass protest march from Maynooth to Dublin to hand in a petition of protest on the deaths in Derry.

Inspired by their hurling colleagues, the footballers made it to the 1973 Sigerson Final only to be defeated by UCD, and went out of the competition in 1974 and 1975 to the same opposition. As newcomers to university competition the GAA clubs in Maynooth became quickly immersed in the new family and embraced the opportunity with great enthusiasm and foresight. This was probably best illustrated in 1974 when, as hosts of the Sigerson Cup competition, Maynooth hosted a weekend seminar on the future of football. The brainchild of team manager Malachy O'Rourke, it was welcomed as a significant initiative across the GAA family.

The development and success of the GAA in the college was built on the commitment of the student body and the strong support of staff members, particularly Malachy O'Rourke, Liam Ryan, Gerard Meagher, Cathal Ó Háinle and the College President, Tomás Ó Fiaich. The infrastructure at the time was quite limited, with all major home matches played at Maynooth GAA grounds. As with all voluntary organisations, fund raising was critical, alongside financial support from the recently arrived capitation grant and a limited amount of sponsorship.

As the 1975/76 academic year settled down, conversations about the upcoming football season had an optimistic tone among the GAA fraternity. Malachy O'Rourke had returned from a sabbatical to take over the reins of the senior football team and, alongside him, trainer Pat O'Brien (Tuam) had returned to studies in Maynooth equipped with new training techniques acquired while studying at Strawberry Hill College in London. From an administrative point of view, Pat McHugh (Clogher) took over as chairman of the Cumann Peile with the late Sean Hegarty (Armagh) as secretary and the author as treasurer. The group of players had in previous years unsuccessfully contested one Sigerson final and two league finals, and while some significant players had departed the college there had also been some good additions to the squad. Despite the optimism, the season got off to a slow start when Maynooth lost the first two games of the league campaign, but after Halloween things improved in the league and sights became fixed on the upcoming Sigerson Cup weekend in February 1976.

The growth in the student population and the strong performance of the Maynooth Intermediate team in the second-tier league were all reflected in the panel selected by Malachy O'Rourke, team captain Dan O'Mahony (Achonry) and Pat O'Brien for Sigerson '76.

Maynooth Sigerson Cup Winners, 1976

That panel was: Dan O'Mahony (Achonry) Captain, Jack Fitzgerald (Kerry), Larry Kelly (Kerry), Tony O'Keeffe (Kerry), Tom Barden (Ardagh and Clonmacnois), Mick McElvanney (Ardagh and Clonmacnois), Francis Henry (Achonry), Paddy Henry (Sligo), Eamonn Whelan (Laois), Martin Nugent (Offaly), Donie Brennan (Sligo), Seán McKeon (Louth), Peter Burke (Ardagh and Clonmacnois), John McParland (Down), Pat Donnellan (Tuam), Liam Kelly (Kilmore), Pat Ryan (Kildare), Frankie Murray (Ardagh & Clonmacnois), Stephen O'Mahony (Achonry), Padraig Leydon (Leitrim), John Clarke (Meath), Michael Marren (Achonry), Sean Hegarty (Armagh) RIP, Paddy McGovern (Kilmore) and Liam Whyte (Clonfert) RIP.

The Sigerson Cup competition in the 1970s was traditionally completed over one weekend in February. The 1976 competition was to be hosted by Trinity College and was to welcome NUU (New University of Ulster, Coleraine) as the newest university in the competition. The Maynooth preparation was multi-faceted: daily training, coaching and preparation on the campus were punctuated by a series of challenge matches, including a number against the Garda at their grounds in the Phoenix Park. In tandem with this, there was a weekend training camp on the beach at Lusk in north County Dublin, even though on the first morning the squad arrived to find the tide was in! Training activity reverted to the grass. One other series of sessions the team captain Dan O'Mahony wryly remembers was exercising to music in Loftus Hall, decades before the world discovered Spotify, aerobics or bluetooth!

The Sigerson Competition was fixed for the last weekend of February 1976, the weekend of a mid-term break in Maynooth, which had a decidedly adverse affect on support for the Black & Amber. The TCD sports campus at Santry hosted the quarter-finals. Maynooth made everyone else sit up and take notice when a contribution of 1–6 from Peter Burke set up the platform for an impressive ten-point victory over UCG. On Saturday, the venue moved to Croke Park for Maynooth and a semi-final date with hosts, Trinity. The large squad paid dividends here, with only four of the team who started against Galway lining out against TCD. Even though reinforcements were called for in the second half, Maynooth, with 1–3 from Pat Donnellan, had eight points to spare at the final whistle.

Awaiting Maynooth in the final in Croke Park on leap day, 29 February, was our old nemesis, UCD. On a wet and windy day, the skill, hunger and determination of Maynooth accounted for a star-studded Dublin squad. Goals from Martin Nugent and John McParland crucially contributed to a 2–5 to 0–09 score line. A celebratory banquet in Malahide was one to remember for everyone involved and, in his rooms, Liam Ryan hosted a welcome party for the Sigerson Cup on its first night in Kildare.

This remains the solitary Sigerson success for Maynooth. There have been reunions, remembering and recollections, but as the fiftieth anniversary approaches, it would be great to see the great old trophy return to Kildare before the golden jubilee.

MEMORIES OF MAYNOOTH (1974)

Agnes Neligan

Russell Library

he college was deserted, the library was locked when I arrived for work on the first day of my thirty-four year career at Maynooth. New Year's Day 1974 was declared a public holiday in Ireland for the first time. Nevertheless, I was told to report for work as normal. Walking through the campus I eventually met a very grumpy gentleman who directed me to the gate lodge for a key. It was also closed. I was sitting on the cold stone steps to the library pondering my options when, finally, a member of staff with a key arrived.

The interior of the library, now the Russell Library, was dark, gloomy and piercingly cold. A storage heater in the office provided the only heating, and to keep hypothermia at bay throughout the day we took turns sitting on it while opening parcels of books that had arrived over the holidays. A cold-water sink and a kettle provided us with hot drinks; there were no other facilities. The following days saw the college come to life as people gradually returned to work and heating and catering resumed, though the lack of these services over holiday periods would long remain an issue for those of us who had to work. Mice were a real problem, especially in our office. Happily, the Professor of Chemistry, Fr Michael Casey OP, kindly offered to help us. He had his own recipe for killing them, and one day arrived with several open boxes containing the concoction, while cheerfully announcing that there was enough there to kill twenty people!

The library was then operating in a state of limbo as the former librarian, Fr Sean Corkery, had retired and his replacement was not due to arrive until March. In view of the many changes taking place in the college at that time it was understood there was an urgent need to develop the library and a report on the future of the service had been commissioned. Unfortunately this had not been delivered. Everything was on hold. The new deputy librarian, Mary Connolly, duly arrived and the librarian of the University of York, Harry Fairhurst, was invited to examine the level of library service and make recommendations for future development. He visited the library between October and December 1974 and presented his report in February of 1975.

The report looked at bookstock, catalogue records, finance, staff, services and accommodation. While his comments did not present an exaggerated picture, as he himself noted, and his recommendations were not extravagant, the report was not received with universal approval. Perhaps the comparison made with the newly established University of York and that of an old residential institution was not always entirely appropriate.

Traditionally access to the main library, now the Russell Library, was restricted to members of staff. With the advent of lay students, it was now opened to all. Several branch libraries existed for students, St Mary's Library for seminarians, Junior Library for undergraduates and a textbook library for HDipEd students. Books were also stored in numerous vacant rooms throughout the college. Fairhurst estimated a total collection of 100,000 volumes. He commented on the grime and widespread 'psocid' infestation and the chilly climate, though this was probably better for the books than for the people who studied and worked in the building. Apart from the scattered locations, finding books was another problem as there was basically only an author catalogue. The classification system did not help either. An additional problem was the arrangement of books in the main library, which were shelved numerically from the bottom shelf upwards. A major task was the reshelving of the entire library.

The report noted that the 1974 budget for the purchase of books and periodicals was £15,000. There was no budget for other items such as normal office supplies, and obtaining funds for even basic items was often a challenge. The library managed the funds and had its own cheque book. The cheques were signed by the bursar and countersigned by an authorised member of staff. To save time, the bursar signed a number of blank cheques at a time. The number signed varied as did the bills in need of payment, necessitating regular visits to his room, ordeals not to be undertaken lightly.

Fairhurst recorded that at the time of his visit there were seven library staff. He noted the absence of any proper conditions of service and poor salaries. My own monthly salary was £183.33 with a take-home pay of £140.14. Working conditions were basic and, as the library was open seven days, working hours included Saturday and Sunday, usually alone. There was no security present during opening hours and many people had keys to access the building when closed. This could lead to unexpected and scary events as when one winter's evening after closing time I went out to investigate a noise when a figure dressed in vestments carrying a candle emerged from the darkness; it was not a spectre but a recently appointed bishop who still had his own key. On a recent visit to Maynooth during the summer vacation I found it in virtual lockdown and felt great nostalgia for those far-off more innocent times.

Borrowing was restricted to staff and postgraduates. They simply signed a register on loan and return so it was not possible to know what was borrowed. There was some discussion on extending this service to all students, but Harry Fairhurst was surprised at the hostility aroused by this proposal.

Study places were cramped, uncomfortable and badly lit. High shelves needing ladders were potentially dangerous. Stairs were narrow and hazardous and there were no fire precautions. He did note that all these issues were appreciated by the college. He raised concerns about the proposal for a separate undergraduate library and strongly advocated the need for a unitary library. He recommended that alternative use be found for the space allocated for a library in the new Arts Building on the North Campus. His plans for an extension to the existing building were never seriously considered, though in view of the financial circumstances at the time this was probably the best he could suggest.

An interesting historical note was his recommendation on the need to invest

Details of the Frieze – Russell Library

in new technology such as microfilm, and audio-visual materials such as disc, cassette tape, open-spool tape, slides, linked-tape slides, film strip and film loop, videotape and video cassette, most of which formats are now confined to history. Computers were not mentioned.

The report was largely ignored, and the deputy librarian departed after two years, leaving another interregnum until a librarian was appointed in 1980. Nevertheless, in the coming years most of his recommendations came to pass, being based on current practice and a genuine need for a better service. Less than ten years later a new library was built which would have been inconceivable in 1974.

Others will write about those early days of change at Maynooth. Mostly 1974 was a challenging year. Many were welcoming and positively disposed. Others not so much. My lowest moment was being told my position was that of a library servant and I should know my place. Nevertheless, we were full of hope and enthusiasm for the future, though with little idea of the many changes and exciting developments that were in store.

REMEMBERING
WHAT I'VE FORGOTTEN (1976)

Evelyn Conlon

In October 1976, I arrived in Maynooth with a five-month-old baby to study for a BA. I had previously attended UCD, straight from St Louis in Monaghan, but clearly that hadn't worked out; my hair-raisingly naive expectation that I would be in Newman's *Idea of A University* had died a quick death, choked on the smell of drying concrete at Belfield. But this time I was prepared. After sadly consigning Newman to the shadows, I had gone to Australia by boat, travelled around it by van and returned to Ireland by bus across Asia and the USSR, so I knew some things. I was ready and, what was even better, I was interested in the subjects I had chosen.

Autobiography is an untidily inadequate word for covering the telling of 'what happened'. What does that mean? Is feeling and thinking also 'happening'? How can I tell what happened in Maynooth? My time there is divided into many pieces, most of them furiously contradicting each other. There was the learning – the lectures, the library, the essays, the overheard conversations, but mostly, for me, there was the new strange world I'd found myself in, that of being a mother. If I'm still shocked by it – and I sometimes am – I was stunned then. After delivery – a word clearly devised to suggest a stork-like simplicity not associated with what has just taken place – I thought that there should be schools of philosophy attached to all maternity wards to allow us some chance of getting language to understand existence. If ever I got to university, I'd study that.

I had come back to Ireland with the intention of returning to education. The idea of having children while doing so would have been a laughable notion. But there I was, registering for a BA, adjusting my blinkers every which way, determined to plough on. In preparation for my first day I had found a mother working at home in Maynooth who would mind my child while I was at lectures. After a week I questioned the viability of what now seemed like a crazy undertaking. But I was foolhardy enough to see a chink of light. It seemed to me that having a crèche on site would be the very best solution. Thus began the effort. I had meetings and wrote letters. A few other women were initially enthusiastic, but had to absent themselves as obstacles mounted and they became worried that the arrangements they had already made could not be rescued if the crèche didn't work out. On the times that I agreed with their fears, I withdrew into the street of dreaming, always a good place to live. I arrived on day one of the crèche's life with a brazen hopefulness. In a short time others did join, one by one, until the edifice was grounded.

And so, with the working arrangement behind me I settled into a routine: drive from Santry, settle the baby with a cheerful Martha, go to lectures, return after the end of the twelve o'clock to feed the baby, take him for a short spin out towards Kilcock if he was having difficulty rolling into his siesta, put him contentedly to sleep for his afternoon nap, run to the canteen and gulp the last of the food, the smell of which had been making me ache. My hunger satisfied, I returned to the halls of learning, where I became like any other student undertaking the study of English, history, sociology and philosophy. I'm afraid the latter turned out to be wrong time, wrong place, having as little relevance to me at that precise moment as Newman had to Belfield.

Over the three years many things happened in my life. I sometimes feel that if I say them quickly, and leave out the domino effects, it will put an acceptable order on them, one that won't exhaust me thinking about them. So, with as much speed as I can, I had another baby in second year, and separated from my husband in third year. I brought the new baby to the crèche and now settled two of them before running to the canteen. I got my essays in on the last required day. I didn't have time to imagine how my life was being spoken about but no doubt it was. Living outside communal standards causes whispers and you have to learn to withstand the gale of them. I was indeed unintentionally existing on the margin, openly, because, unlike others, I couldn't hide. When I turned up for second year with an actual visible pregnancy one lecturer called me into his room. He had a mean-spirited point to make and said, in a certain voice, that he presumed I would now be giving up. His injunction was a gauntlet. In mitigation, I say that men like him, protected from the real world, had a lot to put up with when I arrived in their corridors, certainly more than I had intended. And yes, some opprobrious words came my way, but I prefer to remember the acts of kindness. They were more surprising because I had never expected them.

In writing about my years at Maynooth I contemplated not referring to these personal circumstances, until I realised they were such an overwhelming backdrop it would be flippantly dishonest of me not to do so. But my memory can rise above the daily minute-to-minute organisation, the split personas, and dwell on the studies. With a bow to the artist Joe Brainard's searing short-sentence memoir *I Remember:*

I remember my history lectures, how Mary Cullen, Jacqueline Hill and Vincent Comerford created a vivid past, transposed me to times gone, teaching me things I didn't know and making me curious about what was between the lines.

I remember that in English classes I finally learned about George Eliot and how to enjoy Shakespeare. I learned how to protect the apprentice writer in myself when it clashed with the canon. When the sixteenth-century Tudor lyric got too ludicrous for me I dipped into Marilyn French's *The Women's Room*, the book written directly to me it seemed. They made tantalising opposites.

I remember how one day my heart was entirely on Thomas Hardy's side and I begged him for once, just once, not to make the bad things happen.

I remember listening to John Montague read.

I remember that sociology knocked me off my socks. Mícheál MacGréil suggested we go to court one day as practical experience for his deviance and control module. That day changed my view of the world. Although anthropology and functionalism and anomie come into my head sometimes, it is Courtroom Number 6 that takes front of house always.

I remember that I longed for something in philosophy classes … I still do. Ah, I wish …

I remember chewing barley sugar sweets to relieve the morning sickness during First Arts examinations. And Nora Leneghan coming from Dublin to have my lunch on the table when I came out, so I wouldn't get even sicker.

I remember, towards the end of my pregnancy, Pascal Smyth and his flatmates giving me the key to their house so I could grab the occasional fifteen-minute sleep.

I remember that I also had a life outside all of this.

I remember that I occasionally envied some people, not in that I wanted to be them but more in a 'gosh I wonder what's that like' way.

I remember that the old block of the university was close enough to Newman. I remember the priests from there, some of whom were toying with their vocations, one in particular who was driving many women mad.

I remember that I didn't have the money to go to the graduation ball, but it would have been no place for me anyway.

I remember that a message was relayed to me that if I had a problem with my HDip fees something could be sorted.

What happened in Maynooth is that I learned how to learn, got a grounding in how to refit with Ireland and, astonishingly, got a degree, for which I will always be grateful.

MINDING THE HOUSE
– AND THE FARM

Denis Bergin

Group of Farm Workers (early 1900s)

The story of Maynooth College tends to be told mainly in terms of its academic development, the life of its staff and students within the walls, and its iconic status, however misperceived, as a power-centre of the Irish Church.

However, from its beginnings, the funding of a project described by one of its begetters as 'a new scene … and important in its consequence' was so rapid that the management of its finances was a critical issue. Accounting for income and expenses (including a grant-in-aid from the British government), covering building costs, supervising the administration of college burses and financial aid to students, meeting the demands for housing and sustenance for its hundreds of inhabitants, were all constant and major concerns of the trustees.

Over the 225 years of the college's existence, the weighty responsibilities for these matters have been laid on the shoulders of just fourteen bursars, a dozen of them clerics, and the most recent two a layman and (at time of writing) a laywoman.

Almost from the beginning, when the college received sixty acres as part of the purchase of the Stoyte and Riverstown Lodge properties, there has been an emphasis on acquiring farmland – by 1837 the tract known as 'Collegelands' had grown to 136 acres.

Within a decade of the college's founding, however, it was the beneficiary of the controversial bequest of over 400 acres by Lord Dunboyne, the apostate Bishop of Cork, whose sensational deathbed reconciliation in 1800 resulted in an equally sensational court case regarding the validity of his will. The issue was eventually resolved almost a decade later by a compromise whereby the lands were divided with his family, providing the college with an income of £400 a year from lettings to tenants that continued until the lands were sold in 1933.

The Maynooth College Act of 1845 increased the annual government grant from £9,000 to £26,000 a year, and added £30,000 for new buildings. This allowed the trustees to take 115 acres leasehold and 218 acres as tenants at will from the Duke of Leinster, properties that became known as Laraghbryan West and Laraghbryan East. In fact, the college would be evicted from the latter in 1878 when no acceptable agreement could be reached with the Duke for a continuation (the college eventually resumed its tenancy and bought out the duke's interest in 1918).

In 1903 and 1904 the college bought out its leasehold interest in the lands surrounding the main campus, as well as an additional 100 acres it had acquired at Newtown across the canal, and also invested in an outfarm of almost 500 acres west of Kilcock in the townland of Killick, whose leasehold it bought out in 1933. Between 1935 and 1938 the old farmyard at the rear of the gate lodge was replaced by a new complex off the Kilcock Road, at a cost of over £17,000, with fitting out costing a further £8,000 (the equivalent of about €185,000 at today's prices).

In 1943, the college bought out the leasehold of the Laraghbryan West property and exchanged its Newtown holding for the Chamberlain property at Crew Hill, thereby creating the vast expanse of countryside that would become

Raking the grass on Desert Pitch at the back of Logic House (1940s)

home a quarter of a century on to the first student residences and eventually the entire North Campus. The Killick farm was sold in the early 1980s to help fund the John Paul II Library.

At the height of its landowning existence, therefore, the college had over one thousand acres under its control, almost as much as the Duke of Leinster had in his Carton estate at the other end of the town.

Meanwhile the demands of a rapidly expanding building complex, and the peaking of enrolment in the seminary at 500-plus in the late 1950s, created additional demands on the bursar and his small staff. The first moves in the modernisation of the college administration had begun with the employment of male clerks in the Bursar's Office, located in Riverstown Lodge. The opening up of the college to students from religious orders, and then to lay students studying for the HDipEd, added a new dimension to the administrative burden. By the early 1970s the role of women in administration had been recognised, alongside their growing presence as students on campus, and the first permanent appointments as clerks and personal secretaries often came from among those already part of the college 'family'.

In all of these transactions, there was a human element that has not been well chronicled. The only contact of students with the Bursar's Office was at the annual presentation of bills, when students learned of the subsidy being paid by their bishops and the balance falling to them to settle.

The farm employed more than half a dozen permanent workers under a series of farm managers, though their only contact with the college students may have been confined to their supervision of annual potato-picking expeditions, for which the participating students were rewarded with a slap-up meal in the college refectory.

The college's catering operations were overseen for many years by members of the Daughters of Charity, who also ran the Senior Infirmary or 'List', taken over by the order in 1905.

Staffed by young men who were known informally as 'the Saucepans', the dining rooms gradually yielded to lay management, including a spell involving personnel and trainees from the Council for Education Recruitment and Training for the Hotel and Catering Industry (CERT), as detailed in the article by David Carbery elsewhere in this volume.

Housekeeping for the academic and senior administrative staff was also the responsibility of these young men, with special responsibilities devolving to their supervisors and to senior staff members, including those who served as principal butler in the Professors' Dining Room, valet/chauffeur to the president (up to 1968) and the steward responsible for miscellaneous administrative logistics that included the overseeing of postal collections and deliveries, involving at its height the collecting and sorting of over a thousand inbound and outbound pieces of mail a day. Eventually the housekeeping duties would be transferred to a professional staff, and the catering services outsourced.

Engineering and maintenance operations, including the smooth running of the boiler house and the planting and ordering of the extensive grounds, also had a permanent staff.

The stories of these areas of engagement, most of them now only a faint memory for the students who encountered them briefly in passing, remain largely to be told. But for the employees involved, there is a sense that their service of the National Seminary and its staff and students was more a calling than a duty. That service over so many centuries should be remembered as we undertake the commemoration of significant anniversaries.

ere we present the stories, as told by themselves, of a father and daughter who were part of the story of what might be called Maynooth's hidden infrastructure: Aidan Ryan managed the college farm for a quarter of a century, from just before Ireland's entry into the Common Market until his retirement in 1992; and his daughter Noeleen, an early female employee in the Bursar's Office, continues to serve the institution after forty years of service, over half of them on the staff of Maynooth University, where she manages the Fees and Grants Office at time of writing.

ON THE FARM

Aidan Ryan

Aidan Ryan spent over twenty-five years as manager of the college farm, retiring in 1992. Here he remembers the background to his appointment, and some of the happy memories of his time in the employment of the college, under the supervision of the bursar.

I was born in 1935 in Coolgarrow, Castledockrell, near Bunclody, into a farming family. There were six of us. My father died when I was five and my mother died when I was seven. We were all reared by uncles and aunts and most of them had good arable farms. They were very progressive and even down to this day you can see their farms out on the Enniscorthy road. I went to school in Marshalstown – that was the parish. I left school after the Primary (Certificate) like everyone else at the time and worked on my uncle's farm until I got married. It was about sixty or seventy acres. Some of us went to the tech (technical or vocational school) at night to study engineering. I got very little out of the family farm in the end; when I was eighteen, I went to look for my share and was told that there was only £80 left for me. But we were lucky in that we weren't forced to go into an orphanage and that we were well looked after by our uncles and aunts.

I got married in 1959 to Joan Jordan, a woman I met at a dance in Monageer. We didn't know what we were going to do but I heard about a farming job in a place in Donabate (County Dublin) and I applied for it and got it. The man who owned the farm used to come down to Wexford to hunt, and that is how I came to meet him. There were three or four working there, and we had a house with the job, which was common at the time for farm workers. The farm was about 100 acres. I stayed there until I got a better job in Celbridge from a man with a business in Dublin – he was a Mr Ruttle and he owned a company that was in the confectionery business. He was a gentleman farmer, again with about 100 acres. He knew nothing about farming – wouldn't know the land from the road – but he gave me my head. By this time, we had a daughter Noeleen and we actually lived in the big house itself. I was working on my own there with just a part-time man to help me.

We spent six or seven years there and one day a job came on the paper for a farm manager in St Patrick's College Maynooth and I applied for it. I was invited over by a clergyman and we chatted for a bit and all he said was 'When are you going to start?' I don't know how many others applied for it (I heard there were a few) but anyway I got it. The clergyman was Fr Jim Cosgrove, a man that wasn't popular because he had a no-nonsense way about him, but I always got on with him.

We got a lovely house in the farmyard, which was up a lane on the college side of the Kilcock Road. There was some land there, and a lot more on the other side of the road, in total about 300 acres. The college land joined Timard Lane, which had a small community of its own, not connected to the college farm – maybe three houses on smaller farms that were given to people resettled from County Mayo. Bernard Durkan, the TD, came out of one of these houses. Then the college had another farm of about 600 acres nearer Kilcock in a place called Killick.

I always met Fr Cosgrove out of doors, usually up Timard Lane, to discuss any business we had. We would lean over a gate and chat about anything and everything. We became very friendly and he confided in me a lot. Yet I don't think I ever met him socially or ever attended his Mass.

He had his own social life. He was very friendly with the O'Reilly family who had a few businesses in the town. A woman from his own part of the country came to the Maynooth area as a poultry instructress and married one of the O'Reillys. I think Fr Cosgrove had a hand in that match, and he was always very friendly with them afterwards.

He always made it clear that I was the boss as far as the farm was concerned, and that what I said goes. The first morning I met him, he said 'Where's your [neck)] tie?' I didn't have it on me, but he said, 'Never come out into the yard without a tie.' And I've always worn a tie down to this day, even after I retired.

There were about eleven people working on the farm at the time I took over. It was a big change from Celbridge, and for a while I didn't know where I landed. The college farm was mainly in dairying and the larger outfarm in Killick (nearer Kilcock) was for dry cattle and sheep. There were houses for workers on both farms. Mick Lawless, a dairy man, had the house next to ours. Bill Donovan lived in the town of Maynooth. He was in the fire brigade, so when there was a fire they would ring our house and my wife would go out to get Bill and off he would go on his bike to the fire station. There was a little lodge house and three single men lived there – Sean Buckley, Paddy Mullen and Paddy Delaney. Seamus Carty lived there as well, and is still living there after all those years. Mick Purcell from Kilkenny lived on the outfarm to look after the dry stock.

When I took over, we had about forty or fifty cows milking, mainly supplying milk to the college. I changed all that and built a milking parlour and by the time we were finished the herd had grown bit by bit until we had 160 cows, with two men and a relief working full time in the milking parlour. Now we had more milk than the college needed and so we sold the rest to Dublin Dairies.

We used the old-style churns at the beginning, putting them out on a stand by the road for collection and then of course the bulk cooling tanks came in and the refrigerated trucks would come in at all hours of the day or night and collect the milk. It became a kind of a bargaining thing, and we would sell the milk to the place that paid most.

For a while we had a big operation supplying vegetables and eggs to the college. We grew vegetables in an acre near the orchard and potatoes on the home farm, and Fr Cosgrove would arrange for the students to come down and pick the potatoes. They got a special meal in the college in the evening in return for their labours.

Otherwise we didn't have many dealings with the college, and in all my years there I don't think I knew who the president was or ever met him. I went up to the bursar's office every Thursday to get the men's wages. During the harvesting time meals were sent out to the fields for the four or five extra men working for contractors, ploughing or cutting hay or making silage. Sister Anne was in charge of the kitchen and I got on well with her; she had a great way about her.

I do remember being at an ordination one year and there were eighty-two being ordained. The farm employees were also required to go down to the religious ceremonies in the College Chapel on Good Friday, but we had to make up the few hours later on in the day.

As time went on we expanded some operations and closed down others. We had a man called Paddy Brady working full time butchering cattle for the college, maybe killing three or four beasts a week, but eventually we got out of that, and out of potatoes and eggs, because it was cheaper to buy them in.

We had four tractors, and I had a jeep for travelling around the land. Fr Cosgrove would always be aware of the transport situation, and would say 'that old wagon is getting a bit shook' and give me an envelope with cash or a cheque to get a better one, sometimes one he had marked out himself at O'Reilly's garage.

Of course I was well known in local farming circles as the man from the college, and when I went to Doyle's Mart, which is where Tesco is now, they all knew that I had a few bob and they bid up anything I was interested in. However, it worked to my advantage in other areas, because I was buying ten tons of feed or fertiliser where another man would be buying one. I dealt with Farringtons out in Rathcoffey but sometimes Quinns of Baltinglass, Wicklow, would come in with a better price and I would deal with them.

When the new road was being built from Maynooth to Kilcock, I suggested to Kildare County Council that there should be a tunnel put in under the road to prevent the cows crossing on a main road. After a lot of discussion, a tunnel was built, the first of its type in Ireland at the time.

We also introduced Simmental cattle into Ireland. A man named Murphy from Cork was bringing them into Ireland from Austria and we bought twelve. We did up a special house for them and there was great interest in them. We called them 'whiteheads' but they were not a whitehead breed. We had an open day that was supposed to be about Friesians but there was more interest in the Simmental. Fr Cosgrove loved showing cattle and we had entries in the RDS Spring Show and won rosettes for them.[1]

It was very disappointing when the farm at Killick was sold in the early 1980s. I got a few hints about the sale, but we went ahead and sowed the crops anyway. The new owners took possession in June and harvested the crops that we sowed.

Pat Dalton was the bursar by then and didn't interfere in the running of the farm. He just let me get on with it. I ran it the way I wanted, trying to make as much money for the college as I could. I remember one year when we made a profit of £69,000.

In 1979, when the pope came to Maynooth, I was in charge of making everything look well, because they had to come out around the fields for parking and I used to look after the playing fields as well, keeping them mowed. I was supposed to be in charge of the gardens too but the gardener at the time was Bartle Redmond from Ballygarrett in Wexford, and he had helpers (his two daughters Christina and Margaret still work in catering in the college). Bartle and I were good friends, with the Wexford connection.

I can't complain about my life. I had responsibility and I had money to carry it out, but in the end it wasn't my responsibility or my money. I had a bypass in 1990 and I retired in 1992 when I was fifty-eight.

My wife was a great support to me throughout the years, a great woman. One day I bought a copy of the *Enniscorthy Echo* up the town, and when I brought it home my wife saw a house for sale outside Bunclody. And she said, 'I'm going to buy that house'. I said, 'Where are you going to get the money?' She said, 'I'll get it', and she did. And that is how we came to be back living here.

---

1   One of the professors, commenting on the emphasis Fr Cosgrove placed on his farming duties once quipped 'There was a time we had a farm attached to a college, but now we have a college attached to a farm.'

AT THE OFFICE[1]

Noeleen Ryan

Noeleen Ryan came to live on the Maynooth campus at the age of eight, when her father was appointed manager of the college farm and the family moved to the residence provided in the college farmyard. In 1979 she was co-opted to assist with the organisation of the visit to Maynooth College of Pope John Paul II and has remained on the administrative staff of the college since, now serving as manager of the Fees and Grants Office of Maynooth University.

I was born when my parents lived in Donabate, so I'm a Dub. And an only child. Mam was really a bit of a snob so after we moved to Celbridge she planned for me to go to a private school, St Wolstan's in Celbridge, which was a Holy Faith school. It was so exclusive at the time that there were only three in my primary class. But Mam was a very intelligent woman, and she kept pushing me and Dad. She died in 2013 but she had dementia for a few years before that. Her nephew is a doctor down here in Wexford and he looked after her well in her last years.

Dad drove me to Celbridge every day and collected me in the evening. That was agreed between himself and Fr Cosgrove, the bursar. I didn't know much about what was going on in the college, but one year a relative of Dad's from Wexford joined up and found the seminary life very lonely. So he used to come up to the farmyard in his soutane and my mother would give him a cup of tea and a slice of brown bread, and then give him a few 'supplies' for the week and he would go away happy.

Eventually it got to the stage where he would bring two of his friends. They would come down every Saturday night without fail. The door in the wall between the yard and the college grounds was always supposed to be kept locked but Dad would open it for the boys and close it around eleven or twelve after they had left. They would watch *The Late Late Show* with Gay Byrne and Mam would lay out a feed for them. How they got away with it, I don't know,

1   As told to Denis Bergin at Noeleen's home in Bunclody, 12 October 2019. Some small amendments and additions have been made for continuity, clarification and ease of reference for those not familiar with the era or the locales mentioned.

particularly Dad's relative, who was in his first year there, because they would be afraid of their lives of being discovered. He left after a year and in fact he came back later to work in the university on the administrative side.

I had an aunt in Limerick, a sister of my father's, who was matron in Barrington's Hospital. When I finished the Leaving, she said, 'Send that one [me] down here to make her hardy.' She was a typical hospital matron, but she had been raised on a prosperous farm like her siblings and she knew what she was doing. All the Ryans were fascinated by Maynooth and the farm and they used to visit us regularly there.

My aunt arranged for me to stay at the Dominican Hostel and attend Mrs McNamara's Commercial School. Everyone in my class in St Wolstan's did secretarial courses, except for one girl who was picked out to be a doctor, but sadly she died.

Every year during school holidays in the summer I used to go down to the relatives in Wexford for the months of June and July. When I came back up in August 1979, after finishing my secretarial course, Fr Cosgrove asked my father, 'What's that one at?' And when Dad said that I was just after coming back from Wexford, he said, 'Send her down to the office.' I knew the office from going there with Dad the odd time, and I remember thinking that everyone and everything there was very ancient, including Joe Leonard, who worked with these huge leather-bound ledgers.

My first task was to help organise things for the visit to the college of Pope John Paul II. All the local people got a little ID to allow them to see the pope. They were to come into the Aula Maxima, have their photograph taken and the photo put on a little red card that we then laminated.

After the pope came, Joe Leonard was given a special papal medal for his work during the visit and we were all brought up to the Professors' Dining Room and given privileged access, and the President (later Cardinal), Tomás Ó Fiaich, handed over the medal. Joe lived out on the Kilcock Road beside where the new campus is now, in a house by itself. Tom Flood, who was one of the best-known members of the house staff in the college, lived up there too with his family and his daughter Maria is still on the staff, having worked in *The Furrow* office for many years.

Joe Leonard had been the chief clerk in the Bursar's Office for many years. Liam Greene was also there for some time and became assistant bursar with responsibility for all the general operations on the site like catering and cleaning. He was a single man and he used to write pantomimes for the Carmelites in Dublin. He lived in a room in the college, and when he retired, he got an apartment up the town but only lived for a few years. He was buried in the college cemetery.

Pat Dalton was the accountant and he became bursar later. The others that I worked with were Ray Manning and Noel Kenny; Mary Haslam who was the secretary; Mary Butler, who looked after the general office duties, and Breda Keyes, doing the salaries (her nephew is now working in the college as well).

When the excitement of the pope's visit died down, Pat Dalton, the accountant, asked if I would do a shorthand and typing exam and I did and he said, 'You can work with us now for a year'. They wanted someone to deal with fees and the St Joseph's Young Priests' Society (which gave grants to students), and Ray Manning, the clerk there, said, 'You can handle that'. So I did and I was the first person to work in what became the Fees Office.

They had a big NCR machine where you inserted cards and typed in details, and I would then be able to refer to what fees were due and had been paid, deal with the various bishops' offices, and so on. Sometimes a bishop would come into the office and I remember on one occasion I was standing by while Joe Leonard talked to him. When he left Joe said to me, 'You were very disrespectful to that bishop.' And I, being young and brave, said 'Why?' And he said, 'You didn't kiss his ring.'

When I went there first Fr Cosgrove's sleeping accommodation was upstairs to the left and then on the right was his sitting room. On 8 December 1979 he died. He was found dead in the bath. His was the first corpse I ever saw; I remember going up the stairs with Dad at his wake in the room on the right that is the President of Maynooth University's office now. All the clerics were all around him in their lace. And after he died everything in his rooms had to be logged, and I remember sitting up there by myself doing that (Dad got a memento from among his possessions).

Around the 1980s we became more modern and this little square computer arrived and this fellow came with it to teach us how to use it. I was the young girl and I was going to take it on.

I remember going to the Good Friday ceremonies in the College Chapel with Mam and we'd be sitting up at the back with all the students there in front of us. And I remember Eamon Martin, now the Archbishop of Armagh, leading the singing – he was a wonderful singer. And we always had to go to Mass when a working day was a holy day – we sometimes went to the Junior Chapel where our offices are now.

When Joe Leonard retired, Ray Manning became the chief clerk. 30 September was always the end of the financial year for the college. I process the closing off of the fees ledger every year now and it always has to be done by 30 September. That's an old rule that's still observed.

Then, in 1997, everything changed drastically and the office was split. Myself and Joan O'Riordan went with the National University and the other staff went with the Pontifical University. Joan is a very interesting person as well because her mother worked as a housekeeper to some of the professors; her family were from Copper Alley in Moyglare.

Maureen Mooney is a daughter of Bill Donovan, who worked on the farm with Dad, and she was one of the first women to work in the college. She worked with the President's Office and then with the Registrar's Office, and she ended up working in the Records Office to the day that she retired. Maureen always wore the formal suit and the high heels to work. She married Michael Mooney whose father Jim also worked on the farm, and his sister Mary was the telephonist at the college lodge. Michael ended up working with Maureen in the Records Office as well.

Mary Moriarty was the president's secretary and she was also very traditional in her dress. She had studied Irish at the college and remained friendly with her professor, Fr Tomás Ó Fiaich, so when he became president she worked in his office. She was succeeded by Marie Murphy, who still works on the college campus, in the Research and Graduate Studies Office of the University.

Joan O'Riordan and I, and our colleague Ann O'Shea from the Records Office, decided to have a little celebration when we were twenty years in the present offices (in former Junior Chapel) and we got a whole heap of old photographs together. It was a great reunion with the people that we worked with over the years.

We had an interesting time when we lived in Maynooth in the old days, but in a way it was a kind of prison. The house was fabulous and Mam kept it lovely, but it was removed from both the college and the town, behind a wall, and Mam never drove. I remember when we came back down here to Bunclody Dad sat us both down and he said, 'I'm sorry that you were more or less prisoners down on the farm.' Yet I'm still working there – travelling ninety-plus minutes a day from here to there and the same back, though the new motorway has made it a little easier.

REFLECTIONS ON MAYNOOTH COLLEGE IN THE 1970s

C. J. Woods

It was in 1962 that I became aware of the existence of Maynooth College. This was when I was at Cambridge University attending the lectures of Professor Owen Chadwick on nineteenth-century ecclesiastical history. When, later, I was contemplating doing research for a PhD on the Catholic Church in Ireland, my adviser, Edward Norman, who had completed research in the same field for which he had visited Maynooth's library, told me to avoid the place, as it was not for the likes of me, it was strictly for the college's members. In fact, it was then accessible mainly to professors and postgraduate students – all of them clerics.

Since 1910 Maynooth had been peculiarly both the Irish National Seminary for diocesan clergy and, to enable its students to obtain a BA or BSc, a 'recognised' college of the NUI. In the mid 1960s it was about to begin its long transformation from a Catholic seminary to a fully fledged university in which young men aspiring to a clerical career would become a tiny minority. Its peculiar status allowed it to begin admitting what I might call 'ordinary' students. The first such student I knew personally was Mary-Rose O'Brien, who, unhappy in her history course at UCD, transferred to Maynooth about 1970. Transfixed by 'Tom Fee' (as she referred to the Rev. Tomás Ó Fiaich, the Professor of Modern Irish History) she flourished and emerged with a creditable BA (NUI). Nuns had already been admitted in 1967 to do degree courses. Mary-Rose, earnestly pious and outspoken in her opinions, was one of the first 'non-religious' female undergraduates. She was my main source of information on the state of the college and once insisted on taking me to an Easter midnight vigil, my first introduction to the College Chapel. For some reason, in 1973, I was invited by Professor Ó Fiaich to be a tutor in his department and in 1974 an occasional lecturer. These part-time positions I held under his successors, Patrick J. Corish (1975) and R. V. Comerford (1988), until I retired (2006).

In 1973 the buildings of St Patrick's College Maynooth, were entirely on what is now called the South Campus. The site was delineated on the north side by the

St Joseph's Square

Galway Road and on the south side by Parson Street; the only entrance known
to scholars was through the main gate beside the ruined Maynooth Castle.
Stretching to the west was parkland and beyond that, invisibly, as I understood,
was the college farm that supplied the kitchens. An Irish paradox was that the
Protestant parish church was situated then, as now, beside the Catholic college's
entrance and ostensibly within its campus, which I always imagined gave thought
to clerical students.[1] Maynooth village was still just that and was surrounded
by open country stretching westwards to the distant Atlantic. Buses to Dublin
were infrequent, no trains stopped at the railway station (closed since 1963),
and the Main Street offered next to nothing of interest to academics.

The building I got to know well was Rhetoric, where my department, Modern
History, was located and still is. Among historians the word 'modern' is used as
a distinction from 'medieval' and 'ancient'. If I recall correctly the year when
I began (1973), first-year undergraduates covered what we now call the 'long
nineteenth century' and made some progress into the twentieth. Unimaginably
now in the field of Irish history, their second year was devoted entirely to the
Renaissance and Reformation periods and the final year to the seventeenth and
eighteenth centuries — 'early modern'. Before long 'special courses' were added
to the syllabus. A course in 'medieval' was introduced by Dr Katherine Walsh

---

1   See Patrick Comerford's article elsewhere in this volume.

who would kindly give me a lift from Dublin until, in 1976, she left for an academic career in Vienna. In 1974 I began lecturing on 'Ireland and the French Revolution'. My other special course, 'European overseas expansion, 1417–1700', which brought in Portugal, Spain, England, France and Holland, was, I think, interesting for beginning with a *tabula rasa*, students having no previous knowledge and so no preconceptions. Certainly, for me, it was gratifying for this reason. My only regret is that I have never heard of any student afterwards doing postgraduate work anywhere in this vast field despite my recommendations. Paradoxically, I always tutored and lectured in areas and periods that were distant from my own research fields. My doctoral thesis was on Ireland in the 1880s and I was most familiar with the 'long nineteenth century'.

I was always something of an anomaly. I finished thirty-three years later as the longest-serving member of the department without ever having been full time. By then the Department of Modern History had become simply the Department of History, with no inhibitions about the twentieth century. Ironically, I greatly enjoyed teaching early modern, and my magnum opus (published in 2018) turned out to be largely about the twentieth. Apart from the professor, the only full-time member of the teaching staff when I began was Mary Cullen. A part-time colleague in that small department was Elma Collins. That they were styled 'Mrs' and 'Miss' respectively, not 'Dr', should be a reminder that PhDs were not yet *sine qua non* in academia. At Cambridge both my director of studies and my tutor were just MAs and so plain 'Mr'. Much later one student told me he thought Elma Collins was the best teacher in the department. Her main job was at the Institute of Education in Dublin, renowned for getting good results from previously weak students. This was a reminder that a PhD is not a guarantee that the holder is a good teacher.

The dining hall, a short distance away from Rhetoric, was for all staff, academic and administrative, though clerical professors dined communally in a separate refectory. Academics of different disciplines got to know each better in the dining hall; clerics were rare. An exception was the ubiquitous Micheál Mac Gréil, a Jesuit priest (i.e. not a diocesan), previously an Irish Army officer and generally a man of many parts, chiefly lecturer in sociology, and Santa Claus at the annual Christmas staff party, open to domestics and academics alike. Another memory of the informality of Maynooth College in the 1970s is that milk from cows on the college's farm was available gratis from jugs on the large dining table.

The college library in the Pugin quadrangle was another place with which I quickly became familiar. No longer had I to avoid it. Students read upstairs seated uncomfortably at long tables. Classification of the books was *sui generis*. It was (I now know) the *Ratio studiorum* of seminaries abroad as modified for Maynooth by Thomas Wall, later librarian of the Irish Folklore Commission. It had the merit of according with the syllabuses of theological students. For ordinary students, and for me, it was somewhat mysterious. It became obsolescent as new teaching departments were created. When the large bulk of the stock was removed to a new building the Wall system remained effective in the 'old library' as another relic of the college's past. A personal connection with the college library was that in June 1976 I married Penny Davis who, three months previously, had been appointed to its staff. She was to become the recognised authority on the rare books and other collections of what in the 1980s was renamed the Russell Library.

If there were quarrels in my department, I was never aware of them. A tradition of good relations seems to have been established by Tomás Ó Fiaich (its head since its creation in 1953). Though his public persona was that of a 'political priest' (almost a character from my doctoral thesis), he was in 1973 and later as 'laid back' as any 'singing priest', almost overwhelmingly friendly and a pleasure to work for. He had a genius for remembering people's names, indeed he knew mine before I had even heard of him. A peculiar trait, presumably acquired when studying in Belgium, was always to greet with a handshake. Perhaps this helped him remember names. It was no less a pleasure to work for Patrick Corish, who was by nature rather reserved. When I began at Maynooth he had already been there for thirty-five years, having himself begun as a clerical student. His research and publications were all in the field of ecclesiastical history, largely of Ireland, from which some might have supposed that the extent of his historical knowledge was limited. On the contrary he had what always seemed to be an instinctive knowledge of all other fields of history as well as an ability to reduce any matter to its essentials and to present it with common sense, brevity and wit. A list published in 1990 of his writings (my contribution to his Festschrift) was soon out of date, as in retirement he wrote a substantial institutional history, *Maynooth College, 1795–1995*, published in 1995.

Outside my department there was friction that had much to do with the changing nature of the college. The secular commitment it had acquired in 1910 as a university institution was displacing the religious nature of the original seminary. Its clerical establishment was in inevitable decline. A cause célèbre that in the late 1970s reached the Supreme Court had no impact on me personally, nor did other quarrels, and I never felt a partisan. Just the same I could never but empathise with the priest-professors whose very homes were the college. Their privacy had been invaded and their way of life was being questioned by outsiders whose assumptions and mores were different from their own.

REFLECTIONS ON MY TIME
IN CLASSICS

Martin Pulbrook

held a three-year post-doctoral research fellowship at Trinity College Dublin before coming to Maynooth in 1976, and my friends warned me that Maynooth was very different and might come as a cultural shock. Indeed, it was very different: when I went to the staff coffee room on my first morning, the small group there were talking Irish. But the Maynooth welcome was overwhelming: and not once did President (and later Archbishop and Cardinal) Ó Fiaich, walk past without stopping to have a brief word. And so it was (I heard) for others too. That was the first and striking thing about Maynooth; it was small enough for everyone to be welcome, because all were interconnected.

I wish that things had remained that way, and that Maynooth had grown thereafter by natural process, rather than by accelerated governmental stimulus. In my first year, 1976–77, there were 900 students altogether, including seminarians. In the spring of 1983 the President, Msgr Michael Olden, circulated to all staff members a two-page letter in which he outlined the possibility and 'opportunity' of substantial 'growth' at Maynooth. I was by then a member of the college executive council and spoke passionately and at length at one meeting about the potential dangers of such 'growth'. I gathered that I was one of three members of the lay staff who felt this way. We were inevitably in a minority, and so the decision was made in the opposite direction, and in favour of 'growth'. How I wished that it had not been so!

My French mother (from a Breton Catholic family) was thrilled that I had got the job at Maynooth, declaring 'you will be safe with the priests' – members of her family had been at a similar Catholic seminary in Brittany. This view was compounded by – and indeed originated from – my mother's intense dislike of modern urban England and the social rootlessness that prevailed there. By contrast she always had a 'soft spot' for Ireland, viewing it as a kind of haven in a troubled world.

And, in those early years after 1976, Maynooth was, indeed, a kind of 'haven' to me. I was in a unique position as a member of the lay staff. In a department of four, all my colleagues (William Meany, Thomas Finan and Gerard Watson) were priests; and I was invited into the priests' refectory for lunch on a regular basis, perhaps once or even twice a week in those early days. For an outsider, it gave a unique insight into the very heart of Maynooth.

What my three colleagues built up in the Maynooth Ancient Classics Department in the 1980s – principally orchestrated, it must be said, by Gerry Watson – was little short of a miracle. Maynooth, with its 'Recognised College' status within the NUI, had often been seen as the 'poor relation' of UCD, UCG and UCC – indeed, one Classicist at UCD commented to me on my appointment to Maynooth in 1976: 'any port in a storm'! In the event, the Classics Department at Maynooth turned out to be anything but the 'poor relation'. From small beginnings (we had fifty Greek and Roman Civilisation students, all told, in the 1976–77 year), Classics quickly grew, year by year, until something extraordinary had happened. By the late 1980s, although Maynooth was still small by general standards, a higher percentage of the total student body was studying Greek and Roman Civilisation than in any other Irish or British university. It was a phenomenal achievement, and Gerry Watson and his Classics colleagues have not, on the whole, received the credit due for this achievement. All that now lies in the past, alas!

Classics maintained its eminent position in the college for other reasons too. As from 1975, Gerry Watson had been the first editor of the interdisciplinary arts journal, *The Maynooth Review*, a position that I, in turn, held from 1982–89. Gerry was also a distinguished member of the Classics committee of the Royal Irish Academy, and I, in time, followed him as secretary of that group. When Hibernian Hellenists began to find their twice-yearly meeting place of the Ballymascanlon House Hotel too expensive, it was again Gerry Watson who was instrumental in bringing those meetings to Maynooth. For these reasons, Classics at Maynooth certainly 'punched above its weight', and did so successfully.

Speaking for myself, I disagreed with the decision enshrined in the 1997 Universities Act to grant independent status to Maynooth within the NUI. This was a motivating factor in my decision to take early retirement three years later, but not the principal reason, which I shall come to. I do not think enough general credit has been given to the pre-1997 trustees (the four archbishops and thirteen senior bishops) for the way they ran the college. They were interested simply in academic values without partisanship, and I have letters, and received visits from, individual bishops attesting to this. By contrast, the post-1997 governing body has contained members from too many 'special interest groups', each with their own agenda to push (beyond the purely academic), and the consequences are widely evident.

I have elsewhere (in my obituaries of Fr Watson, Fr Meany and Fr Finan in the *Irish Times*) described the Classics regime at Maynooth under them in the 1980s and 1990s as 'golden times'. It is in the nature of human activity that such times do not last; we should simply be grateful for them when they come, engulfing us in their splendour. And I am immensely grateful for those years at Maynooth, which can be looked back at with a sort of affectionate nostalgia. The harder, drier, more materialistic and less visionary attitude that was to follow was not easy for me; and in 2000 I felt it right to submit my resignation.

I have so many memories of those years. In the 1970s I had bought an old Daimler ambulance and converted it to a motor-caravan for touring the continent. This was used to transport all the books from the old libraries to the new (John Paul II Library) in 1984. In 1982, Bríd O'Doherty, Noel Deeney and I climbed the chapel tower to the very top on a glorious summer's day. We were the last members of staff to do so before the tower was closed for safety reasons. In the early 1990s ten small lime trees were dug up in the course of works near the new library and were to be thrown away. I asked if I could have them, and permission was given. They now form the western boundary of my garden near Mullingar and are thirty feet tall.

My daughter Dorothy started as a first-year science student at Maynooth in the autumn of 2018. In coming back, inevitably, more frequently than at any time since I retired twenty years ago, I have to admit that I hardly recognise the new and changed Maynooth, so different from the Maynooth I knew when I joined the staff forty-four years ago. I indeed count myself fortunate to have experienced Maynooth as it was then.

A SAVING GRACE?

Peter O'Reilly

Iarrived in Maynooth on Tuesday evening, 7 September 1971, and was ordained on 17 June 1979. Back then, a vocation was a bit like COVID-19: I was never quite sure if I had it or not and there was no clear test for it. Formation, as I look back at it, was not a science – exact or otherwise. Human formation (brought to prominence by Pope John Paul II) was incidental and presumed to be something that was effected by classmates on each other. It seems to have been sufficient back then that I 'fitted in'. I remember the first person I knew who 'cut' in the early months, by which I mean 'left the seminary' – perhaps cutting loose. It made a big impact. On his door – and, yes, the more creative types put things on their room doors – he had a sign: 'I used to be conceited, but now I'm perfect'. I suppose I should have seen it coming. Back in the day, students had to get a tea chest somewhere, perhaps from a local shop. During the seminary year, we thumbtacked a tablecloth to it and turned it upside down to double as a nightstand beside the bed. When summer holidays arrived, the chest was used to pack away everything in a designated store room until we got our new room in September. Over the years, I had accommodation in Long Corridor (there were too many of us for the first-year Rhetoric House accommodation and we overflowed to there and had to share rooms); then Logic House; St Patrick's, St Mary's and, in the final year in Senior List as List Monitor (as it was called), what used to be the Senior Infirmary where the Daughters of Charity lived, nowadays the Columba Centre. The plugs in the rooms were for lights or radios only. If you wanted to boil a kettle, that was done on the corridor. I remember one fellow as a prank putting a squirt of washing-up liquid in one such kettle.

Fr Joe Delaney was Junior Dean when I arrived. There were three deans then: Junior, Middle and Senior. Such were the numbers in those times. I remember how near the back door of the College Chapel my seat was on a Sunday morning during my first weeks, a sign of how many clerical students there were then, numbers which included the SMA and other orders (if I remember correctly). The hostels on 'the other side' of the Galway Road came later, after the walkway bridge was built to what was destined to become the new campus. I was there that afternoon when the final beam of it was put in place. Even from afar, I remember the febrile excitement of Msgr Newman (later Bishop of Limerick).

Over my time at Maynooth, the numbers fell, at least by a third and perhaps nearer to a half. (I have the impression, not the figures.) Back then in the middle 1970s, the decline in vocations to the priesthood was well under way. I remember noticing it, but only in terms of the seminary shrinkage. I don't know who was looking at the bigger picture, but I wasn't. It was unthinkable then, unimaginable too, that the 'machine' of the Church would begin to fail. The measure of mission then was more about 'fitting in' than 'filling in'. It was okay to be eccentric – and some of us were (I don't see it so much any more) – but it was de rigueur to be regular at turning up for things. Mind you, Fr Joe Delaney once asked a fellow cleric (HD) to consider his vocation because he was 'too faithful' to his duties: he never missed anything. It was only later that I learned how the words 'always' and 'never' can be so revealing. The student left for the love of his life, as it happily turned out for him (and her). I didn't realise it until years later that Fr Joe was a brother of the Irish broadcaster and author Frank Delaney, someone whom I read and enjoyed listening to in later years. Fr Joe had breadth – both of body and mind. Indeed, the former could make you forget the latter when I knew him. Such a rich human being. Back in the day, we students could only see the monolith authority. Perhaps his departure from Maynooth back to the pastoral life (interesting that I say it that way) had a lot to do with a breadth that parish (as opposed to seminary) life might offer. In one of his dean's talks I remember him saying: Never let it be said that the only thing you can go into in any depth is your armchair. I also remember a guest dean's talk from the then Fr Michael Olden: he recommended that as priests we should always have one comfortable room in the house. Otherwise, you'd always be out. I later learned that even such a room was not always in some parish houses as they then were.

Our Professor of Experimental Physics was Gerard McGreevy, whose stature had been affected by illness in his earlier life. We did not know that at the time, and it was typical of him to just 'get on with it' without self-pity. His first question about most things was 'What's the procedure here?' A man of no ambition other than to do right. Very much a 'church man'. He had been six months on the staff of St Michael's College, Enniskillen, when he was asked to go to Maynooth to help set up the Experimental Physics Faculty at Maynooth. He talked later of his time in Colorado where he did his doctorate in physics; he used to tell of the absolute lack of humidity contributing to many a shock to communicants who got more than the Holy Communion wafer if the priest happened to pick up a

Msgr P. F. Cremin

dose of electrostatic charge while walking along a carpet. He was a very orderly, straightforward person. One of the best teachers. He had a set of notes that he had in a cumbersome ring folder. Hoisting this folder up on to the stand, and then heaving and adjusting himself on to the high seat, he always began by saying: 'The last day we were talking about … '. He had a particular north Monaghan cadence, where his filler word was an 'eh' that could sound like the motor of a garden strimmer. I got to know him in a different capacity after ordination. He was a most gracious host. In his final years, he was the active-retired priest in the first parish where I was parish priest. I enjoyed his company and discovered a hinterland in him to which as students we were blind. He was a great traveller, for example in the US, and in the Far East: he actually got to China. He had a great correspondence with people in foreign parts, especially with members of religious orders and missionaries. It turned out that the establishment man I knew in Maynooth as a student was a caricature of the real man. He was a great priest, who acknowledged to me in later years that the established Church in pre-conciliar Ireland had got 'too high … and needed to come down'.

The changeover to theology in later years was jarring for me, as I had been a science student, not used to essay writing and exposition of philosophical thought as opposed to research and experimental fact. We were well warned that Danny O'Connor, our Old Testament Professor, would have us doing 'drawing and colouring in' to make a map of the Holy Land (like a primary school exercise). One particular Sunday, Fr Danny was on the 9.30 Seminary Sunday Mass. If that Mass were over early enough, it was possible to make it down the village to the number 66 bus to Dublin that left around eleven o'clock (and got you an extra hour in Dublin). Not that Sunday. He was still preaching towards half past ten when it dawned on him that he'd gone on a long time and he said: 'I know I've gone on a long time but sure where would you be going anyway?' That raised a laugh, but not quite enough to relieve the wish to be on the bus. It's funny that then, as now, when people become restive about Sunday liturgy it's around the homily and the music.

Tom Marsh was our dogmatic theology teacher in second divinity. I hadn't been all that confident with theology. Tom stopped me one day. 'Peter,' he said to me, 'I know that you know the stuff, but you have to demonstrate that you know it. Science has made you too brief. You just need to write more. Presume that I know nothing when you're writing for me.' He had such a natural way with him: gregarious, with a love for sport and theatre (as I remember him). He mixed more freely and genuinely with the students in the social context of the village. There was something unpretentious in him that must have jarred with the more aloof and austere professorial tradition as it had developed at Maynooth.

In my third divinity year, Gerard McGinnity was appointed Junior Dean. He wasn't long ordained. I remember him as a fourth divinity student in my first year. Fresh, friendly, vivacious, witty (without being mordant), especially talented and entertaining. As a student prior to ordination, he featured in the cast of plays and as a star turn at a concert or two that I attended in the Aula Maxima. I recall two renditions in particular. One, entitled *Rindercella*, was a retelling of the Cinderella story (from the US, I think) where syllables of words were swapped around within sentences to hilarious effect, especially in his live rendition. The final flourish came in the moral: Don't slop your dripper. The other rendition (which I would love to hear again) was a recitation of three pastiches of the poem 'Three Blind Mice' in the style of three different poets: Wordsworth, Yeats and one other which I forget. The Yeats version referred to the carving-knife-wielding farmer's wife: Slish, slash, slice – A terrible beauty is born.

In my third divinity year I was also taught by John Quinlan, a brilliant

Kerryman. His lectures were quite often prefaced by a potpourri of whatever was on his mind. Sometimes the scent was sweet. For instance, I remember him saying: 'If you learn one (really) new thing every month, you'll be doing well'. Sometimes it was a little more acrid. Complaining about the decline in the decorum of convent life, he mentioned that 'Night Prayer and Lights Out' had become 'Light Prayer and Nights Out', and 'Nuns just sweep off their veils and say, "Call me Dorothy".' I wouldn't have realised back then how Sr Dorothy might have felt. Possibly he didn't either. That year, he was on the Gospel according to John and my clear recollection is that he was brilliant on it: lively, vivid, poetic, erudite, offering a synthesis and a clear thread through.

Still, the person in my memory who complained most around and about the college was Frankie Cremin, as he was called among us. A man with a double doctorate, whose rooms were crammed with books and newspapers as I heard it. 'Have you read them all?' he was asked. His apocryphal reply: 'All of some and some of all.' I don't know how I avoided his harangue about the college, but some of my fellow students did not. 'I don't blame you,' he would say in his gentlemanly but insistent way. 'I blame them. Like a fish, the rot starts at the head.' I think the 'them' was probably the bishops in general. Like a latter-day Jeremiah of the 1970s, he berated how they were presiding over the decline of the Irish Church. There was no easy transitioning out of the high-church days.

Coming towards the end of theological studies, homiletics became important. There are many stories of the then Professor of Homiletics, Ronan Drury, who, though based in Maynooth and identified by Maynooth, was never quite limited or defined by Maynooth. He stood apart from the establishment ecclesiastical sense that was in the Maynooth of that time. In those days, gathered bishops at episcopal conference meetings walked up and down St Joseph's Square after lunch, wearing episcopal ring, full soutane, with fascia, zucchetto and gold pectoral cross. Ronan Drury, not a hierarch of the old order, was more tuned to the coming culture. His wit. After another half nine Seminary Sunday Mass, at which my fellow diocesan Professor of Experimental Physics, Gerard McGreevy, had delivered a long sermon which detailed all (or at least it felt like all) the saints whose images adorned the College Chapel ceiling, Ronan was heard in the sacristy afterwards breathlessly asking for the text. 'For *The Furrow*?' Gerard is supposed to have asked. 'No,' said Ronan, 'for Bord Fáilte'.

As I look back now, I recall that tension between what I might characterise as the pre-conciliar ecclesiastical Church and the post-conciliar Church, possibly describable as a church of the culture. We were all of us in two minds. One was the soutane-wearing clerical student and the other was the jeans-wearing college

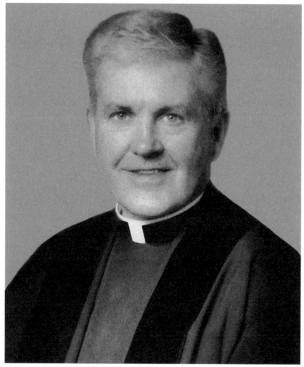

Rev. Prof. Ronan Drury

student. When the soutane passed gradually out of use as daywear – some time around 1977, I think – jeans were banned. The soutane might have been gone but the mentality lingered on, with the appeal of certainty and erstwhile standing in Irish society. In my memory, the greatest rattling of the cage of Maynooth identity came in the drama of the days in the High Court around the status of the then pre-laicised P. J. McGrath and Malachy O'Rourke. Could they still retain positions in Maynooth? Was it a seminary within a college or was it a college within a seminary? Which had priority? I remember being agog looking at rival letters to the *Irish Times* signed by different groups of the clergy staff. An answer was found; order was reasserted; but as to who the winners and losers were? There was a loss coming that none of us could have foreseen.

We had no mobile phones. You had to wear a watch. You could only call home from a telephone kiosk under the stairs outside the refectory, provided someone else wasn't on it before you. Letters were the main way of contact. Bygone days. I'm glad to see the science of personal formation has taken more shape in my lifetime. I wish Maynooth of old had had more of it. It might have been a saving grace.

THE OLD ORDER PASSETH AWAY: REMEMBERING MAYNOOTH, 1972–79

Tom Collins

Though of small stature, Fitzy was a giant in St Flannan's College, Ennis, in 1970. As hurling captain, he occupied the most prestigious position on offer to a student in the college in that era. Neither particularly compliant or devout, he took us all by surprise when he became a clerical student in Maynooth on completing his Leaving Certificate in 1970.

In October 1972 I would begin a lifelong association with Maynooth as a first-year arts student. And on my first day there I became re-acquainted with Fitzy. He had by now corrected his earlier career choice option and was no longer a clerical student. In all other matters, he was an authority on this new world of Maynooth. And so, as I queued to register outside the pre-fab on what is now called the South Campus, I needed some hasty advice on subject selection. I had decided on Latin, geography and English. But my fourth choice must be between two arcane subjects – philosophy or sociology. It was at this juncture Fitzy's authority came to the fore. 'Choose sociology,' he urged. 'It's a total doss!'

And on such small encounters is one's life path determined.

The 1960s had heralded an axial shift in much of Western civilisation as the post-war baby boomers gained their voice. This generation would discover what the social media generations would subsequently take to heart   that in an era of mass communications those who controlled the microphone controlled the message. New technology; new music; new world visions were taking hold. The Civil Rights Movement, the Women's Movement and even the Second Vatican Council were all harbingers of change.

These, and associated developments, are probably what led Liam Ryan, the then Professor of Sociology in Maynooth, to assure all of us in class in 1973 that we had, ourselves, as young eighteen-year-olds, already experienced more change in the previous ten years than we were likely to encounter in the rest of our lives.

Even then, this seemed a somewhat surprising assertion. Indeed, much of what seemed like change was in fact quite familiar – which made it feel like it wasn't change at all. While the Latin Mass had now given way to the vernacular, we continued as weekly Mass attenders and little else in the apparently great sea-change of the Second Vatican Council affected us or was even apparent to us – something which was illustrated to me clearly in 1973 when in first-year sociology we were asked to list those changes. It was a short list! The Civil Rights Movement had indeed migrated from the southern states of the US to the Six Counties in Northern Ireland in the late 1960s. By 1973, this issue was now being transacted along the traditional and depressingly familiar lines of the age-old Irish–English conflict. And while according to Bob Dylan the times were a-changin', it was also reported that he sang with the Clancy brothers, who were then busily internationalising Irish traditional ballads and Aran sweaters around the world.

There is a sense, therefore, in which the 1970s, to some extent, marked not so much the beginning of modern Ireland as that it gave a glimpse, sometimes fleeting, of what it would ultimately look like when it happened! The familiar and the unfamiliar co-existed in a state of something of a ceaseless arm wrestle between differing world views.

The village of Maynooth in the early 1970s reinforced the sense of slow continuity. According to the census of 1971, Maynooth had a population of 1,296. The village consisted of the main street and a few mean lanes hanging on to the street, consisting largely of houses attached at one stage to the Carton demesne. The main street was bookended on the east side by the Cattle Mart, and on its western edge by Kavanagh's Mill. The dust and smells of the corn mill were ever present around the town. Workers there were distinguishable by the thin film of white dust that clung to them, lending them a ghostly appearance as they made their way to and from work each day. Mooney's Restaurant was the only restaurant in the town. The overpowering pungency of boiled cabbage that pervaded it has left a lifelong memory of what we were all working so hard to escape from.

But there was also a grandeur to the street. The gates to the college, flanked by the castle, lent a sense of a triumphal destination to the great lime tree avenue connecting Carton with the college. The college itself, coyly concealing its historic Pugin squares and church behind a somewhat bland front facade, would slowly reveal its architectural riches through two arched passageways either side of Stoyte House.

So Maynooth combined the agricultural, feudal and ecclesiastical in a unique way which accorded it an easy familiarity to a student body then largely drawn from the farms and villages of rural Ireland. As the National Seminary, Maynooth drew its students from all over the country, with the accents of Donegal, Derry and Cork ever present and mingling in the ether of the campus. In the late 1960s the college had opened its doors to lay students. Though it had few faculties, it had a small but steady demand from a generation of young people, most of whose parents had never attended university or possibly never even imagined the possibility. While the introduction of free second-level education by Donogh O'Malley in 1966 is widely acknowledged as a transformative intervention in Irish economic and social life, the university scholarship for those who achieved four honours in the Leaving Certificate, announced at the same time, was also hugely significant. It presented the option of university entry to a cohort of students for whom such an option was not there previously. Maynooth was a ready and safe destination for this new cohort of university entrants. In 1972 the scholarship, administered by Tipperary County Council, paid my college fee of £300 or thereabouts, and awarded a maintenance grant of £250. The cost of full board for a student in a family home in Maynooth – or, more likely, in Leixlip – in 1972 was £7 per week.

The transition to Maynooth then from a rural Catholic upbringing in Tipperary including five years as a boarder in St Flannan's College, Ennis, felt less like a transition than a natural development of what had gone before. It was an environment that cushioned the move through late adolescence to early adulthood and left an enduring and deep affection for the college in an entire generation of its students.

College Chapel from the Long Corridor Arch

In first-year sociology, we were introduced to the thinking of Ferdinand Tonnies. Writing in the late 1880s, he had distinguished between two forms of social solidarity and cohesion – *Gemeinschaft* and *Gesellschaft*. The concept of *Gemeinschaft* referred to societies characterised by close, personal, face-to-face relationships with a strong sense of a shared communal identity. That of *Gesellschaft*, on the other hand, referred to societies that were based on formalised, contractual relationships, where order emerged from elaborate and codified systems of rights and duties.

We understood this distinction as students in the 1970s. We were Ireland's post-war baby boomers, abandoning much of what we had grown up with; seeking the emancipation of anonymity and hugely energised by the intellectual milieu in which we found ourselves. While having a sense that we had a foot in both worlds as described by Tonnies, we had no doubt about the direction of travel.

There were clearly tensions between such opposing world views in the wider society. Within Maynooth itself, we had the suspicion that the ecclesiastical authorities of the college saw the secularisation of the college as a mixed blessing. The cloistered setting of a seminary was now breached by lay students, the majority of whom were female.

The tension on the integration–segregation continuum between the two student cohorts found its clearest expression in the allocation and organisation of space on the campus – a tension memorably captured by Paddy Duffy, the founding head of the Geography Department, as one between sacred space and profane space. As a lay student, one quickly became aware of those spaces that invited entry and those that didn't. The Pugin buildings, while not closed to the lay students, were open to them somewhat on sufferance. There was the constant risk of being challenged by an ageing cleric patrolling the cloisters with the question, 'What are you doing here?' There was no doubting the statement in this question. The grandeur of the Pugin dining hall, off limits to lay students, with its great solemn wooden tables and monastic scale, mocked the prefabricated canteen pushed to the edge of the campus in which Margaret Gaffney presided as a formidable maitre d'hôtel to the lay diners. The footbridge across the main Dublin–Galway road linking the South and North Campuses somehow suggested a split purpose more than a unitary one.

So in the early 1970s the lay population in Maynooth were part of what would now be referred to as a major disruption event in the nearly 200-year history of Maynooth. We were conscious, nonetheless, in the small and personalised world of the college, of major tensions within the clerical community, and that the clerical-lay fault line was not the only such tension. In 1971 the clerical students of the college had gone on strike, mainly on grounds of what they saw as the inadequate theological formation they were experiencing. In 1972, Pat O'Brien, who had been a leading figure in the strike, had been exiled by the bishops to continue his studies in Rome. While many of us felt that Rome wasn't such a bad place to which to be exiled, his case became a cause célèbre in the affairs of the SRC that year. Amongst the clerical professors we could also deduce tensions. While some were personal, they were also doctrinal. Liam Ryan could encapsulate both as he wondered eloquently at lectures why, if 95 per cent of priests would make excellent bishops, they always emerged from the other 5 per cent!

The sense that Ireland was in the early stages of an axial shift was reinforced by the way in which one came to know the world as a student in Maynooth at that time. So much of the academic content focused on the theme of continuity and change. In geography for instance, Willie Smith and Paddy Duffy recast rural communities as exotic and worthy of academic investigation discourse – even if a little quaint. The fact that most of their students had a first-hand acquaintance with these communities, and were, indeed, actively committed to escaping them, meant that lectures were less a case of making the strange familiar than of making the familiar strange. In his lectures on Joyce's *Dubliners*, Peter Connolly would explore Joyce's contention of Dublin as a city built upon a dung heap. With an almost frightening intellectual clarity he would decode *Dubliners* around the themes of paralysis and epiphany to an enthralled class of first-year English students. While in some parts of the college we were being taught that there was a Third World because it was not closely enough aligned with the First World, Fran Walsh in geography was arguing that we had a Third World because it was *too* closely aligned with the First World. In history, Mary Cullen was emerging as an influential and inspirational figure in the embryonic Irish Women's Movement – a movement that would be pivotal in the ongoing transformation of Irish society in the ensuing decades.

So, while the undergraduate years in Maynooth were entirely memorable on so many fronts, it is the academic experience and the encounter with many great minds in the teaching staff of the college that remains the most memorable. While university strategic plans and mission statements were, as yet, part of what would have then looked like a dystopian future, the college seemed to know somehow that its job was less to transmit a body of knowledge of the world than to form a way of looking at the world. Staff and students were not overly encumbered by the burden of summative assessment, something that gave them the freedom to breathe into learning. In my undergraduate years I had a total of two summative assessment encounters – one at the end of first year and one for my BA in September of third year.

In October 1979 Pope John Paul II visited Ireland and included Maynooth on his itinerary. On what looked like a triumphal passage through the country, involving more than one million people in the Phoenix Park and many thousand on a foggy Monday morning on the Maynooth campus at the entrance to the College Chapel, it appeared the fault lines had been surmounted and the long-threatened change was merely a mirage. But what appeared in this visit like a triumphal reassertion of a particular world-view proved, instead, to be a wake. The old order was passing away and the papal visit was merely its high-water mark.

I joined the Maynooth staff on that same day. There was little doubt, even then, that a new order, whose roots were faintly visible on my first acquaintance with Maynooth as a student seven years previously, had now definitively taken hold.

In the following years, as an academic in the Adult Education Department, it soon became clear that Irish people in the 1980s were more likely to look to psychotherapy than religion for guidance as they navigated the complexities and challenges of their lives. But in our work with the students in the department, we did not discard everything. Instead, we tried – however successfully others must judge – to draw on an earlier experience of Maynooth in creating the department. This was one that celebrated the joy of learning and the unique co-learning and co-creation relationship that can arise between a student and teacher given the right circumstances. It maintained the long-standing commitment of Maynooth – sometimes ambivalent – to opening pathways into university for excluded groups. And it was always ready to embrace disruption.

UNDERGRADUATE REFLECTIONS OF AN ARTS STUDENT (1977–81)

Michael F. Ryan

It was October 1977 and I registered as an arts student in the new Arts Building building on the North Campus of St Patrick's College Maynooth. On the town side of this vast greenfield site, there were hostels including The Society of African Missions; Auxilia (girls only); and others for missionary orders. On the Kilcock side of the Arts Building, a relatively primitive students union building also emerged. It would become an important focal point for many a good night out.

There was a palpable sense of new beginnings, not just for us as students, but also for Maynooth as a university. There were also links, however, with the older pontifical Maynooth. Some of our tutorials were located on the old campus. Clerical students from the Pontifical University joined us for lectures in the Arts Building and there was a spirit of integration as lay and cleric sat side by side. The overhead footbridge on the Galway road became a symbol of new synergies between old and new; between tradition and modernity. We generally loved the walk across campus and particularly the daily perusal of the *Irish Times* and *Irish Independent* in the Old Gun Library, complete with scholarly texture and layers of ecclesiastical history. I can still visualise the dim lighting, the black spiral staircase and the ageless wooden reading bench that invited silent reflection.

The two new lecture halls in the Arts Building and the many tutorial rooms were then home to many stimulating lectures in my chosen first-year subjects of English, Irish, geography and sociology. The bright colours and semi-circular walls of the Arts Building ushered in a new style of contemporary architecture, contrasting starkly with the classically traditional forms of the old campus.

In English, Peter Connolly, Mary Fitzgerald, Peter Denman and Angela Lucas were among those who inspired us with enthusiastic explorations of literary genres and literary criticism. In the pre-PowerPoint days of acetate sheets and spirit duplicator carbon-copy, they kept us busy listening and writing in shorthand as we tried to keep pace with their thoughtful insights.

In Irish, Tadhg Ó Dúshláine and Pádraig Ó Ciardha invited us to engage with the wonderful poetry of Seán Ó Ríordáin and Máirtín Ó Direáin. In sociology, Micheál Mac Gréil shared his research perspectives on prejudice and tolerance in Ireland. Eileen Kane excavated our anthropological consciousness and Liam Ryan ensured we were familiar with the founding fathers of sociological thought (Weber, Compte, Durkheim and Marx became agents for the development of our critical insight). He once quipped (before summer examinations): 'While some aspire to achieve distinction, more perspire to avoid extinction!'

In geography, we explored Ireland's field patterns with Paddy Duffy, Ireland's industrial landscape with Fran Walsh and urban landscapes with Denis Pringle. Later we also studied the plains of Canada with Seamus Smyth. We experienced the authentic habitus and passionate interests of each of our lecturers. There were geography field trips to locations like Cong in Mayo and the Burren in Clare, which provided us with deep understanding of geographical processes both physical and manmade. There were also some funny episodes, like the attempt by overly enthusiastic students to lift a tombstone in an ancient burial ground! This daring feat resulted in a long wait at an A&E facility, as a finger was stitched and bandaged. There were also some great late-night sing-songs and sociable encounters with host communities in rural Ireland.

In addition to the various lectures and tutorials, there was many an informal conversation in the canteen (replenished with Mrs Gaffney's famous shepherd's pie). Some of these conversations were profoundly formative as we hovered between current affairs, politics, sociological insight, sporting endeavour and romantic matchmaking! As end-of-year exams approached, there were also long periods spent in the library as we relied on core textbooks for further reading and familiarisation with key models and theories. There were no online resources in those days and thankfully few continuous assessment requirements. There was a sense of time to think and absorb in the year-long academic cycle. When exams came, we all assembled on the old campus in those austere old halls beside the 'Graf' and playing pitches.

As the years progressed, friendships evolved and many of these were deepened in the formative processes of being a student on a similar programme. Mrs Kelly (accommodation officer known as 'Ma' Kelly) helped us find accommodation in the then new housing developments at Maynooth Park, Rail Park, Greenfield and Cluain Aoibhinn. Some students were luckier to secure the in-town locations of Leinster Cottages and its environs, which were adjacent to the socialising hotspots of The Roost, Caulfields or the Leinster Arms.

In those years, Maynooth had a strong connection with rural Ireland, and county affiliations were strengthened by social nights out, based on one's county

An Dr Tadhg Ó Dúshláine, Roinn na Nua-Ghaeilge

of origin. Frequently, we travelled to Harry's in Kinnegad for these events. Some of the largest of these included the Tipperary and Limerick nights out. Maynooth also seemed to attract many students from the Midlands and border counties, particularly Monaghan and Cavan.

The extra-curricular life on campus was also considerable for its time, with many prominent guest speakers from political, social and other backgrounds. I have memories of hearing Garret FitzGerald, John Hume and other heavyweights debate political issues of the day. Student societies were quite active and included The Social Action Group, The Musical Society, The Cuallacht Cholmcille Debating Society, The Historical Society and The Drama Society, and, of course, the sporting clubs for hurling, camogie, soccer, rugby and tennis.

In geography, we also had the annual *Milieu* magazine and in winter the Musical Society hosted the ever popular song contest in the Aula Maxima. The contest was so popular in the late 1970s that a few heats were necessary to select those songs that made it through to the grand final. The Aula was also used as a cinema on Sunday nights for those of us who didn't return home every weekend.

Rag week was usually held during late spring and also provided much fun and entertainment. There were innovative competitions, including dramatic parodies such as Snow White and the Seven Giants, various sporting leagues, and some famous incidents of kidnapping of prominent lecturers or clerical staff. The week culminated in the rag ball and significant proceeds were raised for various charities.

Completing a degree at St Patrick's College Maynooth was a very popular choice with students aiming to become second-level teachers, who completed a three-year undergraduate degree programme. Most graduates continued for a further year to complete the HDipEd. Upon graduation, many graduates could work in schools almost full-time, and return to Maynooth on Monday evenings for the necessary theoretical components. By the 1980s, this model had changed to a more full-time programme, including three days in college and two days learning the art and craft of teaching in chosen second-level schools. I remember being quite inspired by lecturers such as Brother McCann for the philosophy of education and by Jim Callan for curriculum development. Máire Bean Uí Catháin was also the steady pair of hands on teaching methodologies and managed the micro-teaching sessions in Education Hall on the old campus.

Studying in Maynooth between 1977 and 1981 was a really positive process and a privilege at a time in Ireland when access to third-level education was not to be taken for granted. The foundations for further knowledge exploration were firmly established in the company of lifelong friends. This foundation opened many other opportunities and was truly transformative in so many ways.

Almost a quarter of a century later, I returned to Maynooth to complete a doctorate in education and was quite impressed with the ongoing transformation and expansion of the campus. More recently, I have returned as a proud member of the governing authority. The original arts bock is now just a small building, dwarfed in size by impressive infrastructural developments on the North Campus. For me and possibly many other graduates, however, its significance as the foundation of a significant journey in education remains intact.

Arts Building

FOR THE ARTS BUILDING

Peter Denman

here it sits, the Arts Building – low, square, and showing its age – hunkering down on the North Campus, surrounded and largely obscured by its multi-storeyed brethren. I recall a graduation ceremony some years ago when the then president, in the course of an address promising great developments to come, referred dismissively and apologetically to the Arts Building and quoted Frank Lloyd Wright's observation that 'a physician can bury his mistakes, but an architect can only grow vines' to hide unattractive and embarrassing structures. He held out, instead, the prospect of its being hidden from sight by shiny new science buildings. Even as he made his architectural critique, he was seemingly oblivious that he stood in the Aula Maxima, which no one would describe as architecturally elegant.

You may have gathered that I feel protective towards the tired and too-often maligned Arts Building, and I want to present the case for the defence. Our Maynooth careers share a starting date. Goethe described architecture as 'frozen music', and the 1970s Arts Building is like one of those vinyl albums of the decade, enduringly attractive even if its record sleeve is creased and faded. When I arrived in 1977 as a callow temporary lecturer, I was taken across the Galway road to see where my office would be. There was the recently completed Arts Building in splendid isolation on a raised mound in the middle of the grassy expanse that then constituted the North Campus. To the west, tucked against the hedge, was a steel shed that served as the students' union building; to the east, towards the Moyglare road, was a scatter of hostels then owned by religious orders. Between those, the black and white hard-edge style of the Arts Building was a signal of modernity, a new beginning for St Patrick's College. I took up position in an office with a sylvan view across to the 'old' campus, the trees and the spire beyond, my base for the next three decades.

As a creation of the 1970s, the interior of the Arts Building aimed to be open-plan, with different areas flowing one into the other. There was a loosely defined area for staff to sit and gather for coffee mid-morning, and this was just around the corner from the student restaurant, which in turn was a through-way to a reading room and library. The whiff and aroma of boiling vegetables and fried chips from the restaurant kitchen permeated the building each midday. Most notably, and futilely, there were little study and tutorial areas, each consisting of a half-dozen chairs, separated by six-foot square screens but open to all passers-by on the fourth side. This fanciful design, which imagined earnest discussions between students and staff in an unfettered and unsequestered environment, did not survive a year, and it wasn't long before those open areas were shut off to make rooms with proper walls and doors. It was a presage of things to come. The staff area has long since been closed in, and the restaurant area is now a hive of offices.

In those early days, the Arts Building contained multitudes under its flat roof. There were staff departmental offices, lecture theatres and classrooms, the main student restaurant, a large part of the library with a reading room attached, language laboratories, the Registrar's Office, and a post distribution centre (remember, no emails those days, so a steady stream of paper communications had to be moved internally and externally). Student numbers were under

Arts Building (Detail)

2000, and the building was a natural hub for them. Staff numbers in academic departments were also small – generally ranging from three to five. As a result, departments were grouped together, and staff had frequent contact with colleagues in other disciplines. In the Arts Building there were English, Old Irish, Modern Irish, philosophy, sociology and Classics cheek by jowl, in neighbouring offices, with French and German also nearby. This led to real interdisciplinary exchange and understanding. Nowadays departments tend to be hived off into different buildings and different faculties, with little occasion for informal approach and discourse. Furthermore, back in the 1970s and 1980s, professors along the Arts Building corridor were nearly all clerical. While this may have been a somewhat skewed seniority profile, it did mean that there was a degree of interplay between the NUI university elements and the St Patrick's staff, a feature that seems now all but lost.

At student level the Arts Building is still a locus of student contact and interaction. As other structures grew up around it – the John Hume, the science building, Callan, – the layout of the Arts Building with major entrances on two opposite sides means that there is a continuous footfall through it. Because of this it has never become an unvisited backwater. With its three-metre sheltering overhang and paved walkway around the outside, it is one of the few university buildings suitably designed to provide shelter from the storms that all too frequently sweep in from the west. Would that other areas of the exposed campus had been designed with similar foresight for the inevitable weather!

The Arts Building has held on to its unpretentiously descriptive name, while surrounded by the fancifully named Iontas and Eolas and Phoenix, and the honorifically named John Hume and Callan. There was at one stage an informal discussion among staff to propose renaming the Arts Building after a recent and noted leader on the Maynooth campus, but the name suggested provoked such virulent opposition in some quarters that the idea was swiftly dropped. On the topic of naming, I admit there were times when my efforts to communicate the worth and pleasures of literature and the humanities were failing in reception and falling on deaf ears to such an extent that I would mutter that rather than Arts Building it would be better labelled with the Freudian 'Arts Block'. However, such disillusionment was momentary.

Its two lecture theatres are still in service, and for a time they were the prestige venues for guest speakers – E. P. Thompson, Seamus Heaney, John McGahern and many other writers. They also provided a forum for the Literary and Debating Society, with students such as John O'Donohue[1] (*Anam Cara*) and Michael Harding taking the platform.

So, as I worked in the Arts Building over three decades, I developed an affection for it and even admired many of its qualities when others became dismissive of it. Indeed, to invoke Goethe again, the story of our relationship could be described as a *buildings-roman*. The building now stands as a tangible witness to the co-location that has characterised Maynooth even as the academic centre of gravity has shifted in recent years. The building has shown exemplary adaptability, its interior elements going through their several iterations while serving in turn the Recognised College SPCM, then NUI Maynooth and now Maynooth University.

---

1   For memories of John O'Donohue as a student, see the article following by Kevin Hegarty.

'GREAT STUFF'
IN MEMORY OF JOHN O'DONOHUE
— *Maynooth Student 1974–81*

Kevin Hegarty

The Child Jesus
and St Joseph,
St Mary's Oratory

It was an evening in late May 1981 and the ordination class gathered for the last time in the senior common room in St Mary's. It was a get-together fuelled by a little wine and a lot of nostalgia. Together for several years, we were about to go our separate ways.

We wondered what the future held. On what low rungs of the clerical ladder would we soon be perched? There was excitement about the years ahead and trepidation about leaving the familiar. Eventually, there was an awkward silence. How could we bring this final meeting to an appropriate end?

One of our number, Paddy Murray, from the hill country of County Down, was blessed with a whimsical sense of humour, which he used to relieve tense moments. 'I wonder,' he intervened, 'who amongst us will be the first to die.' The gathering collapsed in laughter. If, however, we had taken bets on that macabre question, the longest odds would have been on John O'Donohue. Tall, strong and vigorous, he was a life force who lit up every room he entered. I reckon he was the most gifted Maynooth student of his generation.

Life and death provide tales of the unexpected. So it was that John was the first to go. On a bleak early January morning in 2008, he was laid to rest in the earth of the Burren that had nourished him so lavishly. He had died suddenly while on holiday in France. He was fifty-two.

By then, John had long escaped the clammy embrace of clericalism and won international reputation as a philosopher, poet and public speaker. In a series of books, from *Anam Cara* to *Benedictus* he had sought to mint a new language of religious experience that resonated with the impulses of the modern world. Much of Catholic religious writing had become stale, larded with abstruse theological formulas, deaf to contemporary experience and buttressed by lengthy papal quotations. Pious clichés masqueraded as insights.

John's books burst upon this tired religious publishing world like an array of daffodils in an end-of-winter landscape. The books are a fusion of John's explorations in philosophy, theology, literature, music and art. In *Divine Beauty*, he wrote that 'the beauty of God is reachable for everyone and can be awakened in all dimensions of our experience'.

Underpinning his writing is the Celtic consciousness of the wonder of God in nature and human experience. Growing up in the Burren, on the fringe of the Atlantic, he came early to the Celtic world. From the moment of his birth his eyes were anointed by the beauty he saw all around him. In the exquisite fauna and flora of his native landscape, he discerned whispers of divinity. His books, retreats and lectures across the English-speaking world afforded hope and inspiration to people of all faiths and none.

John and I were friends throughout our years in Maynooth. He quickly found his natural habitat in the university, studying philosophy and English. Unlike many of us he was not daunted by its long and high cloisters, dominated by large portraits of grim-faced nineteenth-century clerics.

Though committed to scholarship, John did not live in an ivory tower. He often touched down in our everyday world, his loud laughter echoing down the corridors of the college. His customary term of approval, 'great stuff', was applied equally to a philosophical idea, a poem, a piece of music, a painting and a good pint.

He had a formidable reputation as a debater in Irish and English. Always informed, eloquent and witty, his presence on the podium usually attracted large crowds.

Even then he had a special sensitivity for those haunted by the anguish in their lives. He also had the capacity to laugh at himself. One of my abiding memories of Maynooth is of John, already in thrall to the rigorous charms of the German philosopher, Hegel, belting out with gusto 'Blanket on the Ground' in the college song contest.

I treasure my memory of a day that he and Michael Harding, also in our class, tried to explain the lyrics of the Boomtown Rats to Msgr Cremin, the Professor of Moral Theology, for whom the decrees of the Council of Trent were the apex of human creativity. In short, however, this renaissance mind came up against the limitations of his genius. He participated enthusiastically in the aptly named, 'bull leagues', probably the lowest form of football on the planet, where he passed the ball with entertaining inaccuracy.

By the time of his ordination, John had outgrown Maynooth and was ready for his next academic challenge. He eschewed the charms of Rome, where the lure of clerical advancement is often the graveyard of intellectual integrity. Instead he tested himself in the austere atmosphere of Tübingen University in Germany. He proved his academic credentials by gaining a PhD (*summa cum laude*) on Hegel. The *Review of Metaphysics* commended his thesis for 'breaking new ground in our thinking about consciousness, the self and what it is to be a person'.

I believe he would have made a wonderful Bishop of Galway. He would have been at home on the banks of the Corrib, a place which has the intimacy of an Irish village and the cosmopolitan flair of a university city. Galway is the cultural centre of the Celtic world of Aran, Connemara and the Burren, which meant so much to him. He had the intellect, the imagination and the charisma to present a convincing vision of Christianity in a secular environment. A bishop's pastoral might have been a work of literature.

He returned from Tübingen to an ambivalent welcome in his diocese. During the papacy of John Paul II, the Catholic Church was a cold house for creative thinkers.

John soon found an audience in Galway for his spiritual explorations, but the Church authorities were unwilling to facilitate his ministry. They sought to appoint him to a busy curacy where he would have little time for extra-curricular activity. They may have hoped that his fertile imagination would wilt under the sodden weight of careful clerical conversation in the presbytery. It was as if Barcelona FC were to confine Lionel Messi to carrying the jerseys for its third-string team.

John was always fearless. He struck out on his own and made the world his parish.

From Guff to Chub
A SEVENTIES' RITE OF PASSAGE

Thomas O'Connor

n the late 1970s, the classic entry route into Maynooth was still matriculation, bought on a Leaving Cert earned in a diocesan boarding school. Historians may recall how a network of these institutions once fed the National Seminary. Originally cut from the same tridentine cloth as the Royal Catholic College of St Patrick, in the years after the Second Vatican Council a gap in conditions and expectations opened up between the major seminary and its minor feeders. While conditions in the junior colleges conformed, in many ways, to the emergency exigencies of the 1940s, Maynooth had mellowed sufficiently to make the experience of living there qualitatively

different from that endured under diocesan boarding school regimes. That's why in September 1977, entering Maynooth as a chub made an impression that students of both previous and succeeding generations find hard to imagine. In 1977, Maynooth was *so* unlike St Finian's, Mullingar, and its avatars. The immediate differences were mainly carnal: in Finian's, there was a sausage of a Sunday morning; Maynooth offered a daily fry, if you could stomach it. Hot water in Finian's was a twice-a-week luxury; Maynooth, on the other hand, imposed new hygiene standards. In Finian's everyone had to tog out, the hot water situation notwithstanding; Maynooth tolerated conscientious objectors.

There were other, less sensual differences. The quality of time, for instance. Despite the fact that much fun was had there, one's spell in Finian's, from lowly guff-dom to the prefectorial exaltation of fifth year, was inevitably more of a sentence than a stay, cut in notches of recollected misery. In Mullingar, time could hang like a leaden curtain, on the long Wednesday afternoons, during the interminably wet weekends and all through the dreary stretch that was called January. Maynooth time, on the other hand, was free from midland backdraft and it was there, for the first time, I think, that time took wing and began, like a swift, to fly. We didn't realise it, but during that fateful September, something, somewhere began to tick. That tick would eventually toll, but nobody fretted. Running out of money or patience were commonplaces, but no one inferred that we would ever run out of time.

If time changed its character with the transition to Maynooth, so too did space. Boarding school survivors will understand what I mean when I say that, in Finian's, space was inhabited promiscuously, in the sense that none of it was private. The dorm, the chapel, the library, the classrooms, the gym, the so-called *palestra*, even the jacks: all were more corridors than rooms, and loitering an almost unavoidable offence. In the diocesan school, you were perpetually on the move around the place, unconnected, by right, to any one piece of it. In late 1970s Maynooth, on the other hand, space was precisely zoned, with lay separated from cleric, male from female, sacred from profane, public from private and, yippee this, communal from the personal and private. However incredible it might seem now, the gift of a personal space, a secure and officially sanctioned retreat from the madding crowd was, to a Finian's refugee at least, nothing short of an El Dorado: the contested space of boarding school replaced by the segregated security of the seminary. Imagine, after the promiscuousness of the dorm, the luxury of one's own room; a library space from which you could not be randomly ejected; a jacks door that wouldn't spring open under some oaf's boot; the insane liberty of going for a walk in a park full of trees on your own, any time you liked. Inebriating draughts of a new, sweet wine that helped conceal, for a while, the persistence of other, subtler, secondary school continuities.

Like responsibilities. You will understand that, in Finian's, the management viewed the free will with which we were all allegedly endowed, as a potential recalcitrant, with disruptive tendencies. School rules were accordingly designed to make its exercise largely redundant, maintaining all students in a state of arrested childhood, which explained, in part, our childish behaviour. Consequently, nobody ever asked us why we were in Finian's. Not only because the 1970s were not especially interrogative but also on account of children not knowing their own minds. Like their Mullingar contemporaries, the Maynooth authorities believed, theoretically, in free will but, unlike their Finian's brethren, had had to make some concessions to its practical exercise. Seminarians might not be considered full-blown adults but were expected to know at least parts of their own minds. About why they were seminarians, for instance. Accordingly, we were all, not unreasonably, required to give an account of ourselves, to a dean, a spiritual director, a visiting confessor … to ourselves. Which was easier said than done. You see, then was a time when the 'system' did a lot of our thinking for us, though less tyrannically, it must be said, than digital platforms now programme our twenty-first-century successors' expectations, self-image and appetites. Back then, it was surprisingly easy to enter Maynooth without really knowing why. Which, to be fair, wasn't St Finian's' fault. After all, the religious vocation, to a certain extent, was a family and a community affair, as much as the individual's. It was considered a little calculating, in fact, to have justifications too readily to hand. A bit evangelical or protestant even, in the Billy Graham sense, of course. So, although free will was a bigger deal in Maynooth than it had been in Mullingar, you still didn't have to have everything thought through. Which was a relief for an eighteen-year-old. Not that custom and habit, apparently discredited by the recent council, weren't assuming new, subtler forms that made us think we were freer. Sometimes imagined freedom is nearly as good as the real thing.

Enough to be getting on with, you might think, all that space stretching, time warping and will bending. But there was one more thing: the North. It might be useful to mention here that, back then, the Finian's hinterland stretched from Drogheda to the Shannon and plunged Munster-wards, to Eglish, near Birr. Northwards, however, it limped past Oldcastle and, apart from the odd refugee from Cavan (those too refined for St Pat's), the state as I knew it, terminated, for all practical purposes, somewhere just beyond Fennor. That changed, utterly, in September 1977 when, for the first time, we met actual Northerners, in the flesh. Don't get me wrong. We weren't total muppets. Even in hermetically sealed environments like Finian's, the world had been breaking in: the Dublin and Monaghan bombings, Guildford, Birmingham … and that was just 1974; the Troubles seeping, like a threat, into our secondary school grunge. But that was the North, not Northerners, the making of whose acquaintance awaited our September 1977 arrival in Maynooth.

I don't know what impression we made on them, but they did awe us a little bit, at least for a while. The main thing they had over us southerners, I suppose, was suffering. It made them appear wiser, which some, in fact, probably were. In the things of life, at any rate. And certainly when it came to a sense of humour. Was it the sheer unfairness of Six-County life that gave their Catholic humour its edge? I loved it, and to this day its recall triggers the uncontrollable laughter that hurls me back to that lost September world. When we learned that the best laugh always hurts a bit. I remember a Derry-man explaining what, exactly, a *black hole* was. And with what withering wit. Some sort of self-administered therapy for him? Maybe. Certainly a transformative, belly-aching laugh for me, and so it remains in memory. We learned more than we could ever teach in return, education being the unequal exchange it is.

'PLAY IT, SAM'
A THEME AND EIGHT VARIATIONS

Patrick Devine

'Sam' here refers not to Arthur 'Dooley' Wilson in the 1942 film *Casablanca*, but to Rev. Professor Noel Gerard Watson (1927–2004), a native of Belfast who was ordained in St Patrick's College Maynooth in 1961 and returned seven years later to head the Music Department of the NUI college for sixteen years until his retirement in 1984. I joined him as a (very) junior colleague for his last seven years there and, despite the disparity in years and experience, we established a close working relationship and strong friendship. While I always knew and addressed him as Noel, to his clerical colleagues in Maynooth he was 'Sam', possibly to distinguish him from another Gerard Watson on the staff, also from the North, who was Professor of Classics.

Var. 1: I first met Noel in December 1973. He needed an organist for the carol service in Maynooth that Christmas, and on the suggestion of Gerard Gillen, who was one of my lecturers in UCD at the time, I was approached for the 'gig'. Noel collected me on Bachelors Walk (in Dublin's city centre) in his sleek and powerful BMW. On the journey to Maynooth he claimed to be a lover of fast cars and, to an even greater extent, of motorcycles. Later I would learn that he attended the TT races in the Isle of Man every June, after all the examination business in the department had been concluded. I couldn't help smiling when I first heard his abbreviated version of the Christmas carol title 'In the Bleak Midwinter', i.e. 'In the BMW'!

Var. 2: Blessed with rugged good looks and a dapper gait, Noel certainly cut a dash. I never saw him in casual attire, and at all times it was clear how important his vocation was to him. One abiding memory is his beginning every class he took with a prayer. Whenever he left my office after discussing some business, I could hear him whistling down the corridor. On one occasion I learned from him that the secret of his success was an eight-letter word, i.e. homework. That advice made a lasting impression.

Prof. Noel Watson conducting a performance of Bach's St John Passion, 1984,
with Ian Partridge (standing to the right) as narrator

As a result of my previously erroneous memory and Noel's diplomatic
correction during one of our conversations I have subsequently taken a certain
delight in one-upmanship when someone misquotes the familiar phrase 'S/he
who sings prays twice'. To reinforce the accuracy of his intervention he even
offered the Latin original, 'Qui bene cantat, bis orat', i.e. 'S/he who sings **well**
prays twice'. That was telling me!

Var. 3: On hearing the news of the death of a student's parent in the North,
Noel and I decided to attend the funeral and we were accompanied by a number
of students. Two carloads set off in convoy from Maynooth early on a Monday
morning, and when we were halfway there we stopped somewhere in Longford
at an isolated public house which had just opened for the day's business. One

unfortunate employee was trying to summon up the energy and enthusiasm to clean up the establishment. We ordered tea for ten and availed of the opportunity to stretch our legs. However, there was no sign or sound of any tea being made, and after what seemed a really long delay Noel was moved to say in an audible whisper, but just out of the employee's earshot, 'Make that one tea and ten saucers!'.

Var. 4: One doubtless innocent but unfortunate remark occurred in a keyboard tutorial. The tutorial took the form of a meeting involving a group of four or five students who would take turns to be examined at the piano on prepared homework by the tutor, here Noel. When it came to one female non-Caucasian student he began by absent-mindedly directing her to put her 'lily whites', i.e. lily-white hands, on the keys! Thankfully no offence was taken.

Var. 5: The above incident notwithstanding, Noel, like a true professional, approached all aspects of his work seriously. This was especially the case when he took choral society practice, usually on Monday evenings in Callan Hall on the South Campus. Incidentally, the membership of the choir included women and men from outside the college, lay people who loved the activity of singing good-quality music in like-minded company. In retrospect it is gratifying to know that the Music Department was engaging in outreach long before the word became a 'buzz' term for third-level institutions.

It was in the context of these weekly rehearsals that I saw Noel most regularly: he directed proceedings, putting the choir through its paces, while I accompanied at the piano. Endowed with a fine singing voice and, more crucially, with perfect pitch, which equipped him with the ability to detect the slightest deviation of intonation, he made the learning process all the shorter and more enjoyable for the members.

One evening as the rehearsal had just begun, a latecomer excused herself as she passed other members in her row in order to get to her regular seat. However, one of those in her path refused to give way, whereupon the following command issued from a clearly irritated and impatient conductor: '[surname of uncooperative student], shift your butt!' There followed a deadly silence from the stunned choir members, but the rehearsal resumed after some uneasy moments. In subsequent days Noel must have received some complaint, possibly from one of the more mature external members, because he began the following rehearsal with a sincere apology to the chastened student before the assembled body. With that, the usual state of equilibrium was restored.

Var .6: The carol service in 1981 was recorded for broadcast by RTÉ television, and Noel asked me to write a carol for the occasion. Using a text by the late Pádraig Ó Fiannachta, former Professor of Nua-Ghaeilge (Modern Irish) in Maynooth, I duly obliged and produced a mildly dissonant setting which, to say the least, received a mixed reaction from the choir members. The memorable verdict of one of the tenors was that the composer must have had an unhappy childhood!

Var. 7: As director of the choral society Noel naturally chose the music for all of the choir's performances. The annual choral and orchestral concert in the spring usually featured one of the canonic works such as the Fauré's *Requiem*, Bach's *St John Passion* and Mendelssohn's oratorio *Elijah*. It is a testament to his courage, as well as to his trust in his musical instincts, that he acceded to a request from two colleagues (Martin Pulbrook of the Classics Department and myself) to undertake and prepare a largely unknown composition, Anton Bruckner's large-scale *Mass in D minor*. This he did, learning the music from scratch like virtually everyone in both choir and orchestra, and the result was the first performance of the Mass in Ireland, on 27 March 1983. I was especially proud of him on that evening.

Var. 8: Noel bequeathed me his personal copy of *The New Grove Dictionary of Music and Musicians* (1980), and although he had informed me of his intention to do this, I was nevertheless very pleasantly surprised when, some months after his death in 2004, I received a request to collect a delivery from Stoyte House, near the gates of the South Campus. *The New Grove* comprises twenty volumes and, for almost a generation, represented the most comprehensive reference tool on music in English for educators, performers, composers, writers and listeners. Although the work has been superseded by a more recent edition (2001), this very generous gift continues to be of immeasurable value and help on a regular basis; definitely a treasure for which I will be forever grateful.

While it might be tempting to conclude on a symmetrical note with another cinematic reference, imagining Noel now mounted on one of his favourite motorbikes in the sky à la *Easy Rider*, it would be more fitting, I think, to quote the title of the penultimate chorus from his beloved *St John Passion*: 'Lie still, lie still.'

SLIDESHOW

Bill Tinley

... in the beginning was the slideshow – lecture halls, canteen, SU, quadrangles, the nocturnal spheres of student societies – a pitch to Leaving Cert boarders, a Knockbeg old boy, Seán McEvoy, acolyte to 'Ma' Kelly and Andrew Egan;

later, the first-choice Maynooth CAO boys on a day trip, February 1983, Rag Week, a film at noon in the Aula, a gowned academic professing to the deserted tiers of Callan Hall, the ubiquity of female students, an impossibly chic library assistant radiant in the studious quiet;

then October, a room in Straffan Way shared with Eamonn Murphy and Pat Holmes, the space between singles so tight it felt like we were tripled-up, tinned sweetcorn on brown bread my supper staple in the garage that doubled as a kitchen;

drawn-out days in the Arts Building, the fug of sodden duffel coats drying in the cloakroom, the *Irish Times* for 25p in the SU Shop, the politics of queueing for 'Ma' Gaffney's canteen fare, tumbleweed through Friday afternoons before the bus to Dublin, lifts home from Guinness's with my uncle;

Professor Corish's refrain that it was said of the Holy Roman Empire that it was neither holy, nor Roman, nor an empire, a reel-to-reel of Plath reciting something about rooks, Frank McGuinness unwrapping 'Adlestrop', the *lectrice* playing Brel, Sr Bríd Doherty dancing to Renaissance music, oblivious as her audience slipped away for the summer;

Top of the Pops in the LA and nights playing pool there, Teresa Keefe from the St Mary's programme on lead vocals at a gig in Slattery's, a soundtrack of '99 Red Balloons', 'Relax', protest occupations, kipping overnight on the floor of Accounts, a fraternal foray up North under the USI banner, seeing the RUC up-close and personal, CND, Amnesty;

Rooney, Fagan and Flanagan begetting the lit mag, *Bitz*, editorial sessions in the SVD, a lost spring afternoon delivering copy to my father's Wicklow printing press, hawking copies to staff at the top of the dining-room stairs, Eileen Kane cooing 'a koo-vawed' over Paul Hoary's 'Couvade';

Prof. Barbara Hayley

Vertú, a literary weekend, Frank McGuinness (again) presiding, that stare as I clacked past him at the Aula door in borrowed football boots to make my only appearance in the seminary league, finding out later that my story had placed second in the Guinness Prize, the £50 cheque a fortune;

two years as Lit Soc president, a spool of poets, story-makers, playwrights, the Friday morning slot that Barbara Hayley granted us, Joe Kane's silver-on-black posters advertising Muldoon, Mahon, Boland, McGahern, Durcan et al., futile hours thumbing in Castledermot, frantic that we'd flunk our role as hosts for the big Heaney reading, *Wintering in Maynooth* inscribed, the news that Larkin had died just weeks after writing to decline our invitation, letters and cards from Beckett and Barry, Hughes and Sirr, Hartnett forgetting his glasses, missing the 66 to Maynooth, the taxi driver he hailed a fan of his since the sixties, Kennelly missing the 66 from Maynooth, standing us rounds in Brady's;

Barbara, with Peter Denman, putting me through my reading paces in a vacant theatre before *Raven Introductions 4* was launched in Trinity, persuading Loughlin Sweeney to employ me in the Development Office, distressed I might have head injuries from a traffic accident only days after graduation, Thursdays tutoring, MA essays on Wilde, Mahon, Moore and Swift, her protective spirit, back from a Scottish holiday to discover she had died in a road crash, my first deep savour of grief, her wedding-gift champagne flutes still charged for family occasions three decades on;

a constellation charting the addresses I've shared, frost on the inside of a Laurence Avenue window, one- and two-bar electric heaters, the embers of a briquette fire hoovered up, a Kingsbry sitting room I set ablaze, sunsets igniting in the big windows of the Main Street apartment over the vegetable shop, our O'Neill Park landlord lighting the stove each morning all summer 1988, three winters of a smoking fire in the 'Castleview' mews;

a four-week stop-gap post in February 1989, back in Development, that ran into a second month, then a further three, a junior lugging brochures to the underbelly of Riverstown Lodge, sleepy July weeks scouring the business pages for cuttings on corporate supporters, dossiers for cultivation dinners in the Parlour, processing covenants, the shock of Cardinal Ó Fiaich's passing;

a segue then to unmapped territory, the hibernating summers set to be disturbed by language schools, teenage Italians, academic conferences, retreats, Tai Chi, Aikido, Buddhism, choirs and chapters, reconnaissance tours with Geraldine Coyne to wings and floors I hadn't known existed on the campus, David Carbery's fiefdom in what had yet to be christened Pugin Hall, a menagerie of keys in Liam Greene's Cold War office, the college stirring as if from a spell, old ways creaking under new pressures, the transition not always seamless;

the weekend Geography conference delegate who returns to her room late Friday night to find a visiting priest asleep in her bed, the busload of Kerry flower arrangers who fetch up for the Bicentenary Flower Festival a year ahead of schedule, the ICMA mavericks who, one night, in pre-CCTV times, apply Chiquita banana stickers to the rings on the fingers of the unsmiling luminaries in portrait frames along the cloisters, poisoned birds dropping from the sky during a national youth weekend (a crackled voice advising over the radio 'don't eat the chicken'), an elderly guest locked out of Senior Infirmary one night, no sign of the nuns, my sidekick scaling a ladder to climb in the kitchen window, security an accessory;

a handshake with scout leader, King Carl Gustav of Sweden, in the dim-lit President's Arch, Seamus Heaney (again) reading in the College Chapel, weeks before he is awarded the Nobel Prize for Literature, the Select Vestry ladies bringing Dominic McNamara and me on a clandestine tour of the Church of

Cardinal Tomás Ó Fiaich planting a tree at the
back of New House with the dean Fr Niall Ahern
and students

Ireland tower, the FitzGerald dead, a first ascent of the college spire, inoculating the sky, wind on a calm day reefing the louvres, half of Leinster on view;

slides and trannies, prints and jpegs, portraits and snapshots, colleagues cajoled into modelling for photoshoots, Pantones and swatches, carpets, curtains, keys and candles, escutcheons and fanlights, phantoms and fictions, a million bed nights and counting;

but shadowing this, the lees of a dream, ghost iambics and enjambments, unfurnished stanzas, an under-pulse of words, sightlines into other realms, a somewhere else that waits to be entered and possessed;

and it's February 2020, thirty-seven years have passed, the carousel has empty slots, slides here and there have been appropriated, the mechanism is snagging, and yet there's time for more, before we stop, before we start again, before we just keep going on …

FINDING MY VOICE AT MAYNOOTH

Liam Lawton

here are many things that can be written about Maynooth, but I would like to think and believe that I discovered my voice in there! As a young country boy leaving home for the first time in the late 1970s and arriving at Maynooth, I was like any young student arriving for the first time and seeing the college with its majestic towers and broad buildings, holding secrets within its walls. Everything was new and life anew lay ahead.

I was a lay student from the beginning and went to study for an arts degree. I

was among the first group of students to study at the Arts Building on the North Campus, as it is now called.

Finding a new freedom and new friends and the acceptance of one's self is a major step forward for any teenager. I was first introduced to the Musical Society at Societies' Day, but I didn't realise then that it was about to play such a major part in my life. The infamous Song Contest was spoken of – people wrote their own original song to compete against others for the coveted trophy among other things.

I entered this contest about two months later and it brought me into a new world. It was the word of creativity, the world of networking, the world of competition, be it carpeted in friendly disposition. There were basically two sections: the first section was where one performed a non-original song (and this was open to all competitors); the second was the original section, where people performed their own original composition. Here I met people from many lands and was exposed to music from different cultures. This is where I began to plough my own furrow with regard to composing and performing.

As the year developed, I was wrestling within myself and all that goes with that too, but eventually I decided that I would study for the priesthood. I was accepted by the diocese of Kildare and Leighin, where I lived, and have lived since.

This again opened new worlds of sight and sound to me – the world of ritual and service. I joined the seminary choir under the baton of Fergus Clarke, who would, in time, turn it over to Sean Lavery. From them I learned much and owe them much also. From Gregorian chant to music for the Divine Office, to all kinds of music that was being prescribed for the liturgy from so many different sources.

I continued to take part in the annual Song Contest and improved my writing skills as each year progressed. The coveted trophy found its way to my sideboard more than once so I was happy in the knowledge that I must have been doing something right!

My twin brother Tom, who was a lay student at the same time I was studying theology, ensured that I was au fait with what was happening in the world of contemporary music. He and his friend Emmanuel McCormack invited me to sing with them at any opportunity I could. In the days before Spotify and its likes, there were nights when there was standing room only as the BBC brought us *Top of the Pops* each week and allowed us to keep abreast with all things contemporary and the various types of music that were being written then. One of my favourite pieces of all time in contemporary music comes from this genre. It is Kate Bush's 'Wuthering Heights', a powerful marriage of imagery, music and lyrics.

Composing for the liturgy was not something I grew into until well after I left Maynooth and was working in Carlow. However, during those years in Maynooth I was exposed to many various types of music and believe now that those early years were very formative for me. To make mistakes, to fail, to come second or third or even last, is a great lesson in itself, and is as important as winning. This is how we grow and learn, as I did.

I was born with a questioning mind and sought the transcendent in music especially. I believe, and still believe it can be touched, especially through our own native language and culture, which was so imbued with the Spirit. I could not understand how some people could look down on our culture just because it wasn't couched in the Latin language or some other classical form. For me, God was as real in the language and music of my own people as he was in the culture and music of other European lands. I still believe this.

This ideology was the catalyst for my continued search and desire to capture this in song and word. It still drives me!

In 1992 I returned to Maynooth to study for the HDipEd and had the opportunity to join the Maynooth Chamber Choir. Again, many different forms of music enriched my palette, and at this stage I had begun to take composition more seriously. In the year 2000 I went to the University of Limerick to study for my MA under Dr Helen Phelan and the late great Professor Micheál Ó Súilleabháin.

Sitting in class in Limerick, I often spoke about my exposure to all kinds of great music in Maynooth and how it formed me. There were people in my group from all parts of the world, and I often wondered if any of them had the wealth and beauty of the world I had come from, though they too had been exposed to different forms of splendour also.

Music is a very subjective force. What some people will enjoy, others might find boring or not to their liking, but the most important thing is to be open to all. This will inform us and help us to be more holistic in life, I believe. If we live with closed minds, we will eventually come up against some challenge that may be difficult to surmount.

As I look back at Maynooth, there are many things that I am thankful for and obviously many things that should have been done differently, but it's there that I learned the beauty of sound. It was there that I learned to seek the talent that lurks within each person. It was there that I learned the meaning of appreciation – how each person is unique but carries within the capacity to make this world a better and more beautiful place.

Music has taken me into many different countries, on to many of the world's leading stages, from Carnegie Hall in New York, to Symphony Hall in Chicago, to LA and beyond. I have been blessed to work with some of the world's greatest musicians and singers, to sing with many beautiful orchestras and to meet some iconic people ... but I am most grateful for the blessed opportunities I was given in my days in Maynooth, in the majestic Aula Maxima, in Callan Hall, in the beautiful Gunn Chapel, in St Joseph's and St Mary's Oratory. These were the days that formed us ... these were the days when we dreamed that our song would be heard, somewhere, some time, some day.

> So fly the soul to its secret abode,
> Seeking some word to lighten the load.
> Could it be, could it be, that God would right the wrong
> Could it be, could it be, that God would hear my song?

FATHER MICHAEL CASEY, MY FRIEND

Rita Joyce Holmes

Rev. Prof.
Michael
Casey OP

n 1980, during one of my first days working in Maynooth College, I walked into a laboratory in Logic House and there was Fr Casey perched on a stool, in deep concentration with a chemical experiment, and that was the beginning of a long-lasting friendship. To all outward appearances a twenty-eight-year-old woman starting out in her career and an eighty-year-old priest at the peak of his profession would not have a lot in common. However, nothing could have been further from the truth for the two of us. We shared our faith, our love of science, and the fact that he was born in the same year as my Granny, Catherine Roberts. Having never met either of my grandfathers, he was in many ways a grandfather figure to me.

He was an extraordinary man – a brilliant chemist, full of humility, caring, kind and a pillar of the college in those times. He had his own way of doing chemistry and he seemed to have an innate ability to knowing the measurements of the amounts of substances that he was adding. At one point he made up a tonic which he drank, as did other members of staff. Fr Casey swore by his tonic but some of us were a bit wary of it as the ingredients were a well-kept secret.

He was fascinated by nature. And he loved to use natural substances, such as natural dyes from beetroot, berries and currants,as natural indicators in his experiments. I'm sure nowadays he would have been classified as gifted. He was a pianist and was still playing the piano when I left the college in 1994. He had an encyclopaedic knowledge of nature, physics, chemistry and biology. He gave lectures to the College of Engineers for many years. He was delighted to do this but was very modest as he would often ask us why we thought they were asking him to teach. He was responsible for the completion of the transfer of Callan's apparatus to the science museum. Indeed, the museum was one of his great passions.

To my great amusement, he was a make-do-and-mend and upcycling enthusiast. I remember him using old beakers as candle-holders and conical flasks for holding holy water. In contrast, when I visited him in the nursing home years later, when we had both left Maynooth, the first time I attended his Mass there he had Waterford crystal candlesticks. The second time he had broken one, which felt much more in keeping with his modus operandi.

I was only one of many friends in the Chemistry Department among both the technical and academic staff. Whenever he needed anything, he knew he just needed to call myself or one of our other friends and colleagues on the technical staff, Ria Walsh, Anne Cleary and Tony Shiels, and we would immediately sort it out for him. Prior to Professor Martin Quinn's leadership, Fr Casey held that role and there was palpable respect and affection between the two of them. He also had many friends, not only in the college, but also in the community. His nieces and nephew were very special to him and he loved them dearly. When his sister died, a group of us from the college went down to Tramore for the funeral and he was very touched by this. I asked him did he visit Tramore often and he said he didn't because he had too many sad memories. Even though he was a very strong person, he also had a very soft and vulnerable side.

A couple of times a year science met religion. He would bless all of our throats on St Blaise's Day and on Ash Wednesday he would administer ashes. As we got to know each other, I confided in him when I was in the very early stages of my pregnancies and he would then give me special blessings. Following the birth of my last three children, Rebekah, Grace and Robert, he christened all three. In fact, my daughter Grace was born the day before his birthday and her middle name Michelle was given after Fr Casey. Whenever I had the opportunity, I went to his Latin Masses as I had taken Latin for my Leaving Certificate and attended them in my youth, and it was a wonderful opportunity.

Over our time working together, he gave me three items. He truly believed in the apparitions at Knock, County Mayo, and he gave me a stone from the wall where the appearance of Our Lady took place; he gave me a recipe for elderberry wine; and he gave me the original master copy of his Christmas card template. These three things encompassed his great faith, his love of the odd indulgence, and his delight in the joy of Christmas.

He had made a pact with Our Lady that he would not take sugar in his tea, despite his sweet tooth, but if someone gave him a treat, he couldn't refuse, out of good manners, so I often snuck him in a meringue. He told me his favourite meal was bacon and cabbage and so whenever I was cooking it for dinner, I would invite him to our house in Maynooth for dinner with myself, my husband Declan and my children, which is also when I would insist he have a sweet treat for dessert.

I confided all the events of my life both good and bad to him. After the death of my Granny, he told me that she had gone straight into the arms of Our Lady, knowing that she shared his deep faith in her. His advice was always to leave everything in the hands of Our Lady. Upon the death of my father, Joe Joyce, he insisted on saying a Mass for him in St Joseph's Chapel, which my father would have been greatly honoured by. And although at that time, it was both a difficult and a comforting thing for me, it is now one of my most treasured memories of my time in Maynooth.

Leaving the college to go to a nursing home truly broke his heart. The college was his home, and the lab and the chapel were his places of worship. Although we both left the college – I left in the summer of 1994 – I still visited him regularly. On one of those occasions I had all four children with me. I left them playing outside of his room, went in to see him, and he asked me if I had the car with me, and said 'Right, you're bringing me to vote'. He was changing his lifelong vote in response to the country being so badly run. I packed all four children into the back seat and off we headed to the polling station in Maynooth Boys' School. He went in, voted, and he came out feeling liberated at this monumental change in his politics. I then asked him if he would like to go into the college and he said he would. The children were playing in the garden at the Infirmary and I accompanied Fr Casey to the chapel. He showed me the seat he always sat in and sat down and cried. When he recovered, he brought me in to the vestry and gave me a book from his drawer on the apparitions, which I have kept to this day. As we walked out of the chapel, we met the butler, Michael O'Riordan, who brought us into the dining room for tea. Some of the priests on

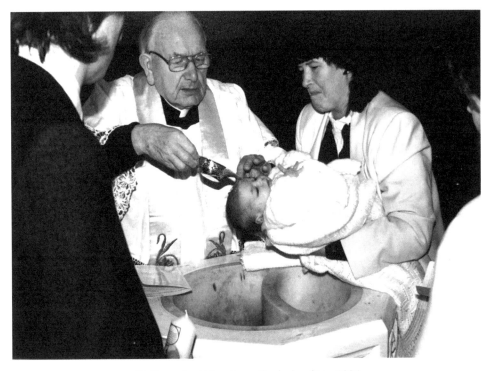

Fr Casey baptising the author's daughter, 1986

the corridor came in to see him. Eventually it was time to leave and head back to the nursing home. I continued to visit him right up until his death. This was not easy as he was always very upset when I arrived, and he always said he did not want to die at Christmas time because of the upheaval it would cause. He died on Christmas Day 1995.

Most years my family and I travel to a small seaside town in the north of Spain for a couple of weeks. There I attend Mass in a small church in the centre of the village where a Latin Mass is said during the summer. They sing the 'Regina Caeli' at the end of the Mass, which always brings a tear to my eye because it was Fr Casey's favourite hymn. And so, winter and summer, many years since his death, his ever kind and powerful presence in my life is still felt.

REFLECTIONS ON A
MAYNOOTH EDUCATION

Thomas J. Norris

My first encounter with Maynooth was with some of its graduates. I refer to priests of the diocese of Ossory who were formed in Maynooth and whom I met when a student in St Kieran's College in the late 1950s and early 1960s. Sitting at the feet of men such as Thomas Brennan, Timothy O'Connor and Joseph Delaney, to name but a few, I enjoyed an encounter with the faith and culture of these priests. In them I met the culture of Maynooth, for they were that college's products and ambassadors.

Those priests manifested a culture that was Catholic, classical and humane. What I mean is that it was a culture weaving together faith and reason, learning and creativity. Later I was to realise that all would have studied Augustine of Hippo who connected the wonder of being human with the even greater wonder of God as love, a Love in love with humanity to the point of becoming flesh and dwelling among us. In some way I began to discover the amazing idea the Almighty has of human beings. Later I was to learn that Aristotle and Plato stressed the the fact that wonder is the beginning of wisdom, with great scientists such as Louis Pasteur and Albert Einstein in full agreement. I was to learn, for example, that the Roman poet, Virgil, could write, '*Omnia vincit amor et nos cedamus amori*: Love conquers all things, so let us surrender to love'. These 'seeds of the Word' revealed the human hunger for the Absolute, the longing for the Everlasting. And that was a first inkling of the dialogue between Jerusalem and Athens, the cities of Faith and Reason, respectively. The teenager, however, did not see Maynooth for over two decades when he went to teach in the Pontifical University.

Hearers of the Word: this title of a famous, even if difficult, work of Fr Karl Rahner SJ reveals a truth about life and living that opens up vistas often closed to us even with the advent of divine revelation. What is that truth? Is it not the precedence of life and living over learning? That precedence challenges all institutes of learning and education. 'In Christ was life, and that life was the light of humanity'

(John 1:4). Light follows life, being life's radiance and reflection. Without the experience of the new life and the new humanity brought by the God-Man to humanity, theology will reduce inevitably to being a collection of concepts. It will overlook incarnation as 'the point of intersection of the Timeless with time' (T. S. Eliot), the intersection that points us towards the amazing idea the God of Abraham, Isaac and Jacob and Jesus Christ has of humanity.

This perspective highlighted the challenge facing Maynooth education in the inclusive and broad sense of the term. Idealistic young men came in numbers through the gates of the college to train for the priesthood. Increasingly young men and women came to Maynooth in search of learning in the 1970s. That influx constituted both challenge and opportunity for the college. How should the faculty cultivate wonder as the antidote to mere information, mere erudition? Is not theology faith seeking understanding according to the ancient principle? The great educators in history aimed at activating the sense of wonder in their pupils. They sought this more than they sought information or erudition. As for their pupils, they then had the chance to discover the marvel of human existence when glimpsed under the radiance of the divine glory of Christ, the Lord of glory. St Irenaeus of Lyons puts it incomparably well: 'The glory of God is man fully alive; the life of man is in the vision of God.'

Any account of Maynooth focusing on the final quarter of the twentieth century has to take into account the exceptional 'world context' of the time, namely, the Second Vatican Council. This great stirring of minds and hearts, fulfilling the *aggiornamento* of a great pope, John XXIII, was going to challenge existing patterns of thought and action. It was to be a 'pastoral' council, and not only in the sense of a different emphasis. While the previous twenty ecumenical councils successfully challenged derailments in faith and morals, this council chose a somewhat different orientation. With keen theological and historical insight, and under the impact of the Holy Spirit, the council launched out into the deep with a certain daring personified in Pope John and Pope Paul VI.

Inevitably, the council did not avoid the historical turbulence pursuant upon all the ecumenical councils of the Church. To have done so would have required great shifts of perspective being present and welcomed. The council's guiding principle was that of unity, whether in the local parish or on the plane of the ecumenical. This perspective and aspiration run through its twenty constitutions and decrees.

The final misery is not to know the origin, the identity and the purpose of our very humanity. There has to be a great paradox here.

Did the sheer weight of scientific achievement as expressed in the wonders of technology cause such a loss and de-formation? How is it that we perceive in the West a growing silence, a deadly silence, the silence about the essentials? Now this is high tragedy indeed: while the benefits of technology are real, they may cause an amnesia. We overlook those questions that refuse to go away but pain us when we forget or, worse still, try to bury them. These are the ineradicable questions of Origin, of Identity and of End or Purpose.

The years during which I was privileged to live and work in Maynooth were not unlike a laboratory session: one could see and verify in some measure the truth of these contentions. With the emergence of the NUIM beside the Pontifical University of Maynooth, a campus capable of dialogue emerged invitingly. It was to facilitate the dialogue of faith and science. Increasingly theology, literature and an ever-expanding array of technical and educational topics encountered one another. They met via the students, if slow to meet via the professors. Here one could see a certain measure of interdisciplinarity emerge and function. Both universities seemed more disposed to initiate projects. The delicate dialogue of theology and science took definite steps forward.

A special privilege of teaching in St Patrick's was the possibility it provided of encountering the students. That encounter was at least as important as information provided in the lectures and tutorials: its absence would cause an 'arctic winter' (St John Henry Newman). For if the message did not connect with persons and their utterly unique life-adventure, focusing, as that adventure does, on their search for meaning and truth and love, it tended inexorably to evaporate into clouds of theory. Do the pupils feel a welcome expressing *agape*? Only that experience can dispose them to search for the meaning of their once-off humanity before the Lord of history who has made us for himself and without whom our hearts are restless – until they rest in his. The danger exists, indeed, for providing answers to questions as yet unasked by students is sure to create a feeling of unreality.

Though I have left Maynooth, I frequently meet its past pupils. They bring to mind the saying of St Thomas More: 'One of the greatest problems of our times is that many are schooled but few are educated.' Maynooth graduates belong to the cohorts of the educated.

Images on pages 338–339: Symbolic representations of the four evangelists in the College Chapel (clockwise from top left: St Luke; St John; St Matthew; St John; St Mark)

ROBERT MUGABE'S VISIT TO MAYNOOTH COLLEGE 9 SEPTEMBER 1983

Dominic McNamara

Robert Mugabe, Jim O'Keeffe and Bishop Donal Lamont
in Maynooth College

rime Minister Robert Mugabe of Zimbabwe requested a private meeting with Bishop Donal Lamont in Ireland, prior to his three-day visit to this country in 1983.

Bishop Lamont was an Irishman who had served as a Bishop in Rhodesia and, like Mugabe, was sentenced to ten years' imprisonment for his outspoken condemnation of Ian Smith's white minority rule. He was later deported. Mugabe wanted to be identified with Lamont, so when Maynooth College was asked to host this meeting, the College President, Msgr Michael Olden, felt honoured to

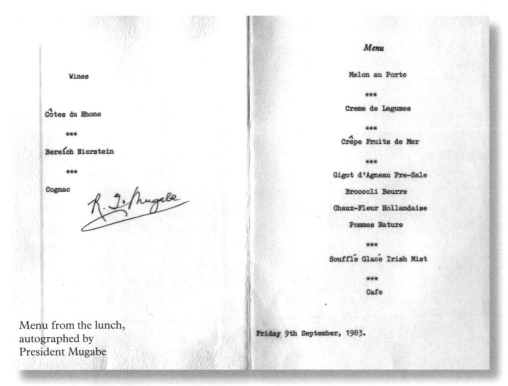

Wines

Côtes du Rhone

***

Bereich Nierstein

***

Cognac

Menu

Melon au Porto

***

Creme de Legumes

***

Crêpe Fruits de Mer

***

Gigot d'Agneau Pre-Sale

Broccoli Beurre

Chaux-Fleur Hollandaise

Pommes Nature

***

Souffle Glace Irish Mist

***

Cafe

Friday 9th September, 1983.

Menu from the lunch,
autographed by
President Mugabe

be asked, and responded positively. Looking back with our 20/20 vision on the man Mugabe became, the college's response may seem incomprehensible.

In retrospect, though, it may be worth reflecting on how Mugabe was regarded in 1983. He had been brought up a Catholic and was educated by the Jesuits. He led the Zimbabwe African National Union (ZANU) in the Rhodesian Bush War against Ian Smith's regime and negotiated the Lancaster House Agreement where he had won plaudits from much of the world for his negotiating skills. Following the 1980 election, he became Zimbabwe's first prime minister, and called for an end to enmity between the races.

For most of the world, his election was a relief. During the following two decades up to the end of the twentieth century, Mugabe was welcomed across the world as he reached out to many countries and world leaders to forge alliances. The following were some significant events:

1981:   Mugabe was nominated for the Nobel Peace Prize;

1982:   Mugabe was hosted at the Élysée Palace in Paris;

1983:   Mugabe made a three-day visit to Ireland where Taoiseach Garret FitzGerald hosted a state reception in Dublin Castle;

Mugabe left Ireland for Washington, where he met with US President Ronald Reagan;

1994: Mugabe was knighted by Queen Elizabeth;

1995: Mugabe was hosted by Bill Clinton in the White House;

1998: On a two-day visit to Ireland, Mugabe held talks with President Mary Robinson in Áras an Uachtaráin, followed by lunch at Iveagh House hosted by Taoiseach John Bruton, with government ministers, and such distinguished guests as the Garda Commissioner, the Army Chief of Staff, and former Taoiseach Garret FitzGerald;

2000: By the new millennium, Mugabe's reputation had collapsed, resulting in EU and US sanctions, which included travel bans on Mugabe himself.

Back in those halcyon days of 1983, the visit of the Catholic Mugabe, the first prime minister of newly independent Zimbabwe, who had called for reconciliation between the formerly warring parties, was keenly anticipated. It was a time when it looked like he could bring peace and justice to Zimbabwe.

Mugabe had requested that his visit to Maynooth was to be kept secret. Yes, he would stay for lunch, but would like a rest afterwards in a private secure place. I was in my early years as assistant to the president and arranged with Sister Vincent in the Infirmary for one of the bishops' rooms to be prepared for him. There were no en-suite facilities in the college at that time.

Mr Mugabe arrived at the President's Arch accompanied by Minister of State at the Department of Foreign Affairs, Jim O'Keeffe, and the party was met by the President, Msgr Michael Olden, who escorted them upstairs to the president's rooms to meet the waiting Bishop Lamont. Monsignor Olden didn't need to introduce the two men who greeted each other warmly. No journalists were allowed at the meeting, and I was the only person who photographed the event, though being much younger at the time, I found it impossible to get the man from Skibbereen out of the picture! The two men were left alone for their meeting, but the bishop recalled that Mr Mugabe said: 'If it had not been for the missionaries, there would be an illiterate government in Zimbabwe today. It was the missionaries who gave us our education and our health service.'

Donal Lamont was born in Ballycastle in 1911. He joined the Carmelite order in 1930, and was ordained in 1937. His mission brought him to Southern Rhodesia where he was appointed the first Bishop of Umtali (later renamed Mutare) in 1957.

The prime minister of Rhodesia, Ian Smith, had declared UDI (Unilateral Declaration of Independence) in 1965, which was opposed by Bishop Lamont. He wrote an open letter to Ian Smith entitled *Speech from the Dock*,[1] in which

---

1   Donal Lamont, *Speech from the Dock* (Leigh-on-Sea: Kevin Mayhew Publishers, 1977).

he told Smith, ' … far from your policies defending Christianity and Western civilisation, as you claim, they mock the law of Christ and make communism attractive to the African people'.

As bishop, Lamont asked his priests and religious not to report the freedom fighters and volunteered to accept responsibility for their actions:

> If the Christian missionary is the informer, the whole community understandably blames him; and they blame not only him but the whole organisation to which he belongs. Not only the church gets the blame, but Christianity itself is condemned as afraid, as an agent of oppression, and is accused of preaching the brotherhood of all men in creation and in redemption, and of contradicting it in practice, even becoming the willing accomplice in the bombing and destroying of villages and in the killing of innocent women and children.

His opposition caused him to be placed under house arrest and charged. To protect others from being incriminated by testifying, he pleaded guilty in 1976, and was sentenced to ten years' imprisonment. On appeal, this was reduced to four years, but unlike Mugabe, Lamont never spent time in prison, and was deported to Ireland in 1977 where he rejoined his Carmelite community. However, many missionaries were jailed for their support of the freedom fighters. In 1978, the year after his deportation, Bishop Lamont was nominated for a Nobel Peace Prize, and his portrait appeared on a Kenyan postage stamp.

Following the meeting in the president's rooms at Maynooth, Mr Mugabe was entertained to lunch where he met the priests of the various faculties in the dining room. The college had also invited representatives of several missionary groups who had served in Rhodesia/Zimbabwe to meet him. After dinner, he addressed the group and again thanked the missionaries and Bishop Lamont for his leadership: 'We thank the missionaries, especially those along the eastern border of Mozambique, who suffered more than anybody else during the war of liberation.'

Mugabe did not want any publicity for this meeting, and as I recall it, none appeared.

Twenty years later, on 14 August 2003, Bishop Lamont died in Dublin. He was ninety-two.

On 6 September 2019, sixteen years after Lamont's death, Robert Gabriel Mugabe died. He was ninety-five.

GOING TO MAYNOOTH

Diarmuid Hogan

e stayed totally silent for a long time, my brother disappeared somewhere, and she cried wet tears. I asked them not to tell anybody. Not for a few days anyway. To give me a chance to sort out things in my head, to tell my friends. But that afternoon my aunt Kitty came down, shook my hand and congratulated me. 'Why did you have to go off and tell Kitty for?' I demanded, after she had tea and went. 'I had to tell someone,' my mother said, 'and Kitty won't tell anybody else.' Twin aunts – two Sisters of Nazareth – both rang that night to say they were delighted and not one bit surprised, it was an answer to their prayers, and they wished me well. Nobody admitted to telling anybody anything but within hours the news had reached their convents in Wrexham and Aberdeen. Mary Murphy, next door, knew too. And Jack O'Gorman, our rival shopkeeper, called me in and gave me a bar of Cadbury's Dairy Milk. He told me I was great. It was no longer my secret.

A long excursion to Maynooth. That September Sunday morning my brother disappeared again. My mother hardly spoke. Anxiety and love had silenced her. My father had always been more a thinker than a speaker, but just before we headed off, on the footpath in front of the house, he held my arm tight and said, 'Come back here whenever you want – this is always your home – no matter what, you will be always welcome home.' I don't remember much else he said that day, nor, to be honest, any other day. But I remember he said that, then.

We stopped on the way. The Prince of Wales Hotel in Athlone. Maybe I should hide in the toilet. Stay there. Not come back out. Ever. Since I was very young this had just been MY thing, in MY head, in MY thoughts, in MY heart. Now it was beginning to belong to other people too. Others were involved. Others who had feelings about it. Opinions. Others to whom it mattered a great deal. Who were now in the spotlight because of it. It was too much. But I didn't stay in the toilet that day. Sometimes I think I should have. I have never gone back to the Prince of Wales Hotel in Athlone.

She was pale and silent in Maynooth that day. Feigning strength but utterly fragile and utterly bereft. Finding it impossible to identify, let alone express, conflicting, overwhelming emotion.

They went away again quickly. Bags out of the boot, a climb to Long Corridor, an invitation to tea in the Ref declined, a polite handshake with Mickie O who said to her, 'Don't worry, he will be fine.' Coping by absconding, my father sat into the car, said, 'We better go, it's an awful long road home.' And they went. Kilcock, Enfield, Moyvalley, Mother Hubbards for tea and toilets, Clonard, Kinnegad, Miltownpass, Rochfordbridge, Tyrrelspass, Kilbeggan, Horseleap, Moat, Athlone, Hayden's in Ballinasloe for the dinner, Aughrim, Kilreekil, Loughrea, Kilchreest, Gort, now County Clare. Stone walls and cousins. Corofin, Kilnaboy, home.

She shed tears that evening. He didn't. He was never a man for tears. Not visible ones anyway. He watched *The Sunday Game* alone. Highlights of that day's All-Ireland – 'the Game of Shame', four players sent off, Galway losing to Dublin by two points. A joyless slog. He went to bed. She smoked her last cigarette and went two doors up the street to Kitty, to drink tea, talk, to describe, to be reassured, to be minded, to be understood. Sisters.

Phone calls not allowed for the first month. Nor visitors. Just letters. She wrote. Twice each week for that month and twice each week, on a Thursday and on a Sunday, for seven years.

Proper letters. On Basildon Bond blue writing paper from O'Gorman's shop. Long letters. Four or five pages. Weather, weather forecast, diagnoses, dramas, dyings, deaths and funerals, courtships, engagements, weddings and baptisms, visitors, the Twins and other aunts, and uncles, and cousins and extended family, the parish priest (Archdeacon Vaughan followed by Canon Kelly), my father, my brother, his girlfriend, once a very detailed account of an emotional resignation from the Hall Committee (she 'flounced out, banging the door but had to come back in again for the keys of her car'), neighbours in hospital, neighbours emigrating, GAA results if relations were playing and news was scarce. Full, vivid, varied accounts of home. And then a list of all those who were asking for me and of all those who were praying for me. Wondering always, in every letter, if I was well, if I was warm and if I was eating enough.

But not just letters. On Friday mornings the envelope came wrapped inside a tightly folded *Clare Champion*. Big pages with biroed asterisks beside anything she considered relevant, interesting or useful. Local planning applications, post-funeral acknowledgements (with an unspoken implication that I should had been there), court reports of 'found-ons' from home being fined, possible summer jobs, anything to do with Our Lady's Hospital in Ennis where she had worked and always a big circle around Diocesan Appointments or news of Eamon Casey. There was often news of Eamon Casey.

First Year Seminarians 1984

And then on Tuesday, a parcel. A proper parcel. Brown paper, stringed and stamped. No sparing with the address – Mr. Diarmuid Hogan, Clerical Student, Diocese of Galway, Kilmacduagh and Kilfenora, St Patricks College, Maynooth, Co. Kildare, Ireland. For seven years of Tuesdays on the common room tables of Long Corridor, Rhetoric, New House, Top Pats, Top Marys and Middle Sanctum, an awkward, obvious parcel for me among the letters and cards and packages for other lads from other places.

And in that parcel? Always two loaves of brown bread. Made on Sunday evening. Wedding ring off. Apron on. Cuffs rolled up. Odlums self-raising flour, bran, milk deliberately soured. Two loaves. Ready for the post on Monday morning.

I told her that there was no need. We were never hungry. Queue in the Ref three times daily. Brown tray. Duck-egg blue delph. Porridge, cornflakes, toast, oxtail, tomato and mushroom soup, chicken chasseur, à la king, maryland and vol-au-vents, stroganoff, cottage and shepherd's pie, roast beef or fatty lamb on Sundays, a fry in the evening, with chips. Jelly, custard, a square of trifle. Club Milks for St Patrick's Day and the Eighth of December. Mr Carbery in the

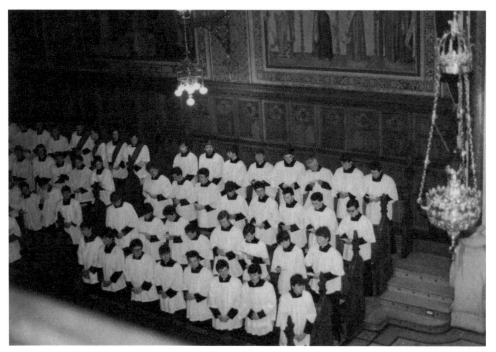

College Chapel 1984

kitchen said his job was to feed us, not to fatten us. So not much lush or fancy. But he and Michelle and Tina and Dolores and Margaret fed us. Plentiful food. No shortage. So I told her there was no need to send bread. Bread needs butter and there is no fridge. Just windowsills for milk. Bread is hard to store, four flights up. It goes stale. Maybe mice. It isn't needed. Send biscuits, or a fiver.

I told her but she persisted with brown bread every Tuesday. I once asked why. She told me that it was because she missed me. That she worried about me. That she had always fed me and minded me. Now I was gone and she wanted to still feed me, to keep me close to her, close to home. She wanted that I wouldn't go too far away. That I would remember where I was from when I was far up there in Maynooth. She feared that in going away, that I wouldn't come home. Michelle was not my mother. She was.

So bread from home, mixed on Sunday evening in the red plastic basin and kneaded out on the kitchen table. Baked with love and anxiety and prayer. Bread posted every Monday to bring the taste of her kitchen, the taste of my home to me, up there in Maynooth, far away. Not Mr Brennan's bread nor Johnston, Mooney or O'Briens. Not another mother's. Hers. Her unique bread. Made by her. For her son. Sent to evoke and strengthen memory, to keep me connected. Reassured. Fed. Embraced. Nourished in body, mind and spirit. Eucharist. Explained by her better that any wise man of Loftus ever did.

They only came back three times – two graduations and diaconate. The journey was too long and they felt a little daunted by the people and the place. Too many priests, too many stairs, too much history. People there were always very nice of course but they were always glad, and relieved, to go home.

She could have died while I was there. She should have died. She had chronic emphysema from years of smoking. She had her very last cigarette that first September Sunday evening and never smoked again. She needed to live and had something to live for. But the damage had long been done. She could have died while I was there, but she didn't. For seven years she held on through hard winters and hospital, through doctors, nebulisers, ambulances and anointings. Praying *go mbeirimid beo* for the summer of 1990.

She shone that June day in Kilfenora, her day, my day. Radiant, a perfect, proud host. She brought an offertory gift to the altar. As the parish choir sang 'Panis Angelicus', she gave to Bishop Casey a loaf of her own brown bread. The work of human hands connecting us to God and to one another. She cried a little that day too, but not much. My father sang 'The Green Hills of Clare' at the reception.

My mother Maureen died exactly eight months later – 'at last all-powerful master, you give leave to your servant to go in peace …'. I said her funeral Mass. She is buried in Noughaval two miles from Kilfenora. My brother and I carried her coffin from the hearse. My father Dermot is now buried beside her.

Maynooth meant every bit as much to both of them as it ever meant to me. Maybe more so. Maybe more so. My own grave has long been marked out beside theirs. I went to Maynooth, but I want to go home. I was once told that I would always be welcome there. May my parents, and yours if they have died, rest in peace. Amen.

Stairs in St Mary's

3D ~ Another Dimension
MAYNOOTH SEMINARY LIFE
IN THE 1980s

Paul Clayton-Lea

From a global perspective the 1980s were, to paraphrase Charles Dickens, the best of times and the worst of times. It was the decade the Berlin Wall fell and the Cold War came to an end but also the years when a new global plague called AIDS was identified, and closer to home the old plague of daily bloodshed and deadly hunger strikes continued to devastate the North of Ireland. In 1986 the Chernobyl nuclear disaster denoted an acceleration of the hands of the notorious Doomsday Clock towards midnight, signalling looming environmental catastrophe, while the advent of the Internet seemed to presage a new information age, which would revolutionise human interaction and global politics. George Orwell's novel *1984*, forecasting the 'thought police' and manipulation of populations through 'fake' news, appeared to have been unduly pessimistic – though ironically it was in that same year that Facebook's Mark Zuckerberg was born! St Patrick's College Maynooth, however, still basked in the afterglow of the historic visit to Ireland in late 1979 of Pope John Paul II, whose personal charisma, towering intellect, energetic papacy and almost successful assassination in St Peter's Square in 1981 galvanised the global Church. Vocations to the priesthood in Ireland seemed plentiful and hundreds of seminarians packed the National Seminary, with an almost eighty-strong seminarian-only college choir alone; flourishing theological, literary, drama, music and football groups accompanied by what in comparison to earlier times and from my personal experience was perceived as a relaxed and humane seminary regime. 1980s' Maynooth appeared to have reached the high-water mark of post-Second Vatican Council seminary life with its dedication to forming an outward-looking, modern priesthood fit for the challenges of the forthcoming millennium. This model of priestly ministry was summed up in the first edition of the student magazine *3D* by one of the most popular and respected members on the campus, Rev. Flannan Markham SSCC.

What the church does not need is uneducated pious priests. These form disaster areas. What it needs is the educated, open, enabling person who is not threatened by new ideas or new situations but is always willing to listen and respond to the Lord as the latter is revealed in the most diverse situations.

In October 1984 a group of seminarians met with the editor of *The Furrow*, Professor Ronan Drury, to discuss the possibility of reviving a student magazine, something that had fallen by the wayside since the disappearance of an earlier version, *Silhouette*, which had provided a student literary forum from the 1940s for many years. The objective of the reborn student publication, as outlined by Michael Murtagh in its first editorial, was to 'paint a picture of contemporary Maynooth in words' and reflect the richness in diversity to be found among this generation of seminarians. Ronan Drury was both enthusiastic and supportive of the project, although unhappy with the initial proposal that the new publication be entitled *The Farrow* or pig's litter, in playful homage to his esteemed publication *The Furrow*. The magazine was eventually entitled *3D*, indicating its intention to reveal a further dimension of student life and thought beyond the traditional class-piece photograph and surface lives of those passing through the seminary. From the relatively small pool of editors and contributors listed over the life of *3D*, some, like Denis Nulty, Alphonsus Cullinane and Michael Router went on to Church leadership roles as prelates, while others built on their early literary forays with the student magazine to become noted writers and gifted communicators – Eamonn Conway, Diarmuid Hogan, Andrew McMahon, Tom Cox and more.[1]

Reviewing the copies of *3D* (which ran mostly annually from 1984–96) it is striking to note alongside the intellectual and literary talent on display the personal nature of many contributions reflecting upon social issues of the day and topics like loneliness, death and suicide, as well as some heartfelt and revealing poetry. There were philosophical, theological and liturgical offerings, political commentary, book reviews and historical items, but for the most part the content was upbeat and lighthearted in tone, though occasionally fervent in religious or sporting ardour as demonstrated by this excerpt from the pen of one who gave himself the name 'Amen Dumbfy':

This sporting column has been alerted to the fact that Knock and Lourdes are not exclusively treated to miraculous occurrences.

---

1   Incidentally, the final issue of *3D* was co-edited by one of the editors of this volume, in 1996.

Holy Family Window by Mayer of Munich in the College Chapel

Consider the strange case of 'Fresher' Gabriel St John. In the recent set-to with St Pat's Drumcondra he received a crippling leg injury and could be seen bravely ploughing through the queue in the Ref at a mere 60 m.p.h on crutches. Within days however he appeared on the Pond for Meath's magic victory over Elphin. Does Mr. St John know something we don't? Or could it be Sr. Vincent's Magic Rub?

The reference to Sr Vincent marked the great affection students had at that time for the Daughters of Charity who provided care in the Infirmary and managed the very busy College Chapel sacristy where, in addition to the highly ceremonial Sunday liturgies and high feast days and seasons, numerous priests celebrated individual Masses daily on side altars. A seminarian was usually appointed as assistant to the presiding sister and an amusing account of his call to this role was given in *3D* by a Meath student, Raphael Mitchell:

On an evening last April I had an unexpected visitor – the Senior Dean, Fr McGinnity. In his usual manner before giving me the news he browsed around the room. Then, sitting down on the bed with that angelic smile he said; 'I'm glad to tell you that the Administrative Council has appointed you Assistant Sacristan to the College Chapel.' Like a tidal wave all of the famous comments about the sacristy came to mind – 'I hope someone who doesn't get up in the morning gets the job … I wouldn't wish that job on my worst enemy … I'd hate that job, you'd be so tied down.' The senior Sacristan whom I didn't know that well was to show me the ropes. Despite all the bad things one had heard he seemed quite calm and even friendly. I said to myself, 'This isn't so bad after all, the Boss seems OK'. But later I was to find out that there was another Boss. However, you will meet her later …

The 'Boss' in question was long suffering Sr Regis, who enjoyed the unenviable task of organising the daily requirements.

Over the years of its existence *3D* provided an abbreviated record of the daily life, concerns, interests and activities among seminarians during that period. The articles and regular features, whilst at times naturally critical or questioning of some aspects of formation, nonetheless emitted a perceptible warmth for the history, traditions and daily life and camaraderie of the seminary. This is particularly evident in the regular 'Maynooth Diary', which recorded significant moments in the life of the college and marked the introduction or departure and sometimes deaths of members of the staff or student body as well as an occasional controversy. In the winter edition of 1987/88, for example, the diary noted: 'The Aula began its film season with the long-awaited *Crocodile Dundee* despite some doubts about its suitability for seminarians as expressed in the *Irish Catholic*'.

The social life of seminarians is usually mentioned in connection with the annual concerts from the chubs or Fourth Divines, where no opportunity was lost to satirise the foibles and eccentricities of many college personages, something taken in good part by most victims. There was also the popular song contest, where the now internationally known Liam Lawton, among others, flexed their early genius for songwriting and performing.

As one might also expect of a young, all-male institution, whether the barracks or the seminary, there were regular and not often complimentary comments about the food; 'Why do all the chickens have four legs and no breasts?' Another issue suggested during the period of the infamous Beef Tribunal when a great cargo of beef went missing that it had in fact found its way to the college resulting in a constant cycle of 'Roast Beef, Beef Stew, Beef Curry, Beef Soufflé, Beef Trifle ...'. The establishment of a 'beefed up' Food Committee was noted in the 1986/87 issue, but meals continued to provide a source of ribald nourishment for *3D*.

The particular significance of this decade in the history of Maynooth and the good fortune of having a surviving student chronicle of the period, I suggest, lies in its marking (albeit unknowingly) the end of a way of seminary life in Ireland wthat had existed in almost the same form for 200 years.

As the numbers of seminarians withered away to a low point by the mid 1990s, *3D* similarly succumbed, owing to the dearth of available editors and contributors. It did, however, largely manage to achieve its aim of providing a glimpse into an otherwise unexplored and unrecorded dimension of seminary and student life.

THOMAS KABDEBO (KABDEBÓ TAMÁS)
A Hungarian Librarian at Maynooth (1983–99)

Regina Whelan Richardson

Thomas Kabdebo at ease in the
John Paul II Library

ntrigued, optimistic and slightly apprehensive, the library staff of
St Patrick's College, Maynooth awaited the coming of the new
librarian, Dr Thomas Kabdebo. A Hungarian, we had been told, and images of
Magyar Posta stamps with colourful birds and butterflies jostled in our minds
with those of Attila the Hun bursting through the library doors. For his part,
his notion of Ireland had been formed partly by Arthur Griffith's writings
on parallel historical events in Ireland and Hungary,[1] and partly by Ireland's
reputation as having the best fishing in Europe. When he arrived, he was no
Attila, but a forceful and imposing figure nonetheless, a man of solid build with
thick swept-back hair and clipped moustache, and the very direct manner of
many of his compatriots.

His early days in Maynooth coincided with the completion of the new John
Paul II Library on the 'Long Meadow' beside the Lyreen River, and his first
undertaking was to oversee the complex move and the establishment of library
services in the new building. He put into operation a very simple but efficient
method of transferring the books shelf by shelf from their old location in the
Arts Building library and what is now the Russell Library to their corresponding
shelves in the new library. During the summer of 1984 teams of library staff
and students could be seen constantly criss-crossing the North and South

1   A. Griffith, *The Resurrection of Hungary: A Parallel for Ireland.* (Dublin, 1904)

Library staff group portrait, academic year 1992/1993.
(*By the Lyreen River, with the College Infirmary in the background*)
Back row (L–R): Patricia Harkin, Valerie Seymour, Paul Hoary, Penelope Woods, Rosemary McManus
Centre row (L–R): Elaine Bean, Susan Durack, Valerie Payne, Jean Kane, Sheila Larkin,
Pauline Murray Davey, Margaret O'Regan, Regina Whelan Richardson
Front row (L–R): Marie T. Finn, Mary Kearney, Etaín Ó Síocháin, Thomas Kabdebo
(Librarian), Andrew Sliney, Suzanne Redmond, Agnes Neligan (Deputy Librarian)

Campuses, ferrying books in the long black boxes immediately dubbed 'coffins'. Nevertheless, a lot of fun was had by the bearers, along with weeks of hard work.

Tom's chief leisure passion was fishing, but on campus he found opportunities to engage in his love of tennis and was an enthusiastic participant in the tennis matches arranged by the university's 505 Social Club, which took place after work at five minutes past five. He engaged in regular doubles games with some of his university colleagues; the slam of the tennis balls, the exclamations, and the tension in the air attested to some very competitive styles of playing on the old courts between The Sheds and The Graf.

His preferred method of communication in the workplace was verbal, and a summons to a discussion was often in the form of a peremptory note placed on one's desk: 'Come to my office at 11', signed with his distinctive initials, TK. I would turn up in his office with absolutely no idea what he wanted, a promotion, an interesting new project, instant dismissal? It could turn out to be anything, from 'I left some pike in the freezer for you today',[2] to '"Killarney John" (an elderly priest of some notoriety) has made a complaint to the president that you had lunch in the Professors' Dining Room.' In the latter case, Tom had

2   He records catching a 3.12kg pike in 'Maynooth lake' (at a local fishery) in 1987 and describes how it was cooked and stuffed with noodles and marjoram. He was out fishing on Lough Ree on Christmas Eve morning the following year, catching a 1kg pike in Lough Ree, which was cooked in a paprika stew and washed down with a strong, fruity Hungarian white wine called Tokaji Furmint. T. Kabdebo, *Fishing for Compliments: Catching, Cooking, Tucking In* (Dublin, 2017).

arranged for me to have lunch with the visiting head of the Hungarian Academy of Sciences, where I was hoping to take part in a staff exchange. In preparation for this, Tom had begun to give me Hungarian language lessons and he had dictated some tapes to illustrate pronunciation. He was very patient, even when I arrived for a lesson unprepared and obviously winging it. It was pleasant to hear him speak in his native language, rather different from his more carefully modulated speech in English, and I think that he was pleased that a member of the library staff was taking an interest.

I had my own copy of *The Resurrection of Hungary*, bought in a second-hand bookshop many years before, and I presented this to him as a thank you for the language classes. Subsequently he invited me to compile the index to a book on Ireland and Hungary. Through this work I learnt much about Hungary, and the historical and cultural links between our countries that it explored.[3] He involved the library staff in a number of publications, as contributors, editors or typists, gave work to local company Cardinal Press, and showed us that publishing anything we deemed worthwhile could be achieved, even in a small way as one's own agent and with a modicum of self-belief. In several ways, this Hungarian librarian enriched my life, giving me the opportunity to engage with the Salamanca Archives, and encouraging me to write; initially on the occasion of the bicentenary of St Patrick's College in 1995 in the publication *Maynooth Library Treasures*,[4] leading to further research and publication on the subject of the Irish colleges in Spain. It was during his time that a librarian was hired on secondment from Trinity College, Dublin to oversee the implementation of a new computer system for the library; this was Andy Richardson, whom I later married, and our first holiday together was to Hungary.

Running in parallel with his career as a librarian[5] was his distinguished literary life; language, writing and publishing were his passions. He forged and recorded Hungarian-Irish historical and literary connections, and through his translations and publications notable Irish poets were introduced to Hungarian readers and listeners, and vice versa.[6] The opening of the Hungarian embassy in 1991 was an opportunity to organise events under its auspices and sometimes he would invite library staff who were interested in Hungary to literary and other events there. He set up a collection of world literature in English translation in

3   T. Kabdebo, *Ireland and Hungary: A Study in Parallels, with an Arthur Griffith Bibliography* (Dublin, 2001).
4   R. W. Richardson, 'The Salamanca Archives', in A. Neligan, ed., *Maynooth Library Treasures: From the Collections of St Patrick's College* (Dublin, 1995). http://mural.maynoothuniversity.ie/5689/
5   During his tenure the Recognised College at Maynooth became the National University of Ireland, Maynooth (1997), with the Library supporting NUIM, SPCM and the Pontifical University, which share the same campus.
6   See his anthology of Irish poems translated into Hungarian: *Tört álmok: Ír költők antológiája* (Budapest, 1988), and his translations of contemporary Irish poets with Maynooth associations, Mary O'Donnell and Bill Tinley.

Staff and students in the College lorry outside the new John Paul II Library
during 'The Move', Summer 1984

the library; the college collection of *Maynoothiana*; a series of library lectures: *Beyond the Library Walls*; and he was a founding member of the *Maynooth University Record*.

He had a great interest in Italian language and culture and had worked as a student tour guide in the Basilica of St Peter's in Rome, the subject of the inaugural illustrated library lecture which he gave in 1984. His coffee mug bore the Italian word *oggi* (today) and he had an alchemist's approach to coffee-making. While he did not introduce the elaborate siphon apparatus he presided over in his home, his coffee break in the library involved the careful brewing of a Dutch coffee brand in a special stovetop espresso maker.

Ireland was his second home, reached after much peregrination, following on his escape to the West after his participation in the 1956 revolution; he spoke of this only occasionally in the library, and shared some memories in an interview to RTÉ Radio in 1986. Thomas Kabdebo died in his eighty-fifth year on 23 May 2018.[7] His experience of the reality of living in post-war Central Europe and his subsequent life, including his time in Maynooth, are captured in his autobiography *No Matter Where I am, I See the Danube*.[8] 'The Danube ... carries the message of Europe ... its language is Europe's river language. This [super-national] message ... is transmitted in all of Kabdebo's books'.[9]

7   See obituary by E. Murphy and R. W. Richardson, '*Thomas Kabdebo (Kabdebó Tamás) 1934–2018*', *An Leabharlann* 27:2 (2018), pp. 39–40. http://mural.maynoothuniversity.ie/10258/
8   T. Kabdebo, *No Matter Where I am, I See the Danube: Autobiography* (Dublin: Phaeton Publishing, 2011).
9   Á. Göncz (President of Hungary, 1990–2000), in the foreword to T. Kabdebo's autobiography.

MAYNOOTH COLLEGE
CHAPEL CHOIR TOUR, 1985

Eamon Martin

I t's hard to believe nowadays that the Maynooth College (Seminary) Choir in the mid 1980s had a membership of around sixty seminarians. Under the direction of the Columban missionary priest, Dr Sean Lavery, the choir aimed to maintain a high standard of choral singing in the College Chapel on Sundays, holy days and special occasions. Dr Lavery had a special love for Gregorian chant and the choir reached a high standard of accomplishment in singing chant in the Solesmes style. In my junior days, the BBC had asked the choir to sing Solemn Latin Vespers of St Patrick for broadcast in the prestigious *Choral Evensong* slot on Radio 3. As a result of this broadcast, the choir was invited to sing at two summer festivals in France in 1985: in Roscoff and in Paris. As senior cantor that year I accepted the task of organising the tour and I kept a chronicle of the events.

The choir set sail on Saturday, 20 July 1985, from Ringaskiddy bound for Roscoff. The Maynooth Choir Concert was to be one of many international contributions to the Breton 'Festival des 3 Mers' which continued through July and August 1985. During our visit to Brittany, we enjoyed a magnificent concert given by a vocal-instrumental ensemble from Bruges, and an orchestral concert by the Orchestre du Chateau Royal of Warsaw. There was time too for some sightseeing, including a trip around the coast of West Brittany with a stop at the ancient monastery of St Guenole (Winwaloe) at Landevennec, which was celebrating the fifteenth centenary of foundation that year.

During the Roscoff concert on Tuesday, 24 July, the choir sang some of the most well-known Gregorian chants: 'Veni Creator' (Hymn to the Holy Spirit); 'Puer natus est' (Introit from the Third Mass for Christmas Day); as well as settings of the 'Ave Maria', the 'Magnificat' and the solemn 'Salve Regina' for Compline. Polyphonic music included Asola's 'Missa Octavi Toni' and a number of Haller motets. It was clear that the audience loved this music, especially when the choir joyfully intoned the great Sequence of Easter Sunday, 'Victimae Paschali'. Here was the perennial song of the Church, sung with all

La Sainte Chapelle

the freshness and vigour of youth. Just as Irish monks sang melodies like these in the monasteries of France in the closing years of the tenth century, the young men of Ireland were once more reminding the French of the beauty of praising God through Gregorian chant.

As we spent more time among the Bretons, we became aware of our shared origins. Many called us their 'Celtic cousins' from Ireland and I was glad we could introduce a Celtic flavour into our concerts. Peter Gannon, a third-year student from Tuam diocese, played some haunting airs on the concertina. Frank Lawrence, from Waterford, played Irish music on the organ, including Stanford's Prelude No. 3. One might have thought that such music would have been out of place in a concert of Gregorian chant, but this was not the case. The modalities of the Gaelic and chant melodies are strikingly similar – perhaps some early Irish influence in the formation of the chants? Ó Riada's 'Ár nAthair' was offered as a prayer and an encore at the end of the concert.

On Wednesday morning, 25 July, we travelled across northern France to the small village of Solesmes, not far from Le Mans, arriving at the monastery – an imposing fortress-like structure on the banks of the River Sarthe – in time for Vespers on the Feast of St James. These days spent in Solesmes were to be the highlight of our travels.

The silence that pervaded the monastery was palpable. The ethos of contemplative life spilled into the daily Mass and hours of the Divine Office which were always sung in Gregorian chant. It was very evident that the monks were singing their prayer as part of a continual offering of their lives to God. Witnessing this had an abiding impact on our own prayer and singing – as individuals and as a group. When Dom Jean Clair, the Solesmes choirmaster, spoke with us, he, too, emphasised this important aspect of the chant. He spoke of the simplicity of melody chosen so as not to dominate or detract from the depth of meaning contained in the text. 'The music,' he told us, 'merely serves the words'. It is this great truth which remains the secret of Solesmes.

Side by side with worshipping God through chanted prayer, some of the monks devote long hours to the careful study of the chanted Mass. Fr Gregory, a young American monk, not much older than ourselves, showed us some of their patient and painstaking work. For the choir this was an opportunity to see, first-hand, Solesmes' work in the fields of paleography and semiology. For those of us who had studied some Gregorian semiology under Dr Lavery at Maynooth, it was fascinating to see the room where Dom Eugéné Cardine and his fellow monks spent their lives attempting to reconstruct the authentic melodies and recapture the rhythms used over one thousand years ago.

On Saturday morning, 28 July, we bade farewell to Solesmes and left by train for Paris – a sudden contrast to the cloistered walls of the monastery! It was in Paris, that evening, in the beautiful setting of La Sainte Chapelle, that we sang the Solemn Vespers of St Patrick as part of the Paris 'Summer Festival'.

A large audience for the concert included many friends from Ireland resident in Paris. It was for us a great honour to have present at the concert the Irish ambassador to France with his wife and the cultural attaché. An invitation from them to attend a reception in the Irish embassy the next day was happily accepted. As we travelled homewards from Paris to Cherbourg on Sunday evening, I was happy and honoured to have been associated with this historic and eventful week in the life of the Maynooth Seminary Choir.

The following year, when Dr Lavery took a sabbatical, I accepted the role of acting director of sacred music and choir conductor for my final year. But of all my Maynooth memories, our summer visit to France in 1985 remains fondly etched in my mind.

In 2013 I returned to Solesmes for Holy Week to make a retreat in preparation for my episcopal ordination. While there I chose for my episcopal motto a line from one of the chants we had sung back in summer 1985 – *Cantate Domino Canticum Novum* – Sing a New Song to the Lord!

A 'DAY IN THE SUN' IN MID-NOVEMBER 1987 WITH RTÉ AND THE CARDINAL

Patrick Comerford

We were a disparate and motley group of half a dozen who arrived from Kimmage Manor in Maynooth for our conferring one dark November day in 1987. In my first year at Kimmage Manor there were thirteen of us on the BD course. Now, three years later, we were just six.

The Theology Faculty at Kimmage Manor has long since been absorbed into other schools and colleges. In the 1980s, it had a special relationship with Maynooth that allowed its students to sit for the degree of bachelor of divinity.

It was an unusual arrangement, and in academic fiction it was supposed to apply only to students preparing for ordination and sponsored by either the Spiritans at Kimmage Manor or the Redemptorists at Marianella. But I had been brash and cheeky enough to knock on the front door one summer evening and ask John O'Brien could I sign up for the three-year programme.

My lecturers and professors were mainly either Redemptorists or Spiritans. The Redemptorist Con Casey coached me through the philosophy requirement Maynooth sought before completing the course in theology. The Spiritan Paddy Ryan taught us Church history. Another Redemptorist, Brendan McConvery, who had lectured on New Testament studies, would present us to the chancellor of the Pontifical University, Cardinal Tomás Ó Fiaich, who would die within three years.

We were the only six from Kimmage Manor that day, and I was the only member of the Church of Ireland. The other five teased: Would I be presented as a Redemptorist? Would I be presented as a Spiritan?

Outside, the late Eddie Kelly of the *Irish Times* was waiting to take photographs. He, too, teased me: would I like my photograph in the paper tomorrow morning – the very paper where I was a staff journalist? The story is still told of an embarrassing moment when Eddie was covering the funeral of Cardinal Conway in Armagh ten years earlier – a gust of wind carried Eddie's hat into the grave, along with the cardinal.

I sat in the chapel comfortably, waiting for our names to be called and for Brendan McConvery to lead us up. My great-grandfather, James Comerford, had worked with the architects A. W. N. Pugin, Richard Pierce and J. J. McCarthy on their churches in County Wexford. After Pugin died in 1852, and Pierce died in 1854, James Comerford moved from Wexford to Dublin, married, and found new architectural commissions with the Board of Works and designing public houses. As I gazed up at the stucco work and ceiling, and admired the craftsmanship throughout the Gothic Revival chapel, I wondered whether James, who became the patriarch of our branch of the family, had ever worked with anyone of this great architectural trio in Maynooth.

As our names were called out, I realised how we were less than half the number who entered the first lectures three earlier. As I was introduced to Cardinal Ó Fiaich, I was greeted with a broad, knowing grin. Yes, he remembered me. He knew of my work with the Campaign for Nuclear Disarmament (CND); Seán MacBride had given him a copy of my recent book; he knew me from the *Irish Times*; he had listened to Christian CND while the Irish bishops were preparing *The Storm that Threatens*, their joint statement in 1983 'on war and peace in the nuclear age', and he had appreciated my comment on it in *The Furrow* later that year.[1]

As we processed out, to applause from our families and our professors, the television cameras were waiting for us too. It was one thing to bump into a photographer who was a colleague on the *Irish Times*; it was another thing to find RTÉ cameras had turned up at our graduation.

We rushed home that evening, not just to share a bottle of bubbly and cut a special cake, but also hoping to be in time for the six o'clock news. However, earlier that day, the loyalist politician and paramilitary George Seawright – whose calls for 'revenge and retribution' made him too toxic for both the Democratic Unionist Party and the Free Presbyterians – had been shot in a black taxi on the Shankill Road in Belfast.

Once again, events in Northern Ireland dominated the evening news. Maynooth had slipped down the list of news priorities, and Cardinal Ó Fiaich's interview must have been heavily edited. Nevertheless, he still got his point across: a large number of women were among the BATh graduates that day, and he expressed his hopes that women with inquiring theological minds would one day find a greater role in the life of the Church. Some of those women graduates served to illustrate his argument.

The six of us from Kimmage Manor could be seen in the background on the

1   Patrick Comerford 'The Storm That Threatens: A Comment', in *The Furrow* Vol. 34, No. 10 (October 1983), pp. 620–25.

Augustus Welby Northmore Pugin (1812–1852)

news report that evening – although, perhaps, only by ourselves and those who loved us. We had our day in the sun, even if it was mid-November.

George Seawright was shot on 19 November and died from his wounds on 3 December; Tomás Ó Fiaich died just over two years later on 8 May 1990. Two men of very different backgrounds, temperaments and values had been brought together on the news for very different reasons on the day of my graduation in Maynooth. As for Eddie Kelly, his trademark hat sat on his coffin at his funeral in January 2010.

Of the six of us from Kimmage Manor who arrived in Maynooth that day, one is a now well-known broadcast journalist, one is working in London on development programmes, and one quickly resigned from active priestly ministry; two are Redemptorist priests; and I was ordained in the Church of Ireland by Archbishop Walton Empey thirteen years later.

Many years after our 'day in the sun', as I was thumbing through some forgotten books on my bookshelves, I came across a well-thumbed postcard from Tomás Ó Fiaich which had been used as a bookmark. My regular return visits to Maynooth have included a quiet day in the chapel on my own self-designed retreat shortly before my ordination, many book launches, as a visiting lecturer, and as a guest when Brendan McConvery was recently awarded an honorary doctorate.

JOINING THE SOCIOLOGY QUARTET

Mary Corcoran

A chair of Catholic Sociology and Catholic Action was first inaugurated in 1937, in St Patrick's College, Maynooth, making it the longest established on the island. Over the years, the Department of Sociology grew in size and stature, eventually helping to found three additional departments (Anthropology, Adult and Community Education, and Applied Social Studies). The hallmark of the department from its inception to the present day is a commitment to both excellence in intellectual inquiry and to the pastoral care of students. Sociology's seventy-fifth anniversary celebrations in 2012 were attended by the President of Ireland, Michael D. Higgins, himself a sociologist.

I began my career at Maynooth in 1990 a few months before Mary Robinson made history as the first woman elected to the Irish presidency. In a smaller way, I was making my own history. I joined a department of four exceptionally gifted men, on a campus that was still heavily male-dominated. The university had yet to undergo a division into two separate structures – the Pontifical University and the National University of Ireland, Maynooth. Most departments were still headed by clerics, and we had a sprinkling of clerical students in our classes. Maynooth back then was relatively small, spatially compact and highly collegial.

The late Liam Ryan was professor and head of department. He had a natural authority and grace and ran the operation in a most gentlemanly way. We worked well under his paternalistic leadership. External examiner visits were a particular highlight during Liam's tenure as we would repair to Barberstown Castle or Moyglare Manor to toast the end of another successfully completed academic year. Liam was a stickler for facts. Facts must always be placed in the service of an argument. This is key to understanding his own approach to the craft of sociology. The sharpness of Liam's intellect and his prescience are evidenced in *Social Dynamite* – his early study of social deprivation in Limerick city, where he emphasised the impact of early school-leaving on the children who exit the system and for its reproduction of social disadvantage across generations.

The commitment to public sociology – which moves beyond the academy and engages with the concerns of real people – was brought home to me by Micheál Mac Gréil SJ, who, like Liam, had learned the craft of sociology during

Rev. Prof. Liam Ryan

Liam Ryan at the Arctic Circle
(August 1981)

Liam ready to drink reindeer milk as an honorary Laplander (August 1981)

turbulent times in the US. As a scholar-activist, Micheál advocated publicly on a wide range of issues from the Irish language, to Traveller rights, to western regional development. His path-breaking sociological inquiries into prejudice and tolerance in Irish society spanned a period of almost forty years. Micheál's grizzly beard and impressive girth made him an imposing presence on campus. Students loved him. An early proponent of experiential learning (a term much in vogue today), he dispatched his students to the courts to observe and reflect on the workings of the legal system. For many, this was a life-changing experience. Micheál was one of those men of the cloth who wore his religiosity with humour, compassion and forthrightness. He could be stubborn, but his natural inclination was always to stand up for those with less power in any situation, whether it was a student, a worker, a Traveller, or someone troubled.

I am reliably informed that the young Michel Peillon caused more than a frisson among the students when he arrived fresh from Paris to teach in the department in the late 1970s. Michel, who retired in 2009, never lost his distinctive French accent. An apocryphal story, often repeated, was that students thought Michel was talking about sociological 'fairies' in lectures when in fact he was talking about sociological 'theories'! Michel possessed that much sought-after quality – a true independence of mind and an ability to pose intellectual questions from different vantage points. At my job interview in 1990, Michel asked me by far the hardest question. What theoretical (as opposed to empirical) contribution did my work on Irish immigrants make to the field? Initially, I was somewhat intimidated by Michel, who had a deserved reputation as a serious and cerebral intellectual. He was extremely widely read and had published a very significant volume on Irish society, *Contemporary Irish Society*, in 1982. He proved to be a most gentle and generous colleague as well as a wonderful research partner and co-editor.

The fourth member of the Sociology Quartet was Tony Fahey, who went on to have a stellar career at the Economic and Social Research Institute and as Professor of Social Policy at UCD. Tellingly, Tony had been a student of Liam's, Michel's and Micheál's. Tony retained (and still retains) a boyish demeanour and an irrepressible enthusiasm for his craft. He is a much sought-after public intellectual who has made a major contribution to public policy studies, while wearing his scholarship lightly. Tony was the kind of colleague who always had your back. When I was at home on maternity leave in June 1992, Tony called to see me and found me with piles of student projects that I was valiantly trying to grade. He swept them all up in his arms, insisting that I had more important things to focus on. A typical collegial act of kindness.

Apart from the professional development and life lessons learned when I joined the quartet, my early years in Maynooth were enriched by wonderful relationships with women colleagues across the college. We regularly met as an informal women's forum to discuss issues of particular interest and concern. The winds of change were beginning to blow through Maynooth in the 1990s and we pushed to have a stronger say in the running of the college. For instance, in 1993 we produced and submitted a document to the Faculty of Arts calling for an equality policy, including the appointment of an equality officer (at the level of vice-president) and an equality committee. Sometimes it can take a while for such new-fangled ideas to bed down within an institution! In 2013, I chaired an Academic Council Working Group that brought forward recommendations for a more system-wide focus on equality, diversity and inclusion. I subsequently chaired the Joint Academic Council/Governing Authority Committee on Equality, Diversity and Interculturalism that devised an updated equality policy for the university in 2018. In the summer of 2019, Maynooth University appointed its first Vice-President for Equality and Diversity.

The Sociology Quartet, which I joined in 1990, contributed significantly to the evolution of the discipline of sociology both within Maynooth and beyond. In an expanded and much changed institution, sociology continues to play a significant role, upholding the tradition of scholarship, promoting public sociology and engaged research, and contributing to policy-making and governance within the university and beyond.

MEMORIES OF 'TOM AND GERRY' AND THE DEPARTMENT OF CLASSICS, MAYNOOTH

Maeve O'Brien

The study of the Greek and Latin languages, of the humanities, was ably promoted in Maynooth, in Ireland and beyond by Professor Thomas Finan and Professor Gerard Watson. Both now sadly passed away, their contributions and personalities are sadly missed: *sed fugit interea, fugit inreparabile tempus* (Virgil, *Georgics*, 3. 284). Both men, newly ordained, found themselves as very young scholars labouring in the groves of academe in 1959. A period of great cultural and social change in Irish education and society coincided with their appointments. While St Patrick's College was still a place for the education of those who wished to study for the priesthood, 1966 saw it offer education to both religious and laity. A Recognised College of the NUI with faculties of arts, science, philosophy and Celtic studies for decades, the Maynooth Gerry and Tom worked in subsequently became a constituent university of the National University of Ireland with the passage of the Universities Act in 1997. Both Tom and Gerry continued to work in the 'new' university as well as in St Patrick's, which is still the National Seminary and a Pontifical University.

Maynooth has been my professional and personal home for the past thirty years. Ancient Classics has been studied in this place since the founding of Maynooth College in 1795. I was conferred with my PhD in NUI Galway, or UCG as it then was called, and after six years working in a temporary capacity, was lucky to secure a permanent post as lecturer in 1991 in the Department of Ancient Classics. In those days the department was led by Professors Finan and Watson. I waited nervously to be interviewed by the great and the good under the chairmanship of College Vice-President, Msgr Matthew O'Donnell. I need not have worried; even as I was expertly interviewed, I was put at my ease. Afterwards, my first meeting was with Professor Watson, whose affability knew no bounds, and Professor Finan, whose clever wit and dry sense of humour I was just beginning to appreciate. When I could translate a passage from the *Annals* of the Latin historian Tacitus, and present it as we walked the

Rev. Prof. Gerry Watson (standing second from the left)
Rev. Prof. Tom Finan (seated second from the left)
Rev. Prof. William Meany (seated third from the left)

fabulous grounds of St Patrick's College, my initiation was complete.

Both men worked in unison to forward the study of Latin and Greek, serving on many college committees; on the Royal Irish Academy's National Committee for Greek and Latin Studies, and on the Central Council of The Classical Association of Ireland. Their foresight meant that Maynooth was among the first to embrace a new subject, Greek and Roman Civilisation, which involves study of the politics, culture and history of Greece and Rome in translation. A huge upsurge in numbers ensued so that, when I arrived in Maynooth, marking up to 400 First Arts examination scripts each summer was not unusual. Making Classics widely read, and fostering links with interested parties on our island as a whole, was a project dear to Tom, and especially to Gerry. They hosted a conference of enthusiasts under the name 'Hibernian Hellenists' twice a year, starting in 1963. Ballymascanlon Hotel, Dundalk, was the 'inter-party' venue for gregarious and convivial gatherings which accompanied some serious scholarly papers. 'The Oracle of Zeus at Dodona', 'The Sound of Greek', 'The Stoic Theory of Knowledge', 'Problems in Ancient Map-Making' and 'Ion of Chios' were among the first set of papers delivered by H. W. Parke (TCD), W. B. Stanford (TCD), M. Tierney (UCD), G. Watson (St Patrick's College Maynooth), and G. L. Huxley (QUB). Professor George Huxley is a great friend to Ireland, Maynooth and the Classics. When he became an Irish citizen in 2018, George was the oldest new citizen of Ireland (*Irish Times*, Thursday, 29 November 2018). We are fortunate to have him in our midst. My opportunity to deliver a paper entitled 'The Day of Laughter in Apuleius' *Metamorphoses*', in 1987, was a memorable occasion for me. Owing to rising costs, the venue for the meetings changed to St Patrick's College Maynooth and subsequently to Maynooth University, ever afterwards being dubbed 'Ballymaynooth'. Here it continued, organised by classicists from Queen's University, Belfast, and Maynooth University until its final meeting on 8–9 March 2013. The island's collegial friendship of classicists was completed by the erudite contributions of Galway and Cork.

Unlike 'Tom and Jerry' in the famous cartoon, our Tom and Gerry were scholarly, collegial and rivals in the very best sense. One Galway wag used to ask me how 'Gerry and the Pacemakers' were doing and, suffice to say, 'You'll never walk alone' captured the happy collegial atmosphere fostered by their generosity of spirit. Martin Pulbrook and Keith Sidwell made up the quartet to which I, as the only woman, was added. Martin is originally from the Isle of Man, and Keith exchanged the Midlands of England for the Midlands of Ireland. Martin and Keith are excellent researchers and impressive lecturers in the areas of Latin poetry, Greek tragedy, and indeed in every aspect of the ancient world, and although they have left Maynooth for pastures new, they were welcoming and generous colleagues to me when I started to lecture in the area of Ancient Classics. I still count them as dear friends. Those were indeed happy days for me in the company of some of the most erudite people one could meet anywhere, then and now.

Sadly, Gerry and Tom are no longer with us and, as I walked with my baby daughter through to Gerry's burial place in St Patrick's College, and went many years later to Tom's funeral in Enniscrone, County Sligo, I did not think about the exam meetings, departmental reorganisation, new courses of study for students, important though these are. I thought of the invaluable trust, generosity and intelligence of these people who dedicated their whole lives to the service of others. Gerry and Tom combined affable personalities with lives dedicated to rigorous scholarship. This created an atmosphere that encouraged a growth in the numbers studying Classics and also made the department a happy one for both colleagues and students – *in tenui labor, at tenuis non gloria* (Virgil, *Georgics*, 4. 6).[1]

---

1   I would like to express my thanks to Professor Salvador Ryan and Dr John-Paul Sheridan for affording me the opportunity to recall all those, especially the Rev. Professors Finan and Watson, who have contributed to establishing the sure foundation the Department of Ancient Classics now enjoys in Maynooth University. Their scholarship, idealism and attachment to Maynooth as a place of learning has made it *magna parens frugum ... magna virum et mulierum.*

MAYNOOTH A TRUE
ACADEMIC COMMUNITY

Brian Cosgrove

erhaps the best place to start my consideration of what Maynooth's university meant to me is to recall my early acquaintance – long before I went to Maynooth – with the late Professor of Classics in the college, the redoubtable Gerry Watson. I had known Gerry's younger brother, George, as a fellow postgraduate in English studies at Oxford in the mid-1960s. Through him I got to know Gerry, as well as Richard Watson (younger than George).

In summer 1969, a group of us of varying ages stayed at a *pensione* in the seaside town of Cesenatico on the Adriatic coast. The aforementioned Richard was one member; and the group also included Gerry, another priest (Kieran Ryan, a physicist from UCD), and an American nun. This being Italy, the wine flowed – Lambrusco for lunch, Chianti for dinner. More importantly, the conversation also flowed, and a rich mix it was, running all the way from jokes to matters of philosophical or even theological import. It would be difficult to impart to the reader the whole tenor of our sporadic and unsystematic musings. In retrospect, I see us as establishing our own imperfect form of an ancient Greek symposium, though, speaking for myself, I did not feel I possessed the kind of intellectual acumen evident, for instance, in Kieran and Gerry. The latter – for me a large bonus – had a special interest in Plato. In my final year at school, I had been drawn to Shelley's *Adonais,* crucial in introducing me to Neoplatonism; and, indeed, I had made a point of reading Plato's *Symposium* in my first year as undergraduate at Queen's in Belfast.

I taught in UCD's English Department, starting in 1967, and UCD had been, to put it mildly, a mixed experience. In due course, with the sudden and tragic death of Professor Barbara Hayley, Head of English at Maynooth, in 1991, events conspired to make the now vacant chair of English at Maynooth a highly desirable option. In fact, ever since my earlier acquaintance with Gerry Watson, the possibility of moving to Maynooth had always been at the back of my mind, the Cesenatico experience acting as a touchstone of what the Maynooth environment might have to offer. In any case, my personal bias was such that

St Joseph's Square facing Long Corridor

I found a certain attraction in teaching in an institution that boasted so many gifted theologians. Last, but not least, I had been (rather harshly, in my view) passed over for promotion to senior lecturer in UCD. Not surprisingly, there sprang from that experience a further incentive to move to a new academic environment.

When I speak of the appeal of the tradition of theological teaching, I mean to indicate a particular kind of bias in my approach to the study of English. It took me a while to formulate the nature of this bias, but I did attempt to do so in the Library Lecture (the equivalent at that period of an inaugural lecture) delivered in the Common Room early on in my tenure. My own deepest and most ingrained tendency in the study of literature is to treat the subject as first cousin, or even sibling, not of history or ideologically based politics, but of philosophy. Such a bias is evident in my high regard for Melville's *Moby Dick*, which I see as one of the most honest and courageous forays into philosophical or, indeed, theological speculation ever penned. I must immediately add that a sense of responsibility restrained me when it came to our departmental syllabus; I had to recognise the importance of such alternative ideological approaches as post-colonialism, feminism and others. It would be unfair to send out our graduates into the world of postgraduate studies without an acceptable knowledge of those emphases in the modern study of literature which are indicated under the convenient heading of 'critical theory'. It was a difficult balancing act.

So, although I did not consciously formulate any policy, the priorities for me became the following: intellectual speculation; an openness, even to perspectives that I might not share; and, as a corollary of the latter, the attempt to maintain a sense of intellectual community. How fortunate I was in that St Patrick's College (as it was known when I arrived) was so thoroughly endowed with a sense of collegiality. Yes, there had been inevitable disagreements; but in my personal experience, I had never felt so fully integrated into a community of intellectual aspiration.

In my first weeks there were small but cumulatively impressive indicators. I experienced nothing but a generous acceptance from colleague Peter Denman, who had been acting head of department for a year before I arrived. Tom Kabdebo, whom I got to know on my first day when he informed me that I was to be *ex officio* a member of the Library Committee, was insistent, in a more informal setting, that the food on offer in the staff dining room was of a significantly better quality than UCD's (he was right). Gerard Gillen, who had made his move from UCD to Maynooth some years earlier than I, went out of his way to assure me that I would be happy in my new academic environment. He too was right.

Throughout my time in the college, I enjoyed nothing so much as sharing a joke with colleagues from History or Music or other departments, perhaps at lunch on conferring days; and more frequently with Philosophers and Ancient

Lebanon Cedar near the College Chapel

Classicists down the corridor in the old one-storey Arts Building (to which Peter Carr had also gratifyingly moved, after he had retired from the Registrarship). That informal relationship with philosophy then achieved formal status when I agreed to share for alternative years a course devised in Philosophy on Philosophical Aesthetics. For me, and I hope for the English students who took the course, it was a welcome opportunity to transcend the constantly shifting shapes of contemporary critical theory, and, rising above the immediacy of one's own culture, see those theories in a broader perspective – the wood, not the trees.

Because English was a subject available to students taking the BA in theology, it was happily part of my duties to attend not only the Exam Board meeting for the BATh, but the delightful lunches with colleagues from the Theology Faculty afterwards. Over the excellent meal and the freely dispensed wine, we engaged in conversations that were not just entertaining but, I like to believe, at times informally educational. In any case, the network of academic community was further extended and, in due course, I was providing an article or two for the *Irish Theological Quarterly*, an international journal of the Faculty of Theology; and shorter pieces and book reviews for *The Furrow* – a habit that extended into my retirement, thanks to the good graces of that periodical's splendid editor, Ronan Drury, a man whose death affected many. I am delighted to say that I have contributed to *The Furrow*, under its new editor Pádraig Corkery, since that sad event.

Have I been sufficiently eloquent in expressing my gratitude to Maynooth, for accepting me so readily into its rich communality? I could, I know, say so much more. But the ineradicable memory of Maynooth I have and always shall have is how happy I was there: happier by far than in Oxford or UCD.

FIRST SUNDAY IN SEPTEMBER 1992

Joseph Collins

When the soul of a man is born in this country there are nets flung at it to hold it back from flight. You talk to me of nationality, language, religion. I shall try to fly by those nets.

(James Joyce, *A Portrait of the Artist as a Young Man*)

uring my childhood days in Newport, County Tipperary, I was serving early morning Masses almost on a daily basis, at least one Mass on Sundays, and benediction on most Sunday evenings. And then there were all the weddings and funerals. It was inevitable that my plaintive demands for my vocation to be tested would eventually be heard. I cannot be sure now what convinced me of my 'vocation'. It may have been the grandeur and authority of the liturgy. Maybe the twinkling candles and the hallucinogenic incense. Whether it was faith or fascination, I did not understand why, but entering seminary was a kind of magical experience where none of the norms of the outside world seemed to apply. That was 1992!

It was the first Sunday in September 1992 when I entered St Patrick's College Maynooth as a student for the archdiocese of Cashel and Emly. Although now a memory over twenty-eight years old, in many ways it seems like only yesterday. It was All-Ireland Sunday and Kilkenny and Cork squared off against each other. My father was perturbed that we were due at the college in the afternoon as he wanted to see the match. Our parish priest, Joe Delaney (a former Maynooth dean) had advised that the President of Maynooth was a Wexford man and the Vice-President a Cork man, so he too thought it poor form that the seminary year should begin on such a day. In the end we watched the match at a relative's house en route; when we arrived at the college I was the last to sign in and, after dropping my bags in the room allocated to me, we headed across to Mass in the College Chapel.

It's difficult to describe the complexity of feelings, thoughts and emotions experienced on first seeing the college gates in Maynooth with the realisation

Mother Teresa of Calcutta's Visit (1993)

that this was where I was going to live for the following seven years. That night as I unpacked my cases in what was a very large and bare room in Long Corridor, I really began to wonder what I was doing in that place. I was homesick and surrounded by thirty-five others who were probably experiencing something similar.

By the end of that first month a sense of camaraderie had developed as we moved from a collection of bewildered individuals to classmates. Friendships were being made that last to this day and, overall, this period was characterised by great enthusiasm for what lay ahead. Ideals were high and hearts lay open in the belief that we were doing something special.

The place was full of mysteries. One chilling one was that of the nineteenth-century suicides in Rhetoric House where two students allegedly took their own lives in the same room, nineteen years apart. A common legend suggests that a diabolic presence had something to do with both students jumping out of the window to their deaths. There was a recurring story amongst the seminary community that the dark stains on the floor of that room (known as the 'Ghost Room') were human blood from one of the students who, prior to jumping had cut himself with a razor, and that, despite being removed by cleaning products, the bloodstains kept reappearing. Did the ghosts of those dead students really haunt the corridors – or was this just another way of keeping us tucked up snug in our rooms at night?

Some of my favourite memories from those days are of clandestine acts that took place from time to time after lights out. After night prayer we were supposed to return to our rooms and maintain 'solemn silence' until rising time for prayer the following morning. The dean, Fr Frank Duhig (formerly of St Munchin's College, Limerick) would prowl the corridor to check what lights were still on. Our surreptitious acts, which usually centred on my room, involved boiling a kettle in the room and entertaining a few classmates with tea and biscuits in whispered voices. Our mischievous anarchy was indeed quite harmless. Over those gatherings we mused on the great questions of the meaning of life and, in many ways, those conversations were much more formative than what we experienced in the lecture theatres in the Arts Building or the class halls in Loftus.

As I think back, I realise that nostalgia often makes us see the past with rose-coloured glasses and we edit it for content. So, some of the stories I recall are perhaps best left unwritten as I may not do them justice in putting pen to paper. Suffice to say that those memories define my past and very often drive how I think of the future.

On the whole, those years in Maynooth were good years. The regime was reasonable and its deficiencies more than compensated for by the intellectual stimulation and personal/human growth. I grew up a lot there, learned a lot about academic things, made some great friends and learned to have a deep appreciation for life and the things that make it up.

Whilst I went on to leave the priesthood, I will be forever grateful to Maynooth for the start in life and, in particular, for the varied, beneficial and thought-provoking education that serves me well today in the world of academia. Maynooth challenged me not to accept easy answers, but to ask tougher questions and then to lead with insight, grace and resolve. In the twenty-eight years since entering Maynooth, the world has changed significantly, but the need for leaders trained to think theologically has not.

OF COMETS AND PRINCESSES

Susan McKenna-Lawlor

I t is probably unique that I personally remember Maynooth as a place associated with comets. In 1986 we had overhead an apparition of the mysterious and wonderful Halley's Comet, which has been observed and recorded by astronomers since at least 240 BC. Clear records of the comet's appearances have been recorded by Chinese, Babylonian and European chroniclers, and there are interesting accounts of it in the Irish Annals where it is described as a 'bright object', rather than by the word *réalt* (a star). These early sightings were not recognised as reappearances of the same object, and the comet's periodicity, which was first determined in 1705 by the English astronomer Edmond Halley – after whom it is now named – is of the order of seventy-five years, thus making it possible for a human to see it twice in his or her lifetime. Such an observer was my late mother, Meta Keane McKenna, who saw it as a young girl in the skies over her native Cork and, when I brought her to see it again from the grounds of Maynooth College in 1986, she greeted it with the welcoming words, enunciated in spirit over the ages in many countries by people of many cultures, 'Oh my beautiful comet!'

According to a model developed in the nineteenth century (The Nebular Hypothesis), the formation of the solar system began some 4.6 billion years ago with the gravitational collapse of part of a giant molecular cloud. Most of the collapsing mass collected at the centre, thereby forming the Sun, while the remainder flattened into a proto-planetary disk from which, by an accretive process, the planets and other solar system bodies were, thereafter, formed.

Comet nuclei, due to largely remaining resident since their formation from the proto-solar nebula in the cold outer regions of the solar system, are considered to constitute the least processed early material available to scientists for study. Precise knowledge of the physio-chemical composition of comets can thus provide insights into the formation of the solar system itself and into the starting conditions for the origin of life on Earth. The first spacecraft observations of a comet nucleus in history was performed by the European Space Agency's *Giotto* mission, which flew at high speed through the head of Halley's Comet in 1986.

Giotto's Adoration of the Magi with Star of Bethlehem

Artist's impression of the spacecraft flying towards Halley's Comet

This mission was named Giotto after the Italian painter Giotto di Bondone who, in 1304, depicted Halley's Comet as the Star of Bethlehem in one of his frescoes in the Scrovegni Chapel in Padua.

I was principal investigator for one of ten experiments on board *Giotto* and carried in that capacity full scientific, technical and administrative responsibility for this (national) instrument – which I called EPONA, after a Celtic goddess associated with the commencement of the solar year. This name is also an acronym for *Energetic Particle Onset Admonitor* – which indicates that a primary objective of EPONA was to measure high energy particles at the comet. During the design, construction and testing phases of instrument development, Irish engineers from my group in Maynooth received at the Max Planck Institute at Lindau in Germany state-of the-art training in the special skills required to build an instrument with the capability to survive the rigours of space. Meanwhile, I established, in parallel in my laboratory, facilities that could be used when the phase of building and testing the actual flight model would be reached, while also sourcing financial support for the setting up on campus of a commercial company called Space Technology Ireland Ltd (Space Tech.) to provide an environment in which Irish space engineers of the future could pursue exciting and challenging careers. Space Tech. continues to operate and has over the years provided successful instrumentation for keystone missions launched by space agencies in America (NASA), China, Europe, India and Russia.

Integration of the Philae lander with Rosetta

The Electrical Support System (ESS)

The acclaimed success of the *Giotto* mission (which later flew on to visit comet Grigg-Skjellerup in 1992) and important pioneering observations secured by Ireland's EPONA, resulted in my being invited by Professor Helmut Rosenbauer, then director of the Max Planck Institute, at Lindau, to take responsibility for a 'mission critical' unit to be flown by the European Space Agency to yet another comet (i.e. to comet Churyumov-Gerasimenko aboard the *Rosetta* mission). Since it is not possible to make a detailed inventory of the constituents of a comet nucleus through making either ground-based or flyby observations, because the materials present in a cometary atmosphere are chemically differentiated from their parent substances, it was innovatively planned to this time deploy a Lander equipped with high-level experiments onto the comet nucleus to seek, inter alia, for the presence there of prebiotic molecules.

My task was to act as leader for the design, construction, test and delivery of the electrical support system (ESS) aboard *Rosetta* that would appropriately convey commands regarding observations to be made by instruments of the lander payload on the comet's surface, while also ensuring that the precious data actually recorded by these instruments would ultimately be configured for safe transmission to Earth. The ESS was, in these circumstances, defined, as already mentioned above, to be 'mission critical', meaning that, if it were to fail, Europe would have no scientific return from the Lander on which many EU countries were flying very costly high-technology instrumentation. In trying to delicately

The Ariane 5 rocket used to launch the
Rosetta spacecraft

Rendezvous of Rosetta with the comet nucleus

convey to my team the awesome responsibility I had now undertaken for them as well as for myself, I asked, 'Do you know that if we get this wrong they will throw stones at us in every major city in Europe?' The answer I received was just right: 'We do not design shirts in a box,' they said. 'We enjoy challenge and responsibility.'

This was, in fact, a very lengthy challenge. The images on the previous page and above depict the lander arriving at the spacecraft for integration with Rosetta, and the launch in 2004 of the powerful rocket which flew for ten years to bring this hardware to the comet. You will also see the ESS we built, and on which so many hopes and dreams were riding, and, on p. 381, an artist's impression of the spacecraft flying towards the comet. The rendezvous of the spacecraft with the comet nucleus is depicted above.

The cruise phase to the comet was exciting, with flybys of Mars and two asteroids to achieve before the landing of *Philae*, and there is much that I could tell you about the thrills and spills of watching the lander bounce on surface contact and set off across the cometary landscape while recording wonderful data along the way. At the close of the mission, as I came to say goodbye to the ESS at the tracking station, it was very touching to be told by one of the staff: 'The ESS was always our favourite unit since, whenever we addressed it over more than a decade, it always answered very sweetly.'

As I write, a beautiful instrument called PICAM, much of which was built at Space Tech., is on its way to planet Mercury aboard the joint ESA/Japanese twin spacecraft mission BepiColombo (BC), and in the next few months we expect to receive exciting information from the BC payload during a flyby of Venus.

I started with a story about my mother and will end with another one, not in any particular association with what is written above but in the spirit of throwing light on a classical Maynooth tale that can now be revealed to have an unexpected dimension. It happened that a friend of my mother came to the house one day to tell that her son had met a 'princess' (albeit from the post monarchy house of Habsburg-Lorraine) on an aeroplane and that this lady would shortly visit Dublin. It was deemed because of her rank that it would not be appropriate to place her in an hotel and my mother was asked if she might rather stay with her to enjoy authentic Irish hospitality and privacy. I was told about the plan and suggested that my mother would tell over dinner the oft-repeated story of how Sissi of Austria sustained a fall while hunting near Maynooth; had been taken to the college for tea and sympathy and had later sent a gift of a magnificent statue of St George to her hosts in remembrance of the occasion. She was thanked for this attention, although it was pointed out that Maynooth is in Ireland where the patron saint is St Patrick, whereas St George is associated with a neighbouring island. In the aftermath of this, Sissi sent a second gift, consisting this time of a set of vestments very liberally festooned with shamrocks. The matter thereafter had rested with both items being put on display. I suggested that, if the Princess might wish to view the gifts, I was sure that she would be very welcome to do so and would request that she be suitably received. The answer was a surprising one: 'Sissi made no mistake,' my mother was told. 'In her part of Austria the patron of hunting is St George and, had the gentlemen looked more closely at the silver buttons on her riding jacket, they would have seen, embossed on each one, a representation of the very statue that had been sent.' Thus, the original gift had been conceived to make a graceful reference to the riding accident. However, when it was realised that this was not understood, Sissi had quietly sent something else she thought her hosts would enjoy more – beautiful vestments with a special emphasis on Irish national heritage.

Maynooth is a place for stories and there are many still untold that it is hoped this book will reveal. Let us look forward together to what we will learn as we peruse its pages.

AN DORAS

(Is cuimhin linn Urnaí na hOíche i Séipéal an Choláiste ...)

Marie Whelton

Many alumni of Maynooth University remember the liturgical beauty, reverential solemnity and deep peace of Saturday Night Compline in the Gunn Chapel where St John Henry Newman's 'Lead, Kindly Light' was often sung. 'An Doras' recounts the experience of two lay female theology students, who happened upon Night Prayer, one Saturday in the mid-1990s, and it tells of the lasting impact the hymn and the prayer-time had on their lives.

Doras ard maorga agus
solas ag lonrú trí na bearnaí mórthimpeall air.
'An rachaimid isteach?'
'An bhfuil cead againn?'
'Bainfimid triail as.'
D'éirigh linn an doras a oscailt.

Séipéal cúng ag síneadh i dtreo na bhflaitheas,
níos gile ná an pasáiste lasmuigh,
ábhair shagart i mbun guí.
Shuíomar sna stallaí cúil.
Faitíos, cúthaileacht, míchompord:
'Ar chóir do chailíní tuata a bheith anseo?'

Cumhracht chéadfach na túise –
An Naomhshacraimint ar taispeáint
in oisteansóir drithleach grianmhar.
Ionadh, suaimhneas, impí:
'An cumha baile i ndiaidh Iarthar Chorcaí agus
an t-amhras faoin eaglais a thógáil ó mo chroí.'

Reredos and ceiling in the Apse, College Chapel

Ceol niamhrach ó phíoporgán –
iomann Béarla nár aithin mé,
macalla ar mo phaidir féin ann:
'Treoraigh a Sholais Chaoin …
dorcha an oíche, is fada ó bhaile mé …
cianamharc, níl uaim, ach a bheith in ann coiscéim amháin a thógáil.'

Léamh agus iontonú –
briathra agus ceol ársa na Coimpléide ag cur i gcuimhne dúinn:
'an Tiarna a mholadh istoíche',
'faire a dhéanamh i bhfochair Chríost' agus
imeacht, faoi shíocháin, mar a rinne Simeon,
tar éis dó radharc a fháil ar Sholas na Náisiún.

Salve Regina –
na focail Laidineacha ar eolas agam
ó thurais, mar dhéagóir, ar Lourdes.
Chan mé os ard.
Chan mo chomhscoláire, freisin.
Sineirgíocht chairdiúil chineálta cheoil.

Cumha na heolchaire imithe.
Tuiscint faighte go raibh cara nua tugtha dom don tríú leibhéal –
cara leis an Té a bhí á chuardach ag an mbeirt againn sa diagacht.
Fós buartha faoin dorchadas a bhí ag creimeadh ionracas na heaglaise,
ach cinnte de go raibh Dia an tSolais i láthair ag an urnaí oíche seo
dár gcuardach agus dár dtreorú chun sáimhe lena lóchrann séimh.

Cúig bliana is fiche ar aghaidh,
tuigim go mbíonn go leor pasáistí dorcha le siúl i rith na beatha,
agus go nglaoitear orainn, sna pasáistí sin, doirse na lúcháire agus na síochána a
oscailt le daoine éagsúla, fós, nuair a theipeann orm é sin a dhéanamh,
cuimhním ar dhoras Shéipéal an Choláiste, ar bhriathra na Coimpléide,
ar mhisneach carad agus cumhdaítear arís mé i ngrá suthain an tSolais Chaoin.

Tagairtí
'Dé Domhnaigh 1'. *Urnaí na hOíche*. Foilseacháin Ábhair Spioradálta: Baile Átha Cliath, 1974, lgh 12–18.

MEMORIES OF THE GRAF

Niall Howard

I imagine that, for many, the oratories and the Gunn are synonymous with prayer and Mass; the Ref reminds most of meal times; and Loftus meant lectures. But what about the Graf? For some, it reminds them of the varied sports played there – be it football, hurling, soccer, rugby, tennis, handball, road bowling, running or walking. But it was about more than that – it is surrounded by college history and personal memory. Whenever I return to Maynooth, the Graf is the one place that always draws me to revisit, and the

The Graf

physical aspects haven't changed that much since I first walked it in September 1992. So, shall we go for a walk?

 Surrounding the Graf we pass important aspects of the college – St Mary's House with its accommodation and the stories of the lads in wartime oil rationing getting up in the frosty mornings with the first task being to break the ice in the wash basins for the morning ablutions; Loftus with the lecture halls and the stories of past professors on the rostrum, themselves trying to transition from Tridentine theology and the 1917 Code for those going out to a very different vineyard. Little changes in the world show themselves in simple ways – over to the side are the apple orchards, once cherished by the kitchen staff and now just too much work in a fast-paced world; only the birds and the occasional domestic baker avail of them now. And stroll off into the Junior Garden with its rockery, glasshouse and cornucopia of colour, where we remember the lovely story of Msgr Patrick Corish gardening one day in September when a new first-year enquired if he was the gardener, and with a wry Johannine smile the president answered, 'You know, Mary Magdalene made the same mistake herself!'

On the other side of the Graf, we walk past a building of true Christian hospitality and care – the Infirmary, with the treasured feminine outreach of the Daughters of Charity – giving medicinal aid to those who were sick, or a welcome relief to those who needed a break from the timetable for a day or two. There is the John Paul II Library, with its treasure trove for the essay or thesis at hand, but also the lovely chance to explore other disciplines for some extra stimulation as one fingered through the shelves on unfamiliar floors. Looking to the main door of the Gunn brings memories of Easter Vigil fires outside, while inside were graduations, ordinations and carols, and down the avenue to the college farm with the stories of students being drafted in for work during strike times.

On into the cemetery with its November college processions, we go to pray for the dead, and I remember being mesmerised the first time I walked the yew-lined entrance to behold O'Growney's fine mausoleum, while others barely got a numbered cross (indeed two didn't even get the number) – students who were meant to be there for seven years but are there now for eternity, while their parents received the 'We regret to inform you … ' letter.

We amble along the impenetrable wall at the bottom of the Graf with the canal and the railway line just beyond – those on the far side of the wall were going on physical journeys, while we, on the inside, were at the fork in Robert Frost's yellow wood wondering which way would make all the difference in our lives. Sociologists tell us that walls, fences and boundaries are interesting features – sometimes they are to keep people (and ideas) out, or sometimes to keep them in. But we were always reminded that the gates were open for those who wished to leave, and during daylight hours the gates were open, too, to welcome the locals outside to explore the Graf for some tranquillity for themselves away from their village-cum-N4 highway.

Those physical features others could equally recount, but what about my own memories, you ask? Well, I smile when I think of the few first-year/second-year soccer games played in the spiritual months, or indeed the di-shields ('di' for 'diocesan'), which were hotly contested – I smile because they were indeed well stuck for a number to have to field me! But the camaraderie and team building were important for us as we settled into community life in the college and into the prospect of diocesan life afterwards. I think of our Junior Dean, Frank Duhig, encouraging manual labour on a Saturday morning, clipping the suckers from the base of the Graf trees, leading us out like McAlpine with his

Fusiliers, knowing that occupational therapy was good for young men who spent so much time in the head, heart and soul – the body needed to be pushed a bit too – *mens sana*, and all that.

But there was more to the Graf for me than that. In the times when the corridors and cloisters felt a little too claustrophobic, the grounds and the quietness gave a most appreciated breakaway for an hour to get some time for myself. It was the place where I could ponder what was going on in class, what was going on within the class group and college, and what was going on in myself – to smile a bit and to wonder a bit. It gave me the opportunity to be out in the beauty of God's creation long before Pope Francis helped us to reflect on the canticle of creation's patron saint. In a college and Church where tradition and continuity were important, it was a gift to behold the variety of the Graf – the springtime bursting forth, the early summertime beckoning exams and the late summertime marking a new year, and the stunning autumnal colours with the squirrels busying themselves for the bare wintertime of hard frost and snow-covered grounds. While the flat Kildare landscape was difficult to bear at times, being out in the tree-lined Graf took me back home for a while to the more personally invigorating hills and waters of the Kingdom.

However, for all the personal time there, the Graf gave the opportunity to walk the paths with others, and to journey with them on life's pilgrim way with trust and a supportive conversation. It was lovely to set out for a walk with others, or indeed to go out on my own, but then to meet others and turn into friendship for a while. I give thanks for the laughs while on the Graf, and for the serious chats too. I give thanks for the people who walked it with me and for the friendships deepened, and I deeply appreciate the solitary time when, like the pair walking to Emmaus, I too was slow to believe the full meaning of it all, and my own eyes were opened.

While wet days kept us indoors to walk the cloisters with its welcome shelter, there was nowhere like the Graf. It wasn't just about the walk.

MAYNOOTH'S BICENTENARY CELEBRATIONS, 1995

Jacqueline Hill

he establishment of St Patrick's College Maynooth by the British government in 1795 marked an important step in the gradual dismantling of the Penal Laws. With the war against revolutionary France disrupting opportunities for the training of Catholic priests abroad, the government was also hoping to dissuade Irish Catholics from supporting the United Irishmen. During the nineteenth and twentieth centuries, the college was to prove remarkably successful in preparing large numbers of priests, not alone for service in Ireland but also globally. Moreover, by 1995, lay staff and students had been playing a part in the college for some twenty-five years, so there were additional aspects of its history to celebrate.

The bicentenary occurred at a time of change in the college. Preparations for the celebrations were already under way when Msgr Micheál Ledwith stepped down as president in 1994. Looking ahead to the formal legislative split between the theological and secular sides of the college (which came about in 1997, when the latter would achieve full independent status as NUI Maynooth), Professor W. S. Smyth became master of what in 1994 was the 'recognised' NUI college at Maynooth, with Professor R. V. Comerford from the History Department as vice-master. Msgr Matthew O'Donnell succeeded Dr Ledwith as president of the Pontifical University. The two heads worked together on an appropriate commemorative programme.

Numerous events were organised to celebrate the bicentenary. They included a series of lectures (which doubled as an elective course in the Faculty of Theology); an exhibition and colloquium on 'Irish identities', focusing on the nature and role of the Orange Order, which was also celebrating its bicentenary in 1995; the publication of books and the production of CDs featuring the college choirs. A commemorative 32p postage stamp, depicting the President's Arch, was brought out for the occasion (first day of issue, 27 July 1995). The annual carol service was recorded by RTÉ to be broadcast on Christmas Eve 1994, and in January there was a joint ecumenical service between the college and St

FIRST DAY OF ISSUE
Lá an chéad eisiúna

St. Patrick's College, Maynooth.
Established 1795

First Day Issue of Bicentennial Stamp

Mary's Church of Ireland, just outside the college grounds. In March, a series of lectures was given at the Royal Dublin Society by Dr Susan McKenna Lawlor, Professor of Experimental Physics in the college, on instrumentation built by the company she had founded (Space Technology Ireland Ltd) for launch on missions flown by the four major space agencies (European, American, Russian and Japanese).

The History Department was invited to organise the lecture series, and Dr Jackie Hill, who had suggested including something on the Orange Order among other commemorative events, and was making the arrangements for that, took responsibility for identifying suitable topics, speakers and chairs. The college authorities had indicated that the main events should, as far as possible, take place on Tuesday evenings in January to March 1995. The overall theme for the lecture series – eight in all – was 'Ireland in the 1790s', and the venue for most of them was Callan Hall on the South Campus. They began on 17 January with a lecture by Msgr Patrick J. Corish, former Professor of History in the college, who took as his theme 'The founding of the Royal College of St Patrick: the religious context'. Msgr Corish's history of the college, *Maynooth College, 1795–1995*, had been published to coincide with the bicentenary. The following week two members of the Economics Department, Dr Gerry Boyle and Professor Patrick Geary, spoke on the topic of 'The Irish currency and economy in the early years of Maynooth'. On 31 January, Ms Mary Cullen, former lecturer in the History Department, considered 'The town of Maynooth', and the following week Dr

Pontifical University Bicentenary Conference: 'Of Truth and Freedom', November 1995.
Front row (L–R): P. J. Hamell (Birr); Professor J. Kitmyer (Washington); Professor F. Schüssler-Fiorenza (Harvard); Herbert McCabe (Oxford).
Middle row (L–R): Thomas Corbett (Maynooth); C. Nolan (Maynooth); J. Corkery (Milltown Institute); Patrick McGoldrick (Maynooth); Professor M. Quesnel (Institut Catholique de Paris); Professor C. Bressolette (Institut Catholique de Paris); Martin Henry (Maynooth); Patrick Jones (Carlow); C. Casey (Marianella).
Back row (L–R): P. Roe (Maynooth); John McAreavy (Maynooth); Professor S. Hauerwas (Duke Univeristy); Professor D. Burrell (Notre Dame); B. Ombres (Oxford); Professor J. Beutler (Sankt Georgen, Frankfurt); Enda McDonagh (Maynooth).

Arnold Horner of UCD, a specialist on the subject, discussed the historical stages involved in 'Mapping Maynooth'.

The master of the college, Professor Smyth, who had published on the topic, took as his theme 'The 1795 origins and subsequent geographical spread of the Orange Order'. He was followed on 24 February by Professor Marianne Elliott of the University of Liverpool, who discussed 'Ireland and revolutionary Europe in the 1790s'. In March, Professor John Coolahan of the Education Department in the college considered the topic of Irish education in the late eighteenth century. The final lecture in the series took place on 14 March, when the subject was the founding (also 1795) of the National Botanic Gardens in Glasnevin, the speaker being Dr Donal Synnott, the director of the gardens. The lectures were very well attended, having been advertised via posters in the town,

'Towards the year 2000: Public Policy in Ireland': one-day Conference presented by past students prominent in political and public life, 15th June 1995.
Front row (L–R): Eamon Ryan, ambassador to Portugal; Mary Hanafin, Fianna Fáil Executive; Joe Costelloe, TD; John Hume, MP, MEP; Patrick Hillery, former President; John Wilson, former Tanaiste; Senator Michael O'Kennedy.
Back row (L–R): John Gallagher, deputy general secretary, Democratic Left; Dominic McNamara; Liam Ryan; John Brown, TD; Patricia O'Connor; Farrell Corcoran; Noel Dempsey, TD; Theresa Ridge, Dublin County Council; Matthew O'Donnell; Maurice O'Connell, Governor, Central Bank; R. V. Comerford.

as well as notices in the local and national press (the *Leinster Leader*, the *Meath Chronicle* and the *Irish Times*).

Timed to coincide with Professor Smyth's talk on the Orange Order, an exhibition of paintings by the Antrim-born artist George Fleming was displayed in the Arts Building on the North Campus. Entitled 'Echoes', the exhibition consisted of a series of paintings on aspects of the images and symbolism of the Twelfth of July. It was opened on 17 February by playwright Frank McGuinness, whose much-acclaimed play *Observe the Sons of Ulster Marching Towards the Somme* had first been staged in 1985, while the author was a member of the English Department in the college. The following day a colloquium was held in Theatre 1 of the Arts Building, North Campus, on the subject of 'Irish identities: Orangeism, its nature and role in Irish life'. Talks were delivered by Msgr Patrick

Corish on the eighteenth-century origins of sectarianism in Ireland; Dr Anthony Buckley from the Ulster Folk and Transport Museum on the iconography and symbolism of Orangeism, and Sam McAughtry, a Belfast writer and broadcaster, who discussed his memories of Orangeism in Belfast. The final talk was given by Professor Cecil Houston, University of Toronto, a specialist in Irish-Canadian studies, who offered a Canadian perspective on Orangeism abroad.

A bicentenary series of books appeared, spread across a number of academic disciplines. They included several from the Theology Faculty, including Thomas Marsh's *The Triune God*; Myles Rearden CM, *You are Mine: A View of the Spiritual Life*, and Gerard Watson's *Greek Philosophy and the Christian Notion of God*. Other books published for the bicentenary included those by Mary Cullen, who brought out a second edition of her local history, *Maynooth: Má Nuad*, and Étaín O Siocháin (from the college library), who published *Má Nuad: Saothrú na Gaeilge 1795–1995*. Dr Philip Dix, from the Biology Department, brought out a guide to bird life in the college, while Dr Paul Gibson (Geography) produced a local geological guide. Finally, a facsimile reproduction (1945 edition) of the celebrated series of essays about different aspects of college life – Fr Neil Kevin's *I Remember Maynooth* – was also brought out to mark the occasion. Overall, the bicentenary was marked by a notably wide range of events and attracted widespread and enthusiastic attention.

THE NATIONAL SCIENCE AND ECCLESIOLOGY MUSEUM AT MAYNOOTH

Niall McKeith

he Museum of Ecclesiology in Maynooth College was founded in 1934, and Rev. William Moran, Professor of Dogmatic Theology, was appointed as its first curator. The museum was to be a repository for various objects of ecclesiastical interest; especially those that were linked with the research and pioneering work of former Maynooth professors. It has also subsequently been enriched by the benefactions of former Maynooth students and friends. Noteworthy amongst the many benefactors we find the name of Very Rev. John O'Ryan PP of the Parish of St Nicholas of Myra in Dublin, himself an ardent collector of ecclesiastical material, who bequeathed his very fine collection to the museum. At present, the museum has two sections, one devoted to ecclesiology and the other to science.

In 1942, on the resignation of William Moran, the trustees appointed the Rev. Patrick J. McLaughlin, Professor of Experimental Physics and later college vice-president, to be curator. This post he held until 1957. He transferred to the museum all the Callan apparatus, including induction coils, electromagnets, the 'repeater', condensers, electric motors and batteries – amongst these his cast-iron cells, which were also manufactured by E. M. Clarke of London, who sold them commercially. These items had been stored in the basement of Stoyte House, then part of the Department of Experimental Physics.

Professor McLaughlin also carried out extensive research on Callan's publications in Sturgeon's *Annals of Electricity*, in the *Philosophical Magazine* and in the *Proceedings of the Royal Irish Academy*. In volume 25 of *Studies* (1936) he gave an account of these and, in 1965, to mark the centenary of Callan's death, he published *Nicholas J. Callan – Priest Scientist, 1799–1864*. It can be truly said that he rescued Callan's pioneering work from oblivion and established beyond doubt that Callan was the inventor of the induction coil.

Rev. Professor Pádraig Ó Fiannachta, curator from 1958 to 1973, published a 'mini-catalogue' dealing with some of the more important exhibits and added some exhibits of national importance to the collection. It is still available.

In March 1974, Rev. Michael T. Casey OP, Professor of Chemistry, was appointed curator. He made an inventory with detailed measurements of all the scientific instruments in the museum associated with Nicholas Callan. This inventory was incorporated in Dr Mollan's *Irish National Inventory of Historic Scientific Instruments, Interim Report 1989*, and may be regarded as the beginning of the scientific catalogue. The final version of the catalogue, *The Scientific Apparatus of Nicholas Callan and other Scientific Instruments*, was offered by the museum as its first contribution to the bicentenary celebrations of the college in 1995. That same year, Dr Niall McKeith from the Department of Experimental Physics (appointed assistant curator in 1990) and P. J. Breen catalogued the ecclesiology collection also as *St Patrick's College Maynooth Museum of Ecclesiology*.

In the 1990s Niall McKeith, Fr Michael Casey and the then Professor of Physics, Jim Slevin, went through the cupboards and laboratories in the Physics Department which, until a dedicated building was built on the North Campus, was still in Stoyte House. They identified those instruments that were of historical and scientific interest and moved them up to the museum to add to those already there. The collection includes a large selection of surveying instruments dating from 1600 to 1986. The 1986 instrument, recently donated to the museum, was the first of its type to incorporate GPS, cost £86,000 and was used to survey the oilfields of Saudi Arabia.

On the death of Fr Casey in 1995, Niall McKeith was appointed curator and the museum was totally refurbished with purpose-designed and -built display cabinets. The refurbished building was opened in 2000 by Taoiseach Bertie Ahern, and College President Msgr Dermot Farrell, and was called The National Science Museum at Maynooth. The new display cabinets enable the collection of scientific instruments to be shown to their advantage. The displays are centered on Callan's batteries, coils and giant induction coil and show his patent certificate for the invention of galvanisation to prevent iron from rusting. The museum now houses the finest collection of scientific instruments on public display in the whole of Ireland. Many of them were manufactured in Dublin, principally by the firm of Yeates and Sons and Spencer, who were originally opticians in Grafton Street in Dublin, and exported throughout the world. Included in the collection is the Marconi radio equipment used to give the first results of a sports competition, namely the winner of the Kingston Regatta in June 1898, for publication in the Dublin edition of the *Daily Express*. In Fintan O'Toole's *A History of Ireland in 100 Objects* (2014), object number 98 was the Intel Pentium Chip manufactured by Intel in its Leixlip facility. Intel presented

Opening of the Museum with Msgr Dermot Farrell, President; An Taoiseach,
Bertie Ahern TD and Prof. Hugh Connolly

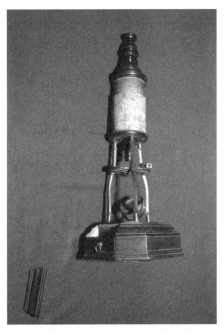

Culpepper Microscope (c.1745)

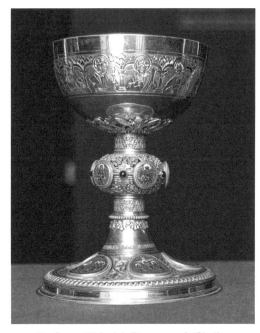

Professor Heinrich Bewerunge's Chalice

the Pentium Chip to the museum in a display cabinet. Intel has also presented the museum with four computers and upgraded them with new ones every five years.

The museum still has, as part of its core holdings, a large collection of vestments, altar plate, penal crosses, mass rocks and papal coins in purpose-built display cabinets. Unfortunately, in 1970, and again in 1980, the museum was subject to robberies. In the latter, over forty of our finest episcopal rings, chalices and numerous gold crosses were stolen and never recovered. For this reason, the display does not fully reflect the history of the college as it once did.

Among the vestments are those presented to the college by the empress of Austria following her visits to the college in the 1880s. Other sets of vestments are those made by ladies-in-waiting to Marie Antoinette, and also those presented by the Queen of Spain, Maria Barbara of Braganza. Also on display is the death mask of Daniel O'Connell, taken within an hour of his sudden death in Genoa on 15 May 1847. The purpose-built cabinet was made by John Lee and was paid for by a kind donation to the museum.

One of the more curious items on display in the museum is a projector, apparently used by Professor Lennon, the then Professor of Physics or Natural Philosophy, who went to Knock, County Mayo, in 1880, the year after the reported apparitions there, to see if he could reproduce the apparition on the side of the church. He was not able to do so. It was believed by some at the time that the apparition was a fake and the result of a slideshow. Lennon proved, to his own satisfaction at least, that the apparition could not have been produced in this manner.

The National Science and Ecclesiology Museum at Maynooth is a real treasure trove, often undiscovered even by those who are already quite familiar with the Maynooth campus. Come and visit us some time.

Facing page: Sundial Detail from Healy's
Maynooth College: Its Centenary History

AN ANTHROPOLOGIST'S MEMORY
OF MAYNOOTH

Lawrence Taylor

'Maynooth will never hire a Jew.'
A prediction that proved wrong. Not only was I hired, but I was among the last professors whose appointment received the imprimatur of the bishops of Ireland. It was 1997, the year that the National University of Ireland, Maynooth, the newest of Ireland's third-level institutions, after a decades' long gestation, was born of Ireland's second oldest (if we forget poor, short-lived St Mary's College, founded on the same site in 1519): St Patrick's College, itself, however modest in size – college, seminary and Pontifical University. A three-in-one mystery.

I took up my position in September of 1998 and soon found that despite the separation, the overlap in space as well as time allowed for a pervasive liminality of the kind that would intrigue any anthropologist. Though I'll confess to being disconcerted by the question 'Father, would you like another rasher?' from servers in Pugin Hall at breakfast (it was my black T-shirt that probably threw them); a mis-categorisation that often occurred in those days when I told folks I met in various parts of the country that I was a professor at Maynooth. While I might be amused by the personal irony of this persistent ambiguity, I soon found that many of my university colleagues were, understandably, more guarded about any continuing influence of the Church – especially in light of the national and international revelations and crises besetting it. I, however, as someone not blinded by either loyalty or fury, was intrigued to find myself operating in a complex web of time and space, where the two institutions seemed to operate in parallel dimensions – a kind of twilight zone where turning a corner into some

point of passage might take one into a very other world.

Over the ensuing two decades of my working life there, my experience was considerably enriched not only by the continuing 'presence' of St Patrick's, but also by the illuminating contrasts between the two 'worlds'. There were sumptuous clerical lunches and dinners with flowing wine and port, sadly absent from ordinary university dining experience, and the marvellous pomp of conferring ceremonies in the magnificent College Chapel (where I might be reassured of my welcome by a bishop's reference to our 'Judeo-Christian' identity). More revealing, however, were the inner workings of both 'sides' of the campus to which, as head of a university department, I enjoyed some access. If the fact of difference was expected, the nature of that difference could be surprising.

I remember in particular the striking contrast between the respective examination boards the first time I attended and participated in both. I suppose I am, like most anthropologists, a committed relativist who regards even, or especially, the deep-seated beliefs of the 'tribe' as potentially cultural constructs, and borders – whether between nations or other human groupings – as always arbitrary. I might have expected a strong commitment to essential categories among the clerics, but on the issue of marks and results, it was my secular university colleagues who revealed a surprising essentialism. If a particular student's marks averaged out to a 38 or 39, or if a student fell just short of moving from a 'second' to a 'first', the registrar (himself a reasonable man and a mathematician who seemed more aware of the slippery human grasp of numbers) asked if any of the concerned departments might consider adding a mark or two to push said student over the line. There would follow a long and tortured conversation in which department heads seemed to take the opportunity to display for the benefit of colleagues the exacting standards and precision of marking in his or her world. You might expect that from a chemist, but it was the representatives of the humanities who were the most assertive in this regard, perhaps anxious to show their scientific colleagues the ultimate reality of their marks, and of the knowledge it measured. This essentialism in their disciplinary vision was often matched by one in their sense of students. With a nearly Calvinist sense of predestination, some academics would describe a student as an essential 'third' or 'second' who, in his marks, was only revealing his true nature, one that we had no business tinkering with.

A brief time afterwards, I found myself among the clerics on the St Patrick's examination board, in which I participated insofar as the theology and arts degree offered at our sister institution involved their students in one or another of the university subjects. Here, among those in whom outsiders might expect a rigidity of belief, I found a casual sense of the relative 'accuracy' of marks as measurements and an apparent bonhomie of shared mission that stood in stark contrast to my secular colleagues. The request for an additional mark or two in this body was invariably met with multiple offers and the elevation of the student in question seemed an occasion of satisfaction rather than conflict.

Of course, it was a particular moment in the history not only of St Patrick's but of Ireland and of the Catholic Church. Perhaps the charitable inclinations of the clerical staff were in part due to the 'buyers' market' in which they, their institution, and the Church now operated. Yet it seemed to me they acted with a genuine sense of the fallible and yet improvable humanity of their students and themselves.

There were, of course, powerful, material reminders of other times around about, when the Irish Catholic Church enjoyed an altogether different status and its hierarchy seemed to revel in a self-assured majesty. The portraits in the cloisters, by which I was one day leading some American visitors as we made our way towards the College Chapel, are one such reminder. We paused before the brothers Fennelly, the late nineteenth-century 'vicars apostolic' of Madras, India, themselves flanked by equally grand depictions of bishops from Denver and Chicago. 'Maynooth,' I pointed out, with only a dash of hyperbole, 'was the greatest unintended consequence of the British Empire. With the founding of the seminary in 1795, they established the centre of what was to be an "Irish Catholic empire" that would stretch from Australia to Canada.'

That notion had occurred to me some days before when I strolled the same corridor after a visit earlier the same day to St Patrick's Cathedral in Dublin, whose many stone memorials to past parishioners include not only that to Dean Swift, but also an array to the soldiers and bureaucrats whose eternal presence there defined the place as 'a' (though certainly not 'the') centre of empire. There were, for example, slabs dedicated to the memory of two soldiers who had survived the Charge of the Light Brigade, along with those of generals, and other loyal servants of Britain's global reach. Back in the cloisters of Maynooth, I couldn't help but think of the 'dark brigades' of missionaries that set out on the 'Maynooth Mission to China' – the precursor to the Columban Fathers. But it was not so much such largely selfless and forgotten men of the cloth, as the complacently powerful global hierarchy whose portraits might seem to view with sad disappointment the ever-diminishing ordination classes whose group photos hung across from them, that promoted the 'unintended consequence' observation.

The powerful position that the Royal College of St Patrick assumed was assured not just by its founding at a moment when global as well as local geopolitics made the Catholic Church less threatening to the British crown, but by the previous elimination of potential rival Church institutions throughout the persecutorial years since the conquest. Now that the Church could be countenanced, and with Catholic Emancipation a few decades later, Maynooth was the only show in town – destined to supply the lion's share of clergy not only for Irish parishes, but for the Catholics of the British Empire, wherever they happed to reside. As largely English-speaking first arrivals to such provincial lands, the immigrant Irish clergy were destined to rise to political prominence within the Church – sometimes to the dismay of other immigrant Catholic groups who came later and/or less well prepared. Hence the Maynooth credentials of so many bishops and vicars apostolic of the English-speaking Catholic world.

That world is of course vastly changed, and St Patrick's is now an aspect of a far less powerful institutional church, just as Maynooth University has grown to be a first-rate university many times the size of its 'mother'. I, the secular New York Jew, now an adopted Irishman into the bargain, continue to be intrigued and even comforted by the enriching presence of the Catholic side of the campus and the intellectual and humane tradition it can represent. Looking around me now, I would say that the child is probably old enough to understand and appreciate the parent, and even to work with it for their mutual benefit.

Detail – Floor of College Chapel

REMEMBERING THE SENIOR INFIRMARY

Gearóid Dullea

Columba Centre (formerly Senior Infirmary)

uring my final year as a seminarian (1998–99), I was asked to live in the Senior Infirmary, or to be, in the old Maynooth lexicon, the 'List Monitor'. The year I spent there was very special, and I have warm memories of that time. That year was also, in some sense, historic, because it was the final year of the existence of the List, the Senior Infirmary.

During my first few weeks there, the late Sr Anne O'Brien DC, Infirmarian, told me that the Daughters of Charity would be leaving the College at the end of that academic year. This would, naturally, be a big wrench for the sisters but it would be an even greater loss to the college. The gentle, strong, caring, professional, faithful, joyful, and Christ-like presence and work of the Daughters of. Charity was something really cherished and esteemed by the students and staff.

In that final year of the existence of the Infirmary there were three sisters: Sr Anne, Sr Sheila, and Sr Veronica. As well as running the Infirmary, the sisters also looked after the various sacristies and chapels of the college. They also followed their commitments to religious life, such as daily Mass, recitation of the Liturgy of the Hours, and community life. I remember being struck by the silence of the Infirmary. Having up to that year lived with classmates in various buildings throughout the college – Long Corridor, New House, St Patrick's and St Mary's – one of the first things that struck me was the silence that pervaded life in the Infirmary: no sounds of student banter or scores of feet travelling to class, or the noise of discussion, disputation or debate. Another of my other key memories is of the heat. Not that it was oppressive, but it seemed that an attitude of 'if we can't cure them here, we'll at least sweat it out of them' prevailed. The temperature in the Infirmary was always kept at a decent level.

Breakfast was taken in the dining room, while I took my other meals in the students' refectory, Pugin Hall. I was to give a homily at Mass in the Infirmary chapel on one weekday each week. If there were sick staying in the Infirmary, one of my duties was to bring Holy Communion to them each day. At nighttime, I had to lock the front door. My tasks were very light indeed.

It is probable that every generation of students has its own store of stories about the Infirmary and the various sisters who ran it in the past: about the difficulty of being admitted as an ill student under one sister infirmarian; of the student pranks such as putting lemonade in the commodes of the bedrooms; or the Infirmary cat that was so well-fed that when an enterprising student once trapped a mouse in the Aula Maxima and then hoped that the Infirmary cat would dispatch it, no such luck: the cat turned up its feline nose at the sight of the mouse and simply waddled back to the civilised climate of its comfortable dwelling.

Yes, that word 'civilised' captures a lot about the Infirmary. There was a sense in which people mattered there, above and beyond the usual measurements and standards that occupied much of our student life.

I can only imagine that the Infirmary was an even more significant institution when Maynooth had greater numbers of seminarians and the life of the college was considerably more regimented. There was a sense in which it acted as a type of 'oasis' or 'safety valve' in the often challenging and demanding rigours of seminary life. There was also the folk memory from an earlier era that recalled the Infirmary being the place where students who died in the college were laid out before being buried in the college cemetery.

For my part, I gained an insight into, and learned from, dedicated religious who brought so much to the college. The sisters were, in the words of Fr Neil Kevin's *I Remember Maynooth*, 'our indispensable friends'. Their perceptiveness, kindness and wisdom added immeasurably to Maynooth. *Caritas Christi urget Nos* (2 Corinthians 5:14), the motto for the Daughters of Charity, had a physical embodiment in their understated and precious presence.

Providence led, ten years later, to my being assigned to work at the Senior Infirmary in its contemporary incarnation as the Columba Centre. So, I moved from being the last of the traditional 'List Monitors' in the Senior Infirmary to working in the same building. The continuity and the change.

R © RTÉ Archives / ref 0501 084.jpg

Queen Mary with members of the Daughters of Charity during the royal visit (1911)

Departure of Msgr Francis Cremin from
the college with (left to right) Sr Sheila
and Sr Anne

MAYNOOTH AT THE
TURN OF THE MILLENNIUM

Tríona Doherty

I almost escaped being a 'Millennial' – that generation that is loosely defined as those born between 1981 and 1996, and whose members are often derided as over-pampered. Born in 1981, I was on the cusp; I was young for my year, and many of my classmates technically belonged to the preceding Generation X, also known as the 'latchkey generation' due to changes in family life from the 1980s onward.

The 1990s, too, were a period of rapid social change in Ireland. The election of Mary Robinson as Ireland's first female president in 1990 had placed increased focus on 'mná na hÉireann'. The latter years of that decade brought the economic boom known as the Celtic Tiger and the tentative emergence of a new, more confident Ireland.

It was an interesting time to study theology in Ireland, though I'm not sure I appreciated that at the time. Divorce had been legalised in 1995, one of the early signs that the Catholic Church's influence on its flock was beginning to waver. The abuse scandals that were to rock the Church had not yet fully come to light, although individual cases such as that of Fr Brendan Smyth had already sent shock waves through the nation.

My own experience of faith in a rural parish had been positive and uncomplicated. The role of the Church in schools was still largely unquestioned. However, by the time I was leaving secondary school we had started to question the status quo, and in religion class we hotly debated topics like abortion, euthanasia and women priests. I remember a classmate expressing the belief that all religions were different paths to one God and being impressed with this new idea.

Amidst these shifting sands, in September 1998, we landed in St Patrick's College Maynooth – fresh-faced teenagers and a handful of enthusiastic mature students – to see what the Irish Church could offer us, and vice versa.

That first year in Maynooth, we picked apart biblical texts and analysed the Creed, highlighted chunks of the documents of the Second Vatican Council

Síolta Committee, second issue (including the author, standing second from right)

and discussed different models of the Church. We tackled moral dilemmas –
the infamous runaway train – and discovered the Church's 'best-kept secret',
Catholic social teaching. My head swam with more questions than answers.

I was combining my theology studies in St Pat's with a BA in anthropology in
NUI Maynooth, which stretched my mind in another direction. While theology
always pointed upwards, anthropology looked outwards to the wider world and
the various ways we humans shape it and make sense of it. Looking back, the
two subjects complemented each other magnificently. The intersection of the
'horizontal' and 'vertical' would delight many a theologian, though at the time I
often felt they were in conflict.

It was hard to ignore the heavy weight of history that surrounded us in St
Pat's, but in many ways it was a typical college experience. The cloisters that

at first seemed daunting were soon simply a shortcut to lectures, as we chatted under the watchful eyes of class-pieces and cardinals. Pugin Hall, or 'the Ref', with its high ceilings and male-dominated atmosphere became a friendly place for a coffee between classes. While the grandeur of St Joe's Square never failed to take my breath away, Dunboyne House and Loftus Hall became a home away from home.

Any dreams I had of blending anonymously into college life were quickly quashed. Within the first couple of weeks, our Scripture lecturer, Fr Seamus O'Connell, knew the names of the seventy or so first-year theology students and would regularly pounce in class to check if we were keeping up. Small tutorial groups meant there was nowhere to hide. Class reps were always scouting for choir members, readers and helpers for Masses and other events.

In second year, arriving to a lecture in Loftus Hall, I was stopped by a priest I didn't know. Fr Stephen Farragher had the idea of producing a yearbook, the first to incorporate students of both the Pontifical University and the seminary, and my name had been 'mentioned'. Would I be interested in getting involved? A committee of lay and clerical students was formed, and *Síolta* was born. The title reflected our sense that the year 2000 was a time of opportunity and new beginnings, with shoots of life springing up in the Irish Church.

Síolta painted a portrait, in picture and word, of the diversity of people that made up the college. It was an exciting project. Under the watchful eye of Fr Farragher, we met weekly to brainstorm and were duly dispatched to coax articles out of staff and students alike. Many of the contributions were witty, like the anonymous 'Ramblings of a Maynooth mouse', while others were more academic. Some honest and moving accounts of college life also made their way onto the pages.

It was my first experience of publishing; making decisions on layout, interviewing visiting speakers like Adi Roche, and speaking publicly at a launch. I remember writing an editorial about how the seeds sown during our time in St Pat's would bear fruit over time. Well, my experience with *Síolta* certainly had a lasting impact – since graduating, the majority of my career has been in journalism, and I contribute to religious publishing to this day.

We did not attend the same lectures as seminarians, but I got to know many of them through *Síolta* and various other groups, like the very active St Vincent de Paul Society. My abiding memory is of Friday-night visits to elderly people and families in Ballymun, an eye-opening reminder that the Celtic Tiger's roar had not reached into every corner of society. Sadly, *plus* ça *change*! Our little group ran homework clubs, food collections, fundraisers and talks, and retired regularly to Caulfield's to solve the world's problems over a pint.

The new millennium was approaching. At midnight on 31 December 1999, I found myself back home with a small gathering in my local parish church. I had agonised over where to spend the evening and, amid horror stories of taxi shortages, I plumped for a low-key family event. It was perfect, a peaceful interlude from the bustle of college life. The following summer I joined a group from the Meath diocese on a bus pilgrimage to Rome for World Youth Day 2000. This was my first experience of the Church outside of Ireland and the 'green shoots' talked about in Maynooth. It was glorious, and the WYD wave carried me into my final undergraduate year.

11 September 2001 was graduation day for my friends in the NUI. I was in Maynooth to celebrate with them, but, without a ticket to the ceremony, I wandered into the village to pass the time. Sitting in a café, the news broke that the Twin Towers in New York had been hit. This was before the immediacy of online news and social media, and a small crowd gathered around the television, watching with horror as the events of 9/11 unfolded.

A few weeks later, the theology class of 2001 graduated in the splendour and pomp of the Gunn Chapel. As we hugged and posed for photos outside the President's Arch, we couldn't have imagined the changes that were to come in the Church, in Irish society and internationally over the following twenty years. Within a few short years, the Ferns Report would be published, closely followed by the Ryan and Murphy Reports, and the face of Irish Catholicism would never be the same again. But that is a tale for another day.

Back in early 1998 as I filled in 'Maynooth' and 'Theology' on my CAO form, I wondered where that choice might lead. All the literature informed us that theology graduates end up in a wide variety of roles – teaching, research, pastoral work, counselling, media, charities, the list goes on – and so it has proven. Ireland's long love affair with the Catholic Church may, as many commentators remind us, have cooled off, but the *síolta* are not without their shoots.

RESPONDING TO THE NEEDS
OF LITURGICAL MUSIC AFTER
THE SECOND VATICAN COUNCIL

Moira Bergin

he Second Vatican Council set a huge agenda for Church music. While hymns in the vernacular were known, though mainly used in devotions, the liturgical reform called for settings of everything that might have been sung by a choir at a Latin High Mass. Now music had to be provided for the priest celebrant, the cantor, the choir and the congregation. Priority was to be given to dialogues like the simple greeting, 'The Lord be with you', to acclamations like the Alleluia before the gospel and the Great Amen at the end of the Eucharistic Prayer. The responsorial psalm was to be something new. New hymns would be needed to fit more clearly into specific elements of the Mass. While music at Mass was the immediate need, music was also an integral part of the Liturgy of the Hours.

Here we record the work of three bodies charged with responding to this agenda and which are linked with St Patrick's College Maynooth.

Advisory Committee on Church Music
The *Constitution on the Sacred Liturgy*, the first document of the council, promulgated on 4 December 1963, called for the establishment of a national commission for liturgy to be assisted by experts in liturgical science, music, art and pastoral practice. The Irish Bishops' Conference set up the Irish Commission for Liturgy in December 1963, consisting of five panels of consultors, including music. The Church Music Panel would become the Advisory Committee on Church Music (ACCM). In its early years it strongly promoted congregational singing and commissioned Mass settings by well-known composers Seóirse Bodley, T. C. Kelly, Gerard Victory and Fintan O'Carroll.

Over the years ACCM has fulfilled its primary role as the consultative body on Church music to the bishops. It has also kept links with the dioceses and parishes through seminars and occasional memoranda and guidelines. *Guidelines*

St Mary's Oratory (2020)

for Payment of Parish Church Musicians was jointly published by ACCM and the Church Music Committee of the Church of Ireland Diocese of Dublin and Glendalough. In December 2015, at Maynooth, ACCM launched *Singing the Mystery of Faith, A Guide to Liturgical Music*. It explains, in a practical way, the role of music in Catholic liturgical celebrations and guides musicians through the pastoral and musical decisions made when preparing music for the liturgy.

In the Jubilee Year 2000, ACCM produced *Seinn Alleluia 2000*, followed by a collection of music for funerals. In recent years its major task has been the production of music for the third edition of the Roman Missal. ACCM prepared *Sing the Mass*, an anthology of Mass settings, including new settings as well as older ones amended in line with the revised translation of the Missale Romanum. This collection was launched at Maynooth at the annual summer school of the Irish Church Music Association (ICMA) on 4 July 2011, five months before the new edition of the Roman Missal came into use. Members of ACCM took an active part in the promotion throughout the country of this anthology. It was also the time when the Church in Ireland was preparing for the International Eucharistic Congress, held in June 2012.

Following the approval of An Leabhar Aifrinn Rómánach, the new Irish translation of the Missale Romanum, ACCM prepared a collection of Mass settings in Irish, *Canamís – Ceol don Aifreann*, launched in January 2019. This brought together for the first time a number of well-known Mass settings as well as newly composed music.

Irish Church Music Association

The Church Music Panel, at the request of Cardinal William Conway, set about the founding of an association to support the work of musicians, choirs and their directors in the field of liturgical music. The ICMA was founded on the feast of St Cecilia, 22 November 1969. A very special contribution of the ICMA was the publication of *Responsorial Psalms for Sundays and Major Feast Days* by Fintan O'Carroll in 1984 and in its third edition in 2006.

The first ICMA annual summer school, was held at Maynooth, on 13–17 July 1970. Through lectures and tutorials, workshops and the daily celebration of the Mass and the Liturgy of the Hours, participants work towards the best standards in liturgical music and celebration and cherish the encouragement received at this annual event.

In earlier years, the summer school was held in various centres throughout the country until in July 1988 it returned to St Patrick's College Maynooth. ICMA celebrated its golden jubilee at Maynooth, 1–5 July 2019. Year after year, the summer school's participants and the guest directors enjoy the beauty of the College Chapel with its refurbished Ruffatti organ for the celebration of the Eucharist, and the reordered St Mary's Oratory for Morning Prayer, the spaciousness of Loftus Hall for lectures and workshops, and Pugin Hall as the summer school feasts on the culinary delights produced by the catering staff.

National Centre for Liturgy

The *Constitution on the Sacred Liturgy*, as well as calling for a national commission for liturgy and diocesan commissions for liturgy, music and art, spoke of establishing an institute for pastoral liturgy. Msgr Seán Swayne, a priest of the diocese of Kildare and Leighlin, ordained at Maynooth in 1957 after his studies of science, philosophy and theology, was able to achieve his dream of such an institute in Ireland. Appointed national secretary for liturgy in 1973 by the Bishops' Conference, he founded the Liturgy Centre at Mount St Anne's, Portarlington. The centre moved to Carlow College as the Irish Institute of Pastoral Liturgy in 1978. It found its third home in St Patrick's College Maynooth when it moved there as the National Centre for Liturgy (NCL) in August 1996.

As well as housing the national secretariat for liturgy for the Bishops' Conference, NCL has liturgical formation as its primary task. It began a one-year programme in liturgy in 1974 and students could take the Diploma in Pastoral Liturgy, recognised by the Faculty of Theology at Maynooth. From its beginning the NCL has reached out to priests and parishes, choirs, composers, artists and architects.

Many of its seminars and study days have taken place in Maynooth, but the centre has also conducted night courses in several places throughout the country. In this work its small staff has had the help of many who are members of its panel of lecturers and liturgy people associated with the various commissions and advisory committees in liturgy and allied areas.

Following the transfer to Maynooth in 1996, the Diploma in Pastoral Liturgy became an award of the Pontifical University. In 2000, the Faculty of Theology approved the award of the Higher Diploma in Pastoral Liturgy and a masters programme in theology, specialising in liturgy. The first graduates of the masters degree were conferred in 2002. Working with the Faculty of Theology, the centre has brought several leading liturgical scholars to present seminars and courses at Maynooth. While most students are from Ireland, in recent years students have also come from Nigeria, India, Pakistan, Indonesia, Sri Lanka and England. Again, though the majority of students are Roman Catholic, several have been from other Churches, including Anglican and Orthodox.

Since 1999, the Department of Music at Maynooth University, in association with NCL, has offered the Diploma in Arts (Church Music). The liturgy component of the course is taught at the centre.

In earlier years the programme at the centre was residential, with participation in daily worship. At Maynooth, common worship is still part of the daily programme. New links with the chaplaincy of Maynooth University means that NCL provides weekday Mass during the academic year, taking place in St Mary's Oratory at midday.

NCL was at the centre of preparation of the publication of the third edition of the Roman Missal in both English and Irish. Several booklets of liturgical catechesis and anthologies of music were published and seminars and workshops were conducted at Maynooth and throughout the country.

On a Personal Note

Recording the links between St Patrick's College and ACCM, ICMA and NCL is very much part of the story of liturgy in Ireland. St Patrick's College has been the base of these agencies of liturgical renewal and formation. It recalls my first visit to the church music summer school in 1982 and every year since it made its home at Maynooth, my years as a student of theology, music, liturgy and church music, membership of ACCM and staff membership of NCL.

Ciarán Reilly

For any GAA player attending third-level education in Ireland, the opportunity to play in the Sigerson Cup is greatly prized, but not always realised. In the long history of the competition, which commenced in 1911, the name Maynooth College appears only once on the roll of honour (1976), a win that is the focus of Tom McGuire's chapter elsewhere in this volume. As an undergraduate student at Maynooth I was fortunate to experience the ups and downs of playing in the Sigerson Cup between 2001 and 2005 and, in the process, had the opportunity to play alongside and against some of the top GAA players of the early twenty-first century. The universal language of the GAA allowed me to transition into the life of third-level education so much more easily.

It was a wonderful time to be involved in the GAA at Maynooth. In late 2001 there was an air of excitement in the university about the team's prospects. The resurgence of Gaelic Games at Maynooth at this time was largely attributable to the sterling work of the Gaelic Games Promotion Officer, Tom Maher. Under his stewardship, Maynooth began attracting footballers from across the country, helped in no small measure by the GAA scholarship scheme. I was the recipient of one of these scholarships, which was a great honour, apart from the financial help it gave to a young student. Tom was extremely courteous to everyone who played Gaelic Games, regardless of their ability, and his contribution is fondly recalled by players whenever there is a conversation about the GAA in Maynooth University. Players from the Maynooth team, including Sean O'Dea from Clane, gave great service in the administration of the GAA club within the university.

With the proper structures in place, players derived great enjoyment and benefit from training and playing for Maynooth. Training sessions were largely held on Highfield or on the Rhetoric 'playing field' before the move to the new facilities on the North Campus. Training on the Rhetoric pitch was far from ideal, but we seemed quickly to forget our surroundings and rowed in with whatever was asked of us. I remember one particular training session where, for almost an hour, a handful of us tried in vain to score a goal on Mayo's David Clarke. His prowess was very evident to us then and it came as no surprise to see him a regular fixture on Mayo teams over the last decade and more and a worthy recipient of two All-Star awards. On another occasion during an early morning session on Rhetoric, in the cold and dark, we watched in awe as the superbly athletic and iconic Kerry footballer Marc Ó Sé lapped, and continued to lap, many of us who were struggling in the conditions. Ó Sé would bellow a laugh as, one by one, we moaned about the intensity of the session. Team meetings in the Casey Dressing Rooms were another source of fun and, despite the best efforts of manager Willie Hughes, and later Niall Carew, it was often difficult to contain the laughter and general good humour that were ever present.

My introduction to university football came about almost by accident. In September 2001 my club, Edenderry, had been victorious in the Offaly Senior Football Championship, the same month that I commenced undergraduate studies at Maynooth. That club victory meant that we set our sights on the Leinster Club Championship, and for that reason I did not attend trials for the university freshers' team. However, some weeks later, Edenderry orgainsed a challenge game against Maynooth University and, having 'caught the eye', I was invited to join the Sigerson panel. On the following Saturday I was picked to play full forward against Celbridge in the Kildare Under-21 semi-final in Leixlip. It was a surreal experience, not knowing anybody's name on the team. I was also handed the free taking responsibilities. I remember the bewildered look of some of the Celbridge players when I introduced myself to my team mates prior to the throw-in. Despite this, I quickly settled in to the team and contributed as we made light work of Celbridge. The final against Confey was a mismatch from start to finish and we ran out easy winners 5–11 to 0–5.

While I look back with pride on that victory, I am also conscious of the fact that the university probably should not have been in the competition at the time given the strength of the panel at our disposal. Of the starting fifteen in the county final most had played under-21 for their county, while Dublin's Alan Brogan was relegated to the bench, having opted to play for his club the previous week. Ironically, I never got to see the presentation of the cup or participate in the celebrations. I had been replaced at half-time to allow me attend a meeting with my club, Edenderry, who were in action in the Leinster Club Football Championship the following day. Indeed, I would have to wait until the local newspapers were published the following week to read about the second half, but I was pleased to see that the *Nationalist and Leinster Times'* report mentioned that in the first half 'up stepped Reilly and scored a classic penalty'.

With the under-21 championship annexed, attention quickly turned to the Sigerson Cup. In January 2002 we defeated Trinity College in round one, 1–10 to 1–3, in a scrappy affair at Santry. From there we travelled to face St Mary's of Belfast in round two and, after a brilliant game against the teacher training college at the 'Ranch', two late points from the emerging Laois star, Ross Munnelly, ensured qualification to the coveted 'weekend' stage of the Sigerson Cup. Afterwards, we stopped in a pub on the Falls Road and were pleasantly surprised to find that UTV news were showing highlights of the game on their evening bulletin. Momentum was now building and we travelled to Sligo for the quarter-final in great hope. However, at St Mary's in Sligo, with sleet and snow falling intermittingly, we found it difficult to break down the UCC defence, led by Kerry's Paul Galvin (Footballer of the Year in 2009) and Cork's Anthony Lynch. Coming on in the second half for Dublin's Barry Cahill, who had received a head injury, I quickly scored a goal, driving a breaking ball to the back of the net. However, it was the chance that I spurned a few minutes later, hitting the side netting, when perhaps a pass inside to a colleague was the best option, that still haunts me to this day. Heading to Sligo that weekend I was very hopeful that we could win the Sigerson Cup and emulate the men of 1976. I was conscious, too, of the Edenderry connection to that win in 1976 when Martin Nugent scored a goal in the final, but there was to be no Sigerson fairy tale as UCC held out in atrocious playing conditions. Looking back now, almost twenty years later, there is a definite sense that a great opportunity was missed on that occasion. While Maynooth would reach the 2003 semi-final, after defeating reigning champions Sligo IT in the previous round, I think it is widely accepted that the 2002 team was one of the best the university ever produced and should have emulated the team of 1976.

There was a great change in personnel over the coming two to three seasons and, as the 2004 campaign approached, expectations were lower, which probably benefited the team. A first round win against Mary Immaculate College, Limerick, 0–13 to 0–6, suggested that this team could go further. Led by Mick Foley of Kildare, Vinny Corey of Monaghan and Sligo's Mark Breheny, Maynooth dominated the opening period, laying the foundation for victory. An abiding memory of the game was that the manager of the Mary Immaculate team, Eamon Cregan, was left fuming after two Kerry players had refused to play because of their involvement in the National Football League. Next up was NUI Galway and we made the long trip to a wet and windy pitch at Dangan, which was not conducive to stylish football. Despite what the *Irish Independent* described as an 'enterprising and committed' effort from Maynooth, NUIG ran out winners on a score line of 2–8 to 0–8. Played in wind and rain, Maynooth started well, and when the mercurial Michael Meehan of Galway limped off injured after twelve minutes we thought that it would be our day. However, we had no answer for Donegal's Colm McFadden, who put in an awesome display, scoring 1–5 of the winners' tally. The 2005 campaign would also end in disappointment in Templemore against the Garda College in the opening round. Led by Aidan O'Mahony of Kerry, the Garda College bullied Maynooth both on and off the ball and ran out winners 0–14 to 1–10.

Looking back, I have very special memories of representing Maynooth University in the Sigerson Cup, but perhaps most memorable were the games played in Highfield on the South Campus. Here, even when a small crowd had gathered, it was enough to generate a great atmosphere. With the trees overhanging the pitch, the supporters along the sideline could almost touch the ball as you raced along by them. There was some consolation in not advancing further in the Sigerson Cup by winning the Kildare Under-21 championship and also a much delayed All-Ireland Fresher's competition, played in May 2002 (in the middle of exams). However, the Sigerson Cup allowed the opportunity to play and develop as a footballer, pitting yourself at training and matches against some of the best players in the country. The Maynooth team of this period included Marc Ó Sé, John Keane, Barry Cahill, Alan Brogan, Bernard Brogan and Alan Dillon, who would all win All-Star awards, while Rory Kavanagh starred for Donegal in their 2012 All-Ireland championship win. Others, including Ger Brennan (Dublin), Declan Lally (Dublin), Colm Parkinson (Laois), Ross Munnelly (Laois) and Paul Noone (Roscommon) enjoyed successful inter-county careers, while many more gave memorable performances in the Maynooth colours – including Shane Gilleran from Roscommon, Peter Dooley and Paudie Swinburne of Monaghan, Michael Gurn and Darragh Doherty from Donegal, Mayo stars Conor Moran and Dermot Geraghty, and Tadgh Brosnan of Meath, to name but a few.

PROFESSOR JAMES McEVOY
AND THE RUSSELL LIBRARY

Penelope Woods

ike a church, the Russell Library, its high hammer-beam roof in shadow and its tall dimmed windows casting diffused light on the reading tables, is a peaceful and serene space. The books, from early presses across Europe, bound in leather and parchment, rest on the shelves, silent companions for the reader.

One such reader was medievalist Rev. James McEvoy, Professor of Philosophy from 1995 until 2005. Soft-spoken with a light Northern Irish lilt, he loved the library – for him it was a retreat. He would slip away from the busy noise and bustle of the university to enjoy the solitude and to work undisturbed. It was also his delight to bring visiting scholars to see the library. He would guide them down its full length and then unhook the red rope and disappear into the 'Patrology' bay to show them his particular favourites: the works of the

RARE BOOKS

pseudonymous writer Dionysius the Areopagite. There were three editions there, each with points of interest to discuss: a 1556 Cologne edition with commentary by Denis the Carthusian – it had belonged to the Irish College in Salamanca; the highly regarded edition by Balthasar Cordier, printed in Paris in 1644, its leather binding carpeted in gold fleurs-de-lis and inscribed as a prize to a contemporary student; and its fellow, in a Venetian edition of 1755. The professor was the leading expert on Robert Grosseteste, thirteenth-century Bishop of Lincoln, who had written commentaries on the writings of Pseudo-Dionysius. He once modestly shared the fact that he had been offered the privilege of wearing Grosseteste's episcopal ring while giving a lecture on him in Lincoln Cathedral.

James (Jim) McEvoy had arrived in Maynooth in 1995 as successor to Msgr Matthew O'Donnell, who had become College President in the preceding year. He was soon invited by the librarian, Dr Thomas Kabdebo, to give the annual Library Lecture, with the added request that it should have a modern resonance. In my memory he had given a wide-ranging discourse on the existence of God. Such is the blurring of time. I located the lecture in the *Maynooth University Record* for 1998 – he had chosen the timeless topic, Chance or Design, and had given an update on the debate, presenting views from both sides right up to the present.

The professor, who, like his Irish medieval counterparts, had studied and taught on the continent, brought international scholars to conferences on medieval topics. One such event was held in 2002 on John Scottus Eriugena, the great ninth-century philosopher and theologian, his Irish origins unmistakable in his double name (he was portrayed on the Irish five-pound note between 1976 and 1993). It was an occasion, as always, to focus on the topic and delve into the book collection to discover the riches there and then display them to those who recognised them as old friends and understood their significance. The books came off the shelves in numbers, their turn at last: Hincmar of Rheims, Ussher on Gotteschalk, Maximus the Confessor, and Eriugena's own *Periphyseon*, finally in print in 1681, in Latin translation for all to read … Édouard Jeauneau, leading Eriugenian scholar, was delighted. As always, the professor set to and the papers were published.

Friendship, or *amicitia*, as portrayed in antiquity and the Middle Ages was another subject on which he was an authority. It was one that extended naturally into his own life. He was a man who encouraged others, always with respect and an old-fashioned courtesy. Sitting in the library one day, checking the proofs of some recent writing on the subject, he paused for a brief conversation and produced a list of different kinds of friendship: fine distinctions, a revelation.

The Russell Library in winter was sometimes shiveringly cold, yet for many years the conservation of books and manuscripts was carried out in the centre of the reading room, all year round. To heat such a vast space would have ruined the books, so instead, as readers were normally few, they were given individual heaters which toasted legs but left backs and shoulders vulnerable to the prevailing draughts. The professor was a stalwart, and the only reader to sit so long that he needed the pair of hand-knitted fingerless gloves kept in reserve for suffering numb hands. It was for this reason that when the staff of three or four assembled in the office adjacent to the reading room for the mid-morning or mid-afternoon break, a lone reader was often invited in to join them for a warming and sustaining beverage. Space was limited. The kitchen was no more than a cupboard which contained a hand basin, and two shelves holding mugs and an assortment of teas and coffee. Staff would pull up chairs to the window seat looking out on the open sky, with the visitor sitting in their midst. The professor would sometimes join us and regale us with stories. He loved the violin, had in fact played it since he was a boy. On one occasion he recalled how, when travelling as a child with his mother to his music lesson, on the train from Larne to Belfast, they would pass the cottage in Kilroot where Swift had lived between 1695 and 1696 – his first parish. It was a strange crossing of paths,

Rev. Charles Russell, President 1857–1880

for my parents had been offered the oval-shaped cottage as their first home in 1950 by a fellow teacher of my father on whose land the cottage stood. They had declined because it was in a poor state of repair. My father had taken a photograph of the interior.

Occasionally the library was used for a book launch, when the topic was appropriate. So it was that the last work published in the professor's lifetime, *The Irish Contribution to European Scholastic Thought*, which he had co-edited, was launched there in 2009. It could not have been more appropriate – Pugin's neo-Gothic library, which housed some of the earliest continental printings relating to Ireland. The professor had already moved north to the Chair of Scholastic Philosophy at Queen's University, Belfast. His health was failing and sadly he was unable to be present at the launch. He died twelve days before his sixty-eighth birthday, on 2 October 2010.

St Patrick by Seamus Murphy

THE HALLOWED HALLS
OF MAYNOOTH

Vincent Doyle

As a student at Maynooth, I often ambled the long halls and looked at the photos of history. Ornate portraits of social history, men who pillared the community, now immortalised youthfully behind a glass frame, as they looked towards me across history at the cusp of their ministry, many of whom have since returned to God. It always fascinated me how the black and white photos immortalised the priest in that given moment and kept him there, so he could look at the budding lay theologian in the twenty-first century, across all that would happen and would be revealed in the meantime. Still, in that picture, in that day, in that new priestly garb with pristine collar, that had yet to cleanse and wipe sin from a soul, history inspired a young mind.

In the halls of Maynooth, between Loftus and Pugin, a path would be worn. It was where I discovered the concept of 'elevenses'. I love that it was within the Church that I found this phenomenon, which, to that point, had evaded me. To pause within the confines of a timetable – to breathe, as the aroma of freshly brewed coffee wafted out the door across the wicker basket bejewelled with Lotus biscuits, ready and ripe like the ardent and confused minds, now scurrying and emptying from systematic theology, armed with more questions than when they arrived.

That is where the real theology came to life, in Pugin. That was the pasture, so to speak, that was the gap of the field or the proverbial vineyard, where your own thoughts were distilled, and theology suddenly morphed from being systematic and academic to being real, practised and pastoral. Over the wafer biscuits, with white crockery cup in hand, itself decorated with the emblem of St Patrick's College on the side, one tried one's best to sound right and to fit in. Still, nobody was excluded from Pugin Hall at elevenses – it really was Church at its best. It is where I suppose I first saw inclusion being actualised in the Roman Catholic Church as an adult. This is where we broke biscuit and sipped cooling coffee, as the clock sped dangerously towards the quarter past the hour mark, quickly refilling before the cups would be left abandoned and pens picked up again to learn and question.

Later, as the years slipped by, I would sit in the window near the priest's refectory close to the door as exams loomed. I hoped one or two kind souls might have a quiet word or point to a specific page as I studied for end of semester exams. I was always careful to have the correct book open with the academic cover facing the refectory door as the respective lecturer emerged, just in case they missed that I was actually studying and, more importantly, what I was studying. Thank you to those who stopped during those long summer evenings when the grass was being cut, and the past versus present match echoed down the long hall past the statue of the Virgin Mary.

Most of all I remember everything making sense; I remember a sense of welcome, a sense of belonging, a belonging that I had known as a young boy when I spent time in the church, near my late father, God rest him. Then, as an adult, Maynooth came home to me; what I mean is, Maynooth wrought the kindness of the Church and reintroduced it to me, and I felt warmed and cared for and indeed loved, as I was as a child. I was taught how to think, insofar as my mind underwent psychological and academic physiotherapy. As the kaleidoscope of theology and philosophy was unveiled over the academic semesters, they were buoyed by English and neighbouring subjects such as sociology and anthropology. They all reflected the resplendence of the Most Holy Spirit, who pointed towards a correct and structured understanding of the Jesus of history and the Christ of faith, who would lead me further.

Academic structures formalised, arranged themselves and grounded transpersonal realities, teaching and informing me how to speak with a fluency about subjects that traditionally might escape the untrained lay person. The coffees and Lotus biscuits became the breeding ground for disciplining one's academic argument for whatever was being discussed. Subjectivity was overshadowed by objectivity. This ability to reason, to systematically understand something and put one's point across, stood to me, nurturing a deepening level of understanding personally and academically.

Now, I continue to work with the Church, rebuilding formerly shadowed and obscured pastoral areas. I try to light into eclipsed aspects of pastoral care globally. I remember those men from the framed photos of history, the kind and genuine faces; I remember the many faces who would later sit by many a fire and wipe many tears and bless many dying hands and souls. I remember those who questioned over a Lotus Biscoff, or occasionally a Bourbon Cream and Earl Grey tea, who are now scattered to the four winds; I remember the lecturers who sat with back to blackboard and who engaged a congregation who became a class. We were all Church then, buzzing and alive, and the Holy Spirit was and

Junior Garden

Loftus Halls

remains there, in those hallowed halls of Maynooth where our echoes can be still heard within these words.

And now I am welcomed back, to my heart's retreat, to the warm window throne where I would sit like a cat at a farmer's window, hoping for scraps of information before an exam; where I was thrown back four questions instead of one answer, bemused.

I remember Maynooth, my home, my academic home, indeed my alma mater; the place that nurtured my body, mind and soul. The place where I lived and was formed.

Now, as I am blessed to engage with Maynooth in a different role, though I remain a student; a student who learns from an episcopal conference only to bring those words from Maynooth – from the lips of the Irish Church – to the hands of those shadowed and pained by stigma, discomfort and regret globally. A balm of pastoral care, enabled by understanding and discussion nurtured years ago, over warming coffee, over lunchtime walks and summertime exams, now soothes psychological abrasions globally from Manila to Milan.

And I will always return home, to Maynooth, to Pugin, to the full halls, adorned with history and hope, where years of questions whisper in the subdued reverence of our conjoined pastoral memory.

As eve falls over the Graf, my back turns to leave, yet my heart and mind remain; somewhere there, amid Loftus halls, always learning, remembering, listening, acknowledging and remaining ever grateful to you, the hallowed halls of Maynooth.

MARTIN SHEEN, MAYNOOTH
AND THE MOVIES

Salvador Ryan

Author with Martin Sheen and Ronan Drury in Maynooth College Chapel sacristy

I t all began on 13 October 2010. I received an email from the Theology Office with a query attached. Berystede Films and its parent company, Newgrange Pictures, were about to begin shooting a film based on an historical event in a 1950s' parish in rural Ireland. The parish priest, recently returned from Rome, and a lover of cinema, would be the central character. They needed an historical consultant, someone with knowledge of parish life in Ireland in the 1950s, who might make themselves available in an advisory capacity to the director and the art and props departments and also, of course, to the actor playing the role of the priest. I read through the email quickly and without much attention: I hadn't the time to commit; I wasn't sure that I was the right person; in any case, I'm not a twentieth-century Irish historian – what could I possibly offer? I already had an email composed in my head which would express my sincere regrets. That was when I came to some lines near the end: 'the role of Fr Barry will be played by Martin Sheen': suddenly I *was* an expert on twentieth-century Irish history and the only person for the job! I lost no time in calling Berystede films to offer my services to the film project *Stella Days*.

Well, it wasn't quite as hasty as that. The film company were also looking for a priest who ministered in the 1950s who would be in a position to guide Martin in the role. I knew that in taking on the job of historical adviser I would be able to (and would need to) call upon a number of people who would be able to advise me in my advisory role! As for the choice of priest-adviser, there was never really any doubt as to who that might be: Fr Ronan Drury – inveterate model of eloquence for thousands of the country's priests since the late 1950s. When I contacted Fr Ronan, he had no hesitation in offering his services, including a commitment to spend two full days on set with the cast and crew as we filmed in Fethard, County Tipperary, which had been chosen to double as Borrisokane, where the events originally transpired.

From the outset, this would be a hectic few weeks. I soon received a long list of questions from the art and props departments on the 'creation' of the interior of a 1950s' Catholic church, complete with high altar, confessionals, confraternity banners etc. (the scenes would be filmed in Holy Trinity, Church of Ireland, in Fethard, which would soon get a Catholic 'make-over'). The concern for authenticity and attention to detail shown by the director, Thaddeus O'Sullivan, and the various departments was remarkable. Great emphasis was placed on the colour of vestments for the different Church seasons, the layout of the altar and the church more generally, in addition to more specific queries; for instance, was the Eucharistic host which the priest used at Mass in the 1950s embossed? If so, what might appear on it? How might a parish priest dress when at home in the 1950s? Would he wear slippers? If so, what kind might he wear? Most importantly, though, Martin would need to get used to wearing a celebrant's vestments and, especially, to vest in the sacristy as if he had been doing this all of his life. He would also need to become familiar with handling ciboria, chalices and patens with confidence. This is why a visit to Maynooth and a hands-on tutorial by Fr Ronan would prove indispensable.

And, so it was, that on Wednesday morning, 3 November, Martin Sheen visited the college, accompanied by Thaddeus O'Sullivan. The college sacristan kindly

Martin Sheen in the College Chapel being instructed on how to celebrate Mass

prepared a selection of 'fiddleback' chasubles for Martin to try on; however, the first challenge for Martin to overcome was the unravelling and donning of the cincture, which Fr Ronan demonstrated fastidiously while his every movement was recorded by iPhone. In the meantime, Martin would practise reciting the audible parts of the Latin Mass which he would be required to pronounce. Martin's own deep religious faith helped him to inhabit the character of the parish priest with some ease; however, his instinctive reverence for such sacred duties could also prove to be a challenge in playing an ageing priest who had been celebrating the sacraments for years. It was here that Fr Ronan stepped in and gently encouraged Sheen to be somewhat more cavalier in his handling of the liturgical vessels, to inject a little of the humdrum and the routine into his sacerdotal performance. It was that day, too, that Fr Ronan very generously offered his pouch with holy oil stocks for use in scenes in which Martin Sheen, as Fr Daniel Barry, anoints an elderly parishioner.

Some weeks later there followed two full days of filming church scenes in Fethard, County Tipperary. Part of the story involves Martin, as Fr Daniel Barry, teaching his parish choir some pieces of Gregorian chant, which they proceed to sing more enthusiastically than melodically, to Fr Barry's increasing frustration. Of course, in order to teach the choir the pieces, Martin first needed to learn them. Some members of the Bohernanave parish choir, Thurles, were selected to appear in the film, and Martin would appear at Mass in the parish two Sundays in a row, after which he would adjourn with the others for 'choir practice' in the local parish centre. It was a slightly surreal experience to stand in a room across from Semple Stadium and lead 'President Josiah Bartlett' of *The West Wing* through the verses of 'Veni Creator Spiritus'. With Martin, of course, there was no rush, no fuss; just a genuine joy in meeting people and spending time chatting to them. Martin's driver during the shoot, a Dubliner appropriately named (for a film shot in County Tipperary) Dan Breen, would frequently remark how much of a pleasure it was to work with Martin, stating that he would happily drive him around for the rest of his life.

The church scenes in Fethard were shot on 22 and 23 November and Fr Ronan was present throughout what were extremely long days. We would arrive at the local hall between six and six-thirty in the morning and, excepting an hour's lunch break, would work right through until seven or eight in the evening. It was fascinating to become aware of the concerns of the art and costume department when casting extras – women with recently plucked eyebrows were a no-no (no female plucking of that kind in 1950s' Tipperary), as were men with beards (not too many of them around at the time either). Hence, for two days only, I sacrificed facial hair for art's sake. One of the female leads in *Stella Days* was the lovely Amy Huberman, who was extremely kind and generous with her time. However, as we broke for lunch the first day, my hopes of having lunch with Amy were dashed when I spotted that Fr Ronan had got there before me (and really there was no contest!) – I am not sure who was more charmed with whom!

By 11 December shooting on *Stella Days*, and, for me, a once-in-a-lifetime experience of the nuts and bolts of film production, had 'wrapped'. What gave me the confidence to accept the role was simply the knowledge that I was in a position to draw on the expertise of so many people to whom I could turn when in doubt. The role that Fr Ronan played in this was crucial. As one of my colleagues communicated to Martin Sheen after lunch in the Professors' Dining Room, 'Fr Ronan is your authentic, but not your typical 1950s' priest!' I will forever be grateful to him for sharing this experience with me; it might be said that this was yet another way to 'drive a new furrow' for Maynooth.

PATRICK JOSEPH CORISH
Priest and Church Historian (1921–2013)

Bill Cosgrave

Junior Garden

I was a clerical student in Dr Corish's ecclesiastical history class for three years from 1962 to 1965. He was a priest of my own diocese of Ferns, and, of course, we Ferns students were proud to have such a luminary in our diocesan ranks. But, more importantly, he was universally held to be a top-class lecturer in his subject, lively, clear and entertaining. In fact, in the view of us students, he was the best lecturer we had in the Faculty of Theology. Indeed, we often said we learned quite a bit of theology from Fr Paddy as he led us through the Christian centuries.

Paddy, as we called him, was born on 20 March 1921 to Peter W. Corish and his wife Bridget (née O'Shaughnessy) in Ballytarsna, near the village of Ballycullane in west Wexford, about twelve miles south of New Ross. His father was a teacher in the local primary school and it was there that Paddy began his formal education. At secondary level he was a student in St Peter's College,

433

Wexford. He was an outstanding student who spent most of his time at the books, as he had little or no interest in sport. He was a quiet, shy and reflective youth.

He entered Maynooth in September 1938. That was the beginning of a lifetime in St Patrick's. It has been calculated that he spent seventy-two years there, only leaving it towards the end of his life, when he had to go to a nursing home in Naas for about three years. He died there on 10 January 2013, aged ninety-one, and, of course, he was laid to rest in the cemetery in Maynooth College itself, which he had served so well for so long.

Paddy Corish had been ordained for our diocese of Ferns on 17 June 1945. He was immediately sent to do post-graduate study on the Dunboyne Establishment in the college. He obtained his doctorate in theology in 1947 with a dissertation on the Doctrine of the Fall in the Greek Fathers before Pelagianism. He was then appointed to the professorship of ecclesiastical history. In 1952 he gained his MA from UCD with a thesis on Bishop Nicholas French of Ferns (1646–78). Fr Paddy held this professorship with great success for twenty-eight years until, in 1975, he moved to become Professor of Modern History in the Recognised College of the NUI, the other dimension of St Patrick's College Maynooth. He continued his work in history there for thirteen years until he retired in 1988. Retirement for him didn't mean inactivity. He took over the position of college archivist and continued his lecturing outside the college and his writing on Church historical matters.

Fr Paddy was appointed President of St Patrick's College Maynooth by the bishops of Ireland in 1967. Finding this new position not to his liking, and not conducive to a productive use of his talents and learning as an historian, he resigned the position the following year and reverted to his professorship. As Maynooth presidents traditionally enjoyed the title of Monsignor, Fr Paddy was conferred with this papal honour. During his one year as president he contacted me, who had just begun teaching moral theology in St Peter's Seminary in Wexford, and requested that I take on the role of Junior Dean in Maynooth, beginning in September 1968. I accepted and remained in that position for the next five years.

Patrick Corish was an outstanding writer in the area of Church history. He has numerous articles and some books to his credit, all informative and illuminating. In the late 1960s, he initiated a major project and took on the role of general editor of *A History of Irish Catholicism*. Some ten or twelve slim, but valuable, volumes appeared, but the project failed to come to full fruition. However, Msgr Paddy made other notable contributions to our knowledge of

Msgr Patrick J. Corish with Hugh Fenning OP at the launch
of Corish's *Maynooth College, 1795–1995*

Irish Church history, especially in his two excellent books *The Irish Catholic Community in the Seventeenth and Eighteenth Centuries* (1981) and *The Irish Catholic Experience* (1985). But his magnum opus was still to come. So, in 1995, he published *Maynooth College, 1795–1995*, a 542-page volume detailing the development of the college from its beginning to the time of writing. He also served as editor of the Irish historical sources journal, *Archivium Hibernicum*, for some years. He was, as one Ferns priest noted, 'a lecturer of international renown; he has made a significant contribution to Irish historical research and ecclesiastical history in general'. Since his death, he is commemorated by the annual Msgr Patrick J. Corish Lecture, which has been delivered by a host of scholars of international repute, including, among others Professor Eamon Duffy (Cambridge); Professor Roy Foster (Oxford); Profesor Euan Cameron (Union Seminary, NY); Professor Caroline Walker Bynum (Princeton);

Professor Morwenna Ludlow (University of Exeter); Professor Robert Bartlett (St Andrews); Professor Peter Brown (Princeton), Professor Candida Moss (Notre Dame and, latterly, University of Birmingham); Profesor Carlos Eire (Yale); Professor Columba Stewart (Collegeville/St John's); and, most recently, Professor David Morgan (Duke University).

Paddy Corish was a Wexford man and retained a deep love for his native county and diocese all his life. He wrote notable articles on Ferns diocesan history and gave many lectures to the local clergy and laity over the years. While he had no opportunity to serve in the pastoral life of his diocese, he was a frequent visitor to his home county and took annual holidays in Rosslare in Kelly's Hotel. Perhaps his love for his native county and diocese is shown, above all, by the fact that in his will he bequeathed his vast personal collection of books to Wexford County Library.

Paddy was basically a shy person and small talk didn't come easily to him. We, as clerical students in the college, admired his scholarship and brilliance as a lecturer, but we were slow to approach him at the personal level. There was a student, it is said, whose bedroom was situated directly above Fr Paddy's and who, to annoy Paddy, used to throw his shoes, one after the other, against the radiator in his room as he prepared for bed. One night he threw the first shoe only – to see what would happen. Within two minutes, Corish banged on his door and exclaimed, 'For God's sake, throw the other one!'

Some people who knew him felt that he tended towards pessimism at times. Bishop Denis Brennan of Ferns remarked at Fr Paddy's funeral mass in Enniscorthy Cathedral that 'Mgr Corish had developed an impish, good-humoured line in pessimism'. Indeed, one of his much-quoted phrases, which he would deliver with a twinkle in his eye, was 'Things are always much worse than they seem!'

He had a great interest in gardening and spent many hours in the Junior Garden,[1] often in the company of Bart Redmond, a college employee and a fellow Wexford man. This aspect of Fr Paddy's life is commemorated by a small monument in the Junior Garden erected some years ago.

Fr Paddy was a humble and modest person of great integrity and practised a quiet, but deep spirituality. In the Naas nursing home, where he was close to his niece who lived nearby, I was able to visit him on a few occasions. On one such occasion he was entertaining another historian, Art Cosgrove from UCD. I remember once when he was commenting on his own work as an historian, he simply said 'I made a contribution'.

---

1   For a humorous tale relating to this, see Niall Howard's contribution in this volume.

THE FIGHT TO SEEK UNDERSTANDING
MAYNOOTH 2008–13

Kevin Hargaden

I arrived at St Patrick's College Maynooth in September 2008. I was on track to become a Presbyterian minister, only the second to study at St Patrick's. I was fascinated with all my courses and squandered endless hours wandering the stacks of the library seeking to read in to the topics of my lectures. Mature students have a reputation for being annoyingly swottish and I cannot defend myself against such an accusation.

I had encountered the work of the American moral theologian, Stanley Hauerwas, before I started at Maynooth, but the library afforded me a chance to read back through his writings. I was captured by how he articulated the importance of church; that Christianity could not be separated from particular communities who exhibit distinctive virtues shaped by the story of Jesus. His extensive writings served as a conversation partner to the vast tradition of Catholic social teaching I was studying, helping this Protestant find his bearings in a pontifical seminary.

The aspect of Hauerwas's thought that gripped me most profoundly was his insistence that non-violence was not just a viable option for Christians, but an essential hallmark of the Church. Before Maynooth, I was largely schooled by whatever books crossed my path. I had read a lot, but without any coherent path or discipline. To my mind, the question of pacifism had been settled by C. S. Lewis, decades before I was born, when he insisted that 'the art of life consists in tackling each immediate evil as well as we can', which closed down any idealistic plans for universal peace.[1]

Hauerwas detonated a bomb under such common-sense arguments. He was not naïive or grounded in some misplaced belief in the goodness of humankind. There was no optimistic narrative of 'progress' funding his position. His argument, spread across scores of essays written over dozens of years, was much more robustly theological. Newly equipped with the theological faculties provided by my courses in Maynooth, I was able to see how his position was

1 C. S. Lewis, 'Why I am not a Pacifist, in *Faith, Christianity and the Church*, ed. Lesley Walmsley (London: HarperCollins, 2002), pp. 281–93.

Students at the back of Humanity House

Top Loftus class hall

sourced from and engaged with the scriptural material far more elegantly than the positions that at first glance seem much more sensible. He did not rely on superficial readings of the Bible, but neither did he wave away difficult passages with convoluted interpretations. His 'Christological non-violence' was not an evasion of war. His concern was that Christians would be courageous enough to trust that they did not have to kill. Those who have participated in Eucharist have pledged to be at peace with one another. Tertullian famously declared that Christ, in disarming Peter, disarmed every soldier. Hauerwas prompted me to ponder what Christian soldier could take up arms having first sat at the Lord's table?

What I did not realise at that time was that Hauerwas had a deep connection to and affection for Maynooth. He had even taught there, back in the early 1980s, at the invitation of his dear friend, Enda McDonagh. An address that they wrote together – scheming it up over dinner in Enda's apartment on campus – serves as a perfect summary for why, in the last generation, the non-violent position they advocate has grown in strength across the churches.

They delivered this address – An Appeal to Abolish War – in October 2002, not at Maynooth, but at the university where they first became friends, Notre Dame.[2] Making such an appeal just a year after the 9/11 attacks required a certain boldness. The US and her dozens of allies in the 'Coalition of the Willing' were heartily engaged in a 'War against Terror'. Declaring that war should end in a country waging a war that by definition can never end (when, after all, will 'Terror' sign the peace treaty?) is an almost comic proposition.

My lectures in moral theology with Padraig Corkery, Suzanne Mulligan and

---

2   The appeal is published in Stanley Hauerwas, *War and the American Difference* (Grand Rapids, MI: Baker, 2011), pp. 40–42. It can also be found in various online sources, including on the website of the Association of Catholic Priests: https://www.associationofcatholicpriests.ie/2018/11/an-appeal-to-abolish-war/

Michael Shortall had equipped me to see that Hauerwas and McDonagh's manifesto was not an act of abstract idealism. Right at the beginning, they rooted their argument in the very core of Christianity: 'We are driven back to that basic conviction that in the death, resurrection and ascension of Jesus Christ, the destructive powers of this world, prominent among them War, were radically overcome.' I was struck that the result they hoped for from their appeal was 'serious conversation ... interrogation and dialogue', which was a good description of what I was experiencing in my lectures.

At no point did Hauerwas and McDonagh think that the end of war would be achieved by an international committee or some list of principles. They finish the essay by pointing out that it was once thought natural to own slaves. That market was (partially) abolished, but they did not present themselves as founders of a modern-day Clapham Sect. Rather, they insisted that Christians do not settle for the what is pragmatic, for common sense, for what seems 'natural'. They foresee a future where the Church develops a tradition of peaceful witness that has political potency, combined with 'attitudes and structures for resolving conflicts non-violently'.

Before Maynooth, I had partially assumed that theology was a quest for truth and what that meant was that it was often simply about getting the right ideas in the right order. In my lectures, in long coffees shared in Pugin Hall, and in those solitary hours enjoying the library that had been built up over generations, I was inducted properly into faith seeking understanding. Theology was active. It was not a theory. I had to put it into practice. All the talk about hypostatic unions or universal destination of goods was meant to take shape in how I thought, what I said, how I spent my money, and how I approached big questions like peace and war.

As I reflect on the five years I spent as a theology student at Maynooth, this is what I appreciate the most. Theology was presented to me as the most fascinating subject available, one that was intellectually satisfying but that had practical implications for my life and the world. As my education unfolded, I ended up doing my PhD under the supervision of Stanley Hauerwas. The character I met in the pages of those books became a mentor and friend and, when he visited Maynooth again, he made it his business to introduce me to Enda McDonagh. Sitting and watching France and Argentina battle (in a non-lethal fashion) at the World Cup with these two theological legends was a remarkable demonstration of the everyday peace practices of conversation and dialogue – even interrogation – that they articulate in their writing and exhibit in their lives.

For them, theology is more than just getting the right ideas in the right order.

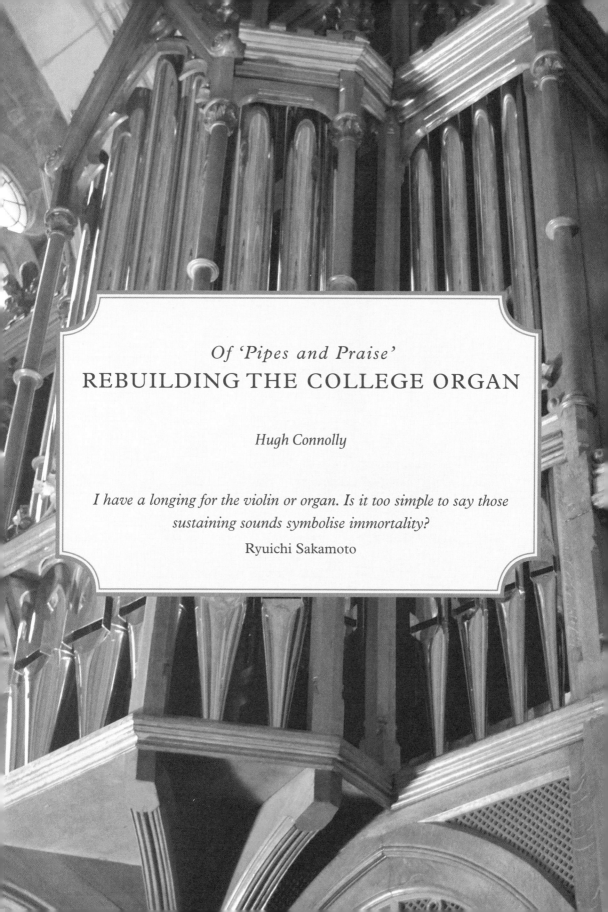

Of 'Pipes and Praise'

REBUILDING THE COLLEGE ORGAN

Hugh Connolly

I have a longing for the violin or organ. Is it too simple to say those sustaining sounds symbolise immortality?

Ryuichi Sakamoto

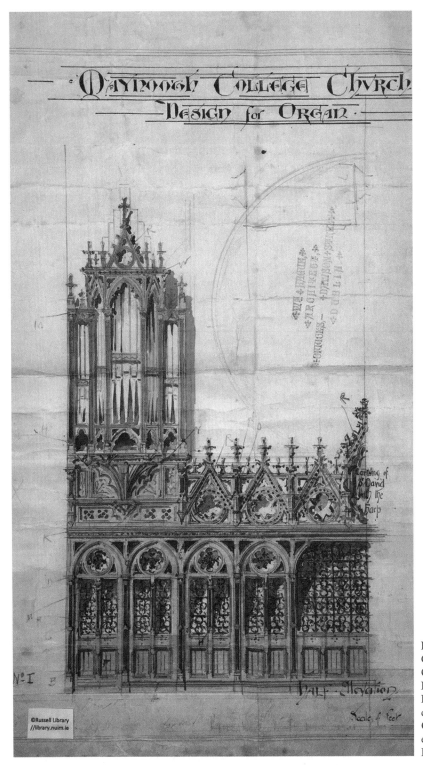

Maynooth College Church
Design for Organ

W. H. Hague
Architect
21 Dawson St.
Dublin

Carving of St David with the harp

Nº I

Half Elevation

Scale of Feet

Previous page:
College Chapel
Organ
Left: William
Hague's
design for the
Organ Case as
executed by Cox
Buckley

Organ Console

Whoever meddles with organs engages with a noble and illustrious instrument whose music has charmed humankind for millennia. *Caveat lector*! Origen, commenting on Psalm 40, concludes: 'The organ is the very Church of God, which at once embraces both the contemplative and active soul.'

The pipe organ is undoubtedly the instrument par excellence of Western Christian worship. In our collective imagination its sound is unmistakably associated with the sacred and the divine. As musical instruments go, the organ has developed in size and complexity more than any other. Throughout this process it has been sustained and improved mainly through its role in Christian worship, at first in the Catholic Church of the Latin Rite and subsequently in the different Protestant confessions.

The organ may have been invented in the third century BCE by Ktesibio of Alexandria. After centuries in the Hellenic it came to Rome and its flourishing empire. Clearly at that time it lacked any sacred meaning. It also differed from our contemporary instruments in that the air was pushed into the tubes not with a bellows, but by water pressure – hence the Greek name *hydraulos*.

Suetonio tells of Nero's great love of the organ. He had apparently an exemplary collection of instruments that he proudly showed off to visitors.

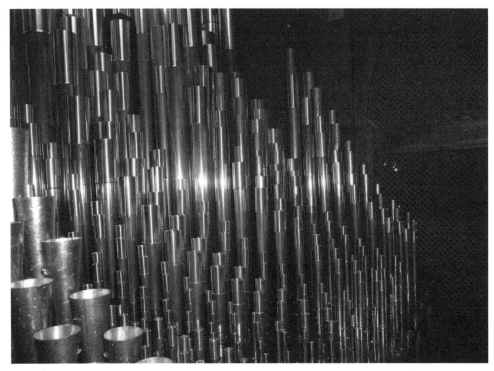

Ranks of pipes during the construction

Throughout the empire the organ soon became a feature of festivals, theatre and even the circus. Iconography suggests that organs were also to be found in the homes of the wealthy.

In the eyes of the early Church, though, the organ remained too closely associated with the 'domestic luxuries' of Roman paganism. In 454 Sidonio Apolinario, bishop of Auvergne, praised King Theodoric for his simplicity: 'His rooms never resonate with those hydraulic organs'.

Perhaps it is unsurprising, therefore, that scholars note a period of silence in the West about organs since the deposition of the last emperor in 476. A couple of seventh-century testimonies eventually attribute the introduction of the organ in the liturgy of the Church to St Vitalian (pope 657–72). While the date is uncertain, the plain truth is that ever since the liturgy and the pipe organ have crossed paths the result has been an indissoluble union that has borne much magnificent and melodious fruit.

Indeed, it is fair to say that today the pipe organ is truly the undisputed emperor of ecclesiastical instruments. It follows, then, that anyone contemplating a refurbishment or rebuild should do so with all the trepidation and extraordinary

The author's name engraved on the largest pipe in the organ

prudence of the surgeon who has as their patient a beloved monarch or patriarch.

As for the Maynooth College organ, it has to be acknowledged that it enjoys neither the venerable age of its ancestors in Bologna, Brescia or Westphalia, nor indeed the sheer immensity of its younger siblings in the likes of Sydney, Philadelphia and Mexico City. That being said, in the eyes and hearts of numerous generations of alumni and professors alike, it has enjoyed a place of genuine affection and esteem.

The Maynooth organ was installed soon after the College Chapel was built (1875–91), under the direction of the first Professor of Music, Heinrich Bewerunge. Built by the Stahlhuth firm of Aix-la-Chapelle around 1890, it was for its time quite avant-garde, using electro-pneumatic controls with the console located at the back of the chapel, well below the pipes in the gallery. This arrangement allowed the organist to be near the choir. However, with the significant distance between console and pipes, there was a noticeable time lapse between pressing keys and sounding notes, rendering it quite tricky to play. A 1970s upgrade eliminated this issue by relocating the console to the gallery.

Over the ensuing decades the organ gradually deteriorated so that some of the stops could no longer be used or else only at one's own risk and peril. A carol service comes to mind where the very last note continued right through the sustained applause and beyond. After the distinctive sound of some frantic footsteps, hastily descending from the organ loft, there came a blood-chilling wail, like the dying moan of some great beast, as the entire instrument shut down and its huge bellows 'gave up the ghost' into the winter night. Thankfully the wonderful instrument had somehow held together until the evening's singing, prayerful reflection and music-making had drawn to a successful close for another season. But it was a wake-up call and a clear signal that refurbishment and restoration could not be further delayed.

Aside from the unglamorous task of fundraising for the rebuild, as President of Maynooth College at the time, I had the privilege of chairing the panel for consideration of the various tenders, a task for which I was not especially experienced. Our panel was nevertheless ably assisted by the unparalleled skill and knowledge of Professor Emeritus Gerard Gillen, who reminded us at the outset that commissioning an organ rebuild was not unlike calling for submissions of poetry. Each organ builder would bring their own tradition and creative imagination to the task, and end results might thus differ significantly. So, indeed, it transpired. Eventually the Ruffatti brothers from Padua were appointed and they set about their task with relish and enthusiasm.

Coincidentally, six months or so later, I was invited to conduct the wedding of a family member in Padua – the home of his future bride. The opportunity to avail of the occasion to visit our dismantled organ in the Ruffatti workshop was not to be missed. After a warm welcome and informative tour of the premises Piero explained how the ancient Venetian city had hosted organ builders since the Middle Ages. In the eighteenth century a highly prestigious organ-building school had been established, founded by Nacchini and continued by Callido and other renowned builders. The unique characteristics of this school formed the foundations for the Ruffatti tradition. In 1940 three brothers – Alessio, Antonio and Giuseppe – founded the Famiglia Artigiana Fratelli Ruffatti, instantly gaining enormous success and producing hundreds of instruments within a short time. Soon their work took on a global reach. The tradition continues today with a second and third generation of Ruffattis, brothers Francesco and Piero and their niece Michela.

A novel idea for fund-raising was the polishing and mounting of some of the disused pipes into a tabletop ornament. Passing through Dublin airport security with several exemplars en route to visit some US benefactors, I was unceremoniously intercepted and swiftly taken aside. When shown images of

Organ Installation

the X-rays I had to admit that the souvenirs did look, for all the world, like mini rocket launchers! Somehow my story held up, though, and the fund-raising trip was, in the end, a resounding success.

After four years of painstaking craftsmanship, much anticipation and resolute fund-raising our rebuild was eagerly unveiled, ceremonially blessed and proudly presented to an expectant congregation drawn from the college, university and broader communities. Olivier Latry, organist at Notre Dame de Paris, gave the first of a series of packed recitals aimed at 'voicing', or putting the restored instrument 'through its paces', and showing it off to a broader constituency. The resounding and enthusiastic applause spoke for itself, and three days later (Wednesday, 30 April 2014) an *Irish Times* review led with the headline: 'Rebuilt Maynooth organ passes the test. The personality of the "new" Ruffatti organ at St Patrick's College Chapel is suave, full, luxuriant and finely balanced.'

It was a fitting tribute to a beautiful old instrument lovingly restored to its former glory and keen to embark upon a new and rich chapter as our magnificent chapel's instrumental voice, proclaiming the word in music and supporting its ongoing song of praise.

CARITAS INTELLIGITUR

S
P

Pulpit of the College Chapel

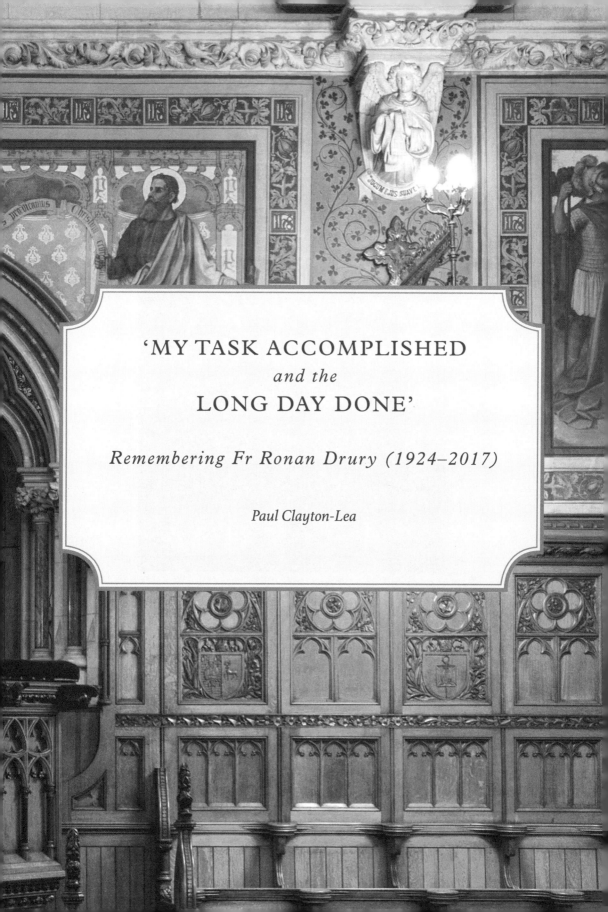

'MY TASK ACCOMPLISHED
and the
LONG DAY DONE'

Remembering Fr Ronan Drury (1924–2017)

Paul Clayton-Lea

Photograph courtesy Meath Chronicle ©

Fr Ronan Drury

At his passing at a youthful ninety-three years in November 2017, Ronan Drury left a genuine and indelible void in the lives of his family, many friends and colleagues. The warm welcome from *The Furrow* office 'den' for visitors high and low, his intense interest displayed with mischievously boyish manner in matters great and small throughout the dioceses of Ireland, and above all his generosity and hospitality towards those who spent time in his company or met him on a daily basis, left a notable vacuum in the corridors and cloisters of his beloved Maynooth as well as the hearts of his friends.

Shortly after his passing, I was fortunate to come across a neat, meticulously handwritten, if somewhat tattered, notebook that he had kept for many years. It was obviously perused regularly. On the first and last pages he inscribed it 'Thomas R. Drury'. Within are found numerous and diverse excerpts from selected authors, saints, scholars and poets. Firm favourite Hilaire Belloc was quoted frequently alongside Rupert Brooke, Shakespeare and O'Casey, Kavanagh, Wordsworth and Dickens, Helen Waddell, Ledwidge and Browning. There is also a host of lesser known or more obscure contributions along with a very few of his own thoughts and reflections. Some passages had been copied onto separate pieces of paper and then carefully glued into the pages of the notebook. The entries all appear to date from the 1940s when he was in his twenties and they end at his ordination to the priesthood in 1947. What is particularly striking about this deeply personal miscellany is their range and profundity, and their influence upon him throughout his life It would not be a great exaggeration to claim that he came to embody their spirit. As we mark the history of Maynooth it therefore seems a suitable occasion to share some of those words that the master wordsmith clearly thought worthy of recording, for, just like the scribe himself, there is a wisdom and a timelessness about them.

In a Maynooth classroom during the autumn of 1982, Ronan firmly, and with a pained expression, memorably instructed our first-year homiletics group that we were not to 'bore the pants off another generation of long-suffering Irish Catholics'. He had a genuine, consistent and heartfelt empathy for the person in the pew and certainly could never have been accused of boring his classroom, audience or congregation, so it was unsurprising to discover this early, unattributed advice to the preacher among his notes:

> One way to make a sermon short is to stop. Live things ought to stop when they have reached their term and they ought not to stop before that. However, if your sermon cannot be stopped any other way you must stunt it. Strike it by lightning; put a worm at the root of it. Anyway, get it stopped.

In similar vein he recorded G.K. Chesterton:

> Merely having an open mind is nothing. The object of opening the mind as of opening the mouth is to shut it again on something solid.

Most telling of all is his barbed quotation from the French philosopher Voltaire, which underpinned his own 'postage stamp' philosophy of sermon writing:

> The necessity of saying something, the perplexity of having nothing to say and a desire of being witty are thrice circumstances which alone are capable of making even the greatest writer ridiculous.

In his role as editor of *The Furrow*, he employed the rule of thumb that less was more when it came to the written word or communicating the most elevated thoughts or complex topic. It was not a process of 'dumbing down', as it's known, but rather of economy of words and challenging the author or communicator to focus relentlessly on their main message, content or point. In a memoir for the volume of essays *Performing the Word – Festschrift for Ronan Drury* (2014), published on the occasion of his ninetieth birthday, his great friend Dr Michael Olden recalled Fr Ronan's rugby days (!), which he said he referred to now and again. However bizarre the togged-out rugged image appeared to those of us who only knew Ronan in his elegant and genteel prime, it helped to explain the dogged tackling that the reverend editor engaged in when dealing with his contributors where their submissions were over long or less than fully comprehensible to anyone other than themselves. Over several pages in his notebook he reiterates the need for this clarity of thought and conciseness of expression. He summed it up in this excerpt from Neil Kevin:

> Two causes of imperfection in the expression of religious sentiment stand out. One is the overstraining of language, mistaking wordage for impressiveness; the other is remaining fossilised in expression.
>
> To catch the mode of the day in speaking, to be neither quaint nor novel, to be familiar with current expressions but not addicted to them, to be not too 'advanced' in diction and not too stale … and then when we come to write, to reflect this contemporary manner of speaking to just the right extent in our writing … that is the only way to excellence in the sphere of religious no less than of secular expression.

Much as Ronan revelled in the world of ideas, books and the creative use of words, he also intuitively understood their limitations and the dangers that they might pose for a priest who became, in the words of C. S. Lewis, so heavenly minded that they were no earthly use. He kept a very telling quotation in that regard from the pen of Robert Louis Stevenson:

Books are good enough in their own way but they are a mighty bloodless substitute for life. It seems a pity to sit like the Lady of Shalott peering into a mirror with your back turned on all the glamour and bustle of reality. And if a man reads very hard, as the old anecdote reminds us, he will have little time for thought.

Hand in hand with his love of words was a lifelong attachment to Maynooth, its inhabitants and history, where he spent most of his long life and achieved such personal and professional fulfilment. In 1945, on the occasion of the 150th anniversary of the college's foundation, he reflected in words that might equally have been applied to himself in later times;

> After a century and a half, Maynooth is old but she is not showing her years. The stones of her buildings may betray the silent touches of time, but the spirit that inhabits the walls is always youthful. Perhaps it is fancy, but when the summer evening closes down and calls the glory from the grey stones, I like to think that the shadows of the past come back again to stroll around under the yew trees.

As it happened, one of our last walks together in 2017 was among those very yews in the college cemetery with its regiment of Celtic crosses and monuments, some dedicated to student seminarians whose graves were relatively new during Ronan's early times as a student. Perhaps it was one of those youthful graves he had in mind when, on the death of a student, he quoted from a fellow student in the 1940s whose words had clearly moved him and whom he described only as 'a student friend':

> He came on loan from God, just for a few years, that we might profit by his example. And then when his time was up God called him back to Himself – and we are lonely.

Students loved his good-humoured readiness to engage with them on their own level while at the same time always encouraging them to be their better selves. If he eschewed the usually intense formality of Maynooth professor/ student relationships, it was never at the cost of respectfulness from either side. Unsurprisingly, over the years he was invited to a legion of ordinations that took him to every diocese if not every parish in the land. The festive excitement and fervour of such occasions at that time are depicted in a poem by John D.

Sheridan which he took from the 1 December 1944 *Standard* and which he says was; 'Written here March 3rd 1945'. Entitled 'The Priestin' of Father John', it offers a hilarious and, at times, poignant account following an ordination, set in the new priest's home parish where everyone claims ownership of the homecoming young Fr John. Verse 3 reads:

> Oul Canon Dan, God bless him,
> Will be fussin' fit to burst,
> And the women batin other
> To get his blessin' first.
> But Canon or no Canon –
> And I'd say it to his face –
> For all his bits of purple
> He'll take the second place.
> Sure even if the Bishop came
> Wi' yon big mitre on
> He wouldn't get the welcome
> That we'll give to Fr John.

The encouragement and support he offered newly ordained priests helps to explain the reluctance of so many past students to relegate Ronan to the past as they did almost all of their other tutors. No class reunion in Maynooth seemed complete without his presence and there were many amiable tussles about whose table he would grace during the Maynooth Union Dinner! His purring enjoyment of these friendly tugs of war was palpable.

A large part of his attraction for young people stemmed from his readiness to embrace change throughout his long life. He had no hankering after a 'golden age' of Church or life itself but welcomed and usually encouraged the positive elements to be found in a changing Church and world. This brief excerpt from a piece intriguingly entitled 'Saints in a Hurry and Married' by the Rev. Neil Kevin was headed by Ronan with his own underlined words: 'Putting back the Clock'.

> No doubt there is something wistful about this old metaphor (putting back the clock), and chivalrous hearts beating in one cause or another have rallied from time to time in its defence; but it remains a metaphor and a dream. The law of nature is forward for better or worse. No age will wear the clothes of a former age. However beautiful they be, they never seem to fit well.

A similar strain runs through another of his selected poems by Rudyard Kipling ('Sestina of the Tramp-Royal'), where we glimpse his appetite for life and openness to change.

> It's like a book, I think, this bloomin' world
> Which you can read and care for just so long,
> But presently you feel that you will die
> Unless you get the page you're reading done,
> And turn another – likely not so good;
> But what you're after is to turn them all.

All who knew him would agree that Ronan Drury was the epitome of courtesy in any company. His lifelong friend, Professor Enda McDonagh, wrote in *Performing the Word*: 'Ronan is a natural or should I say gifted peacemaker. For those individuals, hurt and suffering, he can be a healing presence by word and silence.' He certainly had an almost unmatched record for his attendance at priests' and other funerals.

In thirty-five years, I never heard him utter a profanity or a crude or rude comment or remark about anyone. He delighted in praising those who offered him some small service or kindness and could be almost comically effusive when coaxing articles or book reviews for *The Furrow*, playing at times on the author's vanity or throwing down the gauntlet to others whom he felt would respond positively to his carefully choreographed challenge. Sharp wit and gentle banter were his stock in trade. No one was perhaps less suited to the present age of social media 'trolls' or the contemporary trend in cruel commentary. Maybe a raised eyebrow or a twinkling in the eye that betrayed an imminent waspish comment, but never anything as clumsy or brutal as harsh criticism or unkind judgement. His most quoted source was the Anglo-French Catholic writer, humanitarian and historian Hilaire Belloc (1870–1953) who had written; 'Of Courtesy, it is much less than courage of heart or holiness, yet in my walks it seems to me that the grace of God is in Courtesy.'

Yet, if he was, in essence, a peacemaker and rarely took sides, Ronan was also unwavering about the importance of truth, something frequently and courageously reflected in his publication of provocative articles or contributors occasionally irritating some of those who held authority in the Church. He may have been guided in that regard by a quote from St Jerome, whose words he placed boldly at the head of one page: 'If an offence come out of the truth, better is it that the offence come than that the truth be concealed.'

In an all too rare personal reflection that revealed his sensitivity to the two world wars whose human cost had formed the backdrop to his childhood and youth, he drew comparisons between the writings of his favourite poets Rupert Brooke and Francis Ledwidge. His first short quote from Ledwidge from 'The Lost Ones' is filled with the grief and pain of war:

> But where are all the loves of long ago?
> O little twilight ship blown up the tide
> Where are the faces laughing in the glow
> Of morning years? The lost ones scattered wide?
> Give me your hand, O brother, let us go
> Crying about the dark for those who died.

In a further lengthy reflection on the topic he concluded:

> In several ways Brooke and Ledwidge were similar. Both were harnessing the fires that had been making a riot of their young souls when death intervened. Both marched to the war and the deeper they went into the mire and blood of battle the more the poet in them wandered back to the sad, gay times of their beginning; to the wonder and beauty they had so briefly known – and that the soldier in them was bent on destroying.

This personal reflection was followed by verses from Siegfried Sassoon which were noted as having been written after the Armistice was signed in 1918. Given that the entry was made during the final year of the Second World War it seems to me to have had a special and hope-filled meaning for the young Ronan and the war-weary world of his youth.

> Everyone Sang
>
> Everyone's voice was suddenly lifted
> And beauty came like the setting sun.
> My heart was shaken with tears,
> And horror drifted away
> O but everyone was a bird; and the song was wordless.
> The singing will never be done.

Until he reached his nineties, when his longevity and energy seemed to impress even him, Ronan was not very keen to be reminded of his birthday. This lack of enthusiasm in celebrating the passing of years, even as a young man, is evident in his choice of verse from the pen of Tom Moore :

My Birth-Day

My birth-day!! What a different sound
that word had in my youthful ears,
And now each time the day comes round,
less and less white its mark appears.
When first our scanty years are told
It seems like pastime to grow old,
But as youth counts the shining links
That time around him binds so fast
Pleased with the task, he little thinks,
How hard that chain will press at last.

Such melancholy thoughts rarely lingered. His default position always seemed one of cheerfulness, even joy, in his priestly ministry and his roles as editor, teacher, mentor and friend. Regular sojourns abroad for work or pleasure in the company of friends enhanced his natural *joie de vivre* and love of his faith, exemplified by another quote from Belloc which he penned in large letters;

Where'er a Catholic sun doth shine
There's always laughter and good red wine,
At least I have always found it so
Benedicamus Domino.

This gift of enjoyment of each day and each person – mindful before 'mindfulness' flowered – is found in words that he ascribed to Little Thérèse of Lisieux:

My life is an instant, an hour which passes by,
My life is a moment which flies and is away,
Thou knowest, O my God, that to love Thee on this earth
I only have today.

This inner joy stemmed from a certainty about the God he believed in and served as infinitely merciful and compassionate. It is also revealed in a piece

457

taken from another of his favourites, G. K. Chesterton, which he entitled 'The Joy of Jesus' – a God who smiled.

> I say it with reverence; there was in that shattering personality a thread that must be called shyness. There was something that He hid from all men when he went up a mountain to pray. There was something that he covered constantly by abrupt silence or impetuous isolation. There was some one thing that was too great for God to show us when He walked upon our earth; and I have sometimes fancied that it was His mirth.

While no slouch in terms of theological or moral conceptualisation, especially in relation to discussion of his editorial choices for publication in *The Furrow*, he had a great gift for translating the thoughts and writings of his more erudite contributors into accessible language for his students and congregations. He was in that sense very much a 'man of the people' and never ensconced in an ivory tower. In treating weighty thoughts with a light hand perhaps he took his cue from W. Lyon Phelps, another whom he regularly quotes in the notebook:

> The difficulty with many men is that they imagine their world of thought is the thought of the world.

He enjoyed engaging in whimsical and trivial conversation and in many ways perfected it so that the mild gossip that sometimes ensued became pure amusement with no hint of malice. He happily quoted Cardinal Manning on the topic:

> Harmless gossips buzz on amiably, 'sicut chimariae bombitantes in vacua'; amiable buzzing creatures, the bluebottles of social life.

He was also adept at entertaining his friends with short, humorous verses and limericks to make a point or sometimes divert a heated discussion. One he recorded:

> An Englishman thinks seated;
> A Frenchman standing;
> An American pacing;
> And an Irishman – afterwards!

Another he entitled 'Argument', by Mildred Weston:

> Two stubborn beaks of equal strength
> Can stretch a worm to any length.

Yet another he used to tease his friends from the west of Ireland:

> I think it was Jekyll who used to say that the farther he went West the
> more convinced he felt that the Wise Men came from the East (Sydney
> Smith).

My personal favourite is an unattributed verse entitled 'Sez Me':

> Far duller than people who don't read books
> And viler than those who burn them,
> Are the barefaced, smiling gentleman crooks
> Who borrow and don't return them.

Several saints are significantly referenced and one of the longest passages in his notebook dated 7/3/45, is St Bernard of Clairvaux's exhortation on the Virgin Mary from which the following is taken:

> In perils, in crises, in perplexities, think of Mary, call upon Mary. Let
> neither your mouth nor your heart cease to plead for her prayers, to
> ponder the example of her life. In her steps you cannot stray; invoking
> her you cannot despair; thinking of her you cannot err; clinging to
> her you cannot fall; under her protection you have no fear; with her
> guidance you never weary; with her assistance you reach your goal.

Of the places his absence is most keenly felt, his home parish of Mullagh is high on the list. His sixty-eight consecutive celebrations of Midnight Mass there at Christmas were an annual high point for him and for generations of parishioners. While his native diocese was Kilmore, he explained his place in Meath through receiving his education in St Finian's College, Mullingar, where the scholarships were reputedly more generous than Kilmore. In an *Irish Times* obituary he was quoted as having teasingly told a former Bishop of Kilmore, 'You could have had me for a fiver!' During an interview for Northern Sound local radio three years ago he admitted, 'The whole midnight Mass has a strong emotional element for me. I can see their grandfather's look in the child's eye as they are coming up for communion. It is a very rich experience.' As a young man, perhaps it was Mullagh and his call to priesthood that he was thinking of when he entered a quote from George (AE) Russell:

> A parish where you would find the people ready to cooperate and the young men walking poetry – it is a place perhaps where some very holy priest lived and worked and died perhaps a hundred years ago; and though he is not remembered by name and he is gone into the silence of the past, his work endures and fructifies. We reap today what he sowed long ago.

The splendidly organised funeral liturgies in Maynooth and Mullagh with eulogies and tributes distinguished by their deep sincerity and appreciation of his vocation and friendship will long linger in the memories of those present. Of all his notebook reflections on the topic of death, perhaps the following says best what he would want to say about his leaving:

> So be my passing;
> My task accomplished and the long day done
> My wages taken, and in my heart
> Some late lark singing –
> Let me be gathered to the quiet West,
> The sundown, splendid and serene – Death. (W. E. Henley)

While the following quote did not figure among his notebook selections it seems an apt conclusion for this brief essay written in fondest remembrance:

> He was a man, take him for all in all. I shall not look upon his like again.
>
> (*Hamlet*, Act I, scene 2, line 186)

An earlier version of this article was published in The Furrow *in November 2018. It is reprinted here with kind permission of the Editor.*

Finials (detail of the College Chapel stalls)

REVISITING MAYNOOTH, JUNE 2018

Jim O'Brien

ast week, on my travels, I found myself with an hour or more to spare between visits to properties. It was a fine day, my youngest daughter was with me and our journey was taking us to within sight of the spire of my old alma mater, St Patrick's College Maynooth. A trip down memory lane speckled with sunshine and shadows was too tempting to pass. I turned the car towards the place that saw the youth of me come and go, to show my daughter where her father, and later her mother, faced the mysteries of life that loom large before you when you are all of seventeen.

A potted history of the college and its surrounds poured out of me as we approached the gate. My captive audience of one was treated to short bursts of loose facts about the Geraldine Castle, located just outside the grounds, from where the FitzGeralds of Kildare lorded it over much of the country. Inside

Lady Chapel

the gate, I spotted the ancient yew tree under which Silken Thomas is reputed to have disported himself in his finery. Moving on we saw Stoyte House, the original building granted by His Majesty's Government to the Catholic hierarchy in 1795 so that priests could be educated in Ireland under the watchful eye of the Crown. The British were desperate to staunch the flow of troublesome young clerics disembarking surreptitiously from French schooners with heads full of the kind of revolutionary ideas that caused a Bourbon head to fall into a blood-soaked basket.

Entering St Joseph's Square, any words I said were lost on my young sapling whose breath was taken away by the sight of Pugin's neo-Gothic masterpiece that rose before us on its imposing site. 'O my God,' she said. 'Isn't it beautiful?' I said. 'It is, Dad, it's like Hogwarts for Catholics.' Sweet and tender Mother of Divine God, was I wasting my sweetness on the desert air? But who am I to determine the filter or the prism through which anyone views the world or absorbs history?

I suppose Maynooth was my Hogwarts, where the magic of youth sought to dance under the black cloak of a fraying solemnity. Ambling the familiar corridors with my child, we gazed quietly on the lines of photographs hanging on the walls, preserving my likes in unblemished and unlined eternity.

To my disappointment, the College Chapel was locked. I took a chance that an old friend on the staff might be in residence and dialled his number. He appeared in all his whiteness, the flour of the years sprinkled on him, and he now a professor in shirt and jeans. There are no academic gowns anymore. This lovely Kerryman, who walked under these arches with me in 1975, doesn't need any gown to carry his erudition, or a mortar board to tell the world he speaks at least five languages fluently, and knows things about things that were buried for millennia in the depths of the Dead Sea.

He delighted me, he delighted my daughter and she delighted him. Swiping his card, he took us to the magnificence of the College Chapel with its 494 carved choir stalls, its Italian marble altarpieces and its ornate plasterwork wrapped in Victorian splendour.

There was a time these choir stalls were full – full of young be-robed men whose voices filled the sumptuous arched ceiling with Tantums and Kyries and Glorias. But, for the clip of heels on terracotta, the place is silent now; the decades of a dark theocracy have emptied its stalls as young men choose other paths, while young women have but limited space in these places.

We retired for coffee to the high-ceilinged refectory with its Tudor-like beams and criss-cross diamond window panes. My friend and my daughter talked

The entrance to St Mary's Oratory

about school and holidays and Harry Potter. I was lost among the ghosts gliding around me, forever seventeen.

Rejoining the conversation, we covered as much ground as we could in the last few moments before parting. We talked of his mother in Kerry, Trump, the pope's visit and the state of everything now that Garrett's constitutional crusade has been embraced by a different Ireland.

Making our way out under the arches, we met two of his students, young women in the last phases of PhDs and masters in theology, women whose voices and learning will hopefully speak for my daughters and, indeed, for all of us, in places where exclusion is arrayed in the flimsiest of theological rags.

It was time to get back on the road, to leave this oasis of memory and these moments of unexpected delight. We parted under Silken Thomas's tree, where we too, like the colourful Geraldine, once disported ourselves in all our youthful finery. My friend shook my daughter's hand and told her to mind me. He turned and we embraced warmly, a gesture that would have raised eyebrows and dug furrows in foreheads were we to do so such a thing back in the day when we first came through those gates. We promised to keep in touch. We'll meet in the kingdom; the real one.

This piece first appeared in *The Farming Independent* on 3 July 2018.

THE GOLDEN JUBILEE
OF THE 'SEM. COURSE', 1969–2019

Donal McMahon

he Seminarist Course in Philosophy and Arts was established by the trustees of Maynooth College on 7 October 1969 and therefore marked its golden jubilee in 2019. Patrick Corish's bicentenary history has left us this account: '[T]wo-year courses in which philosophy was dominant had to be set up under the supervision of a seminarist board for the unmatriculated seminarians who were first admitted in the autumn of 1969',[1] while the annual *Kalendarium* has faithfully recorded its academic and administrative life since then. However, apart from such brief notices or official documentation, it has not, so to speak, featured much in the literature – whatever about being treasured in the heart.[2] Now, since a golden jubilee of any kind always, and deservedly, places the principal(s) centre stage, the valuable contribution made by the Seminarist Course to the college and the Church may, on the occasion of its jubilee, be appropriately publicised and all who were part of it congratulated and thanked.

The 'Sem. Course', as it was familiarly called, catered for the many students (diocesan, missionary and religious) who previously would have matriculated on the basis of a pass in the Leaving Certificate but who now, in 1969, following the change in matriculation standards introduced by the NUI in 1965 and rolled out over the following years, were required to have two honours as well.[3] As a result, for the first time since 1910, when Maynooth became a Recognised College of the National University, a distinction was made between degree and non-degree seminarians.[4] Not being able to do a degree course meant a certain parting of the ways from one's peers and

1 Patrick J. Corish, *Maynooth College 1795–1995* (Dublin: Gill & Macmillan, 1995), p. 420.
2 'Those first impressions of life at Maynooth must have been strong indeed, for they have outlasted all that came after them' (Neil Kevin, *I Remember Maynooth*, reprinted Maynooth: St Patrick's College, 1995, p. 26; first published 1937). Kevin's impressions were of the BA course. Hopefully, the Sem. student too has equally deep and fond memories, whether he proceeded afterwards to ordination or returned to lay life (in Kevin's words, '*ad vota saecularia*').
3 For the background, see J. P. MacHale, 'University Entry: The New Requirements', *Studies*, 56 (spring 1967), pp. 85–89. Some students with the requisite two honours did not matriculate for reasons such as lack of a modern language.
4 The distinction is evident in the 1969–70 *Kalendarium*. Under the heading 'Students, First Year', we read: 'University Residential' (pp. 216–17), 'University Non-Residential' (pp. 218–19), 'Seminarist Residential' (pp. 219–20), 'Seminarist Non-Residential' (p. 220).

cannot but have affected the first-year Sem. student's confidence.[5] What's more, matriculation requirements for the Pontifical University being the same as those for the National University, he was facing the prospect of ending up with neither a BA nor a BD. The road less travelled by, he was discovering, had quite a few academic twists and turns. The situation improved in 1979 when he had the chance not only to gain the Diploma in Philosophy and Arts – promoted now from being a college to a Pontifical University diploma – but, provided he achieved the qualifying mark in his second-year exams and was duly recommended by the Supervisory Board of Seminarist Studies for matriculation in the Faculty of Theology, he also had the chance to reach the elusive goal of a BD degree. At last, in 2011, when, no doubt, it was recognised that two years' hard work after the Leaving Certificate was more than equivalent to two honours in it, and when most clerical students matriculated anyway on the basis of mature years, the diploma was accepted for matriculation by both universities. At an early conferring of the college diploma, President Tomás Ó Fiaich made a joke about Tweedledum and Tweedle DD. It is and has always been my hope that, throughout it all, both degree and non-degree students, united in their priestly vocation, were generous and large-minded enough to rise above all these potentially divisive academic distinctions in hearty agreement with St Paul, 'There is a variety of gifts but always the same Spirit' (1 Corinthians 12:4).[6]

Teachers were needed for the new course. Two priests from the Congregation of the Sacred Hearts of Jesus and Mary (SSCC) were appointed in 1969 to teach philosophy: Flannan (Flan) Markham (1935–95) and Patrick (Pat) Bradley (1934–2011). On Pat's resigning in 1982 to take up the position of superior general in Rome, Thomas (Tom) Kelly was appointed in his place. When our paths crossed again many years later, Pat told me the story of the beginnings of the course (noted in my diary for 7 June 2009): 'Went to 12 Mass in Clondalkin. Met Pat after. Gave me lunch. Talked about '69 and setting-up of course. Newman getting Ó Fiaich and McNamara to his room – things taking off. Providence, he says.'[7] A third full-time appointment was made in 1974 of

5   The whole subject can be viewed in a more positive light, however, when it is remembered that 'in the stirrings after the Council seminarians were beginning to question the relevance of a degree in arts or science […] and all seemed agreed there should be an alternative non-degree course in the first years in the seminary' (Corish, pp. 427–28) – a wish granted by the introduction of the Seminarist Course.

6   Pending accreditation of the course, it was many years before Sem. students were recorded in the *Kalendarium* as receiving an academic award. The first time was for the college Diploma in Philosophy and Arts in 1978. From 1979 on, they became the happy recipients of a diploma awarded by the Faculty of Philosophy of the Pontifical University. The *Kalendarium* for the jubilee year 2019–20 shows (p. 212) that, of the eleven students awarded the BD (Hons) in 2018, five did the Seminarist Course. From not being there at all to making up almost half the total number – 'Nice going!', as Flan (and Tom after him) used to say as a form of congratulations.

7   In 1969 Msgr Jeremiah Newman was president, while Rev. Tomás Ó Fiaich and Rev. Kevin McNamara were vice-presidents.

'a teacher of English and French' (the words of the ad in the *Irish Times*), a role that fell to me, with no teaching experience other than what the HDipEd had given me.[8]

'The first two years were, in many ways, the most enjoyable and fulfilling and I have no doubt that the Philosophy and English courses contributed in no small way to that experience' (Michael Router, Kilmore, 1982–84).[9] In the 1970s, Pat, Flan and myself had most of our classes in New Logic Hall (NLH), situated above where the Pontifical University Office (and before that, the college bookshop) is now: benches running down the middle of the room, single desks at each side, and a blackboard between two windows at the teaching end. In the 1980s, while I continued with my first or second years in NLH, the philosophers for their combined classes in certain subjects needed (hard to believe now!) the more spacious Music Hall (today the Conference and Accommodation Centre). 'My memories of the two years I spent on the Seminarist Course are happy ones. […] The only complaint I have is that [Donal] had to teach in a hall that was always a bit cramped, which led to a lot of pushing and shoving in the back seats!' (Colm O'Doherty, Derry, 1981–83). 'I do still have shameful memories of Rag Week – alarm clocks in the lecture room! I pray you don't remember' (Jerry Carey, Killaloe, 1978–80).

Vincent Sherlock (Achonry, 1981–83) remembers Flan teaching in a packed Music Hall.[10]

> He knew who was there and who wasn't. Equally, he knew who was paying attention and, again, who wasn't. He had a knack of keeping his eye on you no matter where you were in the room. Doodling or idling weren't options. 'Vincent, do I see a question on your face?' was his way of letting you know that he knew your mind was elsewhere.[11]

So what a shock it was when such a central presence was no longer there! He died suddenly, aged fifty-nine, on Sunday, 8 January 1995, just before the start of term.

Following the establishment in 1997 of the National University of Ireland, Maynooth (NUIM), and the creation, in consequence, of separate finances and facilities from those of St Patrick's College, the Seminarist Course was allocated Dunboyne House for the staff and Dunboyne Hall (in Loftus Halls) for the

---

8   See Donal McMahon, 'First and Last Year', the *Irish Times*, 1 November 2013, p. 19. English and French had been taught by part-time staff for the first five years of the course.
9   This and the following quoted memories come from priests who either attended an evening in the college on 2 May 2013 to mark 'Forty-Plus Years of the Sem. Course: A Celebratory and Commemorative Gathering', or who sent me their memories afterwards.
10 Vincent was in a combined class of 108 students in 1981–82 and 100 the following year.
11 See https://sherlockshome.ie/good-to-be-there-and-nice-to-be-asked/

The Irish Saints in St Columba's Oratory completed when the chapel was reordered after the Second Vatican Council

students. This was the era that saw a dramatic decline in numbers.[12] Following Flan's death, when meeting the small number of students at the start of every year in my new capacity as administrator of the course as well as teacher, I used to boost their morale (and my own) by complimenting them on being, in Milton's words, 'fit audience, though few'. On the other hand, the rise in age and the consequent maturity of the students more than compensated for the decline in numbers. There were more and more late vocations, one or two of them, indeed, being around the same age as myself, and all of them, as the reader can imagine, a sheer pleasure to work with. Some, quite understandably, were anxious about returning to study after years spent out in the world. 'I was asked before joining what my biggest fear was, and I said academics, as I had never been in any third-level college before' (Tony Gilhooly, Ardagh and Clonmacnois, 2007–09).

There was no better person to allay Tony's fears of philosophy than Tom who, following his appointment to the NUIM Philosophy Department in 1999, was now, in the autumn of 2007, starting out on a new road himself as professor (in both the National and Pontifical Universities). Someone with his very engaging personality and teaching skills perfected over seventeen years in the seminary was certainly very well qualified to make clerical and lay students alike feel at home with philosophy. But again, what a shock! It turned out that Tony attended Tom's last 'Introduction to Philosophy' module. He died suddenly, aged fifty-one, on 21 February 2008 and was granted burial in the college cemetery. It was my very sad privilege to assist his wife, Marian O'Donnell, in devising a Latin inscription for the headstone.

When the conversation in my office brought up Flan, Tom would often exclaim, 'Ah, put on Flan!', i.e. play one of the commercially released cassettes of Flan's retreat talks. Tom would then do an imitation (good-natured, of course) of his voice and mannerisms, and we would laugh away. A clerical student had recorded some of Tom's lectures and kindly gave me the CD, but I find it hard to put that on. Instead, I like to remember him for one of his drawings. How often, again in the office, and even when we were in the middle of serious exam matters, he would exclaim for some vaguely tangential reason, 'I feel a cartoon coming on! Give me a page!' He would sketch away rapidly, touching it up here and there, and then, 'What d'ye think?' And, genuinely, in a way I could never

12 The first-year figures for the decade years (taken from the *Kalendarium*) will give some idea of the overall trend: 46 (1969), 52 (1979), 39 (1989), 7 (1999), 8 (2009), 10 (2019, 8 Diploma, 2 Higher Diploma in the now reconstituted course). The highest first-year numbers were 70 (1980–81, the year that also saw the highest number (110) for the combined class) and 56 (1986–87). In the introduction to the twentieth issue (2002) of the class publication *U2E2* (i.e. You too, second-year English students of the Seminarist Course), I noted: 'What strikes us at once when comparing this [end of] year's second-year class with that of twenty years ago [1981–82] is, of course, the huge difference in numbers: 2 compared to 44.'

quite do in the case of his highly impressive academic publications (on Heidegger etc.), I would applaud this proof of spontaneous and delightful creativity. And file it carefully away.

I have spoken about the three full-time lecturers on the Seminarist Course. When I was left as the only one in 1999, it would simply not have survived without the invaluable contribution from a succession of part-time philosophy lecturers.[13] Thanks are also due to the many occasional lecturers in the elective arts subjects offered over the years. Following my retirement in 2013 and at a crossroads moment for the course in many of its aspects, Thomas Casey SJ was appointed Professor of Philosophy in the Pontifical University and, later, dean of the faculty. The jubilee year 2019 saw the appointment of Philip Gonzales and Gaven Kerr as lecturers. The team was now back to full strength.

So, things taking off again. Providence, I can hear Pat say. The Sem. Course lives on and sets out, renewed and re-inspired, towards its next jubilee.

13 I wish to record my thanks and, speaking on its behalf, those of the College, to Rev. Dr Donal Daly SVD, Dr Michael Dunne, Mr Eamonn Gaines, Rev. Dr Patrick Gorevan, Dr J. Haydn Gurmin, Mr Stephen McGroggan, Rev. Dr Patrick Moroney SVD, Rev. Dr Simon Nolan OCarm, and Dr Denise Ryan. Drs Gorevan and Ryan continue to serve as part-time lecturers. I wish to thank also all those who taught part-time for the first five years of the course.

WE REMEMBER BEWERUNGE

John O'Keeffe

he National Seminary has a number of musical traditions, some more venerable than others, but when the community gathers each November in the college cemetery and the graves are blessed to the accompanying strains of Bewerunge's *Benedictus*, we are, it may safely be asserted, on fairly solid ground. 'As for you, little child, you shall be called a prophet of God the most high. You shall go ahead of the Lord, to prepare his ways before him … he will give light to those in darkness, those who dwell in the shadow of death … '. Bewerunge's setting of Zachariah's canticle, in which he alternates simple, functional musical structures with richer, more effusive polyphonic ones, offers a succinct distillation of the European choral tradition and an enduring metaphor for the art of liturgical music. This and other compositions of our musical founding father, which continue to punctuate the liturgical year at Maynooth, provide timely reminders of the high calling of Church music and of the deep wells from which it may draw water.

Rooted in a solid tradition but called to strike out for new horizons; one wonders what Bewerunge would make of the contents of a filing cabinet held in the music room which chart the evolution of liturgical music in the seminary from the late 1960s to the late 1980s. Alongside the continuing threads of Latin chant and polyphony are found newer compositions in English and Irish: hymns, Mass settings, early essays in responsorial psalmody, and with them, a significant body of contemporary folk compositions. While one can imagine the exacting professor casting a cold eye on some of the material, all entries formed necessary signposts along the journey of a vernacular liturgy trying to find its feet.

Over the past three decades a number of new musical furrows have been opened up: a fully sung vernacular office for Sundays and solemnities; the Church music series *Feasts and Seasons*, itself a response to the call inherent in the Roman Rite for a scripturally grounded, seasonally distinctive repertoire; and, latterly (too late have we loved thee), a more serious engagement with the musical and spiritual potential of Ireland's native language and culture as an authentic means and fruitful wellspring of liturgical praise. These initiatives have interesting roots, ones intimately and organically bound to the lived liturgical

Cassin's cartoon of Bewerunge, with a caption making fun of his strong German accent

experience of the seminary community. Admittedly (*pace*, students of the early 1990s), the first was parachuted in somewhat like a Cecilian missionary endeavour and critiqued (not unreasonably) by an early episcopal visitation as being 'too severely monastic'. Out of the bare roots, however, some blossoms began to appear, and the enterprise gradually assumed a richer and more attractive texture. Human frailty played its part too, as the tradition of sung morning prayer may be traced back to a pair of Middle Oratory cantors who were having difficulty rising on time on Sunday mornings. The cure eventually settled upon was to keep writing antiphons for them to prepare and sing properly, or else suffer the ridicule of their unforgiving brethren. The bar was raised, the men responded and thus began a new Maynooth tradition. *O felix culpa.*

Over those same thirty years, falling student numbers have seen Sunday worship move from the College Chapel, first to St Joseph's, and more recently, to St Mary's, with attendant implications for the seminary choir. The physical constraints and architectural dynamic dictate a musical approach that tends more towards communal expression, with the choir leavening from within while at the same time trying to articulate its distinctive, prophetic role. This has resulted in a steady increase in the quality and richness of daily liturgical song, something for which the student body has an ever-increasing responsibility. For student liturgy leaders, the programming of liturgical music is now an organic, responsive process with the dual goal of answerability to the demands of the liturgy and the need to keep the community nourished, refreshed and, to embrace once more Pius X's descriptor, 'edified'. In such a context, the psalmist's exhortation '*Cantate Domino canticum novum*' moves swiftly from the realm of pious intention to practical necessity. This organic process has led in turn to the composition, commissioning and sourcing of new repertoire suitable not just for the seminary context, but for use in parishes throughout the country, as the success of the published *Feasts and Seasons* collections demonstrates.

Despite occasional crises of conscience and practice over the decades and the negative soundtrack so sadly a part of the national discussion on the Irish language, the Friday morning Irish Mass currently finds itself in a healthy place both ritually and musically, with its unique spiritual fruits being more fully enjoyed and appreciated by a multicultural seminary community. Maynooth's history of service to the national tongue is a proud one – may it and all national agencies work towards a more fully inculturated liturgy, one in which the Irish Church makes more equal use of both vernacular lungs.

We have not forgotten Bewerunge, nor the succession of fine musicians who, each in their own way, honoured his legacy: Tracy, O'Callaghan, Watson, Clarke,

November Blessing by Sara Kyne

Lavery, Martin, Gillen (I might include here also Rev. Frank McNamara, founder of the Mullingar Schola Cantorum). Bewerunge would certainly have welcomed the establishment in 1968 of a fully fledged Music Department at Maynooth as part of the NUI. He would have rejoiced also at the multiplication of excellent choirs over the following five decades (his spirit certainly hovered over the birth of the Chamber Choir and Schola Gregoriana), placing Maynooth at the forefront of choral performance amongst national campuses. On the academic front, it is entirely fitting that his seminal contribution as a musicologist should be acknowledeged and that the main lecture room of the university's Music Department should bear his name.

Bewerunge's music features prominently in a set of recorded broadcasts from the 1960s of the college choir, under the direction of Rev. Charles O'Callaghan, currently being prepared for archiving in the Russell Library. As I write, the coming year will also see the seminary choir present renderings of his *Magnificat,* as well as his published arrangements of Palestrina's 'O admirabile commercium' and 'Exsultate Deo', and in the first week of November, the choir will in good conscience square up once more to his iconic *Benedictus. Sicut locutus est per os sanctorum …*

In the Bleak Midwinter

FIFTY YEARS OF CAROLS AT MAYNOOTH

Gerard Gillen

p to 1966 the student body at Maynooth was exclusively clerical. In that year, in the spirit of *aggiornamento*, the bishops decided to develop the college 'as an open centre of university education', by admitting lay students (both male and female) to NUI degree programmes. Three years later, with numbers of lay students slowly growing, the Professor of Music at the time, the late Fr Noel Watson, decided to form a choral society for the extra-curricular enrichment of lay students.

In Ireland the late 1960s saw the first impact of the thinking of the Second Vatican Council on Catholic religious practice, with an awakening of the post-conciliar ecumenical movement, when Christians of the various denominations began to discover and celebrate those elements of their traditions that united them rather than those that divided them. In terms of worship, Catholics were quick to discover the rich tradition of Protestant hymnody, and slowly began to incorporate a number of well-known gems such as 'Praise, my Soul, the King of Heaven', 'All People That on Earth Do Dwell', 'Lead, Kindly Light', into the Catholic hymn repertoire, and added to these came a number of Christmas carols such as 'Hark! The Herald Angels Sing', 'O Little Town of Bethlehem', 'Once in Royal David's City' (words by Mrs Alexander, wife of the Bishop of Derry) etc., which, ten years earlier, would not have been heard in Catholic churches.

About this time Catholics also discovered that for some generations their Protestant co-religionists had been celebrating Christmas with a service of carols, readings and prayers, a service that was drawn up over a century ago by a former Archbishop of Canterbury, Edward White Benson, when he was Bishop of Truro. The format was soon taken up by the Chapel community of King's College, Cambridge, where it was modified and celebrated for the first time in 1918, as the service of 'Nine Lessons with Carols', and exported thereafter as such to the wider English-speaking world. Catholics in general took to the newly discovered service of Christmas carols with enthusiasm, and saw

Prof. Noel Watson conducts Chapel Choir of St Patrick's College, Maynooth
during a broadcast of the Carol Service (1971)
Pages 476–477: Annual Carol Service in the College Chapel, 2017

in these services ideal opportunities for developing closer relations with fellow Christians, where all were equal and united in celebrating the birth of Christ in praise and thanksgiving. Choirs in particular relished the opportunity the newly discovered service format provided by way of skilful choral arrangements, for them to display the full range of their accomplishments and prowess.

Thus it was that Fr Watson saw that a carol service, based on the Nine Lessons model, could provide a forum and opportunity for the new Choral Society, whose membership was drawn mainly from the lay student body, to have a recognised role in the expanding college community. The service took place for the first time at six o'clock in the evening in the last week of Michaelmas term 1969 in the magnificent College Chapel. It was an immediate success with both the choir and the congregation, which consisted largely of staff and students. The formula of one six o'clock carol service with the Choral Society as sole choir was repeated the following year, and became the pattern for services in subsequent years up to 1984.

On taking over the choir on my appointment as Noel Watson's successor in 1985, it was made clear to me that the annual end-of-term Carol Service was to

Congregations from the Carol Service

be the musical highlight of the first term. However, I was surprised to discover that by tradition the service only involved lay students, with no participation by seminarians, whose number was in excess of 300 at the time. I approached my seminary colleague, the late Fr Sean Lavery, director of seminary music, with a suggestion that the fine 'college choir', as the seminary choir was then known, should also participate, and after some hesitation, he agreed with generosity and enthusiasm, and thus began the practice of multiple choir participation in what has become a great annual college and university occasion, with wide outside appeal. I also saw the possibility of adding a quartet of festive brass and timpani to enrich the musical ensemble, and in this I was greatly assisted by a young senior seminarian from Derry, who was also college cantor and an accomplished musician and trombonist. This gifted young man, Eamon Martin, is now the primate of all Ireland.

Thus the 1985 carol service established the basic formula which has endured to this day, with multiple choirs (the Chamber Choir and the Schola Gregoriana later joining to bring the number of participative choirs to four), brass, timpani and organ, together with various solo voices drawn from across the entire campus

Congregations from the Carol Service

community, combining to weave a musical fabric that is unique in academic institutions in this land.

The then president suggested to me that we move from the increasingly inconvenient hour of six o'clock to half past seven, and that we should repeat the service once, and later, due to its growing reputation in the wider community, that we should do so for a third night. Thus evolved through the 1990s and early 2000s the three nights of carols, readings and prayers, which sustain the service today under the expert and inspired direction of Dr John O'Keeffe, Director of Seminary Music and Choral Director for Maynooth University. That it is a successful formula, timeless in its appeal, is very clear from the consistent and persistent demand for admission from a public hungry for an experience of Christmas and its message that increasing commercialisation of the feast seeks to obliterate.

Maynooth's great choral tradition extends right back to the years of the first Professor of Music at St Patrick's College, the German priest Heinrich Bewerunge, who was appointed in 1888 with the title of Professor of Church Chant and Organ, and whose tenure lasted until his death in 1923, apart from a period during the First World War when he was unable to return to Maynooth following a visit to his native Germany. Bewerunge was a fine scholar whose publications saw him contribute to discussion on the great cultural issues of his day, in addition to building up a choir in Maynooth capable of singing the most complex polyphonic music, while also enthusiastically imparting to seminarians the latest theories in the revival of Gregorian chant. Such was his influence and impact that his legacy is one that was and is deeply felt by his many successors over the past hundred years.

Securing a 'solo slot' in the carol service has long been regarded as a richly sought-after accolade by aspiring young student singers, and through my years as director of the service I held open auditions each November when, year after year, a constant parade of exceptional vocal talent serenaded me as I sat, Louis Walsh-like, listening in judgement to each one. There was always more talent on offer than there were available solos, but, as we moved to three nights, I was able to spread the spoils a little by allocating different singers to each of the three evenings.

It is, perhaps, invidious to single out people, but while acknowledging the talent and expertise of all our soloists through the years, for different reasons I remember the following particularly: tenor Emmanuel Lawler, for the extraordinary maturity and musicality of his singing in one so youthful; the Brady brothers, baritone Paul, now solo baritone at the Oldenburg Opera House in Germany, and his tenor brother, Ciarán (currently teaching singing in the Music Department); fabulous mezzo-soprano Edel O'Brien from Clare; up-and-coming soprano Rachel Croash … and Catherine Martin TD, now deputy leader of the Green Party, whose rendering of a solo verse in 'O Holy Night' still lingers in the memory. And, before my time, there was the immensely talented Regina Nathan.

The three evenings of carols are festive highlights in Maynooth's annual calendar. Those who attend are usually enthralled by the singing and the obvious enjoyment the young singers derive from their role in the evenings' music-making. They are also inspired by the extraordinary beauty of the College Chapel, with its wood carvings, murals etc., surely Ireland's premier architectural ecclesiastical gem. Present-day Maynooth has a total student population of some 15,000, of whom only a very small percentage has ever entered this wonderful spiritual oasis on their doorstep, so to speak. *Occasione amissa!*

THE CLASS–PIECE

John-Paul Sheridan

I had an existential moment last year. My class-piece moved to the west cloister; meaning the last and furthest cloister in the Pugin building. I say existential because I hadn't realised that I was that old. When I was a third-year student, my dean's class-piece was just outside the refectory (now titled Pugin Hall) and we all thought he was ancient! While not a feature unique to Maynooth, the class-piece has been part of the visual history of Maynooth since the first ones appeared. It is not unusual to see people stopping and recognising priests among those hanging on the cloister walls. A casual glance or studied observation often yields the youthful face of a co-diocesan, a seminary rector or former professor, and sometimes a youthful bishop. I once brought one of my students to see her father's class-piece, which, like mine, had made its way down to the final cloister wall. An article about the Maynooth class-pieces is apposite – they are a familiar part of both the history and culture of the college. However, in 2018 the first class-piece that encapsulated two years of ordinations was hung.

Some of these glimpses of college history have begun to fade, partly because of the sunlight and partly because of the processes used in early photography. However, a project was recently begun to photograph the class-pieces and preserve the information contained on them. The project, under the curatorship of Professor Thomas O'Connor (from the 1984 class-piece) is funded by St Patrick's College and is part of a larger project to establish an online prosopographical database of the Irish Catholic clergy. When completed, it will deliver online access to all the class-pieces in full and also to provide thumbnails of individuals, from the first class-piece to 2002. The image of every individual on every class-piece will be linked to the information on matriculation and ordination captured in the lists in the Hamell lists book. The information contained in Hamell's *Maynooth Students and Ordinations 1798–1895* will also be included in the database. Subject to the approval of the college, it is hoped that this information will be accessible online and will be accompanied by a virtual visit facility which will permit a sample of the class-pieces to be viewed *in situ*.

Professor Neil Kevin, from whom we have (somewhat) borrowed the title

1882–1883 Class Piece

for this volume of recollections, offers a far more eloquent observation on the class-pieces:

> Each man had a special photograph taken and the whole gallery of pictures, together with many artistic embellishments of the photographers, were enclosed in one frame. Meet *our* class-piece … These photographs were taken, as I remember, some short time before ordination. There we are, between eighty and ninety in number, every man looking uncommonly serious and preoccupied; as though he were concerned, here and now, to give the world the final and irrevocable impression of what manner of man he was. Up and down through the rows of faces there is scarcely the first flicker of an approaching smile. Even the irrepressible Willie seems to have feared that, if he were found smiling then, he would be smiling for ever. Which would all be wrong; for the generations of students and others, who go, and will go, gazing at the gallery of class-pieces in the corridors of Maynooth, must not find Willie or any man showing signs of levity.

It was a long time before students smiled while having their portrait taken.

Patrick Hamell's *Maynooth Students and Ordinations 1895–1984* has proved to be an invaluable encyclopaedic source of information for this article and for exploring the class-pieces *in situ* over the years. The first photo of a class-piece in the Hamell book comes from 1861 and consists of three sets of names. The first set are the seventy-four students, probably from Third Divinity (which was the habit of the succeeding class-pieces). There are seven students each from the dioceses of Dublin and Down, six from Meath, five each from Armagh and Elphin and a scattering of students from almost all the Irish dioceses. Interesting among the names of dioceses is Duacensis, which translates as the diocese of Kilmacduagh, mentioned here without Galway and Kilfenora. There are other single dioceses mentioned in these early class-pieces: Cork (without Ross), Down (without Connor) and Kildare (without Leighlin).

The next set of names on this first class-piece are fourteen students who left before ordination. A quotation above the names come from the Letter to the Hebrews and translates, 'And one does not presume to take this honour, but takes it only when called by God, just as Aaron was' (Hebrews 5:4). The final set of names are seven students who died during their time at Maynooth. They appear under a quotation from John 11:25, 'I am the resurrection and the life. Those who believe in me, even though they die, will live.' Of the deceased,

1913–1914 Class Piece

A group of ecclesiastics taken on the occasion of the Episcopal Consecration of Daniel Mannix as Archbishop of Melbourne in College Chapel in 1912

two each are from Kildare and Elphin, and one each from Down, Dublin and Raphoe. This was the habit in these early class-pieces; to list the students who left before ordination and to remember those who had died.

As a priest of the diocese of Ferns, one name sticks out, that of Abraham Brownrigg. He entered Maynooth in 1856 in the Logic class, and after ordination became President of St Peter's College in Wexford. He was one of the four founders of the House of Missions in Enniscorthy. Brownrigg went on to be appointed Bishop of Ossory in 1884 as successor to Patrick Moran, who had been appointed Archbishop of Sydney. His portrait appears on the west cloister facing the class-pieces and there is a window in the College Chapel donated by him and the priests of Ossory.

The next oldest is 1878–79, a photographic copy of which hangs in the former office of the vice-president in Stoyte House. This is the earliest one with photos of the students. Considering that the earliest known portrait photographs come from the 1830s, it must have been quite an innovation to use this new medium in the college less than fifty years later. The next one to appear is 1882–83 and includes a portrait of Professor Patrick O'Donnell, who held chairs of Moral and Dogmatic Theology at Maynooth. Having been ordained himself in 1880, he would have been known to this class as a student and his inclusion on the class-piece might have been as a result of his elevation as Prefect and Professor of Dunboyne Scholars in 1884. His inclusion may have been the beginning of the tradition of dedicating the class-piece to a member of staff whom the class considered to have had a particular influence on their preparation for the priesthood. A member of staff was chosen by the class to be included in the class-piece; at times there was a considerable ritual attached to this tradition. In the earliest class-pieces there are some members of staff portrayed, but many have none. In 1973 the Daughters of Charity were included in the class-piece and that was not the last time they appeared. In 1998 Dr John O'Keeffe was the first lay person to be included in a class-piece.

These are just two of the incalculable number of stories that can be gleaned from these moments captured in time. Each face will elicit a family, diocesan, national or even global story. The members of the 1887–88 class may not have realised that one of their number, Daniel Mannix, would go on to be a member of the college staff, later its youngest president, and eventually would be consecrated a bishop in the very College Chapel that he had watched being built while a student. His story is intricately bound up not only in the world he grew up in, but also in his shaping of a Catholic community on the other side of the world. This class-piece hangs on one of the corridors of the St Patrick's building.

The class-pieces are artefacts of social history. Initially, the names and dioceses were in Latin and then, with the rise of a greater consciousness of the Irish language and, notwithstanding the O'Hickey controversy, the names and dioceses appeared in Irish. The Fáinne can be seen on the lapels of many of the students, as can the Pioneer pin. The 1966–67 piece has a photo of the Oliver Sheppard *Death of Cúchulainn* from the GPO in Dublin.

The decoration on the mounts of the class-pieces is often quite elaborate, with highly ornate Celtic knotwork. These borders sometimes have photos of the early Irish monasteries and drawings of the Irish saints. There is a series of frames that display some elaborate carving, including round towers, shamrocks and wolfhounds, reminiscent of Irish linen and Belleek porcelain from the same period.

The class-pieces are unique windows onto college history, and Irish ecclesiastical history more generally. The most populous class-piece is the 1913–14 one, which contains eighty-five Third Divinity students and the President, John F. Hogan, who had been appointed in 1912. Popes and papal nuncios are portrayed, including in the class-piece for the 'Year of Three Popes', and the subsequent visit of Pope John Paul II in 1979. The Irish Synod is displayed in

1909–1910 Class Piece

Staff photograph 1960s

Front row (L–R): Patrick J. Corish, J.D. Bastable, P.F. Cremin, Michael G. Olden, Edward O'Brien, P.J. Hamell, Gerard Mitchell, Patrick Muldoon, James Doherty C.M., James Cosgrove, John McMackin, John O'Flynn, J.G. McGarry.

Second Row (L–R): William Meany, Tomás Ó Fiaich, Peter Connolly, Pádraig Ó Fiannachta, Ronan Drury, Thomas Finan, Denis O'Callaghan, Jeremiah Newman, Brendan Devlin, Terence Cunningham, Patrick Travers, Gerard McGreevy, Richard McCullen C.M., James McMahon, Timothy Crowley, James McConnell.

Back Row (L–R): Cathal Ó Háinle, Donal Flanagan, Sean Corkery, Michael T. Casey O.P., James Coulter, Matthew O'Donnell, Gerard Meagher

Students on the cloister between two class-pieces

the class-piece of 1956, the Second Vatican Council in that of 1963, the Patrician and Marian Years and the Eucharistic Congress in that of 1931–32 . The various college presidents are portrayed, and the passing of members of the college staff and community is also observed. The 1894–95 class-piece has a photo of the Pugin building and another of the College Chapel without its tower and spire. Another has the interior of the college without the Molloy reredos, which had been consecrated by Mannix in 1913 before he left for Australia. Photos of the interior (mostly the chapel) and exterior of the college feature prominently. Both the 1915–16 and 1916–17 pieces include the same photo of the O'Growney mausoleum and the Geraldine castle ruin at the gates of the college.

The class-pieces document the legacy of Maynooth to the Universal Church. The earliest evidence of this legacy are three students ordained for the Archdiocese of Glasgow in 1902 and 1903, and other English, Scottish and North American dioceses would follow. There is also early evidence of various religious orders and congregations. The earliest to be ordained are the Jesuits, Edmund Power in 1900 and Richard Devane in 1901. A number of congregations were founded from the college and these founders can be seen in the class-pieces. Edward Galvin was ordained in 1909 and with John Blowick founded the Maynooth Mission to China (St Columban's Missionary Society) in 1918. There are members of the St Patrick's Missionary Society, Kiltegan, which was also founded from Maynooth in 1932 by Patrick Whitney and Francis Hickey from the 1920 and 1921 class-pieces respectively. Subsequent religious congregations built seminaries and houses of formation near Maynooth and their priests are also to be found among the photos: Divine Word Missionaries, Society of African Missionaries and Salesians. The Vincentians, whose Irish foundation was the responsibility of a Maynooth man, feature not only among the students but also among the generations of spiritual directors who have served the college since the arrival of John Myers and Patrick Boyle in 1887.

Finally, these class-pieces stand as testimony to the words (again) of Neil Kevin about Ordination Sunday, and a favourite passage of the late Professor of Homiletics, Fr Ronan Drury:

> The slowly moving line of priests down through the College Chapel is never-ending; it goes into the four provinces of Ireland; it crosses the seas into neighbouring England and Scotland, and the greater seas into the Americas and Australia, and Africa and China; it covers the whole earth; it goes wherever man has gone; it is unbroken, it is ever renewing itself at the high altar in Maynooth, and setting out again before the fathers and mothers of Ireland, whose eyes are dim at the sight of it.

MEMORIA NOBIS TENEANTUR
PIUS PAPA XII · HIBERNORUM GENS
LONGE DIFFUSA · FAUTORES OMNES
UBICUNQUE TERRARUM · QUORUM
ERGA FIDEM PATRIAMQUE NOSTRAM
PIETATE PRISCAE COLLEGII SEDES
ANNORUM CURSU CL FATISCENTES
DECORE VIGUERUNT INTEGRATO
MCML – MCMLX

he plaque in the Porch of the President's Arch commemorates the benefactors of the renovations and repairs to the college buildings from 1950–1960. As in the case of the construction of the college chapel in the 1870s, and the bicentennial appeal in the 1990s, it was the generosity of the Irish at home and abroad which allowed this work to take place and, doubtless, the work of college alumni who promoted the appeal for funds; a generosity which still continues today.

The Latin inscription was composed by Rev. Thomas Finan, Professor of Classics. The translation is by Msgr Brendan Devlin, Emeritus Professor of French and former Vice-President of the College.

Be held by us in memory
Pope Pius XII · the Irish people
scattered afar · and all our benefactors
throughout the world · by whose
devotion to faith and fatherland
the venerable fabric of this College
wearied by the passing of 150 years
has flourished anew in its refound grandeur
1950 – 1960

Details of Sacristy Door, College Chapel

NOTES ON CONTRIBUTORS

Niall Ahern is a priest of the Elphin diocese, currently ministering in Strandhill, County Sligo.

Denis Bergin is a writer and editor. He lives in West Offaly and the eastern Algarve.

Moira Bergin RSM, is a Sister of Mercy and staff member of the National Centre for Liturgy, St Patrick's College Maynooth.

David Bracken, a former priest of the diocese of Limerick, ordained from Maynooth in 2002, is currently Limerick Diocesan Archivist.

David Carbery worked in Maynooth College from 1968–2002, when he retired as Head of Catering. He now plays golf!

Joseph Collins is Head of Faculty of Lifelong Learning at Institute of Technology, Carlow.

Tom Collins is the former Head of Education at Maynooth University (2006–11), where he served as interim President from 2010–11. In recent years he has been involved he has been involved in establishing The Technological Higher Education Association.

Patrick Comerford is a priest in the Church of Ireland Diocese of Limerick, a former adjunct assistant professor in TCD, and a former lecturer in the Church of Ireland Theological Institute.

Vincent Comerford is a Maynooth graduate and former Professor of Modern History. He lives in County Kildare.

Evelyn Conlon is a novelist, short story writer and essayist. She is a member of Aosdána and is an adjunct professor in the creative writing MFA program at Carlow University, Pittsburgh, Pennsylvannia.

Paul Connell is a priest of the diocese of Meath, President of St Finian's College, Mullingar and Executive Secretary to the Council for Education of the Irish Episcopal Conference.

Hugh Connolly is a priest of the diocese of Dromore he is currently *Aumônier des Irlandais*, or Chaplain to the Irish community in Paris.

Michael Conway is a priest of Killala diocese, now retired and living in Enniscrone, County Sligo.

Mary P. Corcoran is Professor of Sociology at Maynooth University.

Bill Cosgrave is a priest of the Diocese of Ferns, residing at Monageer, Enniscorthy, County Wexford.

Brian Cosgrove, having taught English in both UCD and NUI Maynooth, now lives in retirement in Dublin.

Mary Cullen lectured in History at St Patrick's College from 1968 to 1994 and, with Professor Tomás Ó Fiaich, was instrumental in building the department in its earliest days. She was conferred with the degree of Doctor of Literature *honoris causa* by the National University of Ireland Maynooth on 8 June 2011.

Peter Denman lives in retirement in Maynooth.

Brendan Devlin is a priest of Derry diocese. He was appointed Professor of Modern Languages at Maynooth in 1958, a position he held until his retirement in 1996.

Patrick Devine is an editor, organist and guest lecturer living in Dublin.

Tríona Doherty is a journalist and editor who lives in Athlone, County Roscommon.

Terence Dooley is Professor of History at Maynooth University.

Vincent Doyle, Psychotherapist, is Director and Founder of Coping International, Ltd. He lives in the West of Ireland.

Joseph Duffy is a priest of the diocese of Clogher, ordained in 1958. He served as Bishop of Clogher from 1979–2010.

Gearóid Dullea is a priest of the diocese of Cork and Ross. From 2010–19 he served as Executive Secretary of the Irish Episcopal Conference and and is currently parish priest of Ballinlough, Cork.

Stephen Farragher is a priest of the archdiocese of Tuam, and currently serving as parish priest of Ballyhaunis, County Mayo.

Eddie Finnegan is a retired teacher, married and living in Harringay, North London.

Gerard Gillen is Professor Emeritus of Music at Maynooth University. Internationally renowned as an organ recitalist, he served as Titular Organist at St Mary's Pro-Cathedral, Dublin, from 1976–2018.

James Good was a priest and missionary of the diocese of Cork and Ross, ordained in 1948. He died in 2018.

Patrick Hannon, Professor Emeritus of Moral Theology, St Patrick's College, Maynooth, is a priest of the diocese of Cloyne.

Kevin Hargaden is the Team Leader and Social Theologian at the Jesuit Centre for Faith and Justice in Dublin.

Kevin Hegarty is a priest of Killala diocese and a frequent media contributor.

Jacqueline Hill is Professor Emerita of History in Maynooth University.

Brendan Hoban is a priest of the diocese of Killala and lives in retirement in Ballina.

Diarmuid Hogan is a priest of the diocese of Galway, serving in Oranmore. He is also Diocesan Communications Director.

Rita Joyce Holmes worked as Principal Technician in the Chemistry Department in Maynooth College from 1980–94. She currently volunteers in a primary school and is the happy companion of grandson, Bram Riley.

Niall Howard is a priest of the diocese of Kerry, ministering in the parish of Killarney.

Susan McKenna-Lawlor is Professor Emeritus at the Department of Experimental Physics, Maynooth University. She is Managing Director of Space Technology Ireland, Ltd (STIL) which builds instrumentation for space missions.

Liam Lawton resides in Graiguecullen, Carlow, where he ministers and is Director of Music in the diocese of Kildare and Leighlin.

Paul Clayton-Lea is a priest of the archdiocese of Armagh and a former editor of *Intercom* magazine.

Colm Lennon is a Member of the Royal Irish Academy and Professor Emeritus of Maynooth University.

Tom Looney is a priest of the diocese of Kerry and parish priest of Fossa, Killarney.

Ciarán Mac Murchaidh is a graduate of Maynooth University (Celtic Studies) and is currently Head of School in Fiontar and Scoil na Gaeilge at Dublin City University.

Eugene Magee is a retired travel agent.

Eamon Martin is Archbishop of Armagh, primate of All-Ireland, and Chancellor of the Pontifical University, St Patrick's College Maynooth.

Darina McCarthy is director of Schola Gregoriana, Maynooth. She carries out administrative and archive work for the Galway diocese.

Peter McCawille SMA was a student in Maynooth from 1969 to 1976. He is based in Abuja, Nigeria.

Brendan McConvery is a member of the Irish Province of the Redemptorists and currently works in Redemptorist Communications.

Barbara McCormack is Librarian, Royal Irish Academy, and former Special Collections Librarian at Maynooth University and St Patrick's College Maynooth.

Enda McDonagh is a priest of the archdiocese of Tuam. He was appointed Professor of Moral Theology and Canon Law at Maynooth from 1958–95.

Frank McGuinness is an Irish playwright and poet. Having lectured at the University of Ulster and St Patrick's College Maynooth, he was appointed Professor of Creative Writing at UCD in 2007. In 2019 he was awarded the UCD Ulysses Medal, the highest honour the university can bestow.

Tom McGuire is Head of RTÉ Radio 1.

Niall McKeith, a retired physicist resident in County Meath, was appointed Honorary Curator in 1999.

Donal McMahon taught English in the seminary of St Patrick's College Maynooth, from 1974 to 2013.

Dominic McNamara is retired in Wexford, having served as assistant to five presidents of St Patrick's College from 1978–2013.

Mary (Burke) McQuinn is a happily retired teacher living in Tullow with her husband Christopher, also a Maynooth science graduate.

Michael Mullaney is President of the Pontifical University, St Patrick's College Maynooth.

Michael Mullins is a priest of the diocese of Waterford and Lismore. He has lectured in Sacred Scripture in St John's College, Waterford, and St Patrick's College Maynooth.

Agnes Neligan worked in the library from 1974 to 2008. Originally from County Kerry, she now lives in Lucan, County Dublin.

Is léachtóir le Gaeilge in Ollscoil Mhá Nuad í Tracey Ní Mhaonaigh. Tá spéis ar leith aici i gcúrsaí foclóireachta agus aistritheoireachta, agus i saol agus i litríocht Chorca Dhuibhne.

Thomas J. Norris is a priest of the diocese of Ossory currently serving as a curate in St Canice's parish, Kilkenny.

Jim O'Brien is a freelance journalist and columnist living in County Clare.

Maeve O'Brien has lectured in Ancient Classics at Maynooth from 1991 to the present.

Thomas O'Connor is Professor of History at NUI Maynooth, director of the University's Arts and Humanities Institute and editor of *Archivium Hibernicum*.

Tadhg Ó Dúshláine: breis agus leathchéad bliain caite aige i Má Nuad faoin dtráth seo.

Anthony G. O'Farrell is Professor Emeritus of Mathematics at Maynooth University.

Cathal Ó Háinle is Professor Emeritus of Irish at Trinity College Dublin.

Pádraig Ó Héalaí: Ina chónaí in Indreabhán, Contae na Gaillimhe; Léachtóir Sinsearach ar scor, Scoil na Gaeilge, Ollscoil na hÉireann, Gaillimh.

John O'Keeffe is Director of Sacred Music at St Patrick's College Maynooth, and Director of Choral Groups at Maynooth University.

Thomas O'Loughlin is Professor Emeritus of Historical Theology in the University of Nottingham.

Nollaig Ó Muraíle is a former Senior Lecturer in Irish at NUI Galway, and before that in Queen's University Belfast.

Martin Pulbrook is a lay minister at Blackpool South Unitarian Church. He lives near Mullingar.

Mary O'Rourke is a graduate of Maynooth College. She is a former TD for Longford-Westmeath and has served as Minister for Education, Minister for Health and Minister for Public Enterprise. She currently lives in Athlone and is a frequent media contributor.

Ciarán Reilly is an historian of nineteenth- and twentieth-century Irish history based at Maynooth University.

Peter O'Reilly is presently parish priest of Enniskillen and Vicar General of Clogher Diocese.

Michael O'Riordan has worked in a variety of capacities in Maynooth College since 1954. He took up his position as College Butler at 6:30am on 1 October 1963 and retired at 6:30pm on 30 September 2003.

Regina Whelan Richardson is a printmaker, and was formerly Subject Librarian for Music, and Modern Languages, Literatures and Cultures at Maynooth University.

Aidan Ryan managed the college farm for almost a quarter of a century until his retirement in 1992.

Michael F. Ryan is Senior Lecturer in the Department of Applied Social Sciences at LIT-Tipperary (Thurles Campus). He is also a member of the Governing Authority of Maynooth University.

Noeleen Ryan has worked in the Maynooth campus for over forty years. She is Manager of Student Fees and Grants.

Salvador Ryan is Professor of Ecclesiastical History at St Patrick's College Maynooth.

Pat Russell lectured in the German Department at Maynooth from 1969 to 1972. He lives in Thurles, County Tipperary.

John-Paul Sheridan is a priest of the diocese of Ferns and a member of the Theology Faculty at St Patrick's College Maynooth.

Lawrence Taylor continues to write, in a variety of genres, and divides his time between Tubac, Arizona (near the Mexican border), and Maynooth, Ireland.

Bill Tinley is manager of Maynooth Campus Conference & Accommodation.

D. Vincent Twomey is a Divine Word Missionary priest and former Professor of Moral Theology at St Patrick's College, Maynooth.

Richard Watson has retired from the college and is enjoying his retirement in Maynooth.

Léachtóir le litríocht agus teanga na Gaeilge in Institiúid Oideachais Marino, Baile Átha Cliath, í an Dr Marie Whelton.

C. J. Woods retired from the staff of the Royal Irish Academy in 2006.

Penelope (Penny) Woods has retired from the Library and is currently chair of Celbridge Historical Society.

WE REMEMBER MAYNOOTH
List of Illustrations

All images unless otherwise stated are © Maynooth College Archives.

Library Collection: 20, 270, 420, 421.

Paula T Nolan: Pages 2–3, 4, 7, 22, 587, 85, 86, 89, 169, 251, 253, 311, 318–319, 338–339, 350, 365, 374–375, 376, 386, 399 (*Chalice*), 405, 413, 423, 424, 448–449, 461, 462–463, 486, 489, 494, 495. © Paula T Nolan except for free attributed use by St Patrick's College Maynooth.

Fr Stephen Farragher: Pages 107–111, 115, 265, 399, 407, 409.

John–Paul Sheridan: Pages 1, 215, 404.

Cover Image:	Detail of roundel of St Patrick, ceiling of College Chapel. Photograph: Stuart McNamara. With kind permission.
Page 17:	Organ and Rose Window © Stuart McNamara.
Page 18:	Maynooth College spire from Carton House © Fr Sean Farrell, CM.
Page 32:	Geraldine Castle, Maynooth. Photograph, William Murphy / Wikimedia.
Page 34:	Geraldine Castle, Maynooth linocut © Susan Durack.
Page 37:	St Mary's Church photographs © Rev. Patrick Comerford.
Page 44:	Engraving St Patrick's College, Maynooth / Shutterstock.
Page 47:	Drawing William Makepeace Thackeray / Wikimedia Commons.
Page 51:	Carton House © The Print Creator / Alamy Stock Photos.
Page 59, 61:	Details from Healy's *Maynooth College: Its Centenary History*.
Page 65:	Bewerunge's *Benedictus*. Transcribed by Dr Darina McCarthy into full score layout from a set of T1, T2, B1, B2 parts likely copied in the 1950s.
Page 77:	Prof. Walter McDonald, Frontispiece, *Reminiscences of a Maynooth Professor*. Courtesy: Prof. Thomas O'Loughlin.
Page 80:	College Chapel. Courtesy: Rev. Niall Ahern.
Page 98:	Jelly d'Arányi © Lebrecht Music & Arts / Alamy Stock Photos.
Page 105:	Ray McAnally and Robert de Niro in *The Mission* ©Warner Bros/Kobal/Shutterstock.
Page 117:	Fr John Brady. Courtesy: Fr Paul Connell.
Page 181:	*Midsummer Glory* by Sara Kyne. College Collection.
Page 195:	First Science Class, 1968–9. Courtesy: Mary (Burke) McQuinn.
Page 197:	Letter from Rev. Prof. Jeremiah Newman. Courtesy: Mary (Burke) McQuinn.
Page 199:	Footbridge in Maynooth © RTÉ Archives.
Page 214:	Statue of Goethe © christianthiel.net / Shutterstock.
Page 221:	Pádraig Ó Fiannachta, Cathal Ó Háinle, Crísostóir Ó Floinn and Tomás Ó Fiaich, Courtesy: Dr Tracey Ní Mhaonaigh, Roinn na Nua-Ghaeilge.
Page 241:	Sketch of Rev. Prof. Peter Connolly. Courtesy: Colin Smythe Ltd.
Page 244:	Frank McGuinness © Amelia Stein.
Page 249:	Sketch of Prof. Barbara Hayley. Courtesy: Colin Smythe Ltd.
Page 255:	*Pugin Hall* by Sara Kyne. College Collection.
Page 257:	Catering staff and David Carbery with HRH King Carl Gustaf XVI of Sweden. Courtesy: David J. Carbery.
Page 258:	Catering Students with the staff, 1968. Author standing extreme right at the end of the second row. Courtesy: David J. Carbery.
Page 297:	Msgr P. F. Cremin. Courtesy: Fr Niall Ahern.
Page 309:	An Dr Tadhg Ó Dúshláine, Courtesy: Dr Tracey Ní Mhaonaigh, Roinn na Nua–Ghaeilge.
Page 313:	Arts Building. Photograph: Tony G. Murray Photography, Naas. College Collection.
Page 323:	Prof. Noel Watson conducting a performance of Bach's St John Passion, 1984. Courtesy: John–Paul Sheridan.
Page 327:	Prof. Barbara Hayley. Courtesy: Cecelia Hayley.
Page 329:	Cardinal Tomás Ó Fiaich planting a tree at the back of New House. Courtesy: Fr Niall Ahern.
Pages 330–31:	College Chapel, Maynooth. Photograph: Liam O'Brien. Used with kind permission.
Page 337:	Fr Michael Casey, OP, baptizing the author's daughter, 1986. Courtesy: Rita Joyce-Holmes.

He's at th
row
extr

he second
g on the